THE
WELSH WARS
OF INDEPENDENCE
c.410–c.1415

THE
WELSH WARS
OF INDEPENDENCE

*c.*410–*c.*1415

DAVID MOORE

TEMPUS

For Meg and Fionn

'...the people of Snowdon say that even if the prince were willing to give their land to the king, they would nevertheless be unwilling to do homage to a stranger whose language, customs and laws are totally unknown to them.'

Letter from the council of Llywelyn ap Gruffudd, prince of Wales, to John Pecham, Archbishop of Canterbury, 11 November 1282 (translated from the Latin by Hilary Peters)

Owen Glendower:
I can call spirits from the vasty deep.

Hotspur:
Why, so can I, or so can any man;
But will they come when you do call for them?

William Shakespeare, King Henry the Fourth Part I, *Act III, Scene I*

First published 2005

Tempus Publishing Limited
The Mill, Brimscombe Port,
Stroud, Gloucestershire, GL5 2QG
www.tempus-publishing.com

British Library Cataloguing in Publication Data.
A catalogue record for this book is available from the British Library.

ISBN 0 7524 3321 0

Typesetting and origination by Tempus Publishing Limited
Printed and bound in Great Britain

Contents

Acknowledgements

This book could not have been completed without a great deal of help from others, and I am particularly indebted to Margaret Jones, Anita Hummel (anitahummel@yahoo.com) and Tom Hardiment (tomhardiment@hotmail.com) for the illustrations; to the National Library of Wales for permission to use Margaret Jones's artwork, and to Dr Paul Joyner, Lona Mason and Gareth Lloyd Hughes for their help with reproducing it; to Hilary Peters for permission to use her translation of Archbishop Pecham's letters, and to numerous other colleagues at the National Library for their assistance with many aspects of the preparation; to the Royal Commission on the Ancient and Historical Monuments of Wales for help with the illustrations; to Meg de Messières for help with the maps; to Professor John Davies for reading the manuscript and offering some valuable observations; to innumerable members of staff (past and present) in the Departments of History and Anglo-Saxon, Norse and Celtic at Cambridge University and the Departments of History and Welsh History at Bangor and Aberystwyth – and in particular to Professor Tony Carr and Dr Huw Pryce – for many years of guidance and encouragement; to Lord Elis-Thomas for his interest in this project; to Jonathan Reeve and his colleagues at Tempus Publishing and to Professor Gareth Williams for making the experience of producing this volume as painless and enjoyable as possible; and last but not least to my family and friends – especially Niamh Sloyne, Paul Hocker, Cory Mortis-Wait, Vicky Cribb, James Caswell, Meredith Cane, my mum and my brother Steve – for all their help and advice. I am also very grateful to my children, Meg and Fionn, for sharing my enjoyment of castles and medieval things in general; this book is dedicated to them. Any errors of fact or interpretation in the text are entirely my own.

David Moore
Tre'r-ddôl, 2004

Foreword

By Lord Dafydd Elis-Thomas,
Presiding Officer of the National Assembly for Wales.

Wales: End of a Principality

Historians are obliged to rewrite history in each generation, simply because changes in contemporary events mean that we reread the past in new ways. Since Wales came into existence as a European legislative region in 1999, with a democratic parliamentary government grandly styled a 'national assembly', a new generation of historians is having to reinterpret the history of this nation within the United Kingdom – and not least to itself!

David Moore's gripping account of war, diplomacy and struggle points up two intimately related questions: was there any time when Wales could realistically have become an independent nation state under native rule? And was that best achieved by the creation of a principality under the king of England, which eventually allowed foreign princes to be imposed all too easily? For the future, perhaps Wales could give up both scenarios as it assumes national equality within an interdependent, European, United Kingdom.

The present Prince of Wales is undoubtedly the most Cambro-phile member of the English royal family ever to have held the title, and when he becomes King Charles III he will have the opportunity to go down in history as truly the last Prince of Wales. As Wales enters a new era, Prince Charles might finally end the colonial fiction by abolishing the Principality of Wales.

Note to the Reader

An x between two dates signifies an unspecified time within this period.

Introduction

When Owain Glyn Dŵr was declared prince of Wales by a few close associates at Glyndyfrdwy on 16 September 1400, he initiated a rebellion which was to become conscious of itself as a war of Welsh independence. But this was no new nation struggling to assert itself. Welsh autonomy could be traced back 1,000 years to the period after the Roman occupation, and Gerald of Wales, writing in the late twelfth century, remarked that the Welsh were noted for their love of arms and the ferocity with which they defended their independence. By 1400, however, that independence had long since been lost; it had been sapped and destroyed piecemeal by centuries of warfare, settlement, economic colonisation and legal imposition, beginning with the incursions of the Saxons in the fifth century and culminating in Edward I's conquest of the principality of Wales in 1283. Paradoxically, however, the vision of Welsh independence was broadest when its chances of being realised were at their bleakest. The Glyn Dŵr revolt was a desperate and ultimately doomed attempt to rekindle a sovereignty that had long since been extinguished, yet it nevertheless seared itself into the political and cultural psyche of southern Britain for centuries. Few educated minds in medieval Wales or England were unaware of the prophecies of Merlin, particularly after they were circulated by Geoffrey of Monmouth in the 1130s: the Welsh longed for a son of prophecy to deliver them from their conquerors, and both they and the English saw in Glyn Dŵr an attempt to restore the 'kingdom of the Britons' – the oldest surviving native polity in the Island of Britain – which had once held most of the island, and which aspired to do so again.

Prophecy and reality, however, are very different things. For all the rhetoric, Glyn Dŵr was attempting little more in practical terms than the restoration of the thirteenth-century principality of Wales, the last bastion of native Welsh independence. That task alone was a daunting one, for it required him to succeed where all of his predecessors had ultimately failed. Long before Owain's time – and long before there was any such notion as 'Wales' or the 'Welsh' – the Britons had been subjected to centuries of Roman rule, and when eventually they had carved out autonomous kingdoms among the ruins of imperial decline, many of them had soon lost their lands and their authority to new invaders from overseas. Even in the areas where indigenous rulers maintained their hard-won independence, it had been increasingly fragile, ambiguous, malleable and compromised from the ninth century onwards, and in the end it had proved unsustainable. In this light, it is worth noting that the paradoxes inherent within Glyn Dŵr's own ambitions would have been much more apparent had he been able to fulfil them. Although Owain takes pride of place in the nationalist mythology of later times, it was primarily the struggles of his predecessors which decided the fate of Welsh independence, and in particular those in the four centuries which preceded 1283. The English showed themselves both willing and able to destabilise Welsh kingdoms in the ninth century, and the Welsh made their first submissions to an Anglo-Saxon king in the same period. By 1283, Welsh independence had been eroded to the point that not only was almost the whole of Wales in the hands of a conquering king of England and his barons, but it was universally accepted that a Welsh kingdom could forfeit to the English crown. The relationship between English overlordship and the legitimist aspirations of the Welsh was always a very uneasy one, and its implications struck deep into the hearts and minds of communities and individuals throughout Wales, from the highest to the lowest. The politics of native Wales were perennially torn between prophecy and the art of the possible.

This book is not a military history. Much of it is concerned with the victories, defeats, alliances and compromises of the rulers of native Wales, but its main purpose is to investigate how they illustrate the nature and practice of political independence. What did independence mean? How was it established? How did it function? How did it come to be under threat, and from whom? How did the Welsh protect it? And why did they finally fail? It is a complex story, influenced by the decline of the Roman empire, conquest and settlement by Irish, Saxons, Vikings and Normans, the strengthening and centralisation of England, the changing political, social and economic climate throughout western Christendom, and the way the Welsh defined and redefined themselves and their country. All of these themes appear in the first eight chapters, which trace developments chronologically, but it would be next to impossible to weave all of them satisfactorily into a strict narrative, so the most important concepts – namely the creation of a Welsh nation and the nature of political authority in Wales, with reference to the European context – are given more detailed consideration in the final two chapters.

With hindsight, it is easy to assume that the story of Welsh independence is that of the native principality of Wales, which was given a difficult birth at Montgomery in 1267 and died prematurely with Llywelyn ap Gruffudd in 1282. It is even easier to misread the medieval world in terms of modern concepts of sovereignty and national unity (whether Welsh, British or English), and to forget that – notwithstanding the tendency towards isolationism since the Reformation – both Wales and England were enthusiastic parts of a pan-European cultural, spiritual and political world throughout the period covered by this book. The history of any country can only be understood if it is first remembered that the past itself is a different country. The very existence of Wales as a recognisable entity was never a foregone conclusion, and Llywelyn and Glyn Dŵr were almost a millennium away when the first Welsh kingdoms emerged. The country was always fragmented, and the numerous autonomous kingdoms were as interested in preserving their freedom from each other as they were in resisting foreign intrusion. Furthermore, Welsh subjection to the English was anything but inevitable, and owed a great deal to the remarkably rapid and in many ways very unlikely development of a kingdom of England. Moreover, most of those who took part in the events which shaped the fortunes of western Britain for 1,000 years would scarcely have recognised the anachronistic concept of 'independence' – let alone 'Welsh independence' – any more than they would have considered themselves 'medieval' or 'sub-Roman'. Their kingdoms were 'independent' by default, and their most eloquent expositions of nationality and independence came only when those things were on the verge of being crushed. By then, it was often too late.

The concept of 'Welsh wars of independence' is valid, however, if only because history is necessarily written looking backwards. Welsh kingdoms practised completely autonomous secular government from the time they ceased to recognise Roman rule until the time they accepted English overlordship and eventually conquest, and much if not most of that independence was lost as a direct consequence of war. Furthermore, the subject is topical. Both the prince of Wales and Welsh independence still excite controversy today, and the devolution of power from Westminster to the National Assembly for Wales in 1999 indicated that Glyn Dŵr's vision of a unified, separate Wales has left an indelible mark on British politics, however differently that vision might be interpreted today.

Conflict is a recurring theme in human history, and the medieval period was no exception. Warfare played a crucial part in defining political authority, and it was as vicious in the Middle Ages as in any other age. Contemporary sources report regular instances of massacres, decapitations and mutilations committed by the Welsh and other nationalities in Wales, both against each other and among themselves. Early medieval poets revelled in gory descriptions of battle, sometimes describing casualties as food for ravens and wolves, and the biographer of Gruffudd ap Cynan was particularly graphic in recalling how an Irish mercenary butchered Trahaearn ap Caradog at Mynydd Carn in 1081: '*Gucharki* the Irishman made bacon of him as of a pig'.[1]

Cruelty was often condemned, but violence was an accepted political and governmental tool, and the highest moral authorities sanctioned the use of extreme measures when established authority was threatened. The church considered it perfectly acceptable, for instance, that Louis VI of France had a

Flemish rebel eaten alive by a rabid dog. A man could commit no greater crime than treachery against his lord, and this accounts for the severity exhibited in the treatment of many rebels, notably Edward I's punishment of Dafydd ap Gruffudd, who was hanged, disembowelled, beheaded and cut into four pieces, which were displayed throughout England in 1283.

Such attitudes help to explain the bitterness of much of the fighting in the medieval period, as both Welsh and English rulers sought to intensify their lordship in Wales. Developments in military technology also helped to brutalise warfare, as did the gradual territorialisation of authority. What had been a matter of raids for booty and strikes against members of rival dynasties became full-scale attempts to control whole regions. Total warfare tactics aimed at starving the enemy were employed in successive English campaigns against Gwynedd, and the Welsh in turn routinely adopted a 'scorched earth' policy between the Dee and the Conwy as they retreated into the fastnesses of Snowdonia. The climate in which fighting was conducted is illustrated by the refusal of the garrison of Llandovery to surrender in 1213 unless they were allowed to keep 'their lives and their members intact',[2] and Henry III's campaign against Dafydd ap Llywelyn in 1245 provides a microcosm of this culture of violence. Starving, freezing soldiers of both sides fought desperately over food at the mouth of the river Conwy, and Henry executed several Welsh hostages in the resulting tension. The Welsh retaliated by hanging and beheading their prisoners, cutting some of them into pieces, and this in turn was answered by the promise of a shilling for every Welsh head brought to the king. There are numerous similar examples; atrocities were commonplace, and it is not necessary to go into them all.

This book is intended for a wider audience than would be the case with a specialist monograph, so the use of academic apparatus has been restricted. Footnotes are used only to identify quotations, and the bibliography is select, but there should be enough information to make it fairly easy for readers to pursue their interest in this subject further. The maps give a broad idea of the main divisions of Wales, but for more detail see William Rees's *Historical Atlas of Wales*; similarly, the illustrations are intended to be evocative rather than forensic reconstructions, and the genealogical tables are by necessity not comprehensive. Personal and place names are given in their native forms, except where this might lead to confusion for English-speaking readers. English place names are introduced to reflect prolonged subjection to English rule, so Morgannwg eventually becomes Glamorgan, Ceredigion becomes Cardiganshire, Môn becomes Anglesey, and so on. Inevitably, however, there is an element of inconsistency, the only justification for which is that it reflects the complexity, contradiction and fluidity which in many ways characterised the medieval world.

I

The Origins and Growth of Welsh Kingdoms
c.410–1063

Roman and Sub-Roman Britain

THE END OF ROMAN RULE

Britain was conquered and ruled by the Roman empire for three-and-a-half centuries after the emperor Claudius invaded in AD 43. It was apparently during this period that 'Britain' – by which was meant the Roman diocese of Britannia, separated from Caledonia by Hadrian's wall in the north – was first envisaged as a single unit, and much of the south and east of the island became heavily romanised. But it was always a frontier outpost, and it came under regular attack from Irish, Pictish, Frankish and especially Saxon raiders from the third century onwards, especially after the empire began to collapse in the late fourth century. It was now only a matter of time until the Romano-Britons were left to their own devices. Power was increasingly devolved as central authority weakened, and many of the front-line Roman troops were removed in 383, when Magnus Maximus, a Spanish leader of the army in Britain, invaded Gaul and overthrew the emperor Gratian, seizing much of the western empire for himself. The missing legions were never properly replaced, although Stilicho brought reinforcements for a campaign against the barbarian raiders in 398; they were taken away again in order to counter an invasion of Italy by the Goths in 401. Defensive responsibilities now lay firmly on the shoulders of local officials, many of whom were native tribal leaders. As a result, many parts of Britain seem to have enjoyed a considerable degree of self-determination by the turn of the fifth century. The Britons were recovering their *de facto* independence by default.

In the winter of 406 and 407, a huge Germanic force comprising Vandals, Suebi, Alans, Alemanni and others crossed the frozen river Rhine into the Roman diocese of Gaul, causing such chaos that the very name of the Vandals became synonymous with wanton destruction. Determined to resist this potentially mortal threat to the western empire, the Roman authorities responded over the next few years by withdrawing most of their remaining troops from Britain to the continent. The Britons asked for imperial help against barbarian attacks, and their alarm at the deteriorating situation both at home and in Gaul contributed to the emergence of three usurpers in quick succession from the army in Britain. The last of them, Constantine, imposed himself in Gaul, but his removal of troops from Britain weakened the defences still further. It did not help that Britain was now ruled at a distance, from Arles, or that Irish and Saxon attacks were renewed in 408. Frustrated with increasingly ineffectual Roman government, the Romano-British upper classes revolted against Constantine in 409. Rome itself was sacked by the Goths in 410, and in the same year the emperor Honorius, now resident at Ravenna, advised the Britons that they would have to fend for themselves, at least for the time being. The Romans never came back.

In many ways, the Britons were already well used to managing their own affairs. They maintained trade and other contacts with the continent, and much of the economic prosperity, social sophistication and cultural vitality that had characterised Roman rule remained. For centuries to come, even the barbarian invaders of Britain lived in a world which was recognisably sub-Roman. But the collapse of the empire was inevitably accompanied by considerable political and administrative dislocation. Very little is known about the politics of fifth- and sixth-century Britain – a fact which in itself speaks volumes about the levels of disruption – but most of the vast and complex structure of Roman financial, judicial and urban administration was no longer in place, and defence was now a priority. The most striking symptom of the new political climate was the reoccupation of Iron Age hillforts across Britain between the fifth and the seventh centuries.

IRISH AND SAXON SETTLEMENT

Barbarian raids continued unabated, and in many cases they were accompanied by colonisation. The Irish, in particular, seem to have settled in several parts of what later became Wales. Memorial stones bearing inscriptions in the Irish writing system known as *ogam* indicate a strong Irish influence in Dyfed, Brycheiniog and Gwynedd, and the ninth-century *Historia Brittonum* recounts a tradition that the Irish were expelled from Gwynedd by a certain Cunedda, apparently in the fifth century. Llŷn may even owe its name to an Irish tribe, the Uí Liatháin, who are said to have had a fort in Britain. The dynasties of Dyfed and Brycheiniog claimed Irish ancestry by the tenth century, and further weight is added to the likelihood of Irish settlement in Dyfed by place-name evidence, and moreover by the *Expulsion of the Déisi*, an Irish account which was composed by the ninth century. According to this source, a group known as the Déisi were expelled from Meath to Leinster and thence to *Demed*, where they made themselves kings, probably during the fifth century. Their first leader in Wales is named as Eochaid mac Artchorp, and a Tewdos ap Rhain of Dyfed is claimed as an eighth-century descendant of the Déisi; this ties in neatly with the later Welsh genealogical tradition of Dyfed. Taken together with the erection of memorial stones upon which Latin was inscribed as well as *ogam*, this would appear to suggest that an intrusive Irish aristocratic elite took power in Dyfed during the fifth century, retaining the memory of their origins, but also imitating Roman practices, apparently in an effort to gain prestige by identifying themselves with the memory of Roman rule. Furthermore, Welsh interest in Ireland was not restricted to contacts with settlers. The early Welsh annals all exhibit a particular interest in Ireland, and British missionaries travelled there in the fifth, sixth and seventh centuries. Irish monks later visited Wales, and the story of Branwen in *Pedeir Keinc y Mabinogi* also reveals close connections with Ireland, perhaps dating from much earlier times.

At the same time as Irish influence was increasing in western Britain, unprecedented numbers of Saxons were invading and settling in the south and east. Despite the twelfth-century protestations of Geoffrey of Monmouth, however, there is no evidence of a significant British exodus from these areas, or of widespread genocide, although there was certainly conflict, which could occasionally be very bloody. The Britons were led to a victory in 429 by the Gaulish bishop Germanus of Auxerre, and later accounts in the *Anglo-Saxon Chronicle* tell of Saxon advances in Kent and the south, including numerous fights from which the Britons fled as from fire. Nevertheless, despite the violence, and despite a well-attested migration from the south and west of Britain to Gaul – and especially to Armorica (later known as Brittany) – archaeological and genetic evidence suggests that most of the existing population in the conquered and settled areas remained where it was, gradually assimilating with the newcomers, who do not seem to have overwhelmed it numerically.

The British political reaction to these developments appears to have been mixed, not least because neither the 'Saxons' nor the 'Britons' were homogeneous peoples, either culturally or – more markedly – politically. Infighting appears to have been widespread between factions on both sides. Some Romano-Britons in the fifth century seem to have continued a policy established by the Romans as early as the third century, whereby Germanic tribes were allowed to settle in Britain in return for military service as *foederati*, and these mercenaries could prove useful against both barbarian attacks and rival British leaders, as well as against any attempt to reassert Roman authority from the continent. The British monk Gildas, writing in the middle of the sixth century, describes a fifth-century alliance between a certain proud tyrant and the Saxons, who later revolted against him, and in the eighth century the Northumbrian monk Bede named this man as Vortigern (Gwrtheyrn) and the Saxon leaders as Hengist and Horsa. Other British leaders resisted the invaders. One of them, Ambrosius Aurelianus (Emrys Wledig), is described by Gildas as a Roman dignitary, and he may have been responsible for a British victory at Badon Hill. By the ninth century, this battle was described by *Historia Brittonum* as the last of twelve won against the Saxons by a certain Arthur, who is also said to have met his death fighting Medrawd at Camlann in 537.

These are all semi-legendary figures, and there is no compelling reason to associate any of them specifically with Wales. Many of their deeds are consistent with what is known from reliable historical and archaeological evidence, but it is impossible to be certain about their real identities, roles or importance, or even the fact of their existence. They cannot be placed geographically with any precision, and most of the material relating to them is either very vague and confused or consists of literary, legendary and mythical accretions dating from centuries after their deaths. The all-conquering Arthur, for example, is mentioned in passing in poetry which may date from as early as the turn of the seventh century, but he does not emerge as the chief battle leader (*dux bellorum*) of the Britons until the ninth century, when *Historia Brittonum* claimed that he was personally responsible for every one of 960 Saxon casualties at Badon Hill. Such literary devices were embellished further by the tenth-century *Annales Cambriae*, which say that Arthur carried the cross of Jesus Christ on his shoulders at Badon Hill for three days and three nights. Gildas, however, does not mention Arthur at all – a very surprising omission given that his *De Excidio Britanniae* ('On the Ruin of Britain'), written in the 540s, was particularly concerned with the prowess and Christian virtues of prominent contemporary and recent British leaders in the context of Saxon invasion. Even more significantly, neither Arthur nor Ambrosius was claimed as an ancestor by early medieval Welsh dynasties – another strange omission, since genealogy was one of the most effective tools for legitimising political authority in early Wales. Genealogists were all too ready to claim descent from Magnus Maximus, Brutus, Adam and even God, but none of them mentioned Arthur until he became established as a literary icon in the later Middle Ages.

Whether or not these British leaders were real people, composite creations or entirely fictional characters, there is no doubt that various groups of Saxons had established control of large parts of southern and eastern Britain by the late fifth century. By that time, almost the whole of the western Roman empire had fallen to barbarian invasion. The only exception was Britain, where independent Romano-British rule remained in the north and west; and that, too, would have been considered 'barbarian' by Roman standards. The British kingdoms in what was later northern England and southern Scotland retained their independence until the demise of Strathclyde/Cumbria in the later ninth century, and sixth-century figures such as Urien ap Cynfarch ('Urien Rheged') and Rhydderch ap Tudwal ('Rhydderch Hen/Hael') were fondly remembered in Welsh literature as heroes of *yr Hen Ogledd* ('the Old North'). The earliest surviving Welsh poetry, Aneirin's *Gododdin*, concerns the defeat of the warband of Mynyddog Mwynfawr of Manaw Gododdin (in the region later known as Lothian) at the turn of the seventh century, in an attempt to re-cover the Roman fort at Catraeth (Catterick) from the Anglo-Saxon kingdom of Deira, which in turn was annexed by its neighbour Bernicia in 604 to form Northumbria. Autonomous British rule also persisted in Cornwall until the tenth century, but the longest survival was in Wales, where Gwynedd remained independent until the thirteenth century.

The Emergence of Independent Welsh Kingdoms

CIVITATES INTO KINGDOMS

In the late Roman period, the region which was to become Wales had been part of the province of *Britannia Prima*, which was probably based on a capital (*caput*) at Cirencester. Provinces were normally divided into *civitates*, the territo-rial extent of which usually corresponded with tribal areas. There were two of them in Wales: that of the Silures in the relatively romanised south-east, and that of the Demetae in the south-west, with capitals at Caerwent and Carmarthen respectively. North and central Wales, the land of the Ordovices, may have been rural districts (*pagi*), or perhaps a military zone administered from York. After the Romans left, and perhaps even before, political authority seems to have gravitated towards the inhabitants of the hillforts in many areas, to the extent that Degannwy and Dinas Emrys were given strong political associations in ear-ly Welsh literature. Britain was no longer a colony of an empire which stretched from the Atlantic to the Sahara and the Euphrates; it was now a patchwork of small independent units. The *civitates* were becoming kingdoms.

The establishment of native kingdoms in Britain was helped by the relative independence of provinces and *civitates* from centralised control, in compari-son with the situation elsewhere in the Roman empire. British tribal leader-ship and identities survived through the Roman period in many areas, with the result that political units were less integrated, more self-sufficient and therefore more durable than many of their continental counterparts. This was particularly true in the less romanised west and north, where the survival of native rule was aided further by remoteness from Saxon incursions, as well as by terrain which was both economically unattractive and militarily difficult in comparison with southern and eastern Britain. Archaeological evidence suggests Romano-British continuity at sites such as Dinas Emrys and possibly Degannwy, and many of the first Welsh kings were probably the heirs of late Roman provincial administration. Continuity from the Roman administrative past is also suggested by the fact that the first Welsh kingdoms were defined primarily by territory rather than by population groups.

GWYNEDD AND DYFED

By the time Gildas wrote in the 540s, several Welsh kingdoms were experiencing at least the second generation of native kingship. Maglocunus (Maelgwn) is said to have seized Gwynedd from his uncle, killing many kings in doing so, and Vortepor (Gwrthefyr), king of the Demetae, is described as the bad son of a good father. Most of these new Welsh dynasties seem to have been home-grown. The dynasty of Gwynedd, for instance, probably originated in Môn, although later tradition relates that Cunedda, the ruler of the Votadini in Manaw Gododdin, introduced himself into Gwynedd and brought with him sons whose names (and those of their sons) – including Meirion, Rhufen, Dunod, Ceredig, Dogfael and Edern – matched those of the later kingdoms and *cantrefi* of Meirionnydd, Rhufoniog, Dunoding, Ceredigion, Dogfaeling (Dyffryn Clwyd) and Edeirnion. There is archaeological evidence for a connection between Gwynedd and northern Britain, notably Pictland, in this period, but there is no conclusive evidence to substantiate the Cunedda story, which seems to represent part of a ninth-century attempt to legitimate the rule of the family of Merfyn Frych. Merfyn, like Cunedda, was an outsider, and the rest of the story bears the hallmarks of onomastic tradition – the sons were very likely invented to explain the place names, and moreover to create an impression of unity in Gwynedd and its ninth-century satellites. Nevertheless, it remains that there were significant numbers of incomers, and they may well have affected existing polities in Wales and possibly created new ones. Vortepor was probably a member of an Irish dynasty which established itself in Dyfed, and it is entirely plausible that there may also have been some British migration into Wales as the Saxons asserted themselves in the east. This was a time of flux and change and, although there was a considerable degree of continuity and stability, it is not even safe to assume that every part of Wales had become part of a kingdom by the end of the seventh century.

It is significant that the only two indisputably Welsh kings mentioned by Gildas were those of Gwynedd and Dyfed. It was only ever the rulers of these kingdoms whom the chroniclers styled 'kings of the Britons', and they played a central role in Welsh political life until the thirteenth century, especially after they were brought together dynastically in the ninth century. Maelgwn Gwynedd died of yellow plague around 547, and his successors in the seventh century included Cadwallon ap Cadfan, who extended the power of Gwynedd into Northumbria for a time in the 630s, and Cadwaladr ap Cadwallon, who died in Rome in 682 and was remembered by the native Welsh chronicle *Brut y Tywysogyon* as the last British king to contest with the Saxons for supremacy in Britain. This dynasty continued to rule Gwynedd until the death of Hywel ap Rhodri in 825. Hywel was replaced by Merfyn Frych ap Gwriad, who probably came from Man, and who founded a dynasty which was to dominate Welsh politics for centuries. When Merfyn died in 844, he was succeeded by his son, Rhodri Mawr, who extended the power of Gwynedd into Powys and Ceredigion. Rhodri was the offspring of a marriage between Merfyn and Nest of Powys, and as a result he was able to take Powys when its king, Cyngen, died in 856; similarly, Rhodri married the sister of Gwgan ap Meurig of Ceredigion and seized the kingdom when Gwgan drowned in 872. These successes, together with a victory over the Vikings in 856, ensured that Gwynedd became more powerful under Rhodri than it had been for two centuries. Moreover, in dissolving both Powys and Ceredigion as autonomous political entities, Rhodri demonstrated that there was no greater threat to the independence of Welsh kingdoms than aggression from other Welsh kingdoms. The end of Rhodri's reign was marked by defeat at the hands of the Vikings in 877 and death in battle with the English (probably the Mercians) in 878, but his son, Anarawd, restored the power of Gwynedd. Anarawd defeated the English in 881 and raided south, where Hyfaidd ap Bledri of Dyfed and Elise ap Tewdwr of Brycheiniog were driven to seek English protection from him, only for Anarawd himself to make terms with Wessex, whose military support he occasionally used in his campaigns. When he died in 916, Anarawd was hailed by the *Brut* as 'king of the Britons'.[1]

The Irish line of Dyfed became extinct with the death of Llywarch ap Hyfaidd in 904, and Anarawd's brother, Cadell, took control of the kingdom. Cadell also secured Ystrad Tywi, and the new composite entity came increasingly to be known as Deheubarth — although for a long time the name was as much a geographical reference to southern Wales in general as the name of any particular kingdom. Cadell's son, Hywel, assumed sole rule of Deheubarth when another son, Clydog, died in 920, and a period of conflict between the two branches of the descendants of Merfyn was brought to an end when Hywel took Gwynedd after the death of Idwal Foel in 942. Hywel held both kingdoms until his death in 949, and also added Brycheiniog before 944. Only Morgannwg lay outside Hywel's sphere of influence, and he entered into closer relations with the English. His name regularly appears at the head of the list of secular witnesses to English charters, above the names of other Welsh rulers, and like Anarawd he was styled 'king of the Britons' by Welsh annalists.[2] Hywel's prestige was such that he was known to later generations as Hywel Dda ('the Good'), an epithet which is first recorded in the 1120s, probably inspired by a hagiographical cult. His hegemony quickly fell apart after his death, however. There was immediately conflict between Hywel's sons and those of Idwal, who recovered Gwynedd after a victory at Carno in 949. By 952, Iago and Idwal ab Idwal were attacking Dyfed, and it seems that a victory at Llanrwst in 954 enabled them to raid Ceredigion later in the year. Nevertheless, despite the loss of Gwynedd, Hywel's son Owain established himself in Dyfed. His son Einion attacked Gŵyr in 970 and 977, and he held Brycheiniog by 983, only to be killed in 984 by the men of Gwent, where he seems to have harboured ambitions. Owain ap Hywel survived until 988, and another of his sons, Maredudd, turned his attentions towards Gwynedd, where there had been a long-running dynastic conflict since the killing of Rhodri ab Idwal Foel in 968. Iago ab Idwal had ruled there for a time, but he had been driven out by Hywel ap Ieuaf in 974 and again in 979, and Iago's son, Cystennin, had been killed when he attacked Môn in 980. When Hywel died in 985, Maredudd ab Owain was quick to take advantage. He killed Hywel's brother Cadwallon in 986 and took tribute from Gwynedd and Môn, extending his influence further into Powys by 992. In 994, however, his power in the north was lost when the sons of Meurig defeated him at Llangwm in Gwynedd. At its peak, however, Maredudd's authority had almost rivalled that of Hywel Dda, and he may still have enjoyed some degree of control in the south-east when he died in 999. He too was commemorated as 'king of the Britons'.[3]

POWYS

The origins of Powys are more obscure. The Cuneglasus (Cynlas) mentioned by Gildas may have borne rule somewhere in what was later north-eastern Wales and the English Midlands, either in Rhos or in the remains of the *civitas* of the Cornovii, which had been based on Wroxeter and later the Wrekin. Cynan ap Brochfael can be identified more securely; he was active in north-east Wales in the late sixth century, and he is also said to have attacked Môn, Dyfed, Gwent and Brycheiniog. By the ninth century (or possibly the seventh, depending on which date is accepted for the composition of the corpus of poetry known as *Canu Taliesin*), it was believed that Cynan was a member of the Cadelling dynasty, the founders of the dynasty of Powys. At the same time, however, the ninth-century *Canu Heledd*, a group of poems which forms part of *Canu Llywarch Hen*, associates another dynasty with Powys, mourning the deaths of Cynddylan ap Cyndrwyn and his brothers and their subsequent dispossession by the Saxons. The places named identify Cynddylan's territory as lying in what later became Shropshire, as well as in eastern Powys. An earlier

poem, *Marwnad Cynddylan*, also tells of a Cynddylan, ruler of Dogfaeling, fighting at Lichfield, apparently against the Christian British population there. The
descendants of Penda of Mercia are known to have controlled the Wrekin area
by the late seventh century, and it is possible that they drove out Cynddylan's
Powys dynasty earlier in the century. It is not clear whether these were a branch
of the Cadellings, whether they co-existed with them, or whether they were a
rival dynasty, but it is likely that the removal of Cynddylan would have allowed
the Cadellings to expand southwards into the central borders. Nevertheless,
Powys seems to have remained an ill-defined kingdom. There is no definite use
of the name 'Powys' in relation to either a king or the kingdom until 808, when
Annales Cambriae record the death of Cadell, king of Powys. By that time the
kingdom was being weakened by English attacks, and the last member of the
Powys line, Cyngen, died in Rome in 856. After Rhodri Mawr's seizure of the
kingdom, there were no more independent rulers of Powys until 1063.

OTHER KINGDOMS

According to the seventh-century *Life* of St Samson, a kingdom of Gwent existed in the sixth century, possibly inhabiting the shell of the Roman *civitas* of the
Silures – the name Gwent is derived from Venta Silurum, the Roman name for
Caerwent. If charters in the twelfth-century *Liber Landavensis* can be relied upon
as evidence for the early medieval period, they indicate a power base in Gwent
Uwch Coed which was superseded in the seventh century by kings around the
mouth of the Wye, where the dynasty of Meurig ap Tewdrig extended its influence until no more minor kings are mentioned by the middle of the eighth century. This hegemony included both Gwent and new territories to the west, and
it came to be known as Glywysing, after Glywys, the supposed founder of the
dynasty. Kings of Gwent seem to have co-existed with those of Glywysing in an
inferior role, and the name of Gwent, while still a recognised regional name, was
no longer the name of the dominant kingdom. The kingship of Glywysing was
shared between brothers and cousins after the death of Ithel in 745, and this situation persisted until Morgan Hen introduced a new dynasty and created a unified kingship of Morgannwg in the middle of the tenth century. Morgan died
in 974, by which time Gwent had become separate from Morgannwg; Nowy
ap Gwriad styled himself king of Gwent around 950, and his son and grandsons
followed suit. Throughout this period, there is no record that Gwent, Glywysing
or Morgannwg had any contact on the political level with the rest of Wales until
outsiders intruded themselves into the area in the early eleventh century.

Many Welsh kingdoms were shortlived, and there may well have been some
whose existence is no longer known. Documentary evidence from *Liber Landavensis* attests kings in Brycheiniog by the middle of the eighth century, but

Brycheiniog was often attacked by other Welsh kingdoms, and it eventually submitted to Wessex in the ninth century in the hope of protection; no kings are recorded there after Tewdwr ab Elise, who was active around 925. Other material in *Liber Landavensis* also suggests the existence of kingdoms of Ergyng and Gŵyr, as well as one around Cardiff, in the late sixth and early seventh centuries – there was also a king Ffernfael in Buellt around 800, but nothing else is known of his kingdom. An otherwise unrecorded kingdom of Rhufoniog was conquered by the Saxons in 816, and in this context it may be significant that early genealogical material records more dynastic lines than there were known kingdoms; on this evidence, Rhos, Meirionnydd and Dunoding (Eifionydd and Ardudwy) may all have been kingdoms in the sixth and seventh centuries. Similarly, although the first recorded king of Ceredigion is Arthen, who died in 807, the dynasty traced its ancestry back to Cunedda, suggesting that both the dynasty and the kingdom may have originated in a much earlier period. Such evidence should be treated very cautiously; genealogical trickery was a common Welsh obsession, and another Ceredigion tradition of later centuries asserted that Arthen's father, Seisyll, had annexed Ystrad Tywi to make a kingdom of Seisyllwg – contemporary sources, on the other hand, never refer to the kingdom as anything but Ceredigion. What is certain is that Ceredigion was always a recognised political unit, and has remained so, but that it had no independent kings after it fell to Rhodri Mawr in 872.

LATER DEVELOPMENTS

New dynasties arose in eleventh-century Wales, bringing with them significant changes. The rise of Llywelyn ap Seisyll was meteoric. He emerged from obscure origins – possibly in Powys – to become king of Gwynedd in 1018, and by 1022 he is described by the *Brut* as 'the supreme and most praiseworthy king of all Britain'.[4] By that time he apparently controlled Deheubarth, and defended it against an intruder named Rhain. Gwynedd was held by Iago ab Idwal after Llywelyn's death in 1023, and the balance of power shifted towards the south, where Rhydderch ap Iestyn was considered to rule all of Wales. Rhydderch hailed from Gwent, but he held at least parts of Morgannwg, and he concentrated most of his efforts in Deheubarth, which he held until he was killed in 1033. He was succeeded in Morgannwg by his son Gruffudd, and in Deheubarth by Hywel ab Edwin, who ruled there until 1039. In that year, Gruffudd, the son of Llywelyn ap Seisyll, seized control of Gwynedd, Powys and Deheubarth in a devastating series of attacks. He first took Gwynedd after Iago ab Idwal was killed, and then defeated a Mercian force in Powys before turning south to exile Hywel from Deheubarth. Hywel returned, only to be defeated at Pencader in 1041 and killed in 1044. The new dynasty of Morgannwg still had designs on Deheubarth, however, and it may have been the sons of Rhydderch who lay behind an attack on Gruffudd ap Llywelyn's warband by the men of Ystrad Tywi in 1047. Gruffudd retaliated by ravaging Ystrad Tywi and Dyfed, and he killed Gruffudd ap Rhydderch in 1056, as a result of which he seems to have exercised some degree of authority in Morgannwg.

These events marked a watershed in Welsh politics. The tendency to combine political interests in both the south-west and the south-east was a new departure, reflected in the increasing use of the term 'Deheubarth' during this period. Furthermore, Gruffudd ap Llywelyn's rule over almost the whole of Wales from the late 1050s was unprecedented. It was not matched in its geographical extent by any medieval Welsh king or prince except Owain Glyn Dŵr, and it brought Wales into direct conflict for the first time with the most powerful ruler in Britain: the king of England.

2

Wales and the Anglo-Saxons
c.577-1063

Origins of the Anglo-Welsh Border

According to the A version of the Anglo-Saxon Chronicle, the West Saxon king Ceawlin defeated three British leaders – named as Cynfael, Cynddyddan and Ffernfael – at Deorham (Dyrham) in 577, and consequently gained control of Gloucester, Cirencester and Bath. The Chronicle's account may not be entirely reliable, since it dates from three centuries or more after the events it describes, but the battle of Dyrham is a symbolic milestone in the history of Wales nonetheless. Ceawlin seems to have been based in the Thames valley, and he had apparently already beaten the Britons at Barbury Castle in Wiltshire in 556, and reportedly went on to do so again at Fethanleag (Stoke Lyne in Oxfordshire) in 584. His successes may well have been reversed when he was expelled after a battle at Woden's Barrow in Wiltshire in 592, but the Saxons were in the English West Country and Midlands to stay. By the 620s, or more likely the 630s, Penda of Mercia fought the West Saxons Cynegils and Cwichelm at Cirencester, and he seems to have annexed the surrounding area. The precise details of what happened in the late sixth and early seventh centuries may never be established beyond doubt, but it is clear that the Britons of the south west became separated from those north of the Bristol Channel as Saxon power was extended into the lower Severn valley. This was an important development in the territorial definition of Wales and Cornwall, and it may well have been around this time that a border was drawn on the Wye between what later became Gwent and England.

The establishment of the border between England and Wales was a far more complicated and obscure process than can be pinned down by particular events. Concepts of the 'Welsh' and the 'English' as peoples began to emerge in the seventh century, although neither 'Wales' nor 'England' existed until much later. Relations between them were often violent. In Welsh literary tradition, much of the material in *Canu Llywarch Hen* – notably *Canu Heledd* – points to a protracted conflict in the Shropshire area from which the Welsh emerged dispossessed and traumatised, and place-name evidence also indicates Mercian incursions into Powys in the seventh century. This was far from the whole picture, however. *Canu Llywarch Hen* also suggests that the hapless Cynddylan ap Cyndrwyn was allied with Penda in 642, and the intermingling of Old English and Old Welsh place names in the border area suggests peaceful English settlement at an early date. Moreover, although there is little doubt that the Saxon population was spreading westwards and settling in what later became the English Midlands and the Welsh borders, this does not necessarily reveal much about who exercised political control. Saxons might voluntarily accept the rule of Welsh kings in return for permission to settle; the areas in which they lived might be re-conquered by the Welsh; and Welsh populations could similarly be subjected to the Saxons. English settlement in the Cheshire area, for instance, was well advanced by the early seventh century, and expanded into north-east Wales from then onwards, leaving a preponderance of Old English place names in the region – but political control of the *cantrefi* of Rhos, Rhufoniog, Tegeingl and Dyffryn Clwyd oscillated between the English and the Welsh until the very last days of Welsh independence. Not for nothing was the area between Snowdonia and Chester known as the Perfeddwlad ('Middle Country'). Similarly, the personal names of tenants of Maelor Gymraeg in 1086 suggest that most of them were of non-Welsh origin, whereas the dynasty of the *Magonsaete* (a tributary kingdom of Mercia in modern Herefordshire) had British blood, and numerous Welsh-speaking communities remained on the English side of the border; many of them survived until the eleventh century and beyond, in some cases until fairly recently. The eleventh- or twelfth-century *Dunsæte* Ordinance contains evidence of Anglo-Saxon laws (apparently dating from the tenth century) relating to a border community in Herefordshire where there were both Welsh and English populations, and similar laws are found in *Domesday Book* in 1086. As late as the thirteenth century, the town of Hereford – which by then had been the seat of an English earldom and county for 200 years – was still usually regarded as being *in Wallia*.

The frontier between the Welsh and the English did not so much mark a national, cultural or ethnic boundary as the territorial limit of consistently effective kingship. On both sides of the border, such power was exercised locally. The boundary between Powys and Mercia seems to have become stabilised around the middle of the seventh century, and by 700 the southern part of the border between England and Wales probably lay roughly where it is today; the fact that it has lasted so long is no doubt closely linked to the sharp geographical contrasts in the area, and their effect on cultural differences. The northern frontier was less well defined, and there is no reason to suppose that the present western border of Cheshire represents any early medieval political boundary. In 616, Æþelfrith of Northumbria defeated Selyf ap Cynan of

Powys (and possibly forces from Gwynedd) in a battle at Chester, after which the monks of Bangor-on-Dee, who had come to pray for a Welsh success, were allegedly massacred. This may have dislodged a Welsh dynasty (possibly the Cadelling) from north-east Wales, but there was no immediate imposition of English rule in Cheshire, and these events do not seem to have established a border between the English and the Welsh, or separated Wales from the British kingdoms of the North. Whereas there were early English kingdoms in parts of the southern and western Midlands, there was none in Cheshire.

English Involvement in Wales

NORTHUMBRIA

Æþelfrith had made clear the aggressive intentions of Northumbria towards Wales, and in 632 his successor Eadwine besieged Cadwallon ap Cadfan of Gwynedd in Môn. Bede, writing in Northumbria 100 years later, suggests that Eadwine took possession of both Môn and Man, at least for a time, and the Welsh poems known as the triads also refer to him fighting in Llŷn. But whatever else the Northumbrian influence in north Wales was, it was shortlived. Cadwallon responded with a devastating series of blows which illustrated both his authority and the breadth of his political horizons. Allying himself with Penda of Mercia in 633 or 634, apparently as the senior partner, he invaded Northumbria and killed Eadwine in battle at Hatfield Chase, thereby becoming the only independent Welsh king in recorded history to have overthrown an English royal dynasty. Not content with this, Cadwallon ravaged Northumbria, destroying all opposition, and according to Bede he ruled from York for a time. Northumbria may even have disintegrated into its constituent parts of Bernicia and Deira, but its recovery was swift; in 634 or 635, the new Northumbrian king Oswald fought and killed Cadwallon at Heavenfield near Hexham.

Cadwallon had demonstrated that a Welsh king could exert a significant influence in Anglo-Saxon politics. Had it not been for his intervention, Northumbria might well have asserted itself as the most powerful kingdom in England. As it was, Eadwine's defeat enabled Penda to establish Mercia as the dominant power in the English Midlands for the next two decades, and he appears to have continued his policy of making alliances with the Welsh. Forces from Powys and possibly Gwynedd may have been allied with him when he defeated and killed Oswald at Maserfelth near Oswestry in 642, and his recovery of Welsh treasures from the Northumbrian Oswiu in 655 seems to indicate friendly relations with Cadwallon's successor, Cadfael ap Cynfyn. Cadfael may well have been present when Penda was killed by Oswiu at Winwaed in Northumbria in the same year.

MERCIA

There were no more significant Welsh attacks on England for 400 years after Cadwallon's death. The English, on the other hand, attacked Wales regularly throughout the early medieval period, to the extent that *Domesday Book* records that the customs of Hereford in the late eleventh century included an obligation on the men of the town to accompany the king's sheriff on expeditions into Wales. Indeed, the very name of Hereford defined it in Old English as the ford suitable for troops, who as often as not were crossing the Wye on their way into Wales. Aggression against the Welsh had become institutionalised, and for much of the eighth and ninth centuries it was led by Mercia.

Æþelbald of Mercia came into conflict with the Welsh of Glywysing in the first half of the eighth century, and he was joined in another attack by Cuthred of Wessex in 743, but it was Æþelbald's successor, Offa, who made the greatest impression on the Welsh. Offa united Mercia, and went on to achieve dominance over all the English kingdoms south of the Humber in the second half of the eighth century. His prestige was on a European scale – he was treated as an equal by Charlemagne, who became Holy Roman emperor in 800 – and his influence was inevitably felt in Wales, where he was and still is best remembered for the dyke which bears his name.

A hundred years after Offa's death in 796, Asser, the Welsh courtier and biographer of Ælfred of Wessex, was of the opinion that the Mercian king had caused a great dyke to be built 'from sea to sea' between the English and the Welsh.[1] The dyke certainly existed – much of it is still there – but archaeology has raised many doubts about its purpose and extent, and also the date of its construction. The west-facing ditch and palisade suggests some defensive function against the Welsh, and troops may have been available from villages nearby, but the dyke was not fortified and there was apparently no garrison. Nor does it seem to have been meant as a frontier control with designated crossing points, since many of the apparent gaps in it are not original; although it was not well defended, there was clearly an intention that the dyke should be difficult to cross. Furthermore, its structure varies from place to place, and there are significant gaps in it between Treuddyn and the sea in the north, in Ergyng, and also in the south; Asser's phrase 'from sea to sea (*de mari usque ad mare*)' was a common literary device, often used by Bede and Gildas, and usually intended to convey a sense of great distance rather than an accurate measurement. Some sections in the Midlands seem to have been constructed long before Offa's time, and other parts in the north and south, including the ditch on the eastern bank of the Wye, were probably added on in the ninth century or even later. There is also an entirely separate Wat's dyke to the east of Offa's dyke, which extended it from the Severn to Holywell, probably at a later date. In short, Offa's dyke was not a unitary work, carried out to some master plan; it was defensible without being overtly military; it was intended to restrict cross-border movement without preventing it altogether; it did not demarcate a final and comprehensive boundary between England and Wales; and it was not necessarily built by Offa.

The central portion of the dyke appears to correspond with the Mercian border with Powys, and it is not unlikely that Offa upgraded and extended existing earthworks there, probably in the 770s. This was most likely in response to deteriorating relations with Powys, where, according to a pillar erected by the native dynasty in its own honour in the ninth century, Elise ap Cyngen fought the English and drove them out, apparently in the 760s. Mercia was not a monolithic kingdom, however, and each part of the border enjoyed its own relationship with its Welsh neighbours. The lack of a dyke in Ergyng, and also in the territory adjacent to north Wales, could reflect peaceful relations between Mercia and the Welsh in those areas, whereas the existence of a ditch on the borders of Powys and Gwent suggests a less friendly situation. Whatever Offa contributed to this, his reputation earned him credit for work which was not his, or even of his time. Moreover, from at least the time of Asser, the dyke assumed a symbolic importance far greater than its practical use. By the twelfth century, it was the conventionally accepted boundary between Wales and England, and recognised as such in Welsh law. It was also believed that ordinances had been made in the past under which any Welshman found on the eastern side should be mutilated, although Anglo-Norman chroniclers could not agree whether it was Offa who had ordered the removal of feet or Harold Godwinesson the cutting off of hands. The dyke may not have set an inflexible and impermeable boundary, and it was not always regarded as such, but as a statement of intent it both revealed and exerted an influence over the mindset of the inhabitants of the border.

The apparently defensive nature of the dyke belies the truth about Mercian relations with the Welsh in this period. After killing Dyfnwal ap Tewdwr of Brycheiniog, who had apparently attacked Hereford in 760, Offa launched expeditions into Dyfed in 777 and again into unnamed parts of Wales in 783. These attacks reached further than any English campaign since the 630s, and they were continued and intensified after Offa's death. His successor, Cenwulf, seems to have been responsible for a battle at Rhuddlan in 796 and the strangling of Caradog of Gwynedd in 798, and he returned in 816, seizing Rhufoniog and ravaging Snowdonia. Cenwulf also attacked Dyfed in 818, and the fact that *Annales Cambriae* record the latter expeditions in terms of invasion and laying waste suggests that these were full-blooded campaigns, intent on devastation as a strategic political instrument as much as booty for its own sake. If this was the case, it was rewarded in 823, when Cenwulf's successor, Ceolwulf, destroyed Degannwy and took the kingdom of Powys. The insistence and ferocity of English attacks on Wales had reached a new level, and the independence of Welsh kingdoms was under genuine threat.

The kings of Powys re-established themselves, however, not least because Mercia was able to devote less of its attention to Wales as it came under pressure itself from Ecgberht of Wessex in the 820s and 830s. But the damage had been done. Ecgberht followed his Mercian predecessors in leading troops into north Wales in 830, and it was probably Powys which was subjected by Burhræd of Mercia and Æþelwulf of Wessex in 853. Powys was unable to survive as an independent kingdom after 855, and although it was Gwynedd which profited from its demise, Mercia played an important part in preventing its resurgence and also in continuing to pressurise other Welsh kingdoms. Beorhtwulf of Mercia was probably responsible for the death of Meurig of Gwent in 849, and it was almost certainly one of his successors, Ceolwulf, who killed Rhodri Mawr and his son Gwriad in 878, only for the Welsh to avenge their defeat on the Conwy in 881. According to Asser, it was Mercian pressure which drove the kings of Glywysing and Gwent into the arms of Wessex in the 870s, and furthermore it appears that much of north Wales, and the Perfeddwlad in particular, was controlled by Mercia before the Vikings came to Chester in 893, although it is not clear for how long.

WESSEX AND THE FIRST WELSH SUBMISSIONS

As a result of this English pressure, Welsh kings were drawn into increasingly subservient relationships with their English counterparts. The *Anglo-Saxon Chronicle* reports that Ecgberht turned the Welsh to 'humble obedience' in 830,[2] and Burhræd and Æþelwulf achieved something similar in 853. It was Ælfred of Wessex, however, who received the first formal submissions, and his assertion of superiority was born paradoxically of a position of desperate weakness. A 'Great Army' of Vikings invaded eastern England in 865, and subsequent Danish attacks in the 870s resulted in the emasculation of Mercia, the creation of a new Viking kingdom of York, and the near conquest of Wessex. Wessex needed all the allies it could find, but the situation gradually turned to its advantage as the politics of southern Britain became polarised between Christian Wessex and the pagan Scandinavian sphere of influence. The Welsh stood by as interested onlookers at first, but Ælfred's victory over the Danes in 878 made it increasingly necessary to take sides. At the same time, the southern Welsh kingdoms were suffering from the attentions of Anarawd ap Rhodri of Gwynedd and also Ceolwulf of Mercia, and this, according to Asser, was the immediate concern of Hywel ap Rhys of Glywysing, Brochfael and Ffernfael ap Meurig of

Gwent, Hyfaidd ap Bledri of Dyfed and Elise ap Tewdwr of Brycheiniog when they sought Ælfred's 'lordship and protection' in about 878.[3] The terms of the agreement are not known, but they are likely to have involved little more than promises of mutual support, with Ælfred as the senior partner. Nevertheless, the acceptance by the Welsh of a relationship in which they were subordinate to an English king was an important new development.

In Gwynedd, Anarawd had little reason to fear Ælfred, whose direct influence was always restricted to southern England. But, as his neighbours all aligned themselves either for or against Wessex, Anarawd was forced to follow suit. He made terms with Scandinavian York in the 880s, but by about 893 he and his brothers reconsidered their position and asked for an alliance with Wessex. In many ways, the relationship was reciprocal, not least because Ælfred was keen to detach Anarawd from his association with York. Anarawd received many favours with great ceremony, and he reaped the rewards of his cordial relationship with Wessex in the form of military aid. Ælfred worked with the Welsh against the Danes, notably in the campaign which chased down and destroyed the Essex host on the Severn in 893, and Anarawd also enjoyed English assistance against Ceredigion and Ystrad Tywi in 895. Nevertheless, he was bound to promise obedience to Ælfred on the same terms as Æþelræd of the Mercians. In theory, if not in practice, the most powerful king in Wales now recognised the king of Wessex as his superior.

This relationship persisted under Eadward the Elder. Eadward worked with the Welsh, ransoming the bishop of Ergyng from the Vikings in 914, and at Tamworth in 918 he received the submission of Hywel and Clydog ap Cadell of Dyfed, Idwal Foel of Gwynedd and the kings of the area between Meirionnydd and Gŵyr. It is also likely that there was a previous submission to his sister Æþelflæd, the Lady of the Mercians and wife of the ealdorman Æþelræd, which reinforced the Mercian position in north-east Wales. This area had been unstable since the Scandinavian seizure of Chester in 893, but the city was retaken by the English in 907, and by 919 Eadward was in control of the whole of the surrounding region. Using this as a springboard, he moved into the Perfeddwlad, where Rhuddlan was fortified in 921 as part of a project to strengthen the *burhs* of the whole of Mercia. The Welsh resisted this, allying themselves with the men of Chester – many of whom were of Scandinavian origin – against Eadward in 924, and the English probably did not secure control of the area until they killed Idwal Foel of Gwynedd and his brother Elise in 942. It is possible, although by no means certain, that Wat's dyke was constructed around this time, marking off the reorganised land around Chester from territories controlled by the Welsh. Whenever this dyke was built, it was probably not intended as a final boundary, and it seems to have been superseded by growth westwards as Chester became the administrative centre for at least half of the Perfeddwlad. This interpretation is supported by the inclusion of the hundred of Atiscross, which lay between the Dee and the Clwyd, in *Domesday* Cheshire in 1086 – an arrangement which very likely pre-dated the recovery of the area by Gruffudd ap Llywelyn in the middle of the eleventh century.

When Eadward's son, Æþelstan, became king in 925, Wessex was already becoming dominant in the English Midlands. By the time he died in 939, Æþelstan had forged the nucleus of a kingdom of England, expelled the Scandinavians from York – making himself the first Southumbrian king to rule north of the Humber – and defeated the king of Scots. Only a few decades after his grandfather, Ælfred, had been reduced to hiding from the Danes in the marshes of the Somerset levels, Æþelstan was the most powerful ruler in Britain since the Romans, and he laid claim to imperial authority over the whole island.

In this political climate, it was to be expected that the Welsh would continue to acknowledge their inferior status. Hywel Dda of Dyfed and Owain ap Hywel of Gwent accordingly submitted in 927, and between then and 956 Idwal Foel of Gwynedd, Morgan Hen of Glywysing, Tewdwr ab Elise of Brycheiniog and Cadwgan ap Meurig of Gwent also attended the court of Wessex. Some of them did so several times, witnessing the king's charters, and all of them were seen as lesser kings (*subreguli*). The terms of their submission are not recorded explicitly by contemporary sources, but there were undoubtedly demands for military support, since Idwal, Hywel and Morgan all set out for Scotland with Æþelstan in 934, and Hywel aided Eadmund with troops in Strathclyde in 944. The other function of submission was the payment of tribute. According to William of Malmesbury, who wrote in the twelfth century, Æþelstan summoned Welsh kings to Hereford in 927 and bullied them into promising him a yearly tribute consisting of 20 pounds of gold, 300 pounds of silver, 25,000 oxen and an unspecified number of hounds and hawks; at the same meeting, he is supposed to have set the border between England and Wales at the Wye. If this account is reliable – and that is possible but far from certain – this was the earliest attested tribute agreement between the Welsh and the English, although there is no direct evidence that it was actually paid. The Welsh prophecy poem *Armes Prydein*, composed around the time of Æþelstan's greatest triumphs, refers to taxes that had been collected from Kaer Geri (Cirencester), implying that tribute may have gone to England at this time, and the Welsh of Gwynedd certainly appear to have been used to paying regular tribute to foreigners by the late tenth and early eleventh centuries – although by then it was paid not to Wessex, but to the Vikings.

Submissions always took place in England, emphasising the superiority of Æþelstan and his successors, Eadmund and Eadræd. But they were not extracted by force. Rather, the Welsh voluntarily travelled to attend the king at places as far-flung as Eamont (near Penrith), Exeter, Worthy (in Hampshire), Luton, Winchester, Nottingham, Dorchester and Kingston-on-Thames. They did this partly because of the implicit threat of violence. William of Malmesbury, for example, claims that Idwal Foel was expelled from Gwynedd by Æþelstan, who allowed him to return only under strict conditions, and more reliable sources confirm that Idwal was killed fighting the English in 942. But the presence of Welsh kings at court probably owed as much to other factors, not least the influence of Hywel Dda, who alone among them was seen as a *regulus* rather than a *subregulus* at the coronation of Eadræd in 946. Hywel may have adopted English legal ideas, but he was anything but subservient in his dealings with Wessex. Although he later ruled most of Wales, he held no more than Deheubarth when Æþelstan was confronted by a combined force of Scots, Northumbrians, Strathclyde Britons and the Hiberno-Norse of Dublin in 937. Yet Hywel chose to remain neutral, no doubt waiting to see whether there was greater cause to fear attack from Wessex or the Scandinavians. As it happened, Æþelstan won the greatest battle of the era at Brunanburh, but Hywel clearly possessed both the independence of mind and action to contemplate the defeat of Wessex and the diplomatic skills to renew relations with it in the following years. He was no puppet, but neither did he take the course advocated by the poet of *Armes Prydein*, who wanted the Welsh to join the coalition against Æþelstan and drive the Saxons out of Britain, slaughtering them as far as the coast whence they had come. If he did share such feelings, Hywel did not allow them to rule his head. It is perhaps a measure of his diplomatic ambivalence that Hywel departed from normal Welsh practice by giving one of his sons the Anglo-Saxon name Edwin. Æþelstan had a brother called Eadwine who drowned at sea in 933, and it is impossible to tell whether Hywel's choice of name was a flattering and sympathetic gesture, a calculated act of spite, or mere coincidence.

By the middle of the tenth century, there was little doubt that southern English domination was a permanent fixture in British politics, despite the protestations of *Armes Prydein*. England had originally been a mosaic of small kingdoms, but there was a long-term trend towards amalgamation into blocks, and this culminated in the creation of a precocious kingdom of England by 1000, complete with sophisticated judicial, fiscal, governmental and administrative systems. Claims were repeatedly made for *imperium* over the whole of Britain, but their importance should not be overestimated. The ideas which underlay the imperialist rhetoric seem to have owed as much to a concept of confederation as to any desire to create a kingdom of Britain founded on military conquest, and both the English and the Welsh viewed submission pragmatically. It was not so much a prelude to conquest as a means to an end. For Wessex, Welsh submissions allowed breathing room from Scandinavian pressure and the chance to indulge in megalomaniac fantasy. For the Welsh, although demeaning, they offered the chance to become associated with the trappings of power, and also a certain degree of comfort. A powerful ally who could protect the Bristol Channel and the sea approaches to Chester was a valuable asset, and the Welsh were no doubt aware that Norse victory in England might leave them alone and surrounded by Scandinavian territory. Nevertheless, parallels can be drawn which suggest that the taking of Welsh submissions in the context of an expanding kingdom of England and the lack of a political centre of gravity in Wales posed a potential threat to Welsh independence: in Germany, for example, a serious barbarian threat in the tenth century allowed Otto I to neutralise and incorporate border zones within an increasingly centralised kingdom. But it remains that Wales was not incorporated into England, and very little of its territory ever came under Anglo-Saxon control. In this period, it remained no more and no less than a buffer zone.

THE LOOSENING OF ANGLO-WELSH POLITICAL RELATIONS

Anglo-Welsh relations at the highest level subsided dramatically shortly after Eadræd ended Viking rule in York, and it is noticeable that the period of Welsh submissions coincided very neatly not only with the growth of Wessex, but also with its need for support against the Scandinavians. The death of Eirik Bloodaxe in 954 brought to an end fifteen years of warfare during which seven kings had ruled York in nine separate reigns, and moreover it marked the fall of the last Scandinavian kingdom in England. The greatest destabilising influence in English politics had disappeared, albeit temporarily, and the efforts of Anglo-Saxon kings were now directed towards consolidation of their power in Northumbria. The English no longer had much use for Welsh support, and the intensity of renewed Viking attacks on England during the reign of Æþelræd *Unræd* at the turn of the eleventh century made a return to the hegemony of Æþelstan unthinkable. For the English in this period, Wales was merely a sideshow. The Danish conquest of large swathes of England, and indeed of the kingdom of England itself in 1014, required all of their attention, and Scandinavian attack remained the greatest perceived threat to England until after the Norman conquest. For the Welsh, the loosening of relations with Wessex may have been a factor in the upsurge in Viking attacks in the second half of the tenth century, but there was not much that could be done about that.

There is very little evidence of a genuinely dependent relationship between the Welsh and the English in the latter half of the tenth century and the first half of the eleventh, or indeed of any concerted attempt to create one. Eadræd never styled himself an emperor over the Welsh, and the submission to Eadgar at Chester in 973 seems to have marked a departure from the early-tenth-century model. Eadgar was rowed on the Dee by Iago and Hywel ab Idwal of Gwynedd, as well as Scandinavian and northern kings, but this took place on or near the border of Eadgar's kingdom – not at court somewhere deep in England where Welsh submissions could be treated as normal business – and the whole event had a flavour of foreign policy rather than domestic politics. The ceremony appears to have represented an attempt to create a pan-Irish Sea alliance against the Hiberno-Norse, with Eadgar at its head; he sailed to Chester with his fleet, and the kings who rowed him were all from the northern Irish Sea area. More significantly, perhaps, although Eadgar's coronation at Bath in 973 employed the language and symbolism of empire, no Welsh kings are known to have attended his court or witnessed his charters, and there were no more Welsh submissions until the middle of the eleventh century.

English raids into Wales continued, however: Cadwgan ab Owain of Morgannwg was killed by the English in 949; Ælfhere of Mercia attacked Gwynedd in 967; Eadric Streona of Mercia ravaged Dyfed as far as St Davids in 1012; and in 1035 Caradog ap Rhydderch was killed in what may have been an English foray into Morgannwg. At the same time, the Welsh began to use English help against each other. Edwin ab Einion ravaged Dyfed, Ceredigion, Gŵyr and Cydweli with the help of Edylfi the Saxon in 992, and Hywel ap Ieuaf was similarly joined by Ælfhere in attacking Brycheiniog and Morgannwg in 983. The latter alliance seems to have dated back to at least 978, when Hywel had English support in attacking Clynnog Fawr in Gwynedd. Such co-operation was mutually beneficial, enabling Hywel to assume control of Gwynedd, and bolstering Ælfhere's position in England, where the death of Eadgar in 975 was followed by dynastic faction fighting. By the same token, Hywel's position seems to have been weakened by Ælfhere's death, and he was killed by other English forces in 985. The practice of seeking military support from outsiders was continued in Welsh dealings with Anglo-Saxons, Vikings and the Normans in the eleventh century, and it represented a significant development, introducing a volatile new element into relations between native Welsh kingdoms.

THE RISE AND FALL OF THE WELSH THREAT TO ENGLAND

As far as Anglo-Welsh relations were concerned, the renewal of large-scale Welsh raids on England in the middle of the eleventh century was equally momentous. Facing a Viking raid on Morgannwg in 1049, Gruffudd ap Rhydderch responded by persuading its leaders to attack Gwent and the Forest of Dean instead, and he joined in the campaign himself, ravaging the manor of Tidenham on the Severn, defeating the forces of Bishop Ealdræd of Worcester, and destroying the levies of Gloucestershire and Herefordshire in the process. The success of this expedition seems to have filled Gruffudd with confidence, and in 1053 he attacked Gloucestershire again around West-bury on the Severn. The first of these border raids was largely inspired by the immediate necessity of finding work for a rapacious Viking fleet, and attacks on England also served to cover Gruffudd's eastern flank as he pursued his main objective, which was to take control of Gwent. But the English now re-garded Welsh aggression as a serious problem, and in 1053 Gruffudd's brother, Rhys, was killed in retaliation. His head was taken to the king at Gloucester.

Any doubts that the Welsh could cause real difficulties in England were dispelled by Gruffudd ap Llywelyn of Gwynedd. Soon after becoming king in 1039, Gruffudd smashed a Mercian force at Rhyd-y-Groes on the Severn in Powys, killing Eadwine, the brother of Leofric of Mercia, apparently with the purpose of securing his eastern borders while he imposed himself in Deheubarth. Before long, Gruffudd established himself as the most powerful king in Wales, and he seems to have associated himself with the influential Godwine party in England, enlisting the support of Swegn Godwinesson – who had recently been created an earl at Hereford – on a raid into south Wales in 1046. In 1051, however, Godwine and his sons came into conflict with the king, Eadward the Confessor, and they were expelled from England after what nearly turned into a civil war. Gruffudd appears to have been quick to take advantage of the unrest, since it was very likely he who led a Welsh raid on Leominster in 1052. Incidentally, it may have been on this campaign that the Welsh first encountered Norman military opposition, since Eadward appointed a number of Norman lords in the border area in the 1050s, among whom were Ralf the Timid at Hereford, Richard fitz Scrob at Ludlow, and Osbern Pentecost (probably at Ewyas Harold).

After the rehabilitation of Godwine and his sons in 1052, Gruffudd involved Gwynedd in English politics to a degree not seen since the 630s. Ælfgar of Mercia had received Harold Godwinesson's earldom of East Anglia from the king in 1051, but he lost it when Harold returned in 1052. He recovered it again when Harold was made earl of Wessex after Godwine's death in 1053, but the growing power of the Godwinessons must have given him a sense of insecurity, especially when Tostig Godwinesson succeeded to the earldom of Northumbria in 1055. Before long, Ælfgar was accused of treachery. Whether or not the allegations were true, they were the product of his rivalry with the Godwinessons, and his unease was no doubt shared by Gruffudd ap Llywelyn – indeed, it may have been negotiations with Gruffudd which gave rise to the accusations against him. Any ties which Gruffudd may have forged with the Godwinessons were severed in 1055 when, having been outlawed, Ælfgar sought and received protection in Gwynedd. Then, after waiting for Ælfgar to bring ships from Ireland, Gruffudd attacked Herefordshire. The *Brut* records a fierce battle there, but the *Anglo-Saxon Chronicle* (pursuing its own anti-Norman agenda) asserts that the English fled without a fight, allegedly because the Norman earl of Hereford, Ralf the Timid, insisted that they fought on horseback. Hereford now lay open to Gruffudd. Civilians were massacred, the cathedral was looted – although not before several canons were killed in trying to prevent it – and the town was pillaged and burned down.

Gruffudd had transformed Welsh relations with England. As a result of his alliance with Mercia, Welshmen accompanied Ælfgar's sons, Eadwine and Morkere, when they met Harold at Northampton later in 1055, and further traces of the Gwynedd-Mercia axis can be found for decades afterwards, most notably after Gruffudd's death. Gruffudd's position in Wales at the end of 1055 was almost unassailable. His main rival, Gruffudd ap Rhydderch, had died before the attack on Hereford, and the incursion into the border helped to secure a new pan-Welsh hegemony. The evidence of *Domesday Book* suggests that Gruffudd had also extended the Welsh border eastwards by this time, recovering disputed areas that had been lost to the English in previous centuries, and pushing far beyond Offa's dyke to Wat's dyke. Even the king of England now acknowledged that he was a force to be reckoned with.

Eadward the Confessor's response to the attack in 1055 was much firmer than it had been in 1052, no doubt because of the Mercian dimension. Harold was sent into Wales with an army, but he achieved little more than the erection of a castle beyond the Dore in western Herefordshire, and he contented himself with re-fortifying Hereford. Peace was eventually made at Billingsley in Ergyng. The terms are not known, but they can hardly have been to Gruffudd's detriment. His ally Ælfgar was treated very favourably, and Gruffudd was probably allowed to keep Ergyng, which he had apparently overrun. His influence in the Herefordshire border area was now so great that the English seem to have decided that it was intolerable. In 1056, Harold arranged for the election of his chaplain Leofgar – who was known more for his military prowess than his piety – as bishop of Hereford, and, together with the sheriff, Ælfnoþ, Leofgar immediately entered Wales with another force. It was a disaster, as Gruffudd routed the expedition and killed the leaders. Gone were the days when a powerful border lord could sweep through Wales, taking huge spoils; the incursions of the 1050s were tentative, localised and intended not so much to overawe the Welsh as to keep them in check.

Gruffudd was now almost in a position to dictate terms. In a meeting with some of the most distinguished men in England – Harold, Leofric of Mercia and Bishop Ealdræd of Worcester (soon to become Archbishop of York) – he recognised Eadward as his overlord, swearing to be a 'loyal and faithful under-king'.[4] The term *undercyning* was the Old English form of the Latin *subregulus*, found in the witness lists of tenth-century charters, and some of Eadward's own charters indicate that he liked to be thought of in the same terms as his predecessors – as a ruler of Britain. But there is no evidence that Gruffudd ever paid him tribute or sent him troops, or even that he attended his court. The twelfth-century writer Walter Map says that Gruffudd agreed to become Eadward's man, but only after Eadward admitted his equal status as a king, having made the effort to cross the Severn from Aust to Beachley to meet him in person; Gruffudd supposedly carried him the last few yards. However credible or otherwise this might be, it remains that 1056 saw the only reliably attested submission by any Welsh ruler to an Anglo-Saxon king in the eleventh century, and that the agreement does not appear to have entailed any of the obligations which had existed 100 years before.

Gruffudd's status as a major power was further underlined by his marriage around 1057 to Ælfgar's daughter, Ealdgyþ, and he intervened once again in Mercian politics when Ælfgar was exiled for a second time in 1058. As before, the earl sought refuge in Gwynedd, and Gruffudd launched another attack on the border, this time with the additional support of the Norwegian Magnus Haraldsson. Ælfgar was once more reinstated, and the Gwynedd-Mercia alliance remained unchallenged until his death. Eadward could do little more than keep a respectful distance.

This all changed after Ælfgar's death in 1062. The earl's son and successor, Eadwine, lacked his father's influence, and it was soon apparent that the mutual respect in Eadward's dealings with Gruffudd had been purely pragmatic. With Ælfgar gone, Eadward wasted no time. Harold was granted leave to attack early in 1063, and he launched a lightning strike, burning Gruffudd's stronghold at Rhuddlan and destroying his ships. Gruffudd eluded him and slipped out to sea, but Harold brought a fleet from Bristol around the Welsh coast to Anglesey later in the year, while Tostig led an army into north Wales. This time, Gruffudd's allies deserted him, perhaps tempted by English threats and bribes, and no doubt remembering old grievances. He was killed by members of his own household, and both his head and the figurehead of his ship were cut off and sent to Harold and thence to Eadward. Gruffudd had been the most powerful king ever seen in Wales – Walter Map compared him with Alexander the Great – and at the beginning of 1063 he was at the height of his authority. Yet Harold had overseen his defeat, his death, and the disintegration of his hegemony in the space of eight months. A century and a half later, Gerald of Wales attributed much of the Norman success in Wales to Harold's legacy, and he claimed – almost certainly erroneously – that there were many stones in Wales inscribed with the legend *Hic fuit victor Haroldus* ('Here Harold was victor'). Such was the folk memory of Harold's achievements that John of Salisbury wrote in the twelfth century that so many Welshmen had been killed by his campaigns that Eadward passed a law allowing Welsh women to marry Englishmen. More plausibly, it was also believed that Harold had enacted severe punishments for Welshmen bearing arms into England.

The Anglo-Saxon Achievement in Wales

The size of the 1063 campaign, and the swiftness with which Eadward and Harold took advantage of Gruffudd's weakened position, show that they regarded the limitation of Gwynedd's dominion as a matter of priority. Their concern, however, was to protect England, not to overrun Wales. The campaigns of the 1050s were emphatically not directed against the stronghold of Welsh power, and even that of 1063, which was manifestly intended to destroy Gruffudd's supremacy, was not a concerted attempt to destroy his kingship, let alone Welsh independence. Eadward was reportedly as ready to negotiate with the Welsh as to fight them, and, moreover, like all of their West Saxon predecessors, Eadward and Harold followed a policy of containment rather than conquest, despite their military advantage. It was now clear that English military might could penetrate the heart of Gwynedd and defeat any Welsh king in the field, and Norman lords on the border had also given the English a new and powerful strategic weapon – the castle – the first of which seems to have been built 'ultra Straddele'[5] (probably at Ewyas Harold on the Welsh border) in 1051 or 1052. But English territorial gains in 1063 were much less extensive than those won by Northumbria and Mercia in earlier centuries, and they did not amount to much more than a return to the pre-1039 status quo: Ergyng was reincorporated as part of south-western Herefordshire, the border in the north was pushed back to the Clwyd, and Harold nibbled at the border in Gwent. Harold's main concern was to protect his western border, to promote himself as Eadward's natural successor, and to curb the power of Mercia, which threatened to sever Tostig's earldom of Northumbria from the rest of the Godwinesson lands. All of these objectives were achieved in the 1063 campaign, as – acting on Eadward's behalf – he established himself as the most formidable earl in England and deprived the Mercians of their strongest ally. There was no need to press the victory further.

Nonetheless, the subjection of the Welsh was not in doubt. When Bleddyn and Rhiwallon ap Cynfyn succeeded their half-brother Gruffudd in Gwynedd and Powys respectively in 1063, they were required to promise Eadward as much as the Welsh had ever given before to any other king, to help him by land and sea, and to be obedient. It is significant, however, that Welsh submissions were no longer voluntary – from the middle of the eleventh century, they had to be extracted by military campaigns. Furthermore, even complete victory did not secure English control of territory only a few miles inside Wales, as Caradog ap Gruffudd showed when he destroyed the new hunting lodge built by Harold for Eadward at Portskewett, near Chepstow, shortly before the king was due to arrive there in 1065. Similarly, Bleddyn raided in Ergyng – now firmly restored as part of England, and usually known by its English name, Archenfield – before 1066. The requirements of border security had embroiled the English in areas where the king's writ often did not run, and it was also apparent that, despite their successes, no English king had ever comprehensively asserted a prerogative over his subordinates in dealing with Wales; Eadward had left the leadership of campaigns to Harold and others. The king's authority was undisputed, but it must sometimes have appeared very abstract when viewed from the borders of Wales.

Nevertheless, the Anglo-Saxon kings had established a concept of superiority over the Welsh which was never challenged by an independent Welsh ruler, and this was never more apparent than under Eadward the Confessor. Bleddyn and Rhiwallon were described as Harold's *satellites* in 1063, and English sources say that Wales was 'entrusted' to them by the king. Their rule was firmly under Eadward's *imperium*. Even at the height of Gruffudd's influence, Eadward had always been his overlord, and when Eadward died in 1066 he was said to have 'governed the Welsh'.[6] For all that Gruffudd had been 'king over the whole of Wales',[7] he lacked the political vocabulary and machinery to challenge English overlordship by turning his authority into something more permanent and far-reaching than his own lifetime, power and prestige. The only way to do that would have been to create a new institution: a kingship of Wales, comparable with the kingship of the Scots. Only then could a Welshman deal with the king of England on truly equal terms. But a unitary kingship of Wales was never a realistic possibility, since it would have cut across innumerable vested interests throughout Wales and also in England. Thus, although Welsh subjection to the Anglo-Saxons was not articulated in binding terms of contractual obligation even in 1063, the Welsh were very definitely subordinate.

The twelfth-century Anglo-Norman poet Geoffrey Gaimar finished his account of 1063 with the statement that 'there was no more heed paid to the Welsh'.[8] The next two centuries would show that not to be entirely true, but Wales would never be as strong again. Gruffudd ap Llywelyn had focused English attention on Wales in a new way, and his defeat threw the whole of Wales into turmoil. Over the course of the next few decades, every corner of the country would be contested by numerous parties, including Welsh, Normans, and not least Scandinavians.

3

Wales and the Vikings
852–c.1282

Scandinavian Raids, Settlement and Control

The first significant contact between Scandinavians and Britain and Ireland was brought about by the Viking raids which began in earnest with the ransacking of the monastery of Lindisfarne in Northumbria in 793. By the middle of the ninth century, Danish and Norwegian armies were overwintering in England and Ireland, often settling, intermarrying with native dynasties, and establishing military and commercial bases. The Norse military camp of Dublin was founded in 841, and York was seized in 867, becoming a Viking kingdom from 876 until 954. Large tracts of England, Ireland and Scotland were subjected to Norse rule, and Dublin and Chester developed into prosperous trading centres by the middle of the tenth century. At Chester, in particular, a Welsh population mixed with English and Scandinavians in a vibrant multicultural city. Viking influence now ranged across the whole of Britain and Ireland, and the Irish Sea formed a Scandinavianised cultural, economic, military and political zone of which Wales could hardly avoid becoming part.

The Viking influence on Wales was initially defined by raids, many of which were probably not recorded. Often the intention was simply to collect supplies, and in many cases it was to loot silverware and capture slaves. There was a thriving market for slaves in Ireland, and many of them were Welsh. St Patrick – a Briton – was taken into captivity by pirates from Ireland in the fifth century, and the practice is recorded more widely in the Viking period: Guthroth Haraldsson seized 2,000 slaves from Môn in 987; Maredudd ab Owain of Dyfed paid a penny a head to redeem captive Welshmen from Norse slavery in 989; and Rhys ap Tewdwr paid his Viking mercenaries in slaves in 1088. Important or valuable prisoners could also be ransomed, as in 914, when 40 pounds of silver was paid for the release of Bishop Cyfeiliog of Ergyng after a Viking raid. There were probably similar arrangements when Meurig ap Hywel was captured in 1039, and when Gruffudd ap Llywelyn was taken by the men of Dublin in 1042.

In time, as the Scandinavians became more established in Britain and Ireland, the nature of their involvement in Wales broadened to encompass alliances, mercenary work, trade, colonisation and possibly political overlordship, but the evidence is often scanty and interpretation is sometimes difficult. It is often far from clear what the intentions of Norse raiders were, for example when they killed Rhydderch ap Iestyn in 1033, when they were defeated by Hywel ab Edwin at Pwll Dyfach in 1042, when they ravaged Deheubarth in 1049, or when a fleet from Ireland foundered in south Wales in 1052.

The first firmly attested Viking activity in Wales was the killing of a certain Cyngen in 852. After that, Scandinavian attacks increased dramatically. Rhodri Mawr drove off raiders in Gwynedd in the 850s, only to be forced to flee to Ireland after a battle with Viking forces in Môn in 877, and Ubba, a leader of the Great Army which invaded England in 865, overwintered in Dyfed with twenty-three ships in 878, doing great slaughter before sailing to Devon to attack Wessex. Norwegian raiders came to Gwynedd again in 892, and in 893 a Danish army under Hastein was defeated by an Anglo-Welsh alliance at Buttington in the Severn valley. Hastein retreated to East Anglia, regrouped and headed to Chester, where the English destroyed his army's sources of food. Moving into Wales for supplies in 894, he seized booty in Gwynedd, but he was driven out by Anarawd ap Rhodri and returned to East Anglia via Northumbria. Vikings also ravaged Brycheiniog, Gwent and Gwynllŵg in 896, and Clydog ap Cadell repelled an invasion of Môn by Ingimund, who had been expelled from Dublin in 902. Merfyn ap Rhodri Mawr was killed by Vikings in Gwynedd in 904, and in 914 a fleet from Brittany under Hroald and Ottar ravaged south Wales and sailed up the Wye, where the bishop of Ergyng was captured; the raiders were repulsed at Hereford and Gloucester, and retreated to Steep Holm, where many of them starved before the fleet sailed for Dyfed and then Ireland. There was also an attack on Môn by Hi-berno-Norse raiders from Dublin in 918.

The emergence of a dominant Wessex under Æþelstan, who defeated Olaf Guthfrithsson's Dublin Norse army at Brunanburh in 937, was a significant factor in bringing a period of respite, but Viking attacks were renewed in the middle of the tenth century. Most of these marauders came from Ireland, Man and the Hebrides, and their targets were predominantly churches around the Welsh coast: there were raids on Penmon (971), Caergybi (961), Clynnog Fawr (978), Tywyn (963), St Davids (seven times between 967 and 1091), St Dogmaels, Llanbadarn Fawr, Llanilltud Fawr and Llancarfan (all in 988), and Bishop Morgeneu of St Davids was killed in 998. Raiding continued into the eleventh and twelfth centuries, and at the same time archaeological evidence suggests that trade between Wales and Ireland flourished throughout this period. There are few documentary references to these commercial contacts, but the *Brut* mentions an Irish trade at Aberdyfi in 1109.

Given this level of Viking activity, it is hardly surprising that the Welsh paid close attention to the Scandinavian sphere of influence, and especially Ireland, with which there had already been contact for centuries. The *Brut* does not mention the sacking of Lindisfarne, but it does record the first Viking attack on Ireland in 795 and the deaths of many Irish and Hiberno-Norse leaders between 862 and 1086, as well as a famine in Ireland in 897. The battle of Clontarf in 1014 is commemorated with an unusually sizeable annal, and Welshmen were present there, possibly concerned to protect substantial commercial interests in Leinster. There was a Welsh settlement around Dublin by the eleventh century, and Gruffudd ap Cynan (who had been born in Ireland) threatened to have an Irishman sent over to consecrate the bishop of Bangor in 1120. Moreover, the Welsh interest in the Hiberno-Norse world was reciprocated. The *Chronicle of the kings of Man and the Isles*, for instance, gives more attention to the death of Gruffudd ap Llywelyn than it does to that of William the Conqueror. Nevertheless, although there was a great deal of contact between Wales and the Vikings at the economic, military and political level, there does not seem to have been much cultural interaction. Linguistic borrowing was minimal; there is very little trace of Scandinavian influence on Welsh social and political institutions; and Welsh literature generally makes little of the Hiberno-Norse dimension.

The familiarity of the Vikings with the sea routes around Wales is confirmed by the large number of Norse place names for coastal features, especially in the south-west and the north, many of which gained wide currency. It was probably during the tenth century, for instance, that Môn came to be known to the English as Anglesey, from the Old Norse *Ongulsey* (possibly 'Ongul's island'). Moreover, hoards and graves found in Môn, Arfon and Tegeingl suggest that there was strong and frequent Scandinavian contact with these areas during the first half of the tenth century. There is particularly strong evidence for Môn: Ingimund established a settlement at Osfeilion in 903; Magnus Barelegs of Norway reportedly intended something similar in 1098; Olaf Sihtricsson of Dublin is said to have made a castle with a mound and a ditch at Bon y Dom; and the twelfth-century *Orkneyinga Saga* mentions a settlement at *Jarlsness*. Both the archaeological and the documentary evidence is fragmentary, but it seems likely that there was some permanent Scandinavian habitation at sites all around the Welsh coast, albeit spread very thinly – there were no enclaves or urban centres of the kind found elsewhere in the Scandinavian world.

Despite the absence of large Viking settlements, Magnus and Guthroth Haraldsson were able to exert a significant influence on the politics of Gwynedd in the late tenth century. They acquired an interest in north Wales when they took possession of Man, having been expelled from Limerick in 967, and in 971 and 987 they raided Môn, where they may well have had bases. They allied with Hywel ap Ieuaf in 978 and captured Iago ab Idwal in 979 (he never appears in the historical record again), and Guthroth supported Cystennin ap Iago in Môn and Llŷn in 980. The sons of Olaf Sihtricsson also raided Môn and Llŷn in 961. This is all especially intriguing because no native rulers of Gwynedd are referred to as 'kings' in this period, and between 949 and 1023 Irish annalists departed from their custom of describing kings of Gwynedd as *rí Breatan* ('king of the Britons') – instead, the term is applied to the king of Strathclyde (in 975). In the 970s and 980s, it seems that Magnus and Guthroth may have exercised some kind of control in Gwynedd, and especially Môn, by taking tribute. Guthroth's subjection of Môn 'with great treasure' in 972,' and Maredudd ab Owain's large tribute to him in 989 (which Maredudd helpfully collected himself), appear to be functions of Scandinavian overlordship, and this may also account for Magnus's submission to Eadgar along with Welsh kings at Chester in 973. A certain Sigferth was also present at Chester, apparently in the role of a Welsh ruler, and it may have been in a similar capacity that he attended Eadræd's court in 955. Similarly, Olaf Sihtricsson is said to have been king in Gwynedd.

The model of a tributary relationship between lesser Welsh kings and greater Hiberno-Norse ones certainly fits what is known of Gwynedd in this period, and it was characteristic of kingship in Scandinavia, but the taking of tribute need not represent anything more than opportunism. It was more likely a result of the failure of Welsh dynasties to assert themselves than a cause of it. Moreover, if there was some form of Scandinavian rule, it is important to see it in context. The presence and military influence of the Vikings was sufficient to prevent native Welsh dynasties from enjoying full autonomy, but it did not mean that native dynasties were ousted. There were no Scandinavian kingdoms in Wales as there were in Ireland and England. Significantly, also, only two Hiberno-Norsemen are known to have put forward claims to Welsh kingdoms, and both did so through native institutions. It was by passing himself off as a son of Maredudd ab Owain that the Irishman Rhain staked his claim to Deheubarth in 1022, and Gruffudd ap Cynan was a descendant of Rhodri Mawr.

By the time Gruffudd's father, Cynan ap Iago, fled to Dublin from the clutches of Gruffudd ap Llywelyn in 1039, Scandinavian rule in Gwynedd was effectively ended. But the memory of it remained fresh. Later in the eleventh century, Diarmaid mac Máel na mBó of Leinster was styled *rí Breatan*, possibly referring to rule in Wales itself rather than of Welsh settlements in Ireland, and a late twelfth-century saga tells of an Earl Steifnir holding lands in *Bretland*, which seems to represent either Wales or Strathclyde. A twelfth-century Manx chronicle even lists Môn as being among the possessions of the kings of Norway. Implausible as such claims may seem, in 1098 Magnus

Barelegs received gifts from the Welsh in Môn which may have represented a form of tribute, and the impact of his visit was such that it was believed that he had brought Harold, the son of Harold Godwinesson, with him, and that he intended to conquer the whole island of Britain.

There is no doubt that the sudden appearance of Magnus and his powerful fleet in Môn in 1098 was enough to inflict a crushing defeat upon two Norman earls: Hugh of Shrewsbury was killed, and his body thrown into the sea, and Hugh of Chester was unable to maintain control of Gwynedd for long afterwards. It may be that Magnus intended to resist Norman advances which threatened to bring him into direct conflict with the king of England, but too much should not be read into the events of 1098. Whereas English and Welsh sources understandably read great significance into them, Irish sources do not mention them at all, and *Historia Gruffud vab Kenan* and *Orkneyinga Saga* portray Magnus as arriving accidentally after a long expedition through the Hebrides and Man, with no intention of conquering anything in Wales – he even had to be told where he was, who held it, and who was attacking it. He reportedly said that he had only come to look at Britain and Ireland, and one of his men, Magnus Erlendsson, said that he had no quarrel with anyone in Môn. This is perhaps the most reliable insight into Scandinavian perceptions. Wales was strategically located on the axis of communications between Chester, York, Man, Dublin and Bristol, but in many respects it was peripheral to the Viking world. It was always one of the last stops on a raiding or trading itinerary that could include Norway, Denmark, the Faroes, Shetland, Orkney, the Hebrides, the Scottish mainland, Ireland and Man, and the importance of Môn as a Hiberno-Norse base declined as Dublin traded increasingly with Bristol rather than Chester from the early eleventh century. Môn was valuable as a source of occasional tribute, and Magnus returned there to collect timber in 1102, but it is significant that he made no attempt to take control of it after his victory in 1098.

The Vikings as Allies

The greatest importance of the Norse world in Welsh politics was as a source of refuge and military support. The first attested Welsh alliance with the Vikings was prompted by the foundation of the kingdom of York in 876, which established Scandinavian power from Northumbria across to the Mersey and possibly the Wirral. Eager to protect his kingdom against this threat and also that of a resurgent Wessex, Anarawd ap Rhodri of Gwynedd made a pact with Guthfrith of York in the 880s, but it was to prove shortlived. The alliance is said to have brought Anarawd no advantage, only misfortune, and he submitted to Ælfred of Wessex by about 893. Welsh rulers of the tenth century tended to move in the orbit of Wessex, and they sometimes received English support, but the author of *Armes Prydein* nevertheless saw the men of Dublin as natural allies against the Saxons, along with the Irish, the Scots, and the Britons of Cornwall and Strathclyde. With the power of Wessex weakened towards the end of the century, Welsh leaders could no longer depend on English assistance, and there was a spate of Hiberno-Norse alliances over the next 150 years. Maredudd ab Owain hired Vikings when he ravaged Morgannwg in 992, and Hywel ab Edwin had the support of an Irish fleet against Gruffudd ap Llywelyn at the mouth of the Tywi in 1044. Similarly, Gruffudd ap Rhydderch was aided by thirty-six ships from Ireland when he raided up the Usk and into Gloucestershire in 1049, and Gruffudd ap Llywelyn had the help of eighteen Hiberno-Norse ships when he sacked Hereford in 1055; he also allied with Magnus Haraldsson of Limerick in an attack on Herefordshire in 1058. Gruffudd's fleet in 1063 may well have been Norse, and Cynan ap Iago is said to have had help from Dublin in mounting two attacks against Gruffudd between 1039 and 1050. Hiberno-Norse forces also fought with Rhys ap Tewdwr against the sons of Bleddyn ap Cynfyn in 1088, and in 1093 Rhys was joined by a Hiberno-Norseman named Turcaill mac Eola. Furthermore, Cadwgan ap Bleddyn received support from Muirchertach hUa Briain in 1109, and Gruffudd ap Rhys probably had Irish help as well in 1115, while his sons, Anarawd and Cadell, together with Owain and Cadwaladr ap Gruffudd ap Cynan, employed fifteen Hiberno-Norse ships when they attacked Cardigan in 1138. Cadwaladr was also forced to pay his Irish mercenaries 2,000 head of cattle under duress for their services in 1144.

Cadwaladr's unpleasant experience with mercenaries was not unusual. Gruffudd ap Cynan and Cadwgan ap Bleddyn fled when they feared Hiberno-Norse treachery in 1098, and Gruffudd's fears were realised on other occasions when he failed to reward his followers as promised. Not surprisingly, the Irish were not universally popular; fifty-two of Gruffudd's supporters were killed by the men of Llŷn, and Madog ap Rhirid came home from Ireland in 1110 'unable to suffer the evil ways and evil customs of the Irish'.[2]

The increasing level of contact between Wales and the Hiberno-Norse in the late eleventh century is best demonstrated by Gruffudd ap Cynan's rise to power in Gwynedd, in which Scandinavian assistance played a crucial part. Gruffudd was born and raised in Ireland after his father fled Gwynedd, and the *Historia* says that one of his maternal grandfathers was Olaf Sihtricsson. It also claims that Gruffudd was descended from Harald Finehair of Norway and Brian Bóroimhe of Munster, and that his uterine brothers were kings of Ulster. Some of these claims are dubious, but Gruffudd's biographer's pride in his Hiberno-Norse connections is nevertheless obvious, and the *Historia* is the only Welsh source with sufficient knowledge or interest to distinguish between Irish and Danes. Moreover, Gruffudd left 20 shillings to a church in

Dublin when he died, and what is known of his life is consistent with the assertion that he was on good terms with both king Mwrchath of Ireland (either Murchad mac Diarmait or Muirchertach hUa Briain) and the king of the Isles and Denmark, and that the Irish and Danes mourned his death.

Ireland was usually Gruffudd's first destination when he met difficulties in Wales. According to the *Historia*, his first expedition was launched from there, and after the battle of Bron yr Erw in 1075 he returned to Wexford, where the king of Leinster heard his complaints and urged him to return quickly to Wales. Betrayed by his Welsh allies, Gruffudd was soon back with a King Diermit in Wexford. He made straight for Ireland again after he escaped from prison in Chester, and rowed from Aberdaron after an abortive attempt to wrest control of Gwynedd from the Normans. Yet another journey between Gwynedd and Ireland after a brief visit to Wales was followed by a visit to Gothrei in the 'islands of Denmark'[3] (possibly either Godfrey Meranach, king of Dublin and the Isles, or Godred Crovan of Man). Gruffudd returned there again before 1098, when he and Cadwgan ap Bleddyn again fled to Ireland. The core of Gruffudd's expeditions was essentially Hiberno-Norse. Danes and Irish fought with him at Bron yr Erw, and they included his foster-father Cerit, as well Varudri, the lord of Cruach Breandain in Munster – possibly identifiable as Cathal mac Ruaidhrí O Conchobhair of Connacht. The king of Leinster gave Gruffudd thirty ships for that expedition, and he was fitted out again with a Danish, Irish and Welsh fleet for the Mynydd Carn campaign in 1081, when the Irishman Gucharki killed Trahaearn ap Caradog. Gruffudd is also said to have been involved in a raid by Norsemen from Orkney and the northern isles on Barry and Newport in the reign of William I, and he was given a fleet of sixty ships by Gothrei, and received a further sixteen from Ireland in 1098. It may well have been Gruffudd and Gothrei whose activities reportedly caused Hugh of Shrewsbury concern about the defence of Degannwy in 1098, and one or both of these two may also have been responsible for the death of Robert of Rhuddlan, the *Domesday* tenant of Gwynedd. It was perhaps not entirely coincidental that there was a resurgence of Viking raids on St Davids (1073) and Bangor (1080 and 1089) during the period of Gruffudd's struggle for power, following a lull of twenty years. Finally, the role of the Norwegian fleet (although apparently unexpected and unsolicited) in defeating the Normans in Môn was crucial in allowing Gruffudd a vital foothold in Gwynedd in 1098. It is tempting to believe that there was some contact between Gruffudd and Magnus Barelegs, and this would certainly go some way towards explaining the whole episode.

The Welsh chronicles rarely mention the Hiberno-Norse, so the fact that the *Historia* portrays Gruffudd so often in their company creates an impression that he was by far the most significant user of Scandinavian and Irish support in

Wales. His connections with Ireland might also seem to make him exceptional. It is important to note, however, that Welsh sources other than the *Historia* mention Gruffudd's Hiberno-Norse forces only twice, and there is no reference at all to his Irish background. Furthermore, there is no mention of him in Irish annals, although they do note Llywelyn ap Seisyll, Iago ab Idwal, Gruffudd ap Llywelyn and Rhys ap Tewdwr. Despite Gruffudd's ultimate success, he meant less to the Irish than some of his Welsh contemporaries, and moreover the Welsh themselves do not seem to have regarded his Irish links as unusual. The implication is that contact between Wales and Ireland in the late eleventh century was both considerable and increasing. The only Welsh rulers known to have visited Ireland before the 1070s were Rhodri Mawr and possibly Cadwallon ap Cadfan, but between 1075 and 1110 they were followed by Rhys ap Tewdwr, Gruffudd ap Cynan, Cadwgan ap Bleddyn, Owain ap Cadwgan, Hywel ab Ithel, Madog ap Rhirid, Gruffudd ap Rhys and possibly Gruffudd ap Llywelyn. In fact, nearly all of the major Welsh rulers of this period are known to have used Ireland as a base or a source of troops, and Rhys ap Tewdwr in particular emerges in a very similar light to Gruffudd ap Cynan in all of the sources except the *Historia*. In the Welsh chronicles, both are found twice with Irish mercenaries, and Rhys, like Gruffudd, had relatives in Ireland – his son, Gruffudd, was sent to Ireland by his kin for protection, probably after Rhys's death in 1093.

The increasing use of Hiberno-Norse alliances and mercenaries was part of a Welsh tendency to employ external aid which had begun with the use of Anglo-Saxon help, and which was to continue with many of the arrangements made with the Normans. Furthermore, in the late eleventh century these foreigners almost always came in by invitation, at least at first, and the Norse military influence was as great if not greater than that of the Normans. In 1098, for instance, it was the Irish upon whom the Welsh called for help, and it was they who, when bribed, brought the Normans to Môn. Welsh rulers were as keen to ally themselves with foreigners from Ireland as they were with foreigners from England. Moreover, many of the Welshmen who brought troops from Ireland never used Norman support, and a comparison of the obituaries in the *Brut* for Muircheartach hUa Briain and Henry I in 1135 offers a revealing snapshot of Welsh attitudes: Muircheartach was exalted as 'the man of greatest power and authority and victory of the men of Ireland', whereas Henry was merely the 'son of William the Bastard'.[4]

For their part, the Normans were quickly assimilated into the political habits of the Irish Sea. Arnulf of Montgomery married a Leinster princess in 1102, and in 1098 Hugh of Chester enticed Gruffudd ap Cynan's Danish supporters into changing sides, promising them rich rewards which they never received. The victory of Magnus Barelegs showed that Gwynedd was still influenced as much by the Irish Sea as by England, and Norse attacks continued into the twelfth century. Gruffudd ap Cynan had to fight off raids, for example, and his son Owain is said to have fought against a host of north-men, while *Orkneyinga Saga* says that the settlement at Jarlsness was visited between 1139 and 1148 by Swein Asleifarsson and Holdboði, who burned six homesteads there before breakfast. The same account also mentions a certain Höldt, a freeman of Bretland, around 1140.

The Welsh were finally deprived of support from Dublin, Wexford and Waterford by the Anglo-Norman conquest of Leinster between 1169 and 1172. By that time, however, the military aspect of the Welsh relationship with the Hiberno-Norse was already in decline. There is no reference to Welsh use of Scandinavian help for twenty-five years before 1169, and there are relatively few examples after the middle of the twelfth century. Maelgwn ab Owain sought refuge in Ireland in 1173, Maelgwn ap Rhys employed an Irishman to kill Cydifor ap Gruffudd in 1205, and it is alleged in the late-thirteenth-century *Legend of Fulk fitz Warin* that there were Scots and Irish in the forces of Iorwerth Drwyndwn (who seems to have been mistaken here for his son, Llywelyn ap Iorwerth). Rhodri ab Owain was also supported by a son of Godred Olafsson of Man – probably Reginald Godredsson – in a campaign in Môn in 1193 which was remembered as *haf y gwydyl* ('the summer of the Irish'). Rhodri clearly relied heavily upon Manx support on this occasion, and it is possible that there was still a Hiberno-Norse colony in Môn. Harald, the steward of the king of Norway, also ravaged Llanfaes in Môn in 1208, but by this time the Welsh were no longer looking to Ireland and Man for support as they had previously.

The Decline of Scandinavian Influence

The combined effect of growing Anglo-Norman power and the pan-Eu-ropean renaissance in the middle of the twelfth century was to orientate Wales increasingly towards the east. The last Irish kings to receive obituaries in the Welsh chronicles were Toirrdhealbhach O Conchobhair of Connacht in 1156 and Diarmaid mac Murchada of Leinster in 1171. Thereafter, although an interest in Ireland was maintained, it came to be focused more on the Anglo-Norman colony, and in particular on issues affecting the Anglo-Nor-man lords of south Wales. Welsh attention was also drawn towards a redefini-tion of Wales itself. Faced with new priorities, the Welsh did not find it dif-ficult to abandon old habits.

In Ireland, too, new priorities emerged. A doctrine of a single national kingship was developed during the twelfth and thirteenth centuries, and the Irish expended their energies accordingly. All of their alliances were made with the aim of domestic advancement, and Welsh alliances became expendable as contentions between Irish bishops and Canterbury, and not least Henry II's invasion of Ireland, encouraged the Irish to concentrate their attentions at home. Moreover, neither the Welsh nor the Irish were in a position to offer each other meaningful support. The kings of Leinster, to whom the Welsh traditionally went for help, lost Dublin to Ruaidhrí O Conchobhair of Connacht in 1166, and when Diarmaid mac Murchada subsequently sought help in Britain he turned not to the Welsh, but to the more powerful Richard de Clare, the Anglo-Norman earl of Pembroke. Furthermore, the Irish needed English compliance for trading purposes – to ally with the Welsh against the marchers would jeopardise vital commercial links with Bristol, Cardiff, Chester and Dyfed, and consideration of the growth of Anglo-Norman power undoubtedly underlay the participation of fleets from Dublin and other Irish ports in Henry II's campaign of 1165. Reginald Godredsson was unusual in considering Wales a worthwhile investment. The possibilities that the Welsh might continue to enlist support in the Irish Sea were reduced further when Olaf Godredsson of Man tendered his homage to Henry III in 1235, promising to protect the maritime approaches to England from hostile forces, and undertaking to supply galleys for the king's service if required.

Welsh contacts in the Irish Sea were still strong, however, and the resulting cultural assimilation undoubtedly played a part in the Welsh renaissance of the twelfth century. Examples of this cosmopolitan attitude include the composition of *Historia Gruffud vab Kenan*, probably in the 1160s, and Rhys ap Gruffudd's invitation to the poets and musicians of Ireland and Scotland to attend his court at Cardigan in 1176. Owain Gwynedd also had a bishop of Bangor consecrated in Ireland in 1165. Although Owain was only able to make such gestures at times when Henry II and Canterbury were at odds, the impression of continued interaction is underlined by genealogical evidence. Merfyn Frych was associated closely with Man in the ninth century, and Godred Crovan, the 'friend' of Gruffudd ap Cynan, strengthened existing ties and encompassed the Dublin-Gwynedd-Man triangle in a network of alliances in the eleventh century. Strong dynastic links between Gwynedd, Ireland and Man persisted in the twelfth century. Cynan ab Owain may have had an Irish mother, and Hywel ab Owain certainly did, but it was with the dynasty of Man that the closest links were forged. Rhodri ab Owain arranged to marry a daughter of Reginald Godredsson, probably between 1190 and 1195, and Llywelyn ap Iorwerth attempted to marry the same woman between 1199 and 1203. In the event, the marriage never happened, but Owain ap Gruffudd ap Llywelyn was said by the poet Bleddyn Fardd to have been of Manx royal descent. On the Manx side, Reginald is alleged to have had a son called Hywel, and the association of two of his daughters with descendants of Owain

Gwynedd indicates his eagerness to ally himself with Gwynedd. It is also possible that he had a Welsh concubine or wife. Even in the thirteenth century, when dynastic associations between Gwynedd and Man were few, relations remained close: Godred Olafsson and his foster-father, Lachlan, fled to Wales in 1238; a certain Godred, the son of the king of Man, was in Gwynedd in 1241; Godred Magnusson similarly fled to Wales in 1275; and Edward I feared that Llywelyn ap Gruffudd might receive supplies from Scotland, Norway and Man between 1276 and 1282.

The dynasty of Gwynedd also held land in Ireland. In 1218, an inquisition in Dublin was required to find whether Maelgwn ab Owain had ever been seised of certain lands in Dublin, so that seisin could pass to Llywelyn ap Iorwerth, and in 1215 Llywelyn petitioned in Dublin on behalf of a certain Cynwrig, whose father, Rhirid, is described by later tradition as a son of Owain Gwynedd. The fitz Rery family in Dublin were supposedly descendants of this Rhirid, and their lands at Cloghran, between Dublin and Gruffudd ap Cynan's childhood home at Swords, may have been held by the dynasty of Gwynedd since the time of Owain Gwynedd or even Gruffudd ap Cynan.

This, however, is the only known instance of a major native Welsh family holding land in Ireland other than as part of the Anglo-Norman settlement. Contacts between Wales and the Irish Sea were becoming more infrequent and less active, and the success of Edward I's seaborne campaigns in 1277 and 1282 indirectly reflects the declining influence of Scandinavian fleets in the thirteenth century. The Scottish victory at Largs in 1263 and the cession of Man and the Hebrides to the Scots by Magnus Haakonsson of Norway in 1266 finally removed the danger of a repeat of 1098. The dynastic material indicates a continued Irish and Manx role in Welsh affairs until the very extinction of native rule in Gwynedd, but the greatest legacy of the Norsemen in Wales was more indirect. Their acquisition of Normandy between 885 and 911 eventually led to the Norman conquest of England, and with it the arrival of a powerful new threat to Welsh independence.

4

Norman Conquest and
Welsh Resistance
1063–1155

The Arrival of the Normans

When the Normans invaded England in 1066, the threat posed by Gruffudd ap Llywelyn to the English border counties was a recent memory. Gruffudd's career had created an impression that Wales was a problem that the authorities in England could not ignore, and the Normans were not slow to cross Offa's dyke.

Native Wales was dealt a heavy blow by Gruffudd's death in 1063, and it might be expected that the Normans would conquer it both quickly and easily. After all, they seized the powerful kingdom of England by force of arms in a single day and subdued it within five years, and their continental lands meant that they had more resources at their disposal than their Anglo-Saxon predecessors. They were also renowned as warriors and land-hungry adventurers, and many of them were aggressive and oppressive by nature. Hugh de Avranches, the first earl of Chester, for instance, was described by the Anglo-Norman Ordericus Vitalis as greedy, lustful and violent – he was known as 'the Fat' – and a number of Welsh sources refer to Norman tyranny. Moreover, Wales was vulnerable. It was not only politically, economically and militarily less developed than England, but was also racked by desperate succession disputes. These weaknesses allowed the Normans to seize Gwynedd in the 1080s, and Roger of Montgomery and his sons annexed large swathes of west Wales after Rhys ap Tewdwr was killed in 1093 – an event which was universally regarded as a cataclysmic disaster for the Welsh. There followed a devastating wave of Norman invasion throughout Wales.

The key to Norman power lay in superior military technology, and in particular the castle, which was superbly adapted to conquest, colonisation and subjection as well as to defence. Castles varied greatly in size, and most of the early ones consisted of little more than earth and wood, but their strength lay in the fact that they were built in closely-knit networks and gave their owners a very tangible physical presence. Even the elimination of several castles could not guarantee the Welsh success, as they repeatedly found to their cost. Once the Normans had entered Wales, it was very difficult to remove them.

Despite all of these advantages, however, few of the territorial gains made by the Normans before 1100 were permanent. Even where they were, the Norman barons were often incapable of imposing direct and consistent control over the Welsh. The first two Norman kings increased royal influence in Wales only slightly, and Gerald of Wales believed that none of the Norman kings was either able or motivated to emulate Harold Godwinesson's achievement in subduing the Welsh. Welsh reverses in this period usually owed as much to internal dislocation as to Norman aggression, and even Roger of Montgomery and his sons never matched the achievements of Rhodri Mawr, Hywel Dda and Gruffudd ap Llywelyn, all of whom had carved out larger and longer-lasting hegemonies. The Normans were merely another element in the perennial complexity of Welsh politics, and their achievement in Wales must be measured against the fact that it was another century before Wales moved decisively into the European feudal polity, and that native rule persisted until 1283.

Part of the reason for this lay in the fact that the Normans were distracted by their interests elsewhere, and especially across the English Channel. Roger of Montgomery, the earl of Shrewsbury, is unlikely to have been the only one who found himself running out of men because of his commitments outside Wales. The creation of a network of fortifications was very expensive, and many Normans must have wondered whether it was worth it. Wales was far less tempting than the rich fertile plains of lowland England: its terrain was harsh and unsuited to Norman methods of warfare and agriculture; its very political fragmentation made conquest difficult; and the Welsh were formidable military opponents. Moreover, although castles almost guaranteed a presence in Wales, they did not necessarily ensure more than a toehold. Any conquest of Wales would inevitably take a lot of time, effort and resources.

It is not surprising, therefore, that the Normans did not immediately unleash the full force of their military might in Wales. For all their energy, ambition and fighting prowess, they were often forced to be pragmatic in their relations with the Welsh. The density of castles in the Welsh borders – far greater than in any comparable area in Britain – demonstrates their military commitment to the region, but the minimal level of intervention before 1093 suggests either that the castles were built defensively or that advances into Wales usually proceeded only with great caution. Norman policy towards the Welsh was typically characterised by support and manipulation of native rulers as much as by outright aggression, and most of the Norman involvement in Wales before 1100 can be seen in terms of a pragmatic desire to ensure that dangerous power vacuums were replaced quickly by strong and reliable rulers, whether Welsh or Norman.

Osbern fitz Richard, for example, had royal licence to conquer 'whatever he can take' from the Welsh on the Herefordshire border in 1086,[1] but it was qualified with the condition 'nothing else' – a proviso which seems meaningless unless there was a difference between lands regarded as fair game for invasion and those where there were established powers. The invaders' acquisitiveness and genius for conquest should not be underestimated, but they do not tell the full story of Norman involvement in Wales.

South Wales and the Marcher Lords

The borderland between England and Wales – now known as the march, from the Norman French *marche*, meaning a boundary – assumed a new importance as Norman lords became established there. The marcher lords were driven by a number of forces previously unknown in Wales. They came from a society in Normandy where restrictive inheritance practices compelled many ambitious younger sons to seek their fortunes on the fringes of the Norman world, and it followed that, once England was parcelled out, the next step was Wales. There were also profound implications for Wales in the dispute between the sons of William the Conqueror which led to the separation of England from Normandy in 1087. It meant that the rulers of England increasingly turned their ambitions and resources towards Wales rather than overseas, while those marcher lords who held continental lands became accustomed to exercising authority beyond royal control. Thus was born a new breed of quasi-independent marcher potentates, moving confidently beyond the reach of royal power in Wales, but beholden to the king for their lands in England, and wary of their Welsh neighbours.

The political landscape of the march was inherently fluid. There had been substantial changes in 1063, notably the accession of Rhiwallon ap Cynfyn in Powys and the acquisition of Tegeingl by Eadwine of Mercia, but more important was the mixed political and cultural heritage of the region. The legacy of Gruffudd ap Llywelyn meant that places such as Lydbury in Shropshire – five miles east of Offa's dyke – were still 'in the land of Wales' (*in terris Walliae*) in the late 1060s, and Gruffudd had also held land in Tegeingl and Exestan – both east of the dyke. This confused pattern of 'English' and 'Welsh' lands was not new, and the situation was complicated further by the mixed population of the border. This was a land of opportunity for the Norman newcomers – and the marchers took advantage of it by appropriating lands not only from the Welsh but also from the English border counties – but it was also complex, ill-defined and treacherous.

One of the first Norman lords to enter Wales was William fitz Osbern, earl of Hereford and lord of Chepstow, who died fighting in Flanders in 1071. He was involved in hostilities with the Welsh of Deheubarth and Morgannwg, and seems to have been instrumental in diminishing Welsh influence in Herefordshire, Ergyng and Ewyas, where only two Welshmen – Gruffudd ap Maredudd and a certain Madog – held substantial territory by 1086, probably having acquired it after the fall of Roger of Hereford in 1075. The building in 1067 of the first stone castle in Wales at Chepstow – which was known as Striguil – also suggests aggressive intentions. Yet William is not known to have penetrated into Wales from his castle at Ewyas Harold, or to have exercised any significant power beyond the Wye, and it appears that the Normans in Gwent generally remained on good terms with their Welsh neighbours, in keeping with the custom of the region. Fitz Osbern's castles were built almost exclusively along the border, rather than in Wales, and his Welsh tenants were generally accommodated. Under Norman rule, Welshmen are found as reeves in Usk, Edlogan, Is Coed and Llebenydd, one of them having previously witnessed charters of Gruffudd ap Llywelyn and Caradog ap Gruffudd. Caradog in particular seems to have enjoyed an understanding with the king, William I, and fitz Osbern's grant of several manors to Maredudd ab Owain in Herefordshire may have been made on similar terms. Moreover, the vagueness of *Domesday Book* in describing Norman lordships in Wales almost certainly reflects their tenuous nature. After fitz Osbern's death, Caradog acknowledged no overlord in Gwent, although William's son, Roger, was styled lord of Gwent before 1075. If for no other reason than mutual survival, the Normans' initial relations with the Welsh did not involve unrestrained hostility.

The Normans became involved further west at the invitation of Maredudd ab Owain, who received Norman support when he successfully pressed his claim in Deheubarth in 1069, following a struggle in which Bleddyn and Rhiwallon ap Cynfyn overcame Maredudd and Idwal, the sons of Gruffudd ap Llywelyn. Whatever the Normans hoped to gain from this, they did not gain any direct authority in Deheubarth. Their support for Maredudd was more likely prompted by fear of a resurgent Gwynedd under Bleddyn ap Cynfyn. In 1072, however, some of the marchers – including fitz Osbern – turned against Maredudd, providing his enemy Caradog ap Gruffudd with military help, and defeating Maredudd and other Welsh kings in Brycheiniog. This change of attitude seems to have been motivated by a sense that the balance of power in the native polity of south Wales was shifting. There was a tendency for rulers of Deheubarth to expand into Morgannwg, and the Normans must have been wary of Maredudd's power and ambition by 1072 when he challenged Caradog by leading an army as far east as the Rhymni. Maredudd had to be stopped, although his son, Gruffudd, was allowed to retain his father's extensive holdings in Herefordshire. At the same time, the emergence of Caradog also seems to have made a difference. He ousted the line of Cadwgan ap Meurig from Morgannwg, and his appearance around 1072 as king there presented a potential threat to the south-eastern march. The Normans appear to have concluded that Caradog should be accepted as the new ruler of Morgannwg, and they seem to have encouraged him to direct his attentions towards the west thereafter – it is noticeable in this context that his close relations with them can be dated no earlier than 1072, and that there was no determined effort against Wales from Hereford until the late 1070s. Whether this was due to Welsh power or Norman indifference or incompetence – perhaps because of Roger of Hereford's 1075 revolt – it is clear that stability in south Wales depended on acceptance of Caradog for most of the 1070s.

In west Wales, Roger of Montgomery ravaged Ceredigion in 1073 and 1074, and it is probably no coincidence that no native ruler is recorded there at that time. It seems that Roger may have taken advantage of the situation for short-term profit, or even that he intervened in order to bring stability to an area of unrest. If he was intent on conquest, it is odd that he failed to intervene during the struggle from which Bleddyn ap Cynfyn came to the fore in Ceredigion in 1075, or even after Bleddyn was killed by Rhys ab Owain, the brother of Maredudd, in the same year – especially since the *Brut* asserts that both Rhys ab Owain and Rhydderch ap Caradog, a member of a rival dynasty, held 'the South' when they fought Caradog ap Gruffudd in 1075, which suggests an unusual and less than comfortable situation there. Rhys overcame the sons of Cadwgan ap Meurig, but in 1078 he was himself first defeated by Trahaearn ap Caradog and then killed by Caradog ap Gruffudd, both of whom were killed by Rhys ap Tewdwr at Mynydd Carn in 1081. The claims of some of the Welsh participants in this contest make it plain that it was very open, and it is no surprise that Roger kept an interested eye on these disputes. But the struggle was purely a native Welsh affair. Whereas all of the Welsh protagonists could point to some genealogical claim in Deheubarth, Roger had none, and moreover, the Normans made no serious attempt to take advantage of the unrest. They were probably well advised not to take sides in such a complex and volatile situation; indeed, far from threatening Norman positions, Deheubarth was now diverting Welsh efforts away from the border. After Rhys established himself, the firmness of his rule ensured that there was no Norman attempt to oust him. He reached an understanding with William I, and ruled in peace with both Welsh and Normans until 1087.

From the 1070s until 1093, marcher intervention and expansion in south Wales were minimal. Rhys survived the disruption on the death of William I in 1087, although the demise of the king with whom he had made terms encouraged several challenges. He was exiled to Ireland by the sons of Bleddyn in 1088, but he returned to defeat them, and he killed Gruffudd ap Maredudd and the sons of Cydifor ap Gollwyn in Brycheiniog in 1091. Throughout this time, Norman harassment was negligible. Bernard de Neufmarché made inroads into Brycheiniog as far as Glasbury in 1088, but no further Norman penetration is recorded there until 1093, and, although Gruffudd ap Maredudd had been maintained in England for some time, it was not Normans but the sons of Cydifor who induced him to become involved in west Wales. Much of the territory between Deheubarth and England seems to have become a buffer zone during this period. There was no strong native ruler in Brychein-iog, for example, and the area was inhabited by Normans by 1093, but Rhys ap Tewdwr had promised to pay 10 shillings for the neighbouring *cantref* of Buellt by 1086, and control of Brycheiniog appears to have been disputed until the Normans built a castle there in 1093. Rhys died at the hands of Nor-mans in Brycheiniog in 1093, and his presence there seems to have been part of a tentative process in which new spheres of influence were being defined.

The repercussions of Rhys's death were felt throughout southern Wales. Cad-wgan ap Bleddyn reacted by ravaging Dyfed, heralding a free-for-all among the Welsh of Deheubarth which made Norman intervention in west Wales inevita-ble. Mindful of both the dangers of instability and the prospects of rich pickings, the marchers moved in, and soon most of the region was in their hands. Roger of Montgomery took Ceredigion and Dyfed within months of Rhys's death, and Brycheiniog was almost certainly acquired by Bernard de Neufmarché at this time. Similarly, Philip de Braose was at Radnor and in Buellt by 1095, Hamelin de Ballon set up a castle at Abergavenny, and it was probably in 1093 that much of Morgannwg was conquered by Robert fitz Hamo. Yet after the initial suc-cess, the first years of the Norman presence in south Wales were marked by defeat. All of the Norman castles in Deheubarth except Pembroke and Rhyd-y-Gors (at Carmarthen) were razed or deserted by 1094, the town of Pembroke was ravaged by the Welsh, Norman forces in Gwent and Brycheiniog were annihilated, and even Montgomery was captured. According to Gerald of Wales, Pembroke Castle only avoided capitulation in 1096 because of the ingenuity of Gerald of Windsor – he is said to have flung the last remaining pieces of bacon from the castle in an attempt to persuade the besieging Welsh that the garrison had supplies to spare, and he also contrived that the Welsh should inter-cept a letter informing Arnulf of Montgomery that there was no need to send urgent help. Such desperate measures illustrated the plight of the Normans in the south-west, and the Norman devastation of Gŵyr, Cydweli and Ystrad Tywi in 1095 scarcely reversed the tide of Welsh success.

The events of the 1090s were dramatic, but they did not mark a watershed in Norman attitudes. Wales was still treated as a region to be managed and exploited, rather than subjugated, and several instances of marcher intervention in these years occurred at the request of the Welsh. Robert fitz Hamo seems to have been invited into Morgannwg by Iestyn ap Gwrgant, for example, and it was to Iestyn, rather than to the Normans, that Einion ap Cydifor turned when he made his first request for help. It seems that neither the Welsh nor the marchers regarded Norman interference as necessary or desirable except in exceptional circumstances.

Such circumstances existed in Deheubarth in 1093. Rhys ap Tewdwr's sons were too young to assert their claims, and lost all of their father's lands; Gruffudd fled to Ireland and Hywel was imprisoned by Arnulf of Montgomery, leaving Cadwgan ap Bleddyn to emerge as the foremost Welsh leader in the south thereafter. Cadwgan failed to press his claims effectively, however, and seems to have concentrated his efforts in Gwynedd. As a result, all of the southern Welsh leaders between 1094 and 1097 sprang from relatively obscure dynasties, or distant segments of the major ones, and none of them was able to command widespread support. In the absence of a strong native candidate, the Normans found that they could and must intervene. They could now move in without fear, but permanent conquest was impossible, and they were content to dominate what they could not subdue.

Native Rulers within the March

Despite the reverses they suffered between 1094 and 1096, the Normans made gains which were ominous in the long term. They received the submissions of the men of Gwent, Brycheiniog and Gwynllŵg, and although many of these probably consisted of no more than the traditionally vague promises of allegiance, more binding ties may have been introduced in the more secure spheres of Norman lordship. More significantly, it was noticed that many Norman castles remained intact with their garrisons, and Cadwgan ap Bleddyn needed to make peace with the invaders in order to receive even a portion of Powys and Ceredigion in 1099. Furthermore, the marchers were now committed to the region, and possessed plenty of resources with which they could uphold that commitment. Militarily and economically, the Welsh were at a disadvantage, and, in this sense, contemporaries were justified in seeing the end of an era in 1093, when 'kings ceased to rule in Wales'.[2] The Normans were in south Wales to stay, and although it was only in Morgannwg, Gwent and Brycheiniog that they were able to retain permanent control after 1135, they were well entrenched in those areas. Hamelin de Ballon was succeeded at Abergavenny by Brian fitz Count, for instance, and Winibald de Ballon and William fitz Baderon were succeeded by their sons at Caerleon and Monmouth respectively. Nevertheless, the vague and impermanent nature of both Welsh and Anglo-Norman power in most of the march often made it necessary to reach mutual understandings. The march was not so much a location as a process of intensification of lordship, and in the first century after 1063 that process was only just beginning.

DYFED

The Norman re-conquest of Dyfed was decisive. Their severity against the Welsh in the 1090s, which was unparallelled except in Gwynedd, suggests that resistance was strong, but the castles in the region were all soon repaired. Gerald of Windsor still held Pembroke on behalf of Arnulf of Montgomery in 1097, and he built a castle at Cenarth Bychan in 1108. Arnulf, meanwhile, consolidated his position in 1102 by marrying the daughter of Muircheartach hUa Briain of Leinster – a move which not only provided him with a useful ally but also deprived his enemy, Cadwgan ap Bleddyn, of a source of support which had been useful to him in 1098 and probably 1099.

Nowhere in Wales was the authority of the king of England felt more than in Dyfed. Pembroke escheated to Henry I after Arnulf rebelled in 1102, and a large Flemish colony was introduced in the *cantref* of Rhos between 1107 and 1111. The Flemings, whose presence was intended to reduce the influence of the Welsh, built up the Norman commercial centres, carved out lordships at the expense of the Welsh, and provided the Normans with military support. Meanwhile, the *cymydau* of Pebidiog and Cemais were subjected directly to the king, and the same probably applied to Emlyn, Rhos, Penfro and Daugleddau. The strength of the conquerors' position is shown by the election of the first Norman bishop in Wales at St Davids in 1115, and also by the fact that no Welsh rulers are found in Dyfed in this period. Significantly, Gruffudd ap Rhys made little attempt to re-conquer Dyfed in 1116, despite victories at Crug Mawr and Narberth.

Nevertheless, the effects of a protracted civil war in England during Stephen's reign, and more importantly Welsh pressure after 1136, all but destroyed what had been achieved in Dyfed. A re-conquest by Gilbert fitz Gilbert de Clare was necessary in 1145, and the Welsh canons of St Davids reflected an atmosphere of growing anti-Norman tension when they demanded a Welsh bishop in 1148, citing Norman oppression. There was no doubt that Dyfed was still very vulnerable to Welsh incursions. Gerald of Wales recalled that the diocese of St Davids could only be governed by the sword at this time, and Norman power was in such disarray by 1155 that Maredudd ap Gruffudd was hailed as the lord of Dyfed.

RHWNG GWY A HAFREN

The dynasty which operated in the area known as Rhwng Gwy a Hafren – 'between the Wye and the Severn', comprising Maelienydd, Elfael, Gwerthrynion and Ceri in the central march – fended off Norman attacks despite the proximity of their lands to the English border, and these territories remained unmolested by other Welsh kingdoms. Maelienydd was held in 1136 by Madog ab Idnerth, who took part in an attack on Ceredigion in that year, and the kingdom passed to his son, Maredudd, by 1143. In 1144, however, it was conquered by Hugh Mortimer, who also repaired his castle at Cymaron; this is said to have been the second conquest – the previous occupation (which may have taken place in the 1090s) cannot have lasted long. Although Hugh killed Maredudd in 1146, and captured his eldest grandson, Rhys, in 1145, the re-conquest of Maelienydd was not permanent, and Cadwallon ap Madog ab Idnerth ruled there by 1160. It was a similar story in Elfael, where Einion Clud, another son of Madog ab Idnerth, recovered the *cantref* for the Welsh by 1160 after the Norman castle of Colwyn had been rebuilt in 1144 and Elfael subjected a second time (the first time having probably been in the 1130s), apparently by William de Braose. Cydewain is undocumented, and little is known of Ceri, which seems to have come into the orbit of the rulers of Maelienydd by the 1170s. Thus, the dynasty of Rhwng Gwy a Hafren maintained control of its lands for most of this period, possibly because the marchers were willing or able to intervene only for short periods. Nonetheless, it is notable that all the known sons of Madog ab Idnerth died at the hands of Normans.

BRYCHEINIOG AND BUELLT

It seems that the native dynasty of Brycheiniog was dispossessed in the eleventh century, when Bernard de Neufmarché and the sons of Iestyn ap Gwrgant of Morgannwg ravaged the *gwlad*. The sons of Idnerth ap Cadwgan defeated a Norman force at Aber Llech in 1096, but nothing is heard of them subsequently, and Gruffudd ap Rhys ap Tewdwr emerged as the foremost Welsh claimant in Henry I's reign. Bernard established himself between 1088 and 1093, and Norman rule was continued under Miles of Gloucester after about 1125, although there was at least one attack from Powys, when the men of Brycheiniog killed Llywelyn ap Cadwgan ap Bleddyn in 1099. Native rule was not eradicated quickly – Hywel ap Maredudd ravaged Brycheiniog and fought the Normans on the Llwchwr in 1136 – but Norman control was eventually established firmly. As a result, Hywel was forced to direct his attentions towards Ceredigion rather than Brycheiniog, to which he had a better claim. Similarly, Buellt was retained by Philip de Braose until at least 1130, and no Welsh activity is recorded in the area.

GWENT AND MORGANNWG

Despite the Norman presence in Gwent, native rule persisted and eventually flourished. Morgan and Iorwerth ab Owain ap Caradog ap Gruffudd appear to have negotiated favourable terms with Richard fitz Gilbert, the earl of

Gloucester, in the 1130s, and they added almost all of Gwent to their lands of Gwynllŵg after Iorwerth ambushed and killed the earl at Coed Grwyne near Abergavenny in 1136. The survival of the native dynasties of Morgannwg is also well attested. In particular, an apparently new dynasty emerged and held its own in Senghennydd and the minor lordships of Afan, Meisgyn and Glynrhondda, and it is notable that the Welsh rulers of Afan did not marry into Anglo-Norman families until 1276.

The western border of Robert fitz Hamo's lordship of Glamorgan seems to have lain on the Ogwr until the late 1120s, but Richard de Grainville conquered a large area around Neath as far as the Tawe by 1130. This action was probably induced by an outbreak of unrest beyond the Ogwr after the death of a certain Roger Ifor at the hands of the sons of Iestyn ap Gwrgant of Afan in 1127, which seems to have been part of a struggle for power after the death of Iestyn. Gerald of Wales observed that the Normans were jealous of Welsh lands in this region, and many prominent Normans of Morgannwg participated in de Grainville's aggression, but in 1136 the sons of Iestyn forcibly regained large chunks of the territory previously held by their father, and it was probably in the 1130s that Ifor Bach ap Meurig of Senghennydd recovered Leckwith.

The lordship exercised by the Normans in Morgannwg was far from all-embracing. Their influence appears to have been concentrated into small pockets, forcing them to create large demilitarised zones in frontier areas by making extensive grants to the Cistercian abbeys of Margam and Neath, and this impression is supported by the creation of an exclusively Anglo-Norman colony west of the Ogwr. Further east, Robert fitz Hamo's demesne lands were meagre, and evidence for the dues owed to the lord from his lands and tenants in Morgannwg is sparser still. Even within his shire fee, he appears to have acted more as an overlord than as a direct lord in relations with both Welsh and Norman tenants. Furthermore, Ifor Bach's raid on Cardiff in 1158, when he captured Earl William fitz Robert of Gloucester and the Countess Hawise in response to encroachments on his lands, reminded the Normans that even the great castles could not always afford them reliable protection. Noticeably, however, violence was relatively rare, and it appears that stability was generally preserved by agreement.

Nevertheless, the castles generally ensured marcher domination of the lowland zone in Morgannwg, and this allowed the establishment of Anglo-Norman government. Around the castles, English forms of tenure were introduced in what became known as the 'Englishry' (*Anglescaria*), to the extent that lordship there was not dissimilar to lordship in an English manor. The means of administration sometimes owed much to local practice, but *cymydau* held by Welsh tenure (*Walescaria* or 'Welshry') were just as dependent on the earl as were the others – albeit that comital control was not strong over any of them. Welsh secular influence over the election of bishops of Llandaf was also removed after 1107. Morgan and Iorwerth ab Owain were the first to recognise the implications of Norman power, witnessing charters of both Robert of Gloucester and Roger of Hereford, and, from 1154, Morgan received 40 shillings a year from the king, as well as the same sum from the lord of Glamorgan. The brothers performed homage to Robert, and they were obliged to serve him in 1138. Similarly, Ifor Bach was the 'man' of William of Gloucester, and the earl may have enforced a right to the lands of Welsh tenants who died without heirs – this seems to have been the reason for his possession of Llangynwyd after the death of Owain ap Caradog ap Iestyn.

Welsh relationships with the Normans were not one-sided, however. There is no record of any Welsh submission in Morgannwg before the 1130s, and the fact that Morgan held Usk in Gwent for the earl in 1138 – only two years after he had captured it – suggests that Robert was simply recognising a conquest about which he could do nothing. Morgan was even allowed to style himself 'king' in witnessing a charter of Roger of Hereford, taking precedence over Norman barons of considerable power. He was clearly intent on reviving his grandfather's kingdom of Gwynllŵg-Gwent. Moreover, the polity in which Morgan moved was as much Welsh as Norman. He married his sister to Seisyll ap Dyfnwal of Gwent Uwch Coed, and fought against Senghennydd in 1158, while his defeat by Ifor Bach showed that Senghennydd also remained fiercely self-sufficient. Although the *cwmwd* of Senghennydd Is Caeach was conquered so comprehensively that fitz Hamo established the *caput* of his lordship (*comitatus*) there, Senghennydd Uwch Caeach was to remain a Welsh stronghold until the 1260s. Ifor ensured close links with Deheubarth by his marriage to Nest, a sister of Gruffudd ap Rhys, and Caradog ap Iestyn similarly married one of Gruffudd's daughters. Caradog and his brothers maintained a firm grip on the uplands between the Taf and the Nedd, and they also raided in Brycheiniog. Afan was to remain under native rule with royal liberties until the fourteenth century.

The hotbed of Welsh resistance was the mountains of Blaenau Morgannwg. The twelfth-century lordship of Glamorgan included only the lowland half of the old kingdom of Glywysing, and Welsh lands in the lordship seem to have been administered separately from the Norman ones. This was largely because, despite the Normans' military sophistication, permanent conquest of the uplands required them to defeat the Welsh on their own terms; they could not and did not change the rules. Indeed, they may not have felt any need to conquer the land above the 600-foot contour which, in the eyes of an Anglo-Norman arable farmer, was worthless. Welsh herdsmen and Norman wheat farmers did not always necessarily fight over the same things.

Apart from the forays of Morgan and Iorwerth ab Owain, neither the Welsh nor the Normans of Morgannwg and Gwent played a large part in the uprising of 1136. The Normans who were defeated at Cardigan, for instance, came from the area between the Nedd and the Dyfi, not Morgannwg. This is intriguing in the light of the close relations between Blaenau Morgannwg and Deheubarth, and the participation of Hywel ap Maredudd from neighbouring Brycheiniog. It seems that Morgannwg was not afflicted by the same dynastic upheavals in the native polity as were experienced further west, and furthermore, although Richard fitz Gilbert may have been killed at the request of the Welsh of Deheubarth, the subsequent activities of Morgan and Iorwerth suggest that their main concern was to take advantage of the problems of Robert of Gloucester in England. It is significant in this respect that the south-east was traditionally separate from the affairs of the rest of Wales.

GŴYR

Gŵyr was ruled in 1102 by Hywel ap Goronwy, who seems to have moved into the area from the central march in the 1090s. After his death in 1106, it appears that Roger of Salisbury, Henry de Beaumont and their successors established themselves in at least some parts of the *cantref*, and Henry had a castle at Swansea by 1116. Peace seems to have prevailed until the 1130s, and much of Gŵyr – now known as the lordship of Gower – was retained by Welsh tenants. The social and economic structure of the *cantref* also suggests that much of it was almost independent. Gower was the object of raids by Hywel ap Maredudd of Brycheiniog in 1136 and by Maredudd and Rhys ap Gruffudd, who destroyed the castle of Llwchwr in 1151. None of these men had any claim to the territory, and the impression of vulnerability is borne out by a late-thirteenth-century reference to a Norman re-conquest after a Welsh takeover during the reign of Stephen. Thus, despite the complete displacement of the native dynasty, Gower remained a melting pot of Norman and Welsh influence.

POWYS

Little is known of Powys in the late eleventh century, but it is likely that Bleddyn ap Cynfyn extended his authority there from Gwynedd after his brother Rhiwallon died in 1069. He enjoyed considerable power and prestige, but by 1102 the *Brut* names Powys among the lands in Wales which were in the hands of the sons of Roger of Montgomery. Robert of Bellême, at Montgomery, is said to have harried the Welsh for four years, and he built castles on the border, but the nature of his position there is not clear. The *Brut* leaves no doubt that Robert exercised some form of lordship when it says that he and his brother Arnulf summoned the sons of Bleddyn to their support. But Robert's practical supremacy over Powys was far from complete, and Cadwgan, Iorwerth and Maredudd ap Bleddyn seem to have regarded him more as an ally than as an enemy. Robert is said to have trusted them, and received them with gifts – hardly a necessary gesture had he been absolutely confident of their loyalty – and the ease with which Iorwerth was bought off by the king suggests that their allegiance was not born of subservience. The brothers' participation in border unrest was after all a direct continuation of the policy of their father (as well as that of Gruffudd ap Llywelyn), and there is no mention of Anglo-Norman mediation or encouragement in Iorwerth's reconciliation with Cadwgan and Maredudd in 1102, or in the division of territories which followed it. Although Powys may have been subject to Norman lordship in theory, it seems that most of the time in practice the native dynasty was able to act independently of Norman authority.

Confrontation between Powys and the English had traditionally been the exception rather than the rule, and dealings with Gwynedd were much more frequent. Dynastic links were very close, and Bleddyn ap Cynfyn and his son Cadwgan had each become kings of Gwynedd since 1063. Indeed, Bleddyn was regarded as the head of the Powys dynasty, although he began his career in 1063 as king of Gwynedd. Rhodri Mawr and Gruffudd ap Llywelyn of Gwynedd had both annexed Powys, and, as in the ninth century, the real external threat to Powys in the twelfth century was again to come from Gwynedd. Both Gwynedd and Deheubarth were in turmoil at the turn of the twelfth century, however, and Powys came to assume a leading role in native Wales in this period. Cynwrig ap Rhiwallon and Gwrgeneu ap Seisyll both took part in the power struggle in Gwynedd in 1075, and the rebellions of 1094 and 1098 against the Normans in Gwynedd were both led by Cadwgan ap Bleddyn, whose followers came almost exclusively from Powys dynasties. Cadwgan was to be the focus of native Welsh political life until his death, and he, his brother Iorwerth and his son Owain were to rule Powys almost continuously until 1116, despite the attentions of Henry I. Elsewhere, Powys extended its influence in Rhos, Rhufoniog, Dyffryn Clwyd, Meirionnydd, Arwystli and Cyfeiliog – territories which it had long contested with Gwynedd – as the hold of Gwynedd loosened.

The native rulers of these areas were not easily swept aside, however. Cadwgan claimed authority over Cyfeiliog and Meirionnydd before his death in 1111, giving them to Uchdryd ab Edwin in return for a promise of support whenever he might need it, but Uchdryd's sons were able to repel Owain ap Cadwgan and Madog ap Rhirid when they entered Cyfeiliog in 1110. Subsequently, Owain and Madog achieved little in Meirionnydd, but Uchdryd's

castle at Cymer was destroyed in 1116 by Einion ap Cadwgan and Gruffudd ap Maredudd ap Bleddyn, who then shared Cyfeiliog, Meirionnydd and
Penllyn between them. Arwystli retained its native dynasty under Llywarch
ap Trahaearn, despite the killing of his two elder brothers by Owain ap Cadwgan in 1106, and Llywarch actively opposed Owain in 1109 and conspired
in the betrayal of Iorwerth in 1111. Maredudd ap Bleddyn considered him
such a menace that he ravaged Arwystli in 1113, but Llywarch was still independent in 1116, when he fought for Henry I in Deheubarth; he later sided
with Gwynedd in the dispute over Meirionnydd in 1124. Llywarch's dynasty
survived an internal power struggle to withstand pressure from Powys in the
1120s, and it continued to exercise some autonomy until 1185 under Hywel
ap Ieuaf, who, despite recognising Madog ap Maredudd as his lord, styled
himself king of Arwystli in the early 1140s. Powys also failed to conquer the
Perfeddwlad, where its claims stretched as far as Dyffryn Clwyd. Maredudd
ap Bleddyn and the sons of Cadwgan supported Hywel ab Ithel as a puppet
king of Rhos and Rhufoniog, and succeeded in repelling his rivals, the sons
of Owain ab Edwin, after his death in 1118, but they were prevented from
overrunning the area by the Norman threat from Chester.

Despite this inability to assert itself consistently beyond its borders, Powys
had emerged as a potent force by the 1140s. The death of all but one of
the contenders for the kingship by 1128 allowed Maredudd ap Bleddyn to
assume authority unopposed, and Powys passed to his son, Madog, without
contention in 1132. Madog eliminated his rivals and consolidated the kingdom against attack. He took advantage of disruption in England after 1135 to
extend his dominions as far as the Fyrnwy, and to strengthen his control over
an area which stretched from Arwystli to near Chester, making raids against
Caus in 1137, Bromfield in 1140 and Oswestry in 1149. His brother Iorwerth
Goch also raided in England, and Powys may have been responsible for an
attack on Cheshire in 1146. Through a combination of military strength and
diplomatic skill, Madog was able to discourage intervention from Gwynedd,
the king of England and the marchers, taking only a small part in the political
convulsions of the years following 1136. The peaceful relations established by
his marriage with Susanna, a daughter of Gruffudd ap Cynan, no doubt accounts in part for the infrequency of interference from Gwynedd until after
his death, and there is also no sign that Madog was under any pressure from
Henry I or Stephen. He was joined by Ranulf of Chester in opposing Owain
Gwynedd in 1150, but no bond was involved, and Madog's only concession to
forces outside Powys was to support Ranulf against the king in 1141.

Recognising the limitations of the position in which he found himself,
Madog was not intent on conquest, but consolidation. He came into conflict

with Gwynedd only through the aggression of Owain Gwynedd, who invaded Iâl in 1149 and also attacked in 1157, and his power outside Powys was minimal. Although he established sufficient authority in Cyfeiliog to be able to give it to his nephews in 1149, he seems to have held only a part of the *cantref*, and he had no direct lordship over Arwystli, where he was defeated heavily by Rhys ap Gruffudd of Deheubarth in 1153. Despite his apparent success, Madog recognised that the increasing strength of Gwynedd and the Normans – as demonstrated in Meirionnydd, Iâl and the Perfeddwlad – rendered expansion unwise, and Powys looked increasingly to secure its position by ingratiating itself with the king. Thus Madog received £8 in Henry II's service in 1157, and Iorwerth was given 40 shillings and the manor of Sutton in Shropshire for his part in the campaign, while the king enabled Madog's sons to procure arms for the war, and Owain Cyfeiliog may have received 5 marks from Henry in 1157 and 15 shillings in 1160. Despite its strength in the early twelfth century, Powys was caught between greater powers, and its days as a major kingdom were numbered.

The dynasty of Powys was heavily involved in Ceredigion in this period. Nearly all of the Norman castles there had been destroyed in 1094, but by 1096 they were once more intact, and Cadwgan ap Bleddyn's claim to Ceredigion in 1099 was realised only with Norman recognition. By 1102, however, it was Iorwerth ap Bleddyn who gave it to him, and Cadwgan's growing strength is shown by his continued and unopposed hold on the *gwlad* even during Iorwerth's imprisonment after 1103. The presence of Nest, the wife of Gerald of Windsor, at Cadwgan's banquet in 1109 indicates that he was on amicable terms with the local Normans, whether through mutual fear or understanding. Any semblance of peaceful co-existence was destroyed in 1109, however, when Owain ap Cadwgan abducted Nest from Gerald's castle of Cenarth Bychan, slept with her, and burned the castle; Gerald himself only managed to escape by climbing down the latrine. Owain was said to have been infatuated with Nest, but there was probably a political motive as well. Cadwgan may have given Owain his full support in attacking Norman interests, although they may have differed over how to go about it; or alternatively, father and son may have been deeply divided over the wisdom of fraternisation with the Normans, especially since Nest, a descendant of both Rhys ap Tewdwr and Rhiwallon ap Cynfyn, might provide Gerald's offspring with a better claim to Ceredigion (and maybe even Powys itself) than had the dynasty of Powys.

Whatever Owain's motives, the consequences were disastrous. Richard, the sheriff of Shropshire, sought to avenge the insult by bribing Llywarch ap Trahaearn, Uchdryd ab Edwin and the sons of Rhirid ap Bleddyn to attack Owain and Cadwgan, and the pair fled to Ireland. Cadwgan was later restored to Ceredigion by the king, but in 1110 he was unlucky enough to be in Henry's presence when news arrived that Owain had killed a bishop in Dyfed. He was deprived of his lands on the spot, and Ceredigion was given to Gilbert fitz Richard. Cadwgan was reconciled with the king once more and returned to rule Powys after the death of Iorwerth in 1111, but he died shortly afterwards, a broken man, whose natural inclination (according to the *Brut*) was not to hurt anyone. Owain was subsequently restored to Powys, and he remained in control there until 1116, when Gerald of Windsor finally took his revenge by killing him in a chance encounter. In the meantime, Gilbert fitz Richard re-fortified Llanychaiarn (Aberystwyth) and Dingereint (Cardigan), and took control of ecclesiastical lands in Ceredigion, while a Flemish colony was established in the *cwmwd* of Is Coed. Norman rule in Ceredigion withstood an attack by Gruffudd ap Rhys and his allies at Aberystwyth in 1116, and it continued to flourish until 1136, when the assassination of Richard fitz Gilbert – who was lord of Ceredigion as well as earl of Gloucester – was followed by a crushing defeat at Cardigan.

GWYNEDD

Despite the circumstances of his accession to Gwynedd in 1063, Bleddyn ap Cynfyn was anything but a puppet of foreign powers. He may have been a target of Norman aggression in or before 1068, but there is no sign of lasting Norman incursions. Bleddyn harassed Chester constantly and allied with Eadwine of Mercia against the Normans in 1068, and there was no Norman involvement when he was killed in 1075. Although Robert of Rhuddlan once ambushed him, the presence of great quantities of booty with Bleddyn's force suggests that Robert's action was one of retaliation against a raid, rather than an attempt to conquer Gwynedd. Bleddyn's position was weakened when Mercian resistance to the Normans collapsed in 1070, but he seems nevertheless to have eliminated all opposition in Gwynedd after defeating the sons of Gruffudd ap Llywelyn in 1069. He was aided in this by his brother, Rhiwallon, perhaps indicating a move towards co-operation between Gwynedd and Powys, and this is further implied by his ability to attack Herefordshire in 1068. The fact that he was operating in Ystrad Tywi in 1075 strongly suggests that he was secure in the north, and his glowing obituary in the *Brut* portrays him as terrible in war, enlightened in peace, and widely respected as the holder of 'the kingdom of the Britons after Gruffudd [ap Llywelyn]'.[3] Like Rhys ap Tewdwr, he ensured stability, and – also like Rhys – his position had been recognised by the king (in 1063). His presence explains Hugh of Chester's negligible westward progress beyond Rhuddlan before 1075, and his death was followed by confusion, as Gruffudd ap Cynan, Trahaearn ap Caradog and Cynwrig ap Rhiwallon all put forward claims to Gwynedd. Indeed, the latter two are said to have split Gwynedd between them.

Gruffudd ap Cynan approached Robert of Rhuddlan for support in 1075, but his attack on Rhuddlan later that year led to the withdrawal of Norman assistance, and, despite achieving some control of Llŷn, Arfon and Môn, he was defeated by Trahaearn at Bron yr Erw. There were a number of Norman incursions into Gwynedd during the next few years, notably a raid on Llŷn by Hugh of Chester, and Robert of Rhuddlan is said to have taken the lands of Welsh lords, made them submit and kept them in chains, defeating Trehellum (Trahaearn?) and capturing a certain Hywel (ab Ithel?). Roger of Montgomery may also have taken advantage of the unrest to seize Arwystli at this time, but it is noticeable that Norman involvement in the dispute between Trahaearn and Gruffudd was non-existent when it reached a head at Mynydd Carn in 1081.

Within months of Gruffudd's victory, however, the earls of Shrewsbury and Chester saw a chance to seize Gwynedd for themselves. Before Gruffudd had a chance to assert his new authority fully, they tricked and imprisoned him, and Gwynedd was controlled by Normans for most of the next two decades. Hugh of Chester erected castles there, Robert of Rhuddlan acquired Rhos, Rhufoniog and *Nortwales* by 1086, and the Breton Hervé was imposed as bishop of Bangor in 1092. Gruffudd had great difficulty in reasserting himself. He eventually escaped from prison, but he was forced to flee to Ireland, and lived as a fugitive in the caves of Ardudwy when he finally attempted to return. Between 1081 and 1094, the only known challenge to Norman supremacy in Gwynedd was the killing of Robert of Rhuddlan by a certain Grithfridus (Gruffudd ap Cynan?), who was raiding Rhuddlan and Degannwy, and Norman control remained considerable even after the Welsh revolts of 1094 and 1098. The earls of Chester and Shrewsbury ravaged Môn in 1098, and Hywel ab Ithel was forced to flee from the Perfeddwlad in 1099. Despite the Norman defeat in Môn in 1098 at the hands of Magnus Barelegs, Gruffudd ap Cynan depended upon Hugh of Chester for his position when he returned in 1099, and he and Cadwgan ap Bleddyn were given lands only after making peace with 'the French'.

Yet Norman power was not invincible. In 1075, one of Gruffudd's first acts after defeating Cynwrig ap Rhiwallon was to take the *cantrefi* bordering England, and he then destroyed Rhuddlan Castle. The raid on Llŷn does not seem to have shaken the authority of Trahaearn ap Caradog, and Robert's death indicates the fragility of the Norman position in Gwynedd, as does the eventual ease of Gruffudd's escape from Chester. It is interesting that his rescuer, one Cynwrig Hir, hailed from Edeirnion, where Gruffudd had been captured – this *cwmwd* was held by Reginald the sheriff in 1086, and Cynwrig's action may reflect Welsh dissatisfaction with Norman rule. In 1094, the conditions for revolt were ideal. There were no major Norman leaders in north Wales – Robert of Rhuddlan was dead, and Hugh of Chester and the king, William Rufus, were in Normandy – and it may be that Gruffudd ap Cynan had recently returned to Gwynedd from prison. The Welsh of Gwynedd, unable to bear the 'tyranny and injustice of the French',[4] rose up and destroyed their castles, and a Norman relief expedition was subsequently defeated by Cadwgan ap Bleddyn at Coed Ysbwys.

Although the earls of Chester and Shrewsbury seem to have restored some control, they were forced to bring in troops to relieve castles which were being attacked, presumably by the Welsh. Gruffudd ap Cynan returned to drive the Normans out of Môn between 1094 and 1098, and the earls returned in 1098, intent on avenging their losses. Gruffudd and his allies, Cadwgan and Maredudd ap Bleddyn, were compelled to retreat, but a Scandinavian force routed the Normans in Môn, inducing another Welsh revolt led by Owain ab Edwin. Gruffudd ap Cynan appears to have acquired Môn in 1099, and Hugh of Chester was obliged to remove all of his goods from Gwynedd to Rhos – and even there the local population turned increasingly towards Gruffudd. Gruffudd's position was now much more secure, and he is not known to have fled to Ireland again. Hugh's death in 1101, to be succeeded by his son, Richard, a minor, further undermined Norman authority, and in 1102, Pope Paschal II arranged for Bishop Hervé to be removed to England; he was translated to Ely in 1109. Gruffudd's prestige was now such that he was consulted about the translation of the teeth of saint Dyfrig from Bardsey to Llandaf, and he secured the election of a Welshman, Dafydd, as bishop of Bangor in 1120. Although there were royal expeditions, Gruffudd was not troubled by the marchers again during his lifetime.

The catalyst of Norman intervention in Gwynedd was disruption in the native Welsh polity, but that polity did not simply collapse, either before or after the Norman onslaught. The Normans usually acted as part of it, not against it, and although they were often quick to take advantage of Welsh weaknesses, they joined forces with the Welsh as often as they fought them. Robert of Rhuddlan was first invited into Gwynedd in 1075, and it was Meirion Goch, not the Norman earls, whose idea it was to lure Gruffudd ap Cynan to be captured. Similarly, it was Owain ab Edwin who brought the Normans into Gwynedd in 1098, possibly only to further his own dynastic claims: he was very quick to turn against them. Direct control of Gwynedd was not a realistic proposition for the Normans, and it may never have been their long-term objective, since, according to Ordericus Vitalis, their main concern was to defend their lands in England. Indeed, the possibility that stability could be as important to them as conquest might explain Hugh of Chester's retreat in 1098 after Owain ab Edwin's establishment as a stable ruler.

For many years after 1098, Gruffudd ap Cynan's hold on Gwynedd was less than complete. His influence depended largely on a few local power bases, especially Môn, Arfon and Llŷn, and even as late as 1121 he is only recorded as holding Môn, although Hugh of Chester gave him some land around 1098 and Henry I is said to have given him Llŷn, Eifionydd, Ardudwy and Arllechwedd before 1114. Little is known of Owain ab Edwin at this time, but it is significant that, although Owain died in 1105, his son, Goronwy, appears as a leader of equal stature with Gruffudd in 1114. Gruffudd was not easily rid of these dynastic rivals, and his position does not seem to have been properly secured until 1125, when his eldest son, Cadwallon, killed Owain's three sons. There was a further attempt to minimise opposition from that quarter in the same year when Gruffudd married Owain's daughter, Angharad; in turn, one of the couple's sons, Owain, later married Cristin, the daughter of Goronwy ab Owain. The fact that the bishopric of Bangor remained vacant from 1109 to 1120 also suggests some turbulence within Gwynedd, but perhaps the best measure of Gruffudd's authority there is that it was sufficiently strong to dissuade the sons of Bleddyn ap Cynfyn from attempting to recover their father's patrimony.

There was some limited territorial expansion under Gruffudd, but no attempt to emulate Gruffudd ap Llywelyn in acquiring other kingdoms. Gruffudd's external relations were conducted primarily through his sons, and he made good use of dynastic marriages. His daughters, Susanna and Gwenllian, were married to Madog ap Maredudd of Powys and Gruffudd ap Rhys of Deheubarth respectively, but only Gwenllian married a man who represented no direct threat to Gruffudd's position as king of Gwynedd. This was a period of consolidation rather than expansion, as Gruffudd's involvement in Ceredigion makes plain. Some interest in the region is suggested by his biography, *Historia Gruffud vab Kenan*, which claims that he secured a promise of half of Rhys ap Tewdwr's lands in 1081, and later ravaged Rhys's *cyfoeth*. He is said to have visited Deheubarth again, apparently accidentally, on a journey from Ireland to Gwynedd, when the wind carried him to Porth Hodni, and he reportedly won three battles there against unidentified opponents. Neither the causes nor the consequences of these events are given, and there is no mention of Gruffudd's activities in Deheubarth in any of the other sources after 1081.

Gruffudd made greater efforts to reassert the authority of Gwynedd in the Perfeddwlad, but with mixed results. He is said to have expanded as far as the English border on his first expedition, and the lesser kings to whom he gave support were probably in this region. He may also have been responsible for a Welsh attack on Chester in 1094, and his son, Cadwallon, was later active on the Dee. By the time of his death in 1137, Gruffudd was able to make gifts to several churches east of the Conwy and in Powys, including Meifod, Llanarmon (yn Iâl?) and Dineirth (Llandrillo yn Rhos). Yet the Perfeddwlad was fiercely contested, and Gwynedd did not establish firm control there until Owain

Gwynedd's campaigns in the late 1140s. Although Hywel ab Ithel fled to Ireland in 1099, and is not heard of again until he was killed fighting the sons of Owain ab Edwin in Rhos and Rhufoniog in 1118, there is no indication that Gruffudd was able to impose himself in the meantime. Norman attempts to secure the Perfeddwlad by establishing a new bishopric of St Asaph were similarly unsuccessful. Hywel may well have been a client of Powys by the time of his death, and it is significant that Gwynedd made very little attempt to intervene in Powys itself. Cadwallon ap Gruffudd was killed in Nanheudwy during a rare incursion in 1132, and it seems that Powys was the stronger kingdom in the early years of the twelfth century. Maredudd ap Bleddyn and the sons of Cadwgan rivalled Gwynedd's influence in the Perfeddwlad, and the mediator between the two kingdoms before 1127 was a Powys man, Daniel ap Sulien, bishop of St Davids and archdeacon of Powys. Had Powys not been afflicted with dynastic problems before 1132, it might have posed a more serious threat to Gwynedd.

Only in Meirionnydd does Gruffudd seem to have been able to exert an influence at the expense of Powys. When the Powys dynasty attempted to assert its authority there in 1124, Gruffudd's sons responded by joining forces with Maredudd ap Cadwgan against Maredudd ap Bleddyn, and they also made a pact with Llywarch ap Trahaearn. They allegedly tried to drive all of Powys into exile, and the harsh retribution exacted on Llywarch by Maredudd ap Bleddyn and the sons of Cadwgan suggests that he may have been on the point of becoming a client of Gwynedd.

Although the territorial expansion of Gwynedd was limited, Gruffudd and his sons emerged as prominent figures in early-twelfth-century Wales as Gwynedd became the natural refuge of native rulers in trouble. Geography played an important part in this, as Snowdonia provided a natural fortress against Norman incursions from the south and east. In 1114, Owain ap Cadwgan sheltered in Gwynedd during Henry I's campaign, and, with Goronwy ab Owain, he joined Gruffudd in agreeing to stand together. Similarly, Gruffudd ap Rhys asked Gruffudd for help in 1115; his request was accepted at first, but he was then refused, hunted down and almost dragged out of Aberdaron church. Maredudd ap Bleddyn also requested help in 1121, and other lesser kings came to Gruffudd for protection, help and counsel. There is no evidence of a formal contract, and the *Historia's* idea that Gruffudd enjoyed overlordship in Deheubarth (including a promise of homage from Rhys ap Tewdwr) can be discarded, but it is clear that he was in a position to dispense generosity to rulers from all over independent Wales. His sons, Owain and Cadwaladr, are also said to have helped all those who fled to them, and concrete evidence of this is provided in 1136, when Gruffudd ap Rhys came to Gwynedd again for assistance. The brothers now took a more active interest in Deheubarth, attacking Walter's castle, Aberystwyth, Dineirth,

Caerwedros and Cardigan in two campaigns, and crushing Norman power in Ceredigion; Cadwaladr later built a castle there. The Normans of Chester were also defeated, and Owain and Cadwaladr are portrayed as the senior partners in alliances with Madog ab Idnerth, Hywel ap Maredudd and his sons and Gruffudd ap Rhys, when they are called 'the splendour of all Britain and her defence and her freedom'.[5] During his father's lifetime, Owain was already becoming accustomed to the role he would play as leader of a Welsh alliance in 1165. Gruffudd himself is said to have devoted his latter years to peacemaking, and Gwynedd enjoyed peace and prosperity by the time of his death in 1137. He had risen to power by force, but it was through caution and firm diplomacy that he consolidated his position and remained on friendly terms with his neighbours. The respect in which he was held by even his enemies is illustrated by the presence of the prior of St Werburgs, Chester, at his deathbed.

These achievements were jeopardised by discord between Owain and Cadwaladr after Gruffudd's death. The brothers fell out in 1143, apparently because of Cadwaladr's killing of Owain's ally, Anarawd ap Gruffudd. Cadwaladr was expelled from both Ceredigion and Gwynedd, but he returned with help from Ireland to force an uneasy peace. Owain, however, eventually destroyed his army and established himself as supreme in Gwynedd in 1144. Cadwaladr's attempt to regain his position in 1147 was foiled by Owain's sons, and, although he recovered some land in Ceredigion in 1149, he was driven into a closer relationship with the Normans. He was with Ranulf of Chester at Lincoln in 1141, and he is supposed to have married into the Clare family, while he also granted lands at Nefyn to Haughmond abbey, and eventually sought refuge in England, where he witnessed a charter of Ranulf of Chester in 1151x1153 and received £7 a year from the king in 1155 and 1156. He may have regained some of his lands in north Wales in 1157, possibly with the help of the king, but by that time Owain was firmly established as king of Gwynedd.

The absence of significant Norman intervention in Gwynedd for several decades during this period is striking – especially when compared with the crucial role played by the Hiberno-Norse in 1143 and 1144 – and it is also noticeable that, unlike his descendants, Gruffudd ap Cynan did not marry into Anglo-Norman aristocratic society. His world was still primarily that of the Irish Sea polity. Yet the influence of the Norman world was growing, and Gruffudd found it advantageous to be connected with it: he gave patronage to churches at Chester and Shrewsbury, and the *Historia* is keen to point out a distant and dubious connection between his ancestors and the Norman kings. Increasing Norman power, together with the re-emergence of Gwynedd as a hegemonic power and the persistence of strong centripetal forces within the native dynasty, were to prove central themes in the remaining years of Welsh independence.

Wales and the Norman Kings

WILLIAM I AND WILLIAM II

William the Conqueror was quick to recognise the strategic value of the Welsh border. Control of the march could prevent his disaffected vassals from receiving help from Wales, and William therefore established marcher earldoms at Chester, Shrewsbury and Hereford. The king did not enter Wales himself until 1081, when he undertook a pilgrimage to St Davids, the motives for which were as much political as religious. A large Hiberno-Norse force had landed there earlier in the year, helping Rhys ap Tewdwr and Gruffudd ap Cynan to victory at Mynydd Carn, and William seems to have been concerned partly to ensure border security and partly to remind the Welsh of his overlordship. English sources say that he took levies, freed many hundreds of men (presumably Norman captives) and slaughtered his enemies, who remain anonymous. This was William's last campaign in Britain, and the Welsh probably expected to be left alone after making the customary promises of allegiance, but they had no doubt learned in 1063 that they needed royal recognition and acceptance of their authority. The arm of the king was becoming longer and stronger.

The process by which a new *modus vivendi* was sought is illuminated by *Domesday Book*, which records that 'Riset de Wales' gave the king £40 in 1086.[6] Riset was almost certainly Rhys ap Tewdwr, and the terms were very probably instituted in 1081. Welsh sources place William's pilgrimage after Mynydd Carn, suggesting that the king was confirming Rhys in what he had already won. It was evidently felt that Rhys's victory had eliminated all serious rivals, and that he was a man with whom William could and must achieve a sustainable peace. Yet the significance of the agreement is less than clear, and it may have been deliberately ambiguous. The payment is reminiscent of the £40 paid by Robert of Rhuddlan for *Nortwales*, which he held of the king, but there is no indication of what exactly Rhys was paying for, and it is only *Domesday Book*'s terminology (*reddit*) which suggests that he actually produced the money. Even if he paid William in 1081, he may have withheld payment after that. Furthermore, it is difficult to imagine to whom he could have paid it – even in 1086, the Normans in south Wales had not penetrated much further west than the Usk. William could persuade himself that Rhys had recognised that native authority in west Wales was something for which he paid the king, whereas Rhys could view the payment as no more than another tribute. The agreement is not inconsistent with the statement of Henry of Huntingdon that William subjected Wales to himself, but it did not amount to royal domination of west Wales. William and Rhys recognised each other as established and stable authorities, and it may or may not have been coincidental that Rhys was to rule in peace for the remainder of the Conqueror's lifetime.

The king's main objective was to protect England, and he seems to have been content with containment on his borders with both Wales and Scotland. William's visit to St Davids cannot have been entirely unconnected with the death of Caradog ap Gruffudd at Mynydd Carn – as ruler of Morgannwg since 1071, Caradog had occupied a key position in an area which bordered both England and Deheubarth, and his removal meant that Rhys ap Tewdwr was now well placed to move into Morgannwg. The 1081 expedition seems to have been intended to keep Rhys in check, and William also used it to shore up the Norman position in Morgannwg by building a motte at Cardiff. The aim was consolidation, not subjection. Cardiff was a very advanced outpost, and royal intervention in Wales under both William I and his son William Rufus was initiated only as a response to real or potential disruption in England, including the threat of unrest in Morgannwg (in 1081) and attacks on the 'land of Chester' (in 1094) and Montgomery (in 1095). Similarly, Rufus's Welsh campaign of 1097 was probably a screen for the erection of castles on the border.

William I seems to have exercised some kind of lordship in south-eastern Wales, which had become segmented after 1063. He was able to make grants to local rulers, and he was allegedly served by Cadwgan ap Meurig of Morgannwg, Caradog ap Gruffudd of Gwent Uwch Coed and Gwynllŵg and Rhydderch ap Caradog of Gwent Is Coed and Ewyas. Caradog is said to have risked losing everything which he held of the king when he harboured Roger of Hereford's men in 1075, and his status seems to have diminished from that of a king (*rex*) to a mere ruler (*regulus*). Precisely what was held of the king, and on what terms, remains a tantalising question. There is no sign that any authority was imposed over Caradog beyond that which existed already, and his foray into Deheubarth in 1081 would scarcely have been possible had he been under pressure from the Normans in the east. His defiance of the king was punished when William Rufus attacked Gwent in 1075, but if anything this highlights the absence of direct royal authority: the king could arrest, try and imprison the mighty Odo of Bayeux in 1082, but his power over Caradog went no further than the length of his sword. Similarly, the king could do little when Bishop Walter of Hereford fled from him into the depths of Wales. The Normans made little territorial impact on the area by the middle of the 1080s, and it seems that William I's objective was merely to lay claim to the lands held in Gwent by Harold Godwinesson before 1066. Moreover, relations between the Welsh and the Normans were usually friendly. Caradog used Norman help against Deheubarth on more than one occasion, and he attended the consecration of a Norman ecclesiastical foundation after 1075 as an honoured guest. Although Norman military power was formidable, Caradog was anything but a subservient tenant – and if this was the situation in Morgannwg, royal influence could hardly have overawed Rhys ap Tewdwr in the west.

In Gwynedd, William I is said to have forced Gruffudd ap Cynan to make peace, probably in 1081, and he may even have been party to Gruffudd's capture. By 1086, Robert of Rhuddlan's tenure of 'Nortwales' indicates that Gwynedd was in the gift of the king, and Rufus is also said to have given 'NortWales' to Hugh of Chester. As in Deheubarth, the *Domesday* agreement in Gwynedd probably dated from 1081. Unlike Deheubarth, however, it most likely constituted a Norman baron's licence to conquer, rather than recognition of an established Welsh king, although it may have been made with either Gruffudd ap Cynan, who was at St Davids with Rhys ap Tewdwr in 1081, or perhaps with Trahaearn ap Caradog between 1075 and 1081. It is also possible that the Normans imposed Owain ab Edwin as a client in 1098. In any case, although the Welsh disliked and resisted Norman rule, there were no complaints about its legality.

William received the tribute of all the Welsh in the same manner as previous kings of England, but he made no novel claims regarding *imperium* over them. The Norman kings assumed the right to decide who should rule Welsh kingdoms, but this was merely a continuation of the policy of Eadward the Confessor, who apparently selected Bleddyn and Rhiwallon in 1063. Moreover, whatever the rhetoric, the reality was that both kings were extending their recognition, rather than imposing their own candidates. There is no record that Rhys ap Tewdwr held his lands of the king (*ad firmam* or *de rege*) as Robert of Rhuddlan did, and it seems that the *Domesday* agreement involved little more than a general promise of obedience, in return for support and recognition. Even if the agreement were interpreted as a feudal contract, it was not entirely unprecedented: Eadward the Confessor had given Gruffudd ap Llywelyn lands across the Dee, and had exercised the right to take them back. It may also be significant that the £40 was payable 'to king William' – it was a personal arrangement, and it was destroyed when William died. Even in Gwynedd, the *Domesday* agreement made very little practical difference. There was nothing to prevent Gruffudd ap Cynan from killing the *Domesday* tenant and taking the kingdom himself, and the regal status of independent, native Welsh kingship survived intact. Nevertheless, William seems to have been aware of the need to institute a more meaningful overlordship. He was the first English king to cross the border for centuries, and he was also the first to be called 'king of Wales' by Welsh sources. He contemplated a more active approach than had his predecessors, and that in itself was a new departure.

William Rufus inherited his father's interest in Wales, and his campaigns of 1095 and 1097 demonstrated his ability to exert direct influence. These were full-scale expeditions involving large numbers of men, and they were intended to achieve the formal submission of the Welsh. The assertion of the *Anglo-Saxon Chronicle* that the Welsh revolted and chose leaders from among themselves, together with the provisions made in 1063, suggest that there may have been a feeling in England, or even a form of agreement, that Gwynedd was held in chief (*in capite*) of the king, and that the Welsh had no right to choose or accept their own kings without his consent. Nevertheless, the lack of a stable supremacy meant that in practice the issue could only be decided by force, and Wales was not a priority for Rufus. His personal involvement in Wales was minimal, and he was preoccupied with problems elsewhere. The Welsh were unlikely to submit to his ineffectual campaigns, and they boasted on one occasion that they forced him to retreat without taking even one cow. Although his reign witnessed a dramatic growth of Norman power in Wales, Rufus did not significantly increase royal influence there by the time of his death in 1100.

Royal involvement in Wales was increasing nonetheless. William I built a castle at Degannwy, and Rufus's influence is apparent in the choice – made by Hugh of Chester – of his chaplain as bishop of Bangor in 1092. Furthermore, the siting of Norman castles may indicate a central strategic vision which could only come from the king, parallel to the situation in Northumbria and Scotland, where royal direction proved invaluable in a fluid and volatile border area which was often subject to unrest and attack. William I was adept at establishing trusted supporters in sensitive areas throughout his dominions, and both he and Rufus installed close associates in the march, where William fitz Osbern, Walter de Lacy and others were instructed to fight the Welsh. There were also sheriffs, with lands and therefore influence in the front line of expansion, whose task was to maintain the vestiges of royal control, and several Welshmen held lands *in capite*. Royal authority was widely respected in the march. It was often taken for granted that Welsh malefactors should receive justice from royal officials, and William fitz Osbern needed the king's permission to maintain certain customary dues of 'king Gruffudd [ap Llywelyn]'. Similarly, the laws and customs of Hereford included provisions for the sheriff to take armed forces against the Welsh, and, significantly, the proviso that if the sheriff does not go into Wales, then nobody may.

Nevertheless, rather than become involved in Wales themselves, the first Norman kings left it to their subordinates. This was largely because their concerns elsewhere made it very difficult to devote time to Wales. William I was preoccupied by the process of conquering England, dealing with numerous rebellions, campaigning against Anjou, Poitou, Brittany and the king of France, arranging a difficult succession, undertaking a massive assessment and reorganisation of English local administration, and fending off Swein Estrithsson of Denmark, who claimed the English crown and threatened invasion in 1069 and 1070. Similarly, Rufus visited Gloucester several times in 1093, but he did not intervene in Wales in that year despite the crisis in Deheubarth – he preferred to allow his barons free rein while he concentrated on dealing with an invasion by the Scots. Moreover, the status of the marcher lordships as liberties meant that much depended

on good faith and mutual understanding between the king and his barons. Hugh
of Chester is said to have held Rhuddlan and north Wales of the king, but his
activities are rarely described as being on the king's behalf, or under his authority. The same could be said of Hugh of Montgomery, who received Shrewsbury
in 1083, or Robert of Rhuddlan. Furthermore, the king was indebted to many
of the marchers for their help in 1066 and against later rebellions, so royal constraints on their power-bases were often slight. There was no *terra regis* at all in
Shropshire, and the royal castles of Degannwy and Rhyd-y-Gors signified no
more control than had Eadward the Confessor's hunting-lodge at Portskewett
– the builders were earls and barons, not the king. Rufus seems to have lacked
both the interest and the financial wherewithal to commit himself decisively
while his barons were being defeated in south Wales in 1096, illustrating the
fact that the king was in no position to direct, restrain or support the marchers as a cohesive invasion force. Given that the Norman and Angevin kings did
not achieve complete military control even of England until the middle of the
twelfth century, the lack of royal influence in Wales was hardly surprising.

HENRY I

Henry I made a deep and unprecedented impression on the minds of twelfth-
century Welshmen. Writing after Henry's death, Gerald of Wales recounted that
he had achieved the final subjugation of Wales, whereas the subsequent reign
of Stephen brought disorder and violence. The *Brut*, calling Henry 'king of
England and Wales' and 'Henry the Great', relates that his power was such that
he 'subdued under his authority all the island of Britain and its mighty ones'.
He was 'the man against whom no one could be of avail save God himself',[7]
capable of contemplating the very extermination of the Britons, and it was no
coincidence that the Welsh advances between 1136 and 1155 occurred during
Stephen's troubled reign rather than during Henry's lifetime. Nevertheless, the
true extent of Henry's personal rule in Wales can be overstated.

Although Henry paid a lot more attention to Wales than any of his predecessors, it was not a priority for him, and most of his dealings there were
with Norman lords. Nowhere in his dominions did he seek territorial expansion, nor could he afford to treat recalcitrant vassals particularly harshly, even
in England. Everywhere, the theme of his reign was consolidation – in fact,
he contributed little else to English kingship. There was no concerted effort
to overrun Wales, and the marcher momentum was faltering at the time of
Henry's accession in 1100. His main concern was to prevent troubles in Wales
from threatening England or royal power in Wales.

Henry's most immediate achievement was to intensify the intrusiveness of
royal government in the march. Shrewsbury and Pembroke escheated to him in

1102, together with lesser lordships, and Chester was taken into royal wardship in 1101, while royal favourites were intruded into vacant lordships. The king also arranged marriages and claimed authority over marcher lands; many charters of marcher lords were issued with his consent, and important agreements were often made in his presence. The full apparatus of shire administration was installed at Pembroke by 1130, and, to a greater or lesser degree, Dyfed was made subject directly to the king. By 1109, Carmarthen was a centre of royal government, and a borough was established at Kidwelly. By 1130, the region was known – at least to royal officials – as Carmarthenshire, and royal revenues were collected from a large area. The king's most spectacular and effective measure was the plantation of a large Flemish colony in Dyfed and Ceredigion after 1107. Some of these areas were justifiably described as a second England, and Henry's influence was such that marcher lords felt it necessary to assume the position of royal officials in Wales whether they were recognised as such or not. Arnulf of Montgomery, for instance, called himself an earl despite his general indifference to the king.

Royal overlordship over the Welsh church was also extended. Henry established the right of the king to control the election of Welsh bishops and to receive their fealty, and he secured their allegiance to Canterbury, which began to make serious efforts to press an ancient claim that Wales was within its province. The authority of Canterbury over Wales was taken for granted in 1125, when the English clergy proposed the transfer of Bangor from the province of Canterbury to that of York, while the translation of saint Dyfrig's relics from Bardsey to Llandaf required the consent of Canterbury. Ecclesiastical subjection was underlined and intensified by the consecration of all Welsh bishops by the Archbishop of Canterbury, their profession of canonical obedience to him from 1107, and their unprecedentedly regular attendance at English royal and provincial councils from 1102. Henry also appointed his own close advisers to Welsh bishoprics. Although far from representing complete royal domination, these developments signalled that the Welsh church was being drawn further into a relationship of subservience to both Canterbury and the king.

Both marchers and Welshmen were addressed as Henry's subjects, and he was skilled in ensuring that important positions were occupied by friendly parties. Ordericus Vitalis claimed that his reign was characterised by an ability to entrust authority to men whom he had 'raised from the dust', but in Wales he did not have the influence simply to choose and control his own men. Gerald of Windsor was typical. In 1105, he was given Pembroke by the king, who provided him with a wife who represented a passport to social integration with the Welsh – but Gerald had held Pembroke since at least 1097, when he acted as constable for Arnulf of Montgomery, and in 1102 Arnulf had sent him to Ireland on a mission which was clearly against the king's interests. Gerald's castles are not known to have had

royal licences, and, apart from Henry's insistence that Gerald was his officer in
1109, there is no evidence that Gerald was ever under strict royal control. Similarly, Henry's grants of Ceredigion to Gilbert fitz Richard and Cantref Bychan to
Richard fitz Pons may well signify no more than recognition of the fruits of independent marcher actions. Marcher power was such that Miles of Gloucester could
call upon the service of forty-five knights from his Welsh lands alone, and Henry's
authority over the marchers was so weak that he needed Welsh support even to
take Bridgnorth. It is also possible that it was the Welsh, rather than Normans loyal
to Henry, who defeated the sons of Roger of Montgomery at Pembroke in 1102.
Only the Flemish plantation in Dyfed seems to reflect real royal power in Wales,
and even the Flemings went on to establish jurisdictions beyond the reach of the
king; men such as Letard *Litelking* are unlikely to have acted as Henry's devoted
servants. The degree of royal control over the administration of the march is also
open to doubt, since many of the sheriffs were appointed by earls, and the real
business of government was conducted at the local level by castellans.

It was the marchers, not the king, who held the key to Anglo-Norman power
in Wales. There was no territorial conquest against the Welsh in the name of any
Norman king, and it was the marchers who were responsible for the vast majority of ecclesiastical foundations in south Wales, as they were in England. English
chroniclers concurred with Gerald of Wales in recognising Henry's death as an
important factor in the Welsh successes of 1136, but they singled out the death of
Richard fitz Gilbert de Clare as decisive. Although Henry's reign saw the erection
of castles at Newport, Swansea, Kidwelly, Carmarthen, Llandovery, Manorbier,
Haverfordwest, Cardigan, Aberystwyth, and many other sites, especially in Dyfed,
nearly all of these were built by marcher lords and bore their names, including
Ralph, Walter, Richard de la Mare, Stephen and Humphrey. Most if not all of
these castles were probably adulterine, and it is instructive that even in Normandy,
where the king (in his capacity as duke) claimed the right of all castle building,
he was nevertheless obliged to accept numerous adulterine castles, especially on
the borders. Robert of Bellême made a mockery of the supposed need for royal
licence to build castles in Shropshire, so Henry's control further west can hardly
have been complete. The almost total absence of royal castles in the Welsh march
– compared with an abundance in other strategic areas such as the south coast of
England and the Scottish border – reinforces the impression that Henry's direct
influence there was limited. The royal castles of Degannwy and Rhyd-y-Gors
were held by the Welsh for much of the time, and the coherent network of
strategically distributed Norman castles in Wales almost certainly owed more to
military, geographical and economic common sense than to royal direction.

The nature of Henry's dealings with Wales is well illustrated by his involvement in Ystrad Tywi, which provided a corridor between Norman territories

in Pembroke and Glamorgan. The king made a series of 'grants' in the area, but it appears that they were determined more by the vagaries of native Welsh politics than by an inflexible royal will. Henry gave Ystrad Tywi to Iorwerth ap Bleddyn in 1102, but the emergence of Hywel ap Goronwy soon afterwards persuaded the king to recognise him instead as ruler of Ystrad Tywi, Cydweli and Gŵyr. Hywel was no royal appointee. Although he is said to have been given Rhyd-y-Gors, he seems to have held it already – the castle had been evacuated by its royal garrison in 1096, and it was not repaired until 1105. Richard fitz Baldwin restored Norman rule at Rhyd-y-Gors in 1105, ejecting Hywel from all the castles in the area, but he returned home without attempting to set up a permanent lordship, which suggests that Hywel was still a menace. The Welsh challenge was finally ended when Hywel was killed by the garrison of Rhyd-y-Gors in 1106. There were no prominent native contenders after the deaths of Hywel and his rival Gwgan ap Meurig, and the ineffectiveness of the Welsh in Ystrad Tywi after 1106 is indicated by the fact that none of the Normans who recovered it had a distinguished military record. As elsewhere in the march, it seems that the Normans intervened only when the native polity was weak, and royal policy blew with the prevailing wind.

The dearth of native challengers in Ystrad Tywi persisted until the return of Gruffudd ap Rhys ap Tewdwr from Ireland in 1114x1115. Gruffudd set about establishing friendly relations with influential local figures such as Gerald of Windsor, but two years of peaceful negotiation for the recovery of his inheritance failed, and he was forced to flee again, returning to assault Norman positions in Dyfed and Ystrad Tywi – including Narberth, Llandovery, Swansea, Carmarthen and a castle in Gower – in 1115 and 1116. The castles held out, however, and Gruffudd's subsequent attack on Ceredigion was defeated, as was a second bid for lands there in 1136. He is not known to have acquired more than a single *cwmwd*, in Cantref Mawr.

The initial impression given by the chronicles is that Gruffudd was resisted in Ystrad Tywi by a firmly entrenched Norman colony under strong royal control, but this is rather simplistic. It is unlikely that Henry would have given land to Gruffudd – a rebel, and a failed one at that – unless he had first established a hold on it. Moreover, it appears that the king underpinned his rule by enlisting the services of native Welsh magnates. The *Brut* sees all of the Welsh who sided with the Normans in 1116 as subordinates: Maredudd ap Rhydderch ap Caradog is said to have held Cantref Bychan under Richard fitz Pons, and others served at Norman castles. The Normans depended on these men. At times of danger, most of the castles were maintained not by Normans, but by the Welsh, and unease about their trustworthiness is suggested by the restriction of each Welsh ruler's tenure of Carmarthen to two weeks. The success of this policy hinged on the calculation that the Welsh desire to repel Gruffudd ap Rhys was stronger than the temptation to rebel against the king.

This was Henry's strength. He was a good judge of men, and in 1116 he was confident of the animosity of the local Welsh towards Gruffudd. Rhydderch ap Tewdwr and his sons, Maredudd ap Rhydderch, and Owain ap Caradog ap Rhydderch ap Iestyn had particularly vested interests. Rhydderch, for example, was Gruffudd's uncle, and he had lost land to his brother Rhys ap Tewdwr, so this segment of the native dynasty was determined to prevent the return of Rhys's descendants. It was Gruffudd's attempt to dislodge such ingrained native interests which caused contemporaries to dismiss his followers as 'young hotheads'.[8] Similarly, Owain ap Cadwgan and Llywarch ap Trahaearn opposed his subsequent foray into Ceredigion, although Gruffudd did not lack Welsh allies there, since Cydifor ap Goronwy and Hywel ab Idnerth were keen to exploit the weakened hold of Powys on Ceredigion after 1109. Such a policy of 'divide and rule' saved the king considerable effort and expenditure, and moreover, he probably had no choice but to endorse the *status quo*.

This reliance on native rulers suggests that the administration and even the military capability of the Normans in Ystrad Tywi was deficient. In 1137, they were so weak that Welsh and Normans alike saw Gruffudd as king of Deheubarth, despite his apparent failure to conquer more than the *cantref* of Rhos in Dyfed, and despite the defeat of his wife, Gwenllian, at Kidwelly. Norman government in the area had always been tenuous. In 1130, the men of Cantref Mawr still owed the king a fine of 40 shillings for killing a Norman perhaps as long ago as 1106, and it was almost certainly never paid. Many Welshmen, such as Bledri ap Cydifor, a royal interpreter (*latimer*) in 1130, served the king, and there was a great deal of integration, but this merely indicates the depth of Welsh resistance – elsewhere, such as in England and Dyfed, the Normans preferred not to retain natives in important offices. The rapid disintegration of Norman authority after 1137 is therefore understandable. Minor segments of the native dynasty renewed their bids for power, and Gwynedd also became involved, but it was the sons of Gruffudd ap Rhys who held the field. Ceredigion was seized in 1136, Carmarthen (which was destroyed in 1137 and 1146) was in the hands of Cadell ap Gruffudd by 1150, and Cadell also ravaged Kidwelly, while his brother, Maredudd, controlled Ystrad Tywi by 1155. Rhys ap Gruffudd eventually emerged supreme, aided by a considerable degree of luck – he was only able to assume control of the lands conquered by his brother, Maredudd, because of the early deaths of two of his elder brothers. But the resurgence of the descendants of Rhys ap Tewdwr demonstrated the shifting military situation in west Wales and the precariousness of the Norman position there. The destruction of Norman power even in Carmarthen and Dyfed was due to indigenous political processes at least as much as to unrest in England, and

Gervase of Canterbury was not entirely accurate in saying that the Welsh went back to their old ways in 1136. They had never really left them.

Nevertheless, Henry I broke new ground both in his willingness to dirty his hands in the complexities of Welsh politics and in his ability to assert himself as the most formidable party in Wales. Iorwerth ap Bleddyn feared the king and his law, and Madog ap Rhirid is said to have felt that he had wronged the king in killing Iorwerth in 1111. Such anxieties were well founded. The most innovative and perhaps revolutionary aspect of Henry's reign was the implicit assertion of direct territorial supremacy. The king 'gave' Llŷn, Eifionydd, Ardudwy and Arllechwedd to Gruffudd ap Cynan; he reportedly attacked Gwynedd because Gruffudd had taken lands without permission; he 'gave' Powys, Ceredigion and half of Dyfed to Iorwerth in 1102; Owain ap Cadwgan and Madog ap Rhirid are said to have feared that he would take their lands, imprison them or even put them to death when they fell foul of him in 1110; Iorwerth was given Powys in 1110 and was commanded not to conspire with anyone on pain of forfeiture and death; Cadwgan ap Bleddyn made great entreaties to obtain Ceredigion from Henry in 1109, and was forced to give £100 and a promise not to aid his son Owain; Cadwgan was then given Powys in 1111, and Ceredigion was given to Gilbert fitz Richard; Henry gave Powys to Maredudd ap Bleddyn on Cadwgan's death, and then divided it between Owain and the sons of Rhirid, taking hostages and tribute, and he gave it to Owain again in 1114; and Gruffudd ap Rhys was given a single *cwmwd*, Caeo, in Cantref Mawr, only for the king to remove him from it in 1127. The *Brut* chronicler was so impressed by Henry's authority to dispense lands that he even has him command that no one was to dwell in Ceredigion at all.

Henry was keen to exploit political divisions in Wales. In 1114, he subdued Owain ap Cadwgan, Gruffudd ap Cynan and Goronwy ab Owain by telling them each in turn that the others had made peace when they had not, and Madog and Ithel ap Rhirid, Llywarch ap Trahaearn and Uchdryd ab Edwin were similarly encouraged to fight Owain ap Cadwgan in 1109. Owain and Llywarch were also persuaded to unite their forces against Gruffudd ap Rhys in 1116. Such cajolery worked best where incentives were offered, and Henry was not short of them. His greatest influence was as a provider of patronage, and it was the promise of substantial rewards, together with the fear that others might get preferential treatment, which persuaded Owain ap Cadwgan to submit in 1114 and later to accept Henry's invitation to accompany him to Normandy and to be made a knight. Perhaps the best example of Henry's shrewd manipulative skills was in 1102, when he first outbid Robert of Bellême for the support of Iorwerth ap Bleddyn – who was offered Powys, Ceredigion and half of Dyfed without rent or payment for the king's lifetime – and then hoodwinked Iorwerth, taking Dyfed and Pembroke back and giving them to a Norman.

Yet the apparent ease with which Henry manipulated the Welsh belied a weakness, and the Welsh knew it. By 1115, Gruffudd ap Cynan was well aware that, as the *Brut* says, 'it was the custom of the French to deceive men with promises'.[9] It was easy and inexpensive for the king to beguile with promises which were never kept, and Gruffudd was not persuaded when Henry attempted to procure his help in catching Gruffudd ap Rhys. Henry's promise to raise Llywarch ap Trahaearn and Uchdryd ab Edwin above their peers in return for help against Owain ap Cadwgan in 1109 was similarly hollow, since he never gave them any protection at all against the men of Powys, and the promise to enrich Owain for military help in 1116 came from a king who could not prevent the constable of Pembroke from assassinating Owain on the very campaign he was to be paid for. Perhaps such promises were made cynically, but the fact remains that only one of Henry's threats and promises is known to have been carried out, when he made Owain a knight. Nor does the acceptance of bribes necessarily mean that the Welsh were at the king's bidding. It is debatable whether Henry could have forced Gruffudd ap Cynan to surrender Gruffudd ap Rhys, or the men of Arwystli and Meirionnydd to fight Owain ap Cadwgan, had they not already been willing to.

The ability to apportion lands did not reflect any permanent executive royal power over the Welsh. For nearly all of Henry's thirty-five-year reign, the absence of any mention of the king, or of royal officials, in accounts of the convoluted and often bloody internal politics of Powys gives the impression that the Welsh were left to their own devices. Henry took no part in the struggle for power within Powys which followed the exile of Cadwgan ap Bleddyn and Owain ap Cadwgan in 1109; nor did he interfere in the division of the lands of Madog ap Rhirid in 1113; nor did he incite the killing of Madog which made this possible; nor did he assert any control in the re-apportioning of the lands of Einion ap Cadwgan in Powys and Meirionnydd in 1124 – Ithel ap Rhirid was given no more than moral support in this instance, and obtained nothing. Henry's administration is known to have promoted conflict in Powys only once, after Owain ap Cadwgan abducted Nest in 1109, and this case was exceptional: it was a response to an insult against both a royal officer and one of Henry's former concubines. Moreover, while the king's use of the dissatisfied rulers of Arwystli and Meirionnydd and an unsuccessful segment of the Powys dynasty may represent a case of 'divide and rule', it was the only occasion on which he was able to implement such a policy.

The humiliation of Cadwgan and Owain was a powerful demonstration of royal supremacy, but it also illustrates the limitations of Henry's power over the dynasty of Powys. Cadwgan's payment was tiny in comparison with the tributes which were supposedly paid to Æþelstan, and Henry was unable to prevent Owain's raids. Moreover, the king's failure to destroy Cadwgan seems to have been due as much to Cadwgan's resilience as to Henry's goodwill. It was easy to dispossess a man who knew that he risked imprisonment or worse if he attempted to leave the royal court without making large concessions. But it was less easy to ensure that he remained dispossessed, and it is significant that Cadwgan and Owain were rehabilitated in the following year. For nearly all of the period 1099–1116, Powys was held by Cadwgan, Iorwerth and Owain, who owed their position to their own strength, not to the king. Iorwerth was able to force Robert of Bellême to come to terms with the king, and it is unlikely that he would succumb meekly himself. The lands which Henry took back from Iorwerth in 1102 lay not in his power-base in Powys but far away, next to the Anglo-Norman castle of Pembroke, which had recently fallen to the king; and when Iorwerth was deceived into attending a royal court in Shrewsbury in 1103 to hear actions against him, the verdict against him and his subsequent imprisonment were imposed 'not by law, but by possession',[10] according to the *Brut*. Henry was unable to overcome Iorwerth by legal means, and, moreover, the 'possession' (*medyant*) referred not to Powys but to disputed lands in Dyfed. Similarly, although Henry's opposition to Owain in 1109 caused Cadwgan and Iorwerth to be fearful, it was directed at Ceredigion rather than Powys itself, and the greatest threat to Cadwgan and Iorwerth was not Henry but their own relatives: it was Madog ap Rhirid, the son of their elder brother, who killed them both in 1111 – without Anglo-Norman connivance. Similarly, the revival of Powys under Madog ap Maredudd was probably due more to the removal of internal divisions within Powys than to Henry's death.

Henry launched two military expeditions against the Welsh, with mixed results. His 1114 campaign was seen by the Welsh as an attempt to drive them into the sea, but the result was no more than another payment of tribute, and then only after Owain ap Cadwgan had twice rejected the king's terms. The campaign of 1121 also made only a slight impression, suffering embarrassing military reverses in spite of its size, including a narrow escape for the king himself, whose armour saved him from an arrow in the chest. Gruffudd ap Cynan paid no tribute when he made peace in 1114 and 1121, although hostages were taken on the latter occasion, and the *Brut* contradicts itself about 1114, saying first that Gruffudd submitted before Owain, yielding nothing to the king, and then that it was Owain's submission which persuaded him to make peace, which included a large tribute. Henry's overlordship was not in doubt, but he was far from able to impose terms on the Welsh at will. Nor was this his main intention, since both royal campaigns were primarily intended to bolster the marcher lords. The war of 1114 was instigated by Gilbert fitz Richard's complaints against Owain ap Cadwgan, as well as those of Hugh of Chester against Gruffudd ap Cynan and Goronwy ab Owain, and it is significant that the *Historia* follows its account of the 1121 campaign by declaring that the earls of Chester and Shrewsbury, the men of Powys and Trahaearn ap Caradog's men had all failed to overcome Gruffudd ap Cynan. Henry I apparently did not deserve a mention.

Sheltering in the natural fortress of Gwynedd, Gruffudd ap Cynan was brought into direct contact with Henry only by the action of third parties: namely the flight of Cadwgan ap Bleddyn from Powys and of Gruffudd ap Rhys from Deheubarth to Gwynedd in 1114 and 1115 respectively, and Maredudd ap Bleddyn's request for Gruffudd's help in 1121. It might seem that Gruffudd was concerned to avoid conflict with Henry at any price, since he was very quick to make peace in 1114, and he refused to fight with the men of Powys against the king in 1121, threatening to attack them if they came near him. However, his readiness to comply with Henry's wishes did not mean that he lived in fear of him. There was no pressing reason to refuse a request from an acknowledged overlord, and there were plenty of reasons not to. It was no more than common sense to accept a bribe to hand over Gruffudd ap Rhys to Henry, and also to refuse to become involved in a costly and unnecessary war in Powys, especially since Gruffudd had no reason to help the descendants of Bleddyn ap Cynfyn, who had posed much more of a threat to his position in Gwynedd than any king of England had. This non-hostile attitude towards the king was generally reciprocated. Henry's campaign of 1114 was directed primarily against Powys, and although the expedition of 1121 was provoked by an attack by Gruffudd on Cheshire, the fact that Henry did not interfere in the rivalries within Gwynedd or in Gruffudd's attacks against Powys in the 1120s suggests very strongly that he lacked the will to do so. There was no desire for a repeat of 1063. The *Historia*'s claim that Gruffudd was on friendly – and by implication reasonably equal – terms with all his royal neighbours seems justified, and this relationship was achieved by detachment as much as by obsequiousness.

The traditional forms of English overlordship were intensified and extended during Henry's reign. Welsh visits to the royal court were revived and became more frequent: Iorwerth ap Bleddyn, Cadwgan ap Bleddyn, Owain ap Cadwgan, Gruffudd ap Cynan and Gruffudd ap Rhys all attended Henry's court, some of them more than once, and they were often summoned rather than invited. Hostage-taking also increased. Whereas Eadward the Confessor is known to have received hostages only once, and William I not at all, Henry I received Henry ap Cadwgan ap Bleddyn as a hostage in return for Iorwerth ap Bleddyn's release from prison in 1110, Owain ap Cadwgan followed suit in 1111, and hostages were promised by Maredudd ap Bleddyn and Madog ap Rhirid in 1111. Henry exacted more of the same in 1121. Demands for payment increased, too: Henry did not miss the opportunity to force Cadwgan ap Bleddyn to pay £100 in 1109, and Iorwerth ap Bleddyn similarly gave 100 marks, 300 pounds of silver (or its equivalent in horses, oxen and other livestock) for his release from prison in 1110. Money was also promised by Maredudd ap Bleddyn, Owain ap Cadwgan and Madog ap Rhirid in 1111, and Maredudd and the sons of Cadwgan gave about 10,000 animals in 1121.

Henry's increased assertion of his supremacy highlighted the subordination of the Welsh in an unprecedented way. Rather than shifting the paradigm of overlordship, however, he merely brought existing relationships into sharper focus by insisting on them more often. Royal lordship, which Gruffudd ap Rhys supposedly wanted to leave in 1115, might have reached into more corners of Wales under Henry I, but it meant essentially the same as it had under his predecessors. Although it might seem that payment was usual – Maredudd ap Bleddyn and Owain ap Cadwgan promised money and hostages in return for Powys, and Henry offered to give Owain his land free in 1114, so that the other Welsh would envy him – there was no attempt to reinstate the *Domesday* payments for any part of Wales. There could be no direct lordship without payment of rent, but there was no obligation to pay £40 *per annum* to Henry as there had been to William I. The Welsh gave tribute to Henry only in exceptional circumstances, and then only as one-off payments. Although he was called king of Wales by chroniclers, Henry had no contractual relationship with the Welsh. He never used any formal title himself with respect to Wales, and his overlordship was ultimately flexible, stretching and contracting in response to the varying fortunes of the king and his dependants. The balance of power might change, but royal overlordship had altered very little since 1063.

The Significance of the Coming of the Normans

Although native Wales was severely weakened after 1063, Welsh kings remained at the centre of developments. The Normans were simply another factor in a very fluid Welsh polity – and not the only non-Welsh element – and they were rarely able to extinguish indigenous authority. Furthermore, although the involvement of Norman kings in Wales showed that they appreciated the problems which had arisen in the Confessor's reign, the tradition of royal non-intervention was generally maintained. Royal policy was not aimed at conquest. It was little more than a concomitant of the establishment of Norman baronial interests there, and most of Wales was beyond the reach of regularly enforceable royal authority.

The reign of Stephen drove home the fact that it was the marchers who held the key to Norman power in Wales. Gilbert de Lacy and the earls of Hereford and Gloucester were at odds for much of the period after 1135, and Anglo-Norman divisions and preoccupations precluded co-ordinated action and even allowed the Welsh to ravage Cheshire for some time. The king despatched Baldwin fitz Gilbert and Robert fitz Harold on forays into Wales, but neither achieved any lasting success, and Stephen's dependence on marcher

support compelled him to create (or rather recognise) Gilbert de Clare's earldom of Pembroke in 1138. Stephen's failure in Wales was a direct consequence
of the 'anarchy' in England during his reign, but it did not come about for
want of personal leadership. Rather, it highlighted the inadequate governmental
machinery he had inherited. Impressive campaigns could be mounted when
there was no other pressing business for the king to attend to, but at a time
when the Anglo-Norman world was split by disputes which had been gaining
momentum since long before Stephen took the throne, the king had no choice
but to rely on the marchers to look after themselves, and they in turn found
their attention divided and their resources stretched. In the end, Clare lands
could only be defended by Clare men, even if they were sent by the king. In
that respect, Stephen was very much like his predecessors, only less fortunate.

The Norman position in Wales did not appear impressive in 1155. Territorial
gains had been made since 1066, but most of them had been lost; the marcher
sphere of influence was ill-defined; military limitations restricted the extent of
both royal and baronial power; the native Welsh polity remained volatile; and
the relationships between the Welsh and the king were still conducted within
the confines of a political structure inherited from the time of Æþelstan. But
appearances can be misleading. Despite all its flaws, the Normans' bridgehead in
Wales – underpinned by their ubiquitous motte and bailey castles – was formidable, and this in itself was a radical change. Furthermore, Norman incursions
provided the catalyst for a gradual but profound shift in the social and economic
life of the country. Many new boroughs were created in the march, and land
which had rarely or never been used before was settled and cultivated as migrants
from England and overseas flowed into Wales – part of a growth in population
throughout Europe in the twelfth and thirteenth centuries. The profits from these
developments inevitably benefited the Norman lords within whose dominions
they were encouraged, and not the native Welsh. English military and economic
power was not in doubt. At the same time, the creation of private Anglo-Norman
lordships in Wales attracted the attention of an increasingly efficient and effective
central government, with the result that the possibilities for royal overlordship
were enormously enhanced. The king was now engaged in a struggle with both
the Welsh and his own barons in Wales, and although he was not yet ready to press
for outright victory, it was inevitable that his massive resources would be deployed
increasingly heavily there. Moreover, whereas the Anglo-Saxons had developed
the theoretical supremacy of the king of England over Wales, the Normans had
now provided a practical imperative for it to be implemented. The seeds had been
sown for the eventual destruction of Welsh independence.

The Balance of Power
and its Destruction
1155–c.1200

Wales and the Angevin Empire

Welsh contacts with the king of England increased under Henry II, who restored order in England after his accession in 1154. Although there was little discernible change in the terms upon which the parties dealt with each other, the subordination of Welsh rulers was reinforced simply by the fact of its being regularly repeated. This in turn enabled Henry to insist upon submissions being done at the time and place of his choosing, often at one of his residences deep in the heart of England, and it appears that he endeavoured to introduce a new precision into his overlordship. Demands were now made for homage as well as fealty, and a new role was created for Rhys ap Gruffudd of Deheubarth as a royal representative. Nevertheless, overlordship remained essentially a loose concept, and the rise of Gwynedd and Deheubarth to a position stronger than they had enjoyed since 1063 focused attention on the lack of a firm contractual relationship between the Welsh and the king.

Henry could not dominate Wales directly, and the existing secular and ecclesiastical spheres of influence were generally accepted. Nevertheless, the accession of an Angevin king, whose influence eventually spread beyond Normandy into Anjou and most of France as far as Spain, meant that Wales was now part – however loosely – of an insular and continental hegemony. Increasing royal domination was inevitable, especially as Wales was now becoming a useful source of troops for both the marchers and the king, who possessed an unprecedentedly large stake in the march after acquiring custody of Pembroke and Gwent Iscoed in around 1176 and Glamorgan and Gwynllŵg in 1183. At the same time, the sheer size of the Angevin dominions meant that Henry and his sons, Richard and John, spent even more time abroad than their predecessors. Until Normandy and the other continental lands were lost in John's reign, the Angevins were more concerned to reward their supporters than to enforce Welsh subservience, although a closer interest in Wales was shown after the invasion of Ireland, which necessitated an unobstructed path to Milford Haven and Pembroke.

The king's main objective in Wales was to restore and maintain stability after the turmoil of Stephen's reign. Indeed, it was Henry II's aim everywhere to restore the *status quo* of 1135. He was concerned to prevent disruption in the secular politics of native Wales, and determined not to allow the bishopric of St Davids to be given archiepiscopal status, which might focus Welsh national aspirations – the metropolitan claims of Canterbury had given rise to calls for a new Welsh archdiocese since the 1120s. Direct action was occasionally necessary, but the rewards and punishments which Henry meted out were always influenced primarily by the requirements of maintaining equilibrium throughout his dominions.

ROYAL EXPEDITIONS

Henry embarked upon several campaigns in Wales, the purpose of which was to intimidate rather than conquer. In military terms, they were generally ineffectual, but they succeeded in reasserting royal authority after the malaise of Stephen's reign. During the campaign which sought to subdue Gwynedd in 1157, Owain ap Gruffudd (now better known as Owain Gwynedd) confidently held Henry as far east as Basingwerk and Hawarden in Tegeingl, and the fleet sent to Môn was mauled – Henry fitz Henry (the illegitimate son of Henry I and Nest of Deheubarth) was killed, the king himself nearly lost his life in an ambush, and the royal army narrowly avoided a disastrous defeat. Henry eventually broke through to Rhuddlan and secured both Tegeingl and a submission from Owain, but these gains amounted to little more than an equable peace. A second campaign was similarly unsuccessful in 1165, when the king appeared first at Rhuddlan and was then faced down by a powerful Welsh confederation at Corwen. Harassed by the Welsh and battered by storms in the Berwyn mountains, Henry eventually gave up and returned home, taking his revenge by gouging out the eyes of his hostages. Only twice were his campaigns militarily successful. Deheubarth was subdued without hostilities in 1163, and Iorwerth ab Owain was dispossessed of Caerleon in 1171, although the latter victory was soon reversed. Royal campaigns could frighten the Welsh for a time – which in itself was a worthwhile objective, as it reminded them of the basis of royal overlordship – but experience showed that even the most elaborate and awe-inspiring military expeditions often achieved nothing of lasting value.

This ineffectiveness was not due to ineptitude. Henry demonstrated his considerable martial skills in France in 1173, and his army of 1165 was drawn from England, Normandy, Flanders, Gascony, Anjou, Poitou, Aquitaine and Scotland. Furthermore, Henry showed his commitment to dealing with Wales by taking the unusual step of requiring more than forty days' service from many of his troops in 1157. He was a formidable enemy. It was only royal expeditions that induced the Welsh to retreat to Snowdonia, and their fear of the king is unquestionable, not least because they relied heavily on the English border counties for food. The limited military success of royal campaigns was due mainly to the conditions under which they had to be waged. Wales was noted for its mountains, bogs, forests and unfavourable weather, which made the conventional Anglo-Norman reliance on cavalry impracticable. As a result, it became standard practice for royal campaigns to include large numbers of lightly armed troops, following the approach pioneered by Harold Godwinesson in 1063. The Welsh, in contrast, had always been adept at warfare in this environment, and their ability to subsist on very little and to move rapidly, together with the practice of transhumance, made retreat to the mountains easy. They were renowned soldiers, skilled in the use of guerilla tactics and powerful weapons such as the longbow, and Henry II wrote to the Byzantine emperor Manuel Comnenus that they were so fearless that they would fight a fully armed enemy despite being unarmed themselves. According to Gerald of Wales, the Welsh were also aware that their freedom was at stake, and their resolve to preserve it was heightened by a growing sense of nationality. The Normans were understandably wary of the risks involved in guerrilla warfare. Moreover, the Welsh could defeat them on their own terms, having become skilled in strategic castle-building and siege warfare, used to pitched battles, and not unfamiliar with the use of heavy cavalry. Although the Welsh were occasionally convinced that royal campaigns were intended to destroy them, the king himself knew that that was practically impossible.

HENRY II AND GWYNEDD

Relations between Gwynedd and England remained distant. Henry received hostages and tribute from Owain Gwynedd in 1157, and, while most sources say that no more than peace was made, it is also alleged that Owain performed *hominium*. This might indicate homage, but it is more likely that Owain became Henry's 'man' in a looser sense. Such a concept was known in Wales, and the terminology of feudal relationships was anyway not standardised – and in any case, Anglo-Norman writers often used familiar feudal terms to describe very different forms of agreement. Semantics apart, Henry was in no position to dictate terms in 1157. Welsh chronicles say that he made peace with Owain, rather than the other way round, and Owain's subsequent actions were not those of a subservient vassal. The *Annals of Margam*, which otherwise record only events in the south, refer to him as 'Owain of Wales' (*Oweyn de Wallia*)[1] in this year, and native princes went out of their way to show him respect. *Annales Cambriae* even call him 'prince of Wales' (*princeps Wallie*) in 1157. Henry's

main aim was simply to receive Owain's recognition as king. No new formal
relationship was established, and it seems that the customary forms of submission were observed. Nevertheless, the introduction of new terminology
is interesting, as it may suggest a desire to redefine the relationship between
Gwynedd and the king.

Henry may have been instrumental in the restoration of Owain's brother,
Cadwaladr, but this is far from certain. It is possible that Cadwaladr was given
Tegeingl, which the king seems to have conquered in 1157, but his only known
lands in Wales were in Ceredigion and Meirionnydd, where royal influence
was almost non-existent. Henry did not benefit from his reinstatement, and
it cannot be assumed that he wanted to help him. Indeed, Cadwaladr lost a
manor in Shropshire at this time, and in any case Dafydd ab Owain controlled
Tegeingl by 1165 and Rhuddlan was destroyed by the Welsh in 1167.

Owain Gwynedd wanted a more far-reaching understanding with Henry,
and he was quick to transfer the captive Einion Clud of Maelienydd to royal
custody in 1160, recognising that deference to the king was preferable to
becoming entangled in difficult border areas. As a result, he may have performed homage (*homagium*) in 1163, and he is said to have encouraged Rhys
ap Gruffudd of Deheubarth to do the same. Moreover, Owain's establishment
as a national leader after leading the Welsh at Corwen in 1165 allowed him
to insist upon privileged terms. The war of 1165 appears to have been little
more than a flexing of muscles, since neither Owain nor Henry seems to have
wanted direct conflict. The king's attack was provoked by Dafydd ab Owain's
ravaging of Tegeingl, and neither side pursued the hostilities with commitment; Henry's frustrated mutilation of hostages was no more than a warning.
The most important aspect of this episode was the war of words. Having
accepted perhaps unprecedentedly humiliating terms in 1163, Owain was
keen both to stress his military power and to redefine his status, styling himself
'king of Wales' (*rex Gualliae*) and adopting the regal first person plural in his
correspondence. Gerald of Wales calls him 'Owain the Great' in the context
of 1165, and his power did not go unnoticed in England, where the Annals
of Chester styled him 'king of Wales' in his obituary. In this atmosphere of
mutual but wary respect, Owain and Henry seem to have been aware of the
possibility of reaching a formal accord, and it was probably in an attempt to
establish a bargaining position that Owain recognised Louis VII of France as
his overlord in 1168, sending messengers promising aid against Henry and
even offering hostages. The message to Henry was clear. Unless a closer and
less demeaning relationship was established, Gwynedd's compliance could not
be taken for granted. The point was emphasised by the failure of the Archbishop of Canterbury, Thomas Becket, to influence the election of the bishop

of Bangor between 1165 and 1167, and also by the futility of Becket's threats of censure against Owain for what was, in the eyes of Rome, a consanguineous marriage with his first cousin. Becket's authority was diluted by his deteriorating relations with the king, and neither excommunication nor an archiepiscopal ban could prevent Owain from being buried in Bangor cathedral.

After Owain's death in 1170, his son, Dafydd, also sought closer links with Henry. The vulnerability of Dafydd's power-base in the Perfeddwlad, coupled with the territorial fragmentation caused by his brother Rhodri's control over Snowdonia and Môn, made friendly relations with the king desirable, and Gerald of Wales reports that Dafydd was unwilling to become involved in Anglo-Welsh conflicts. His support of the beleaguered king in 1173 also suggests that his position in Tegeingl in 1157 was dependent on promises to Henry. Dafydd won himself prestige in the Angevin polity by pressurising Henry to allow him to marry Emma, the king's half-sister, in 1175, and he was the only Welsh prince not to visit Gloucester for admonishment by Henry in the same year. Nevertheless, Dafydd was made to feel the weight of Henry's authority in 1177, when he became the first king of Gwynedd known to have sworn fealty outside Wales during a visit to the royal court at Geddington and Oxford, where he was given Ellesmere in Shropshire as a dowry.

HENRY II AND DEHEUBARTH

Henry's policy of intimidation also led to an expedition into Deheubarth in 1158, as a result of which Rhys ap Gruffudd submitted, giving hostages in return for recognition in Cantref Mawr and elsewhere. Hostages were given again when the king took an expedition to Pencader in 1163. On this occasion, Rhys did not resist, and his position was apparently recognised in return. Rhys is then said to have performed *homagium* at Woodstock later in the year. This is the first reliably attested homage by a Welsh prince, and it meant that Rhys was no longer a mere subordinate. In becoming Henry's 'man', Rhys now recognised the king as his feudal superior and he was bound to serve him against all men. This homage was almost certainly performed under duress – Rhys's surrender was achieved by deception, and he travelled to England as a prisoner – but it appears nonetheless to have represented a formal recognition in Cantref Mawr rather than a humiliation. The *Brut*'s mention of a royal promise is in keeping with Rhys's immediate and unopposed seizure of Dinefwr and Cantref Mawr upon returning home, and moreover, Rhys responded to Henry's failure to honour the promise by re-conquering Ceredigion in 1164. He went on to recover the whole of Deheubarth, and he may also have been among the Welsh kings (*reges*) who offered hostages and aid to Louis VII. Henry's initial ease in browbeating Rhys was due for the most part to the temporary weakness of Deheubarth, and

it was not to be repeated as Rhys strengthened his hold upon the kingdom.
The king's overlordship was not in doubt, and he was more than willing to
assert his right to apportion lands in Wales, but in practice his ability to do so
depended entirely upon the strength of the native Welsh. As impressive as it was,
the homage of 1163 belied an innate weakness in Anglo-Norman authority in
west Wales, and it was never invoked again.

When Rhys 'made friends with the king' in 1171 and was made a royal justice (*iustus*) in 1172,[2] it was from a position of strength, and the terms were
extremely favourable. Although Rhys promised fourteen hostages, 4,000 oxen
and 300 horses, only thirty-six horses were taken, and, rather than receiving
hostages, Henry returned Hywel ap Rhys (who must have been taken hostage
in 1158 or 1163) to his father. The rest of the tribute was deferred until the king's
return from Ireland. Rhys was now a royal official, but there is no mention of
oaths, and, although he is said to have received Ystrad Tywi, Ceredigion and the
cymydau of Ystlwyf and Efelffre in Cantref Gwarthaf from the king, it is clear
that his authority as ruler of Deheubarth no longer depended on royal grants
– if it ever had. Nor was his position as justice dependent upon such grants,
and it was comparable in this respect with that of Hugh de Lacy, whose authority as *justiciarius* in Ireland in 1172 was entirely separate from his position as
lord of Meath. Far from representing an intensified form of submission, Rhys's
new status – unprecedented in native Wales – was conferred because he could
offer Henry both stability and support against the power-base of the marcher
invaders of Ireland. In return, it gave him a measure of protection against the
marcher lords, and authorised him to exert his influence in areas beyond the
immediate confines of Deheubarth, thereby implicitly providing royal sanction for his predominance in the central march. Thus, it was as justiciar that he
met Archbishop Baldwin of Canterbury in Elfael and again in Ceredigion in
1188, mirroring the actions of the justiciar of England, Ranulf Glanville, who
escorted Baldwin through England. Henry acknowledged the dominance of
Deheubarth again in 1175, when Rhys brought all the recalcitrant princes of
south Wales to Gloucester, and the presence of William of Gloucester, William
de Braose and other marchers at this meeting suggests universal recognition of
the new *status quo*. Most significant for the long term, perhaps, was the fact that,
in making Rhys a royal justice, Henry was asserting that authority over native
rulers was somehow dependent upon royal approval, and that overlordship was
to be understood chiefly in terms of law and jurisdiction.

A hundred years after the destruction of Gruffudd ap Llywelyn, a new stability seemed to be emerging in Wales. Anglo-Norman advances had been substantial, but they had lost momentum, and a distinction came to be drawn in the
latter part of the twelfth century between three recognised spheres of influence.

Firstly, the march (*marchia Wallia*) was now regarded as an entity in its own right, separate from areas under native Welsh rule (*pura Wallia*) – although geographically there was not one march, but several – and the second and third spheres appeared when most if not all of *pura Wallia* fell into the orbits of Gwynedd and Deheubarth respectively, as Rhys ap Gruffudd and Owain Gwynedd asserted themselves in the 1160s. It is possible – although unlikely – that the king recognised this as early as 1163, when Rhys and Owain are said to have come to him with many lesser princes in attendance, and recognition may have been given in 1177, when Rhys accompanied Dafydd ab Owain in attending the king at Oxford and these two alone performed liege homage (*homagium ligium*). It is significant, however, that Rhys and Dafydd, alone among the Welsh contingent, were given new lands at this meeting, and it is likely that the homage was performed only for these – not for Gwynedd and Deheubarth. The king was prepared to give preferential treatement to the most prominent Welsh rulers, but he was not yet ready to give formal acknowledgement of any polarisation of power in Wales – as ever, he preferred to divide and rule.

The council of 1177 was an unparallelled royal propaganda victory. In summoning all of the Welsh, Henry demonstrated his indisputable superiority, and the omission of the occasion from Welsh sources is a sure indication of royal success. Henry wanted stability, but he did not want a unified Wales, and his grants to Rhys and Dafydd were both mischievous. Discord was fomented between Dafydd and his brother Rhodri, and the king also set out to generate friction between Gwynedd and Deheubarth by giving Meirionnydd to Rhys; within a year, Rhys and the sons of Owain Gwynedd were fighting over it. Henry had achieved his aim, retaining Rhys's goodwill and upholding the stability of the south while maintaining royal dominance by means of a policy of divide and rule. Rhys, like Dafydd, was classified as a mere 'ruler' (*regulus*), and the minor princes continued to owe allegiance to the king. Despite Rhys's obvious influence, his satellites were described merely as his relatives (*nepotes*) – which they were – rather than in wider terms of political authority. Furthermore, Rhys's position as a royal justice in the south was not parallelled in the north, where the political situation was entirely different. There was no formal constitutional recognition of a new *status quo*, and Gwynedd and Deheubarth did not stand in the same relationship to the king. Yet they were coming to be recognised as permanent fixtures, and moreover, they were coming to be seen as the constituent parts of a single native polity. In the eyes of at least one English chronicler, Dafydd and Rhys were now regarded as 'king of North Wales' (*rex Nortwalliae*) and 'king of South Wales' (*rex Swtwalliae*) respectively.[3]

Henry and Rhys maintained amicable relations from 1171 until the king's death in 1189. It was with the express purpose of preserving the accord that Rhys sent his son, Hywel, to serve Henry in Normandy in 1173, and he also sent troops in 1174. The prince even apologised to Henry for failing to control his sons, but there was always tension. Rhys was well aware of his ability to manipulate the Anglo-Normans after the invasion of Ireland, and, after refusing Diarmaid mac Murchada's request in 1167 to release Robert fitz Stephen, who was eager to go to Ireland, he freed Robert the following year on condition that he supported him against the king. He also captured several Norman castles between 1182 and 1184, and it was only the threat of a royal expedition which forced him to return them, to promise to help defeat his allies, to deliver hostages and to renew his fealty at Worcester. Even then, although he was willing to negotiate with Henry at Gloucester, Rhys had no intention of fulfilling his promises, and Ranulf Glanville was sent to quell another outbreak in both north and south Wales in 1186. In turn, the king sought to undermine Rhys's position in 1188 by enticing his son, Maelgwn, with annual payments of £20, although only £10 was ever paid. The first priority of each ruler was the welfare of his patrimony, and Rhys's position as a royal official was always secondary to his role as a native prince – for all his prestige, he never received any payment from the Exchequer.

All of the Anglo-Welsh agreements of this period were personal and verbal, and the settlement of 1171 consequently meant nothing after Henry's death. At Oxford in 1189, Rhys found that, unlike Henry, Richard I did not want to see him – he may have suspected Rhys of secret collusion with his brother, John, with whom he is known to have had a private peace agreement. Rhys returned home indignantly, and Richard himself was absent from England for most of his reign, leaving representatives – notably Hubert Walter, the justiciar and Archbishop of Canterbury – in his place. Although the king employed Gerald of Wales in attempts to make peace with the Welsh very early in the reign, and John met the Welsh for the same purpose in 1193, Rhys was never close to the new regime. Nevertheless, Anglo-Welsh relations had entered a new era. Even in relating Rhys's rebuke by the new king, the English chronicler Roger of Howden calls him 'ruler of South Wales' (*regulus de Suthwales*).[4]

Polarisation within Native Wales

GWYNEDD

Having eventually overcome the opposition of his brother Cadwaladr within Gwynedd in the 1140s, Owain Gwynedd established himself securely in the kingdom. He also cultivated good relations with his neighbours by marrying in turn the daughters of Llywarch ap Trahaearn and Goronwy ab Owain, and after 1144 he was able to address himself to the Perfeddwlad. He seems to have raided Cheshire in 1146, when the Welsh were defeated at Nantwich, and he constructed a castle at Tomen-y-Rhodwydd in Iâl in 1149. Control of the region was consolidated by the defeat of Ranulf Gernons of Chester and Madog ap Maredudd at Coleshill in Tegeingl in 1150. Owain now held the whole of the Perfeddwlad and Iâl, and his position was strengthened by the accession of a minor at Chester after the death of Ranulf in 1153 – the Norman bishop Geoffrey of St Asaph (better known as Geoffrey of Monmouth), who was appointed in 1152, was never able to visit the diocese. By 1165, and probably as early as 1157, the region passed to Dafydd ab Owain. Owain's castle in Iâl was destroyed by Iorwerth Goch ap Maredudd ap Bleddyn in 1157, but this seems to have been only a minor reverse, since Owain destroyed the abbey of Basingwerk in 1166 and Dafydd held Dyffryn Clwyd by 1165; Dafydd also had a castle at Rhuddlan by 1188. Control of the Perfeddwlad was subsequently uncontested.

Owain's authority in central Wales grew, but it was still fitful and fragile, and it varied from one place to another. He and his sons seized Cadwaladr ap Gruffudd's castle at Cynfael in Meirionnydd in 1147, and Owain is said to have defeated an English army in Arwystli after a victory over the English in Môn, presumably in 1157. It is no coincidence that Hywel ap Ieuaf of Arwystli was in the pay of the king in that year. Hywel himself was defeated in 1162, possibly by Owain, but he remained in power, although he may have been subjected to Owain's overlordship at that time – the exact nature of the relationship is difficult to determine. Similarly, although Owain invaded Edeirnion after the death of Madog ap Maredudd in 1160, and was prominent in the capture of the royal castle of Carreg Hwfa in 1163, it was Maredudd ap Hywel who emerged as lord of the *cwmwd*. It later fell to Owain Brogyntyn of Powys. In the central march, Gwynedd benefited from the death of Madog ap Maredudd in 1160 and the defeat of the Mortimer rebellion in 1155, and Cadwallon ap Madog of Maelienydd saw Owain as the natural recipient of his political prisoners as early as 1160. It is also possible that the Owain ap Gruffudd who conquered Cyfeiliog in Powys in 1162 was Owain Gwynedd, but it is more likely to have been Owain Cyfeiliog, since the *Brut*'s reference to him repairing Tafolwern a second time implies that he had held the area before. Gwynedd's authority beyond its borders seems to have expanded and contracted piecemeal during this period, indicating a growing influence in northern and central Wales which could sometimes but not always be enforced by subjection. The picture is fragmentary, but what is certain is that Powys and the central march had little choice but to back Owain Gwynedd in 1165.

The increasing importance of Gwynedd was due both to its internal stability and to its role in the recovery of much of Deheubarth from the Normans. The sons of Gruffudd ap Cynan had widened their field of action to the south as early as the 1130s, but they remained cautious – their promise of support to

Bishop Bernard of St Davids in 1140, for example, was prompted by opposition to Bishop Meurig at Bangor, rather than any aims in the south. But they did acquire lands in Deheubarth. Cadwaladr ap Gruffudd held part of Ceredigion by 1143, which he gave to his son, Cadfan, in 1149, and Hywel ab Owain Gwynedd held all of Ceredigion in 1151 – he was heavily involved in Ceredigion Is Aeron from at least 1143. Conquest was not sought for its own sake, however. Owain and Cadwaladr returned home immediately each time after successful forays in 1136, 1137 and 1138, and Hywel acted similarly after successes in 1145 – with his brother, Cynan – 1146 and 1147. Intriguingly, also, the *Brut* describes Hywel and Cynan's attack on Cardigan in 1145 as a victory, even though they did not take the town. Attitudes towards Deheubarth were clearly complex.

Gwynedd's presence in Deheubarth coincided with the rise of the sons of Gruffudd ap Rhys. Gruffudd, who married a daughter of Gruffudd ap Cynan, had sought help in Gwynedd in 1136, and most of the activities of Owain's sons were to the benefit of the native dynasty, with whom they usually worked and co-existed until 1151. Hywel and Cynan acted without local support in Deheubarth only once, in 1145 – before the appearance of Cadell ap Gruffudd in 1146 – and subsequent operations seem to have been planned and led by the dynasty of Deheubarth. All of Hywel's support for the sons of Gruffudd was against targets outside Ceredigion, and all of his hostile actions against them were defensive. He helped Cadell to capture Carmarthen (in Ystrad Tywi) in 1146, and joined Cadell, Maredudd and Rhys when they took Wiston (in Dyfed) in 1147, yet he lost Ceredigion Is Aeron to the brothers in 1150, while Uwch Aeron fell in 1151, and his final foothold, in the *cwmwd* of Penweddig, was lost in 1153. It seems strange that Hywel apparently supported a dynasty which dispossessed him as soon as it could, and he must have realised that the sons of Gruffudd were better placed to profit from his actions than he was himself. It may be that he was overconfident in his own ability, but this alone does not explain his support for the native dynasty. The underlying influences behind Hywel's actions seem to have lain in Gwynedd.

Owain Gwynedd wanted a stable border with Deheubarth, where the disruption after 1136 made direct intervention essential. Furthermore, mere stability was not enough. Owain knew that, once the civil war in England was over, well-established marcher families would pour resources into south Wales on a scale which the Welsh could not match. If Gwynedd was not to become surrounded by Anglo-Norman territory, the Normans in Deheubarth – and in particular the Clares in the bordering *cantrefi* of Ceredigion – must be overthrown. Thus, his victories in Ceredigion, his possession of Uwch Aeron, his destruction of a castle in Mabwynion in Is Aeron, his attack on the Flemings, his ravages as far south as the Llwchwr, Carmarthen and Pembroke, his taking of taxes from Pembroke and his alleged slaughter of 7,700 Englishmen were all at the expense of the Normans. He is said to have been supreme in the south, although the *Brut* mentions only his capture of the castle of Gwyddgrug in 1146. By implication, the overthrow of Norman power meant either conquest by Gwynedd or the restoration of the dynasty of Deheubarth. The rise of the local dynasty – and simple logistics – made direct lordship unfeasible, and Owain accordingly held no lands in Deheubarth himself. Clearly, he did not harbour serious ambitions to emulate Hywel Dda and Gruffudd ap Llywelyn by taking the kingships of both Deheubarth and Gwynedd. Instead, he forged close links with the native dynasty, and arranged for his daughter to marry Anarawd ap Gruffudd by 1143. Anarawd's death in that year and the absence of an immediate native successor forced Owain to look elsewhere for a man to rule Ceredigion. Cadwaladr was already there, but his rift with Owain made him unsuitable – he was ejected in 1144 – so Owain selected Hywel ab Owain, and appears to have directed him to continue to support the sons of Gruffudd. Such an attitude would explain his apparent indifference to Hywel's expulsion in 1151. Hywel, for his part, seems to have reacted by fighting against Owain in 1157, and he is probably to be identified as the Hywel ab Owain who appears in receipt of hefty royal payments and gifts in 1157 and 1160.

These attempts to counter burgeoning English power were matched by Owain's increasingly tight control within Gwynedd itself. For instance, the prac-tice of appanage, whereby family members were apportioned territories on the fringes of the kingdom, eased internal threats by distributing troublesome fac-tions centrifugally, and this in turn created buffer zones against outside forces. Thus, Dafydd was given the troubled Perfeddwlad, while Hywel and Cynan were placed in Ceredigion and Meirionnydd after the dispossession of Cadwaladr, and Maelgwn ab Owain may have been accommodated in Ireland. The prevention of dynastic contention between 1150 and 1170 was a considerable achievement. Owain may have been among the first Welsh rulers to select a single heir, and he smoothed over potential dynastic problems by imprisoning his son, Cynan, in 1150 and mutilating his nephew, Cunedda ap Cadwallon, in 1152. Furthermore, there seems to have been an upheaval in administration at this time, and Owain was probably involved in the evolution of a close-knit network of interrelated townships in Gwynedd on the Anglo-Norman model. He also upheld his tra-ditional right to receive clerical oaths, despite the opposition of Canterbury, and he may have adopted some feudal practices, while the flowering of scholarship in mid-twelfth century Gwynedd illustrates the abundance of educated and talent-ed men at the prince's disposal. The adoption of the style 'king of Wales' suggests that Owain perhaps envisaged not just a greater Gwynedd but the eventual cre-ation of a kingdom of Wales. The need for such an institution had been apparent for a century, and Owain gained acceptance as a national leader and established the first known relations between a Welsh ruler and a continental power. That he shared the vision of the thirteenth-century princes is suggested by his use of the style 'prince of Wales' (*princeps Walliae*) by 1166.[5]

Such ambitions were jeopardised by dynastic crisis after Owain's death in 1170, triggered by the killing in the same year of Hywel ab Owain – who seems to have been designated as heir – by Dafydd ab Owain. The immediate candidate appears to have been Gruffudd ap Hywel, but he is not known to have acted, and Owain's eldest surviving son, Iorwerth Drwyndwn, was excluded by a physical deformity. The next in line, Maelgwn ab Owain, was ineffectual and lost Môn in 1173 and the kingship in 1174 to his younger brother, Dafydd, who imprisoned him. Dafydd had direct rule only in the Perfeddwlad, since his younger brother, Rhodri, held Gwynedd west of the Conwy – known as Gwynedd Uwch Conwy – as late as 1188, but he was nevertheless king of the whole of Gwynedd after 1174. Territorially, however, Gwynedd was shared out between his relatives: Iorwerth held Arfon, lands in Ardudwy, and Nant Conwy, while Cynan already held Meirionnydd, Llŷn, Ardudwy and Eifionydd, which he passed to his sons. Considerable problems were posed by Rhodri, who took Llŷn by force, and, notwithstanding a brief imprisonment by Dafydd in 1175, expelled Dafydd from Gwynedd Uwch Conwy later the same year. He also encroached upon the lands of Iorwerth and took a daughter of Rhys ap Gruffudd as a concubine or wife in an attempt to gain support, apparently against the sons of Cynan. With Dafydd's help, Gruffudd and Maredudd ap Cynan expelled Rhodri from Môn temporarily in 1188x1193. Undeterred, he returned with Hiberno-Norse support in 1193 – when he was again defeated – and arranged to marry a Manx princess by 1195.

These struggles – especially Rhodri's intransigence – affected the wider influence of Gwynedd. The court poets record that Dafydd was involved in Hugh of Chester's conquest of Maelor in 1177, and fought several battles in Edeirnion, while Llywelyn ap Iorwerth may have made incursions in the march, and Gruffudd ap Hywel ab Owain is said to have fought in Powys – he was possibly among the princes who joined a royal attack against Powys in 1196. But the propaganda did not tell the whole story, and it seems that many bordering regions, such as Edeirnion, Penllyn and Iâl, became detached from the orbit of Gwynedd as the kingdom underwent internal upheavals in the late twelfth century.

POWYS

The deaths in 1160 of both Madog ap Maredudd and his eldest son and heir, Llywelyn, led to the fragmentation of Powys. A territorial division was made between Iorwerth Goch, Owain Cyfeiliog, Gruffudd Maelor, Owain Fychan,

Owain Brogyntyn and Elise ap Madog – respectively, Madog's brother, nephew and sons. Gruffudd Maelor established himself in the northern half of Powys, and Owain Fychan and Owain Cyfeiliog shared the southern portion, apparently working in tandem. Together, they drove the English out of Carreg Hwfa in 1163, and in 1166 they ejected Iorwerth Goch from Mochnant, which they divided between them. Thus, Owain Fychan obtained Mochnant Is Rhaeadr, Caereinion, Mechain and Cynllaith, and Owain Cyfeiliog was restricted to Cyfeiliog and Mochnant Uwch Rhaeadr.

The failure of any of the dynasty to assert overall control was inevitably damaging. Gwenwynwyn and Cadwallon, the sons of Owain Cyfeiliog, killed Owain Fychan in 1187, but they were unable to control his lands west of Oswestry, which were seized by Gruffudd Maelor by 1188, and such disunity allowed the satellites of Powys to become detached from its influence. Gruffudd ap Hywel ab Owain established himself in Penllyn, and, although the threat posed by Hywel ap Ieuaf of Arwystli was apparently sufficient to induce Madog ap Maredudd to build a castle at Cymer in Caereinion in 1156, it was the disruption after 1160 which enabled Hywel to take Tafolwern in Cyfeiliog in 1162. Although Hywel was repelled by Owain Cyfeiliog, who reaffirmed the subordination of Arwystli, the divisions within Powys were a great weakness, and the kingdom was divided irredeemably into two. Gwenwynwyn ab Owain Cyfeiliog made the southern half of Powys into the kingdom of Powys Wenwynwyn in 1195, and Madog ap Gruffudd Maelor similarly became ruler of the northern portion, Powys Fadog, in 1197. Division of kingship was a rare phenomenon in medieval Wales, and it demonstrated that the plight of Powys was serious.

Powys also suffered from its location between England and Gwynedd. Despite the position accorded to it by the laws, it was no longer the equal of the major native powers. Owain Cyfeiliog, Gruffudd Maelor ap Madog and Madog ap Iorwerth Goch all appeared in the train of Gwynedd and Deheubarth in 1177, and Powys came to depend on external support, walking a political tightrope between Gwynedd and the king. After supporting Gwynedd and raiding into England in 1165, for example, Iorwerth Goch, Owain Cyfeiliog and Owain Brogyntyn were remarkably quick to make favourable terms with the king.

The crushing of Gwenwynwyn ab Owain in 1198 demonstrated that attempts to recapture the former glories of Powys were futile. Gwenwynwyn seems to have accepted the partition as irreversible, and turned all his attentions against the English border around Welshpool, where he became such a menace that Hubert Walter, the justiciar, intervened in 1196. In an attempt to arrest the declining fortunes of Powys, Gwenwynwyn moved into Arwystli when Owain o'r Brithdir died in 1197, and he supported Maelgwn ap Rhys in his capture of both Aberystwyth and Gruffudd ap Rhys in 1197. This worked to the extent that the royal administration was obliged to restore Carreg Hwfa to Gwenw-ynwyn; it was traded for the captive Gruffudd ap Rhys. But Gwenwynwyn knew that his position was precarious, and he felt obliged to court favour by transferring Gruffudd into the king's hand immediately. His rise was viewed in England with concern, and his seizure of Maelienydd in 1198 – after the death of Maelgwn ap Cadwallon in 1197 – followed by his attack on William de Braose's castle at Painscastle in Elfael prompted swift action in defence of the border. As a result, Gwenwynwyn was routed by an English army led by the justiciar, now Geoffrey fitz Peter. There was no longer any doubt that the future of Powys would depend on alliances with greater powers.

DEHEUBARTH

The presence of the Anglo-Normans in the march created an increasingly cosmopolitan environment in the region, making the development of Anglo-Welsh links a matter of social and military necessity. This was true through-out the march and the adjacent territories – Madog ap Maredudd of Powys, for instance, is said to have had four languages – and the south-west was no exception. In Deheubarth, Rhys ap Gruffudd (also known as the Lord Rhys) proved to be both flexible and eclectic, and he was especially adept at dynas-tic politics. His son, Gruffudd, married Matilda de Braose by 1189, and his daughter, Angharad, married William fitz Martin of Cemais, apparently after 1191. Moreover, his dealings with the king involved Rhys in a vast aristocratic society, and cosmopolitanism was encouraged by Welsh contacts with the royal court as emissaries and hostages. Gerald of Wales recounts that Rhys was perfectly at home in the Anglo-Norman world, making polite conversation in French and joking with members of the Clare family at Hereford in 1186. The preaching of the third crusade through Wales by Archbishop Baldwin of Canterbury in 1188 also broadened Welsh horizons, as well as tightening English ecclesiastical domination – Baldwin was the first archbishop to visit St Davids. Furthermore, many Welshmen received their education in England and France. Among the results of this influx of ideas was a close resemblance between Welsh and English legal texts and practices, and also Rhys's adoption of the Anglo-Norman notion that illegitimate sons could be excluded. Rhys was particularly receptive to foreign influences. His Christmas court at Cardigan in 1176 was inspired at least partly by the French *puys* – and in particular by the court of Eleanor of Aquitaine – and his jester, John Spang, seems to have been of English origin. Furthermore, Anglo-Norman monks brought many clerical versions of French *chansons de geste* into Wales, and Geoffrey of Monmouth's *Historia regum Britanniae* is an outstanding example of cross-fertilisation between Welsh, English and continental literature. The close link between this trend and the tightening of political bonds is shown by the unprecedented interest in France displayed by Welsh chroniclers between 1171 and 1182 – the very period of Rhys's friendliest relations with the king.

Rhys found himself the sole native ruler of Deheubarth when his brother and predecessor, Maredudd, died in 1155. The death in 1163 of his nephew, Einion ab Anarawd, removed his last potential domestic rival, and he ousted the Normans from most of Deheubarth by 1158. Although Roger fitz Richard de Clare reinforced Ystrad Meurig and seized Humphrey's Castle, Aberdyfi, Dineirth and Llanrhystud – all in Ceredigion – and Walter Clifford made incursions into Cantref Mawr, Rhys responded by capturing Llandovery and all the castles of Ceredigion. The destruction of the castles of Dyfed and an attack on Carmarthen in 1159 forced the Anglo-Normans to sue for peace, and, despite losing Ceredigion and even Cantref Mawr in 1163, Rhys took Dinefwr back within months and recovered Ceredigion from Roger in 1164. His position was confirmed by the capture of Cardigan and Cilgerran in 1165 and the defence of the latter against a force from Pembroke in 1166, and there were no more marcher attacks until after the death of Henry II. The failure of the Anglo-Normans to react was due partly to their invasion of Ireland, and also to the deaths without surviving male issue of Richard fitz Gilbert of Pembroke in 1176 and of William fitz Robert of Gloucester in 1183 – the lordships of Netherwent, Pembroke, Glamorgan and Wentloog were retained in royal custody, and the lordship of Brecon became separated from the earldom of Hereford in 1165. Most important was Rhys's accord with the king, which both reflected and magnified his considerable strength.

The dominance of Deheubarth was accepted by the rulers of Powys, who followed Rhys to Oxford in 1177, but direct intervention in Powys from Deheubarth was minimal. Rhys's possession of Tafolwern in Cyfeiliog in 1167, together with the defeat and submission in 1171 of the persistently troublesome Owain Cyfeiliog, suggests that he controlled the *cwmwd* for some time, but this is unlikely to have been more than overlordship; Owain may have recovered Cyfeiliog when he retook Caereinion in 1167, and Gwenwynwyn certainly held Tafolwern in 1185. Rhys's main interest was further south, where, by 1175, the list of his satellites was impressive. Einion Clud of Elfael and Einion ap Rhys of Gwerthrynion each married his daughters, while Cadwallon ap Madog of Maelienydd was his first cousin, and his nephews (by his sisters, Gwladus and Nest respectively) included Morgan ap Caradog of Afan, Seisyll ap Dyfnwal of Gwent Uwch Coed and Gruffudd ab Ifor of Senghennydd. Another of Rhys's sisters married Caradog ap Iestyn of Afan, and one of his nieces was married to Trahaearn Fychan of Brycheiniog by 1197. Not all of these links were designed by Rhys, or even by his family, since many dynasties were already closely linked by marriage. Indeed, the small size of the ruling class and the obligation of its members to marry within it made intermarrying inevitable, and the fact that Rhys had eight daughters made the creation of a wide dynastic network almost unavoidable. The relationship with Cadwallon apparently derived from the marriage of Madog ab Idnerth with a daughter of Gruffudd ap Cynan, another of whose daughters, Gwenllian, married Gruf-fudd ap Rhys and became Rhys's mother. Similarly, the fact that Morgan and Gruffudd were Rhys's nephews was mainly a result of marriages between their fathers and daughters of Gruffudd ap Rhys. Nevertheless, such ties did much to bolster Rhys's position as leader of the Welsh in the south.

Rhys's superiority was based as much on interdependence as domination. This was most apparent in his relationship with the dynasty of Rhwng Gwy a Hafren – an area which was increasingly known as the middle march – where Cadwallon ap Madog and his son Maelgwn eventually accepted Rhys's authority without ever becoming puppets of Deheubarth. Cadwallon had authority in Ceri by 1176, when he helped Gerald of Wales to seize the church of Llanfihangel, and he took Elfael after capturing his brother, Einion Clud, in 1160. Einion escaped and appeared at Corwen in 1165 as ruler of the *cantref*, but his subordination to Cadwallon was made clear in the re-foundation charter of the Cistercian house of Cwm Hir in Maelienydd in 1176, and Cad-wallon assumed control of Elfael on Einion's death in 1177. After Cadwallon's death, Maelgwn seems to have lost Elfael by 1188, when Einion o'r Porth ruled there, but he established a hold on Gwerthrynion by 1194 with the help of his brother Hywel. These successes enabled the native rulers of the middle march to resist intervention from Deheubarth. Rhys did not intervene when Einion Clud was captured in 1160, nor when he died in 1177, nor when his son, Einion o'r Porth, was killed by his brother in 1191. Although he does seem to have moved into Gwerthrynion in 1177, when he built a castle at Rhaeadr Gwy – probably after the death of Einion ap Rhys – Rhys lost the area to the sons of Cadwallon in 1194. The only clear sign of Rhys's author-ity in the region is the presence of Cadwallon, Einion Clud and Einion ap Rhys in his train in 1175, and that of Cadwallon alone in 1177. Yet there was a firm relationship between Deheubarth and the middle march, and their simultaneous collapse in the 1190s was not coincidental. Rhys needed the region as a buffer zone against England, and the native dynasty there looked to him for support against the Anglo-Normans. Weakness in either would be detrimental to the other. Thus, the decline of Deheubarth enabled Roger Mortimer to conquer Maelienydd in 1195 and William de Braose to acquire Elfael between 1191 and 1196. Rhys's attitude of non-intervention was rapidly discarded thereafter, and he rebuilt his castle in Gwerthrynion and attacked

Elfael. In short, it seems that Cadwallon accepted Rhys as a nominal overlord in the interests of mutual security.

It was this *status quo* in the middle march which was endorsed by the king in the 1170s. Rhys's influence was recognised when he was appointed justiciar of the whole of autonomous south Wales, and he met Archbishop Baldwin in this capacity at Radnor in 1188. Nevertheless, Cadwallon was still ranked alongside the rulers of Gwynedd and Deheubarth as a *rex* or *regulus* in 1177. The king's harsh treatment of his killers – followers of Roger Mortimer – in 1179 reinforces the impression that Cadwallon occupied an important position, although Henry was probably mainly concerned that the killing was done in England while Cadwallon was under a royal safe conduct. Even so, Henry's anger is intriguing in view of the general hostility between the Welsh and the march, characterised by numerous minor raids. It seems that the middle march was a region over which neither Rhys nor the king could assert real control. Similarly, Rhys rarely intervened in Brycheiniog, Gwent and Morgannwg, and his office of *iustus* did not encompass the march. Nevertheless, he exercised an important role there as a focus of disaffection against the Anglo-Normans. He led the native rulers of these areas in 1175, and he was also held responsible for the behaviour of the Welsh of Morgannwg on other occasions. He and his sons were keen to take advantage of unrest there between 1182 and 1184, but Rhys could not hope to dominate the march, and his relations with native rulers there were negligible.

Rhys recognised Owain Gwynedd as his superior in 1165, and spent three weeks with him besieging Rhuddlan in 1167. But most of the time he was no subordinate, and his co-operation seems to have been motivated by self-interest. Neither Rhys nor Owain could defeat the other, and they seem to have accepted each other's sphere of influence on an understanding of mutual non-intervention. This was first seen in Ceredigion in the 1140s and 1150s, and also possibly in Owain's inaction when Rhys attacked Cyfeiliog in 1153, and the Dyfi was established as a definite border when Rhys confronted Owain there in 1156. Admittedly, Hywel and Cynan ab Owain were present in the predominantly English force which sought to subdue Rhys in 1159, but the situation was still relatively fluid at that time, and in any case there was no further aggression. For his part, Rhys's bid for Meirionnydd in 1177 and 1178 was his only hostile act against Gwynedd, and came only when Gwynedd was divided after Owain's death. It is in this context that his presence at Rhuddlan and his refusal to support Rhodri ab Owain against his brother Dafydd should be seen. In general, Rhys seems to have accepted the influence of Gwynedd and appreciated the value of its stability.

Moreover, it seems that the unanimity displayed in the attack against Owain Cyfeiliog in 1167 marked an intention on the part of Deheubarth and Gwynedd to co-operate in eliminating the threat of Powys. Rhys and Owain are said to have entrusted Caereinion to Owain Fychan, while Tafolwern – and therefore probably the whole of Cyfeiliog – was given to Rhys. Arwystli, where Cadell ap Gruffudd had been influential in the 1150s, seems to have been left to the attentions of Gwynedd after 1162. The increasing polarisation of power was symbolised by the the the division of the spoils between the poets of Gwynedd and the musicians of Deheubarth at Rhys's court at Cardigan in 1176 – no-one from Powys won anything – and the conception emerged of Rhys and Owain as the rulers of 'south Wales' and 'north Wales'. This tendency towards polarisation was shared by lesser kingdoms, too, notably in the assumption by the dynasties of Maelienydd and Afan of authority over the middle march and the Welsh of Morgannwg respectively. Given the development of such power blocks and an increased sense of national identity, it was a natural step to aspire to leadership of the Welsh. Thus, Owain led the unique pan-Welsh confederation of 1165, and both he and Rhys styled themselves prince of Wales.

Despite the lack of formal constitutional recognition, therefore, the idea of a north-south division in Wales was accepted in practice by all parties after the 1170s. Dafydd ab Owain styled himself king of North Wales (*rex Norwallie*) in 1177x1190 and prince of North Wales (*princeps Norwallie*) in 1186x1194, and he was still called *rex de Nordwales* by royal officials in 1194. At the same time, it was usual for Rhys to be known as prince of South Wales (*princeps South Wallie* or *Suthwallie princeps*). The king was always unwilling, however, to recognise any aspiration for a unitary Welsh polity – in confirming a charter in which Rhys styled himself *princeps Wallie* in 1184, Henry pointedly referred to him only as Rhys ap Gruffudd.

NATIVE RULERS IN BRYCHEINIOG, GWENT AND MORGANNWG

The dynasty of Brycheiniog had been reduced to client status by marcher power, but the Welsh retained considerable liberties and influence. A charter to Brecon priory in 1143x1155 reveals at least seven Welshmen in the earl of Hereford's *curia*, and native communities owed no more than military service and monthly attendance at the seigneurial court. Even in the thirteenth century, the Welsh of Brycheiniog did not hold their land of the lord, and they were allowed to assess and answer for their own subsidies, and also to collect their own farms. Trahaearn Fychan typified his dynasty's obstinacy by marrying a niece of Rhys ap Gruffudd – probably the daughter of Seisyll ap Dyfnwal – but William de Braose made clear his authority as Trahaearn's lord by seizing him at Llangors and ordering a humiliating public execution at Brecon in 1197.

Seisyll ap Dyfnwal reclaimed Gwent Uwch Coed in the 1170s and forged matrimonial links with both Gwynllŵg and Deheubarth. Although his son, Morgan, was involved in Gwent Is Coed in 1171, Seisyll's main ambition was to recover Abergavenny. In attempting to throw off Anglo-Norman overlord-ship, however, he could expect fierce opposition, and his killing of Henry, a brother of Roger of Hereford, in 1175 provoked a decisive response. The king summoned Seisyll to hear statutes at Abergavenny, thereby emphasising his subordination, and royal officers then attempted a final solution of the problem: when the unsuspecting Seisyll, his sons, and many of the *uchelwyr* of Gwent Uwch Coed arrived at Abergavenny Castle, they were summarily massacred. Although the Welsh took their revenge by capturing Abergavenny in 1182, their success was shortlived. Native resistance in Gwent Uwch Coed was effectively crushed, and this was undoubtedly the work of the king, into whose prison Seisyll had already been thrown in 1172. William de Braose does not emerge well from the episode, but Gerald of Wales states specifically that Henry and his men – not de Braose – were to blame for the massacre, and it was the justiciar, Ranulf Glanville, who put down the rising of 1182.

Iorwerth ab Owain faced similar opposition in his attempts to preserve control of Caerleon, Gwynllŵg and Gwent Is Coed, and his success in doing so was due almost entirely to his prowess in war. The death of his brother, Morgan, in 1158 brought the whole of Gwynllŵg and Caerleon under Ior-werth's rule until he was forcibly deprived of Caerleon by the king in 1171. His response was to devastate Caerleon and ravage the surrounding country with his sons, Owain and Hywel. Henry II could not afford to recognise his *de facto* power, however, since to do so would guarantee the opposition of William of Gloucester, whose lands, like Caerleon itself, stood on the vi-tal route to Ireland. The king therefore addressed the issue as soon as he returned to Wales in 1172, and Iorwerth, still engaged in hostilities, was sum-moned for talks. Before they could meet, however, Owain ap Iorwerth was killed by William of Gloucester's men. All hope of a peaceful settlement was abandoned, and Iorwerth and his other son, Hywel, ravaged Gloucester and Hereford. Iorwerth went on to recapture Caerleon in 1173, and Hywel seized the whole of Gwent Is Coed and took hostages from the local *uchelwyr*. The position of the dynasty was further enhanced when Hywel mutilated Owain Pencarn, Iorwerth's brother, in 1175. Henry was forced to accept native rule, and annual royal payments of 40s to the dynasty continued into the thirteenth century. Despite Hywel's loss of Usk in 1174 and the Anglo-Norman capture of Caerleon in 1175, Iorwerth had retained or recovered his authority, and Hywel held castles in Morgannwg for Henry during the disturbances of 1184 and 1198. However, the failure to take castles and the vulnerability to attack did not bode well for the future of the dynasty, and Hywel had little choice but to remain neutral in all Anglo-Welsh affairs except those that concerned him directly.

The dynasty of Senghennydd was forced by expediency into compliance with the Anglo-Normans. Gruffudd ab Ifor Bach succeeded his father by 1175, and he may have hoped to extend native rule in the *cantref* to its old boundaries, but he was compelled to accept the rapidly increasing authority of the earl of Gloucester, who appears to have appropriated parts of Senghennydd Is Caeach into his own demesne lands. Cadwallon and Maredudd ab Ifor were in royal service in 1187 and 1203, and, although Cadwallon held a castle in 1198, much of Senghennydd appears to have been drawn inexorably into Anglo-Norman hands.

The strongest resistance to the Anglo-Normans in the march was presented by Morgan ap Caradog ap Iestyn of Afan. Morgan inherited a firm power-base west of the Ogwr, but native influence in the lowlands was reduced significantly as many of the numerous Welsh population there sold out to English lords. This erosion of Morgan's authority was compounded by a general transfer of power from native kindreds to their lords, and furthermore, disputes between Welshmen in the coastal plain were now subject to the earl of Gloucester's seigneurial court. Morgan was therefore increasingly confined to the uplands, and his uneasy relationship with the Normans is illustrated by an undated incident in which, having given a hostage to Earl William, he rebelled, and William mutilated the hostage. Glamorgan was not easy for the Anglo-Normans to control, however. The Welsh burned a barn of Margam abbey in 1161, and also the abbey's vill of Kenfig in 1167, and Morgan seems to have been prominent in the rebellion of 1182 and 1183, when the Welsh attacked Neath, Kenfig and Ogmore. The revolt was carried on to Cardiff and even into Gwynllŵg, where Newport was attacked, and it was only put down by a substantial army led by Ranulf Glanville. Norman control in this region after the death of Iestyn ap Gwrgant was always tenuous, and the chronicler Benedict of Peterborough relates the outbreak not to the death of William of Gloucester in 1183 but to an attempt by an unnamed Englishman to build a new castle – no doubt Ogmore – in 1182. It was apparently around this time that Morgan acquired lands in and around Ogmore, probably including the castle of Ogmore itself, and the Welsh re-conquest was so decisive that late twelfth-century records make no mention of the Umfravilles, the previous Anglo-Norman lords. Thus, Morgan and his descendants seem to have retained these lands for some time.

The Destruction of the Status Quo

The death of Henry II in 1189 removed an important player from the Welsh political scene, and Rhys ap Gruffudd reacted quickly and effectively. No longer able to depend on cordial relations with the king, he attacked and gained control of Cantref Gwarthaf, Kidwelly, Gower and Rhos, capturing

Carnwyllion, St Clears, Laugharne and Llansteffan in 1189, and by 1192 he had built a castle at Kidwelly and taken Nevern, Llawhaden and probably Swansea. His sons, Hywel and Maelgwn, captured Wiston and Ystrad Meurig respectively in 1193. Similarly, in 1196, Rhys took Carmarthen, Colwyn, Radnor and Painscastle, attacked Herefordshire, and routed Roger Mortimer and Hugh de Sai. The destruction of the *status quo* had not diminished Rhys's power, and the Anglo-Norman menace had been almost nullified. William de Braose's attacks on St Clears in 1195 and Swansea in 1196 were the only acts of aggression against Rhys, and the Anglo-Normans were distracted by unrest in England, where Roger Mortimer was accused of siding with the Welsh.

Militarily, Deheubarth was secure enough. Dynastically, however, it was not, and the issue of the succession was to be its downfall. It appears that Rhys intended that his eldest legitimate son, Gruffudd, should succeed him at the expense of the older but illegitimate Maelgwn, who was allotted no lands and was apparently obliged to give hostages to Gruffudd. Maelgwn understandably resented this departure from traditional practice, and his rivalry with Gruffudd began as early as 1188, when each brother seems to have been eager to ensure that the other went on crusade. It became necessary for Rhys and Gruffudd to imprison Maelgwn in 1189, and Gruffudd then transferred him to William de Braose's prison. Maelgwn's escape in 1192 brought chaos: Rhys himself was imprisoned by his sons in 1194, and stability was replaced by shifting alliances, deals, exchanges of hostages, deceit and connivance. Rhys's death in 1197 finally removed any semblance of unity, and the unprecedented length of his obituary in the *Brut* illustrates the sense of desolation at his loss. Maelgwn and Gruffudd remained in conflict until the latter's death in 1201, and, despite the fact that the succession was disputed only between these two, continued dissension between them and their descendants eventually led to the dismemberment of Deheubarth.

Maelgwn's intransigence destroyed any hope of a smooth and peaceful succession. There was now nothing to prevent territorial disintegration, and his part in this earned him almost universal hostility. Native Welsh chroniclers had their own dynastic axes to grind when they blamed Maelgwn for the loss of Cardigan (1200), Llandovery and Dinefwr (1204), but their criticism was based soundly on the fact that it was Maelgwn who had broken the peace. His brothers only opposed Rhys and Gruffudd after he had already badly damaged Rhys's authority, and the capture of Dinefwr – the political heart of Deheubarth – in 1195 by Rhys Gryg and Maredudd is consistent with the view that the other brothers were concerned to restore order as much as to wreak havoc.

The failure of any individual to dominate Deheubarth inevitably weakened the kingdom, and both Gruffudd and Maelgwn became dependent on the king to an unprecedented degree. In his desperation to leave his kingdom intact, Rhys arranged in 1197 that Gruffudd should be 'made heir' (*factus haeres*) by the king.[6] Gruffudd therefore accepted that his status as heir was derived at least in part from the authority of Richard I, and it could now be assumed that the king was entitled not only to recognise Welsh princes, but to take part in the procedures by which they were selected. Maelgwn, too, seems to have been dependent, since, after capturing Gruffudd in 1197, he ensured that he was handed over into royal custody by 1198. He also relied on aid from Gwenwynwyn ab Owain, and it was apparently this association which turned the king against him. Gruffudd was accordingly released in 1198, and he took the whole of Ceredigion except Cardigan and Ystrad Meurig, but Deheubarth remained divided, and Anglo-Norman forces were able to occupy Dinefwr in 1197x1198. The king was ready to recognise Gruffudd as Rhys's heir at first, but he subsequently switched his support between Gruffudd and Maelgwn, either in an attempt to undermine native rule or in an effort to keep up with the continually changing situation in Deheubarth. Whatever the king's motives, it was the implacability of Maelgwn's resistance which was primarily responsible for the creation of new precedents of royal authority, and the wisdom of Rhys's decision to break with tradition in excluding him is therefore open to question.

The Emergence of Llywelyn ap Iorwerth in Gwynedd

As the eldest son of the eldest surviving son of Owain Gwynedd, Llywelyn ap Iorwerth might have considered himself the legitimate heir to Gwynedd, but his claims were not accepted without a fight. Later generations would know him as Llywelyn Fawr ('the Great'), and he displayed his military prowess from an early age. He was reportedly in arms by the age of ten, and Gerald of Wales reports that he was only 12 when he harassed his uncles Dafydd and Rhodri in 1188. In 1194, Llywelyn appeared at the head of an alliance which included Gruffudd and Maredudd ap Cynan and possibly Rhodri ab Owain, and after defeating Dafydd – probably at Aberconwy – he expelled him from the whole of Gwynedd except three castles, which presumably lay in Tegeingl or Dyffryn Clwyd. Dafydd was captured and exiled in 1197, and finally driven out in 1203 – he and his son, Owain, spent the rest of their lives in England – and Rhodri, who was probably the unidentified opponent defeated at Porthaethwy and Coedaneu in Môn, was removed from contention by 1195. Llywelyn seems to have taken Dafydd's lands for himself, while Gruffudd ap Cynan ab Owain held Meirionnydd, Môn, Arfon, Arllechwedd and Llŷn. Maredudd ap Cynan ruled Eifionydd, and Ardudwy and Nant Conwy probably remained in the hands of Iorwerth Drwyndwn.

Llywelyn's nearest rival for the kingship after 1197 was Gruffudd ap Cynan, and it seems that Gruffudd held rule in Gwynedd. It was Gruffudd, not Llywelyn, who promised – but did not perform – homage to the new king John in 1199, and Llywelyn performed neither homage nor fealty in a separate agreement with John in the same year. Furthermore, in applying to Cîteaux for permission to build Cistercian monastic houses in 1199, Gruffudd was styled *princeps Norwallie*. Llywelyn was not unsuccessful – he captured Mold from Ranulf of Chester in 1199 – but the forces he sent to help Gwenwynwyn were decimated in 1198, and there is no firm evidence that he ousted Gruffudd from Gwynedd Uwch Conwy. He won a victory in Arfon around this time, but this cannot be seen as decisive without the debatable assumption that his charter to the abbey of Aberconwy dates from 1198x1199 and not later. Thus, it seems that Llywelyn did not rule Gwynedd until at least early 1199, and probably not until after Gruffudd's death in 1200.

With Gruffudd dead, Gwynedd Uwch Conwy now lay open to Llywelyn, and by 1202 he had eliminated all opposition. He ejected Maredudd ap Cynan from Llŷn and Eifionydd on a charge of treachery in 1201, and Maredudd also lost Meirionnydd on a similar charge in 1202 – although he was ousted by his nephew, Hywel ap Gruffudd ap Cynan, the hand of Llywelyn is not hard to detect. For his part, Hywel could not resist the annexation of his father's lands in 1200, and he had little option but to adhere to Llywelyn. Maredudd vanished into obscurity, but his sons, Llywelyn Fawr and Llywelyn Fychan, secured a place in Meirionnydd under Llywelyn's lordship. Llywelyn's cousin Gruffudd ap Rhodri is said to have received lands in Eifionydd – probably at the expense of Maredudd – but neither he nor Owain ap Dafydd posed any threat. Llywelyn consolidated his position by gaining, or rather creating, powerful ecclesiastical allies, especially in the abbey of Aberconwy, and by 1200 he was in a position to be regarded by Pope Innocent III as the most prominent of the Welsh princes.

6

Llywelyn ap Iorwerth and his Legacy
c.1200–1257

Llywelyn ap Iorwerth's Rise to Supremacy

WELSH RELATIONS WITH JOHN

The administrative machinery of English government acquired an increasing precision at the end of twelfth century, and John used it to push at the boundaries of royal interference in Wales almost as soon as he became king. In 1199, he claimed to concede and confirm the lands, castles, tenements and rights of both Powys Wenwynwyn and Gwynedd, and he requested the homage of Gwenwynwyn ab Owain and Gruffudd ap Cynan, asserting that they should promise service in return for their lands. Llywelyn ap Iorwerth also promised homage to John 'as to his liege lord' in 1201,[1] conceding that he had no right to harbour fugitives from England. These contracts were similar in many ways to that made between Henry II and Rhys ap Gruffudd in 1163, but they were different in several important respects. The Welsh now acknowledged not only that the king was their feudal lord but also that they held their lands by feudal contract. They had become tenants-in-chief in the same manner as English barons, and they could expect to be treated accordingly – hence the agreement with Llywelyn required for the first time that the leading men of Gwynedd should do fealty to the king as well as to the prince. Furthermore, in offering Welsh litigants the option of English law – which would be judged by the royal court or by royal officials sent to Wales – John established a legal precedent for royal intervention throughout native Wales. Finally, the terms were to remain in force not just for the lifetimes of the signatories but also under their heirs, and they were committed to writing and preserved in the royal archives for future perusal by the king's lawyers. Royal overlordship was now being infused into the very political fabric of Wales.

These submissions were not entirely detrimental to the aspirations of Gwynedd, however. At its heart, John's claim of feudal seisin was little more than a repeat of his predecessors' assertions of overlordship, and Llywelyn gave only the traditional promise of support. Moreover, Llywelyn needed a more precise constitutional framework in which to work out his relationship with the king. Any permanent hegemony in Wales needed royal acquiescence, and submission was inevitable if native rule was to survive within the constraints of English overlordship. Furthermore, although homage increased Llywelyn's subservience, the precedent could be used to his advantage if he could extract the homages of other Welsh princes for himself. In time, the intensification of royal overlordship was to help in the theoretical development of a principality of Wales under Gwynedd.

Although the king had established a legal pretext for undermining Welsh independence, he does not seem to have been intent on pursuing it. He was quick to recognise first Gruffudd and then Llywelyn as prince of Gwynedd, and his promise in 1201 that he would not interfere in internal disputes there indicates that the legal clauses were primarily a bargaining counter. They would not be applied until the situation had altered radically. Nevertheless, John showed his wariness of Gwynedd in 1199 when he confirmed Gwenwynwyn in possession of lands which had been conquered from the king's enemies – presumably Gwynedd. A divided Wales was preferable in royal eyes to domination by Gwynedd, and Llywelyn's seizure of Powys in 1202 was therefore a cause of concern to John, especially in view of the weakness of Deheubarth. There was a mutual desire for a new accord. The king faced growing difficulties in France, and he could ill afford an open conflict with Gwynedd, while Llywelyn, who was now established on the English border, could expect resistance comparable to that faced by Gwenwynwyn. His success had brought him into direct confrontation with the king and the marchers, and royal recognition of his position would be necessary if it was to be maintained.

Llywelyn was therefore quick to do homage when the king returned to England from France in 1204, and John's illegitimate daughter Joan (who became known to the Welsh as Siwan) was promised to him in marriage, with the castle and manor of Ellesmere – which had been held by Dafydd ab Owain – as a dowry. More importantly, when they were married (probably in 1205), Joan brought an alliance with the king, the importance of which was such that Llywelyn abandoned plans to marry a Manx princess. John, although understandably cautious, seems to have been satisfied that Powys and Gwynedd were stable by 1208 after Llywelyn re-conquered Powys and acquired Ceredigion Uwch Aeron. Both sides were now ready to redefine their relationship. There were apparently negotiations in 1209, and the prince joined John's campaign in Scotland in the same year. Llywelyn had won the king's friendship, receiving a gift of falcons from him in 1210, but there was no recognition of his conquests as parts of an extended Gwynedd. Although he was probably required to do homage later in 1209, he was still no more than prince of Gwynedd.

Llywelyn's ambitions destroyed this *entente* in 1210. The circumstances are unclear – it is possible that he allied with William de Braose – but the justiciar, the bishop of Winchester and Ranulf of Chester moved into the Perfeddwlad and defeated Llywelyn in Creuddyn. Ranulf constructed castles at Degannwy and Holywell, and Llywelyn retaliated with attacks on the earldom of Chester in 1210 and 1211. The threat posed by Gwynedd was now a major priority for the king. John assembled an army at Chester in 1211, and the Welsh retreated to Snowdonia, taking their possessions with them, including all the livestock. By the time John's army reached the Conwy, it was unable to feed itself, and the soldiers were reduced to eating their horses. The king retreated, only to return at harvest time with a better prepared force which swept into Gwynedd Uwch Conwy, where Bangor was burned and the bishop, Robert, was captured and ransomed for 200 hawks. Llywelyn was humbled and alone. Moreover, in the scale and thoroughness of his preparations for war, John had laid the blueprint for future royal campaigns in Wales. The king now possessed both the legal justification and the military means to destroy Welsh independence.

The mutual exclusivity of John's and Llywelyn's aims was obvious: Wales was to be dominated either by Gwynedd or by the king. John was determined to stop the expansion of Gwynedd, and he imposed crippling terms. Gwynedd would escheat to the king should Llywelyn die without heirs by Joan, and in 1212 Owain ap Dafydd and Gruffudd ap Rhodri, Llywelyn's disinherited cousins, were granted Rhos, Rhufoniog and Dyffryn Clwyd, together with licence to take further lands from Llywelyn if they could. Although the latter arrangement proved ineffectual, Llywelyn was forced to grant the Perfeddwlad to the king in perpetuity, and John built castles there, many in places where there had been no previous fortification. He also demanded 30 hostages, as well as a promise of 20,000 cattle – 3,000 of which were given immediately – and 40 steeds, together with an annual render of falcons. Gwynedd was humiliated, and despite further talks in 1212, there was no prospect of a negotiated return to the *status quo*.

Llywelyn had little option but to take military action. Despite John's success, experience taught that the lack of a foothold west of the Conwy made English control of the Perfeddwlad insecure, and the garrisons – particularly the one at Aberconwy (Degannwy?) – did not help themselves by deliberately provoking the Welsh. Llywelyn easily recaptured most of the region in two months in 1212, completing his re-conquest by taking Degannwy and Rhuddlan in 1213. He enhanced his position further by obtaining papal absolution from his homage to John, and the interdict which Pope Innocent III had placed on John's kingdom in 1208 was lifted from Llywelyn's lands and those of his allies. Not content with this, Llywelyn put forward a claim to be taken seriously on the international stage by making an alliance with Philip II (Augustus) of France. John was in no position to respond. Hampered by the interdict and baronial discontent, he was reduced to impotent displays of anger, executing many Welsh hostages – he reportedly refused to eat or drink until the job was finished – and ravaging the coast of Gwynedd. A formal treaty was out of the question, however. The lifting of the interdict from England in 1214 left Llywelyn as no more than a rebel, and the king's difficulties at home meant that he was in no position to negotiate any meaningful agreement. Llywelyn obtained only the release of hostages in 1214 and a truce in 1213, which was extended throughout 1214 and 1215. Officially, he remained an enemy of the king.

Unable to come to terms with John, Llywelyn made a pact with the English barons in 1215. The king's defeat allowed peace to be established, and Llywelyn received his reward in the favourable clauses relating to Wales in Magna Carta. The remaining hostages were to be released, all lands of which the Welsh had been disseised illegally since 1199 were to be restored, and all Welsh charters which had been delivered for the security of the peace were to be returned. Disputes would be decided in the march by English, Welsh or marcher law, depending on the location of the lands in question. The Welsh were also bound to restore lands they had taken unjustly, but this did not detract from what was in effect a royal concession of the Perfeddwlad and other recent conquests. Nevertheless, this was no more than a prorogation of the truce. The disseised lands were recovered by force, so their status was never discussed; there was still no recognition that Llywelyn's conquests constituted anything more than mere territorial acquisitions.

Llywelyn was now supreme in Wales. He recovered his former territories by 1217, and swept all before him in the south. Royal lordship in Ystrad Tywi, Dyfed and Ceredigion capitulated in 1215, and a second campaign in 1217 encompassed Brycheiniog, Gower and Dyfed. Llywelyn also prevented the appointment of a royal candidate as bishop of St Davids in 1215 – Iorwerth of Talyllychau was elected instead – and the sympathetic Cadwgan of Whitland was installed at Bangor in the same year. Most importantly, the prince established himself as the leader of the Welsh as early as 1212, and he even took their homages in 1216. The king now faced both the threat of a united native Wales and a fundamental challenge to the nature of his overlordship. John was in desperate straits, and could do nothing, but this very incapacity denied Llywelyn the treaty he sought.

For all the weaknesses apparent at the very end of John's reign, his power was such in 1211 that he commanded unprecedented obedience throughout England, Scotland, Ireland and Wales. The extension of royal influence in Wales was the result of a number of factors: the king's large stake in the march; the concentration of resources in England after the loss of his lands in France by

1204; the confiscation of ecclesiastical temporalities during the interdict; the growth of English national sentiment; the increased ambition and efficiency of royal government; and not least John's often underrated personal qualities. But one of the most important factors was instability within Wales itself. It was not external pressure but dynastic unrest within Deheubarth, for example, which induced Maelgwn ap Rhys to quitclaim the castle of Cardigan to John in perpetuity in 1200, in return for Ceredigion, the *cwmwd* of Is Hirwen and the castles of Cilgerran and Emlyn. The acquisition of Cardigan provided the king with a strategic focus in west Wales for decades, but it was not John's primary intention to weaken the native dynasty; rather, his main concern in Deheubarth seems to have been to resist the expansion of Gwynedd. Hence he recognised Gruffudd ap Rhys in 1199 and 1200, and supported Maelgwn only when Gruffudd proved ineffective. When Maelgwn similarly failed to make an impact in 1200, John gave William de Braose licence to conquer all he could from the Welsh, as well as the lordships of Glamorgan, Wentloog and Gower in 1202. Whether Deheubarth was ruled by the Welsh or by the Anglo-Normans, the king's main desire seems to have been that it should provide a stable counterbalance to Gwynedd.

The divisions within Deheubarth made this impossible, however. Between 1203 and 1206, Maelgwn renewed his alliance with Powys, captured Llandovery and Llangadog, built castles at Dineirth and Abereinion, and eliminated potential rivals, but he suffered badly at the hands of Gruffudd's sons, Rhys Ieuanc and Owain. The situation was complicated further by Rhys and Owain's conflict with Rhys Gryg between 1208 and 1210. Despite co-operating in the capture of Dinefwr, the brothers contested with Rhys for Llangadog and Llandovery, and they subsequently opposed both Maelgwn and Rhys consistently until 1215. Furthermore, this disruption led to the involvement of external parties: the men of Kidwelly killed Maredudd ap Rhys in 1201, Cilgerran was captured by William Marshal in 1204, and Llywelyn ap Iorwerth seized Ceredigion Uwch Aeron in 1208. Realising that none of these combatants could control Deheubarth, John withheld support almost completely from all of them, and none of the native dynasty was required to perform homage. De Braose also made little headway in Deheubarth, and the king had little choice but to wait for the disruption to resolve itself. John's increasing troubles in France after 1202 did not make things any easier for him, and Maelgwn took advantage of royal weakness in 1206, breaking his truce with the king.

The threat posed by Gwynedd in 1210 made this situation intolerable both for the rulers of Deheubarth and for the king. Maelgwn promptly remade peace with John, and he and Rhys Gryg supported the royal campaign of 1211, but Llywelyn's influence was such that most of the dynasty of Deheubarth now supported Gwynedd. John therefore resorted to direct intervention. Falkes de Breauté, the sheriff of Cardiff, who had taken the role of William de Braose since the latter's downfall in 1207, was sent into Deheubarth in 1211. The objective was not conquest but the resolution of the succession dispute, and peaceful means were preferred to violence. Falkes was to bring Rhys Ieuanc and Owain quietly into the king's peace, but when this failed he was authorised to force them to surrender both themselves and Ceredigion Uwch Aeron to the king. Frustrated by continued instability in Deheubarth, John was now attempting to dominate the region himself. Rhys Gryg was helped in capturing Llandovery in 1210, and a royal castle was built at Aberystwyth in 1211, only to be burned down soon afterwards by the Welsh. Despite his reconciliation with Rhys Ieuanc and Owain in 1211, John granted their lands in Ceredigion Uwch Aeron to Maelgwn, and he went on to re-grant them to Rhys Gryg in 1212, overlooking the fact that it was Maelgwn and Rhys who had destroyed his castle at Aberystwyth. Similarly, Falkes and Ingelard de Cicogné, the sheriff of Hereford, supported the sons of Gruffudd in 1213 against Rhys Gryg, who was required to give Llandovery to them. He refused, was defeated, and sought refuge with Maelgwn before attempting to renew his alliance with the king, only to be imprisoned by royal officials; his lands were given to Rhys Ieuanc in 1214. John's deft manipulation of the Welsh followed the pragmatic royal tradition of divide and rule, and his transferral of power from native rulers to royal servants was reminiscent of Henry I. More importantly, the military and administrative involvement of royal government in Wales had been intensified, and laid the foundations of future policy.

Powys was forced into association with the king by the power of Gwynedd. Madog ap Gruffudd Maelor of Powys Fadog received ten marks in 1205, and both he and Maredudd ap Rhobert of Cydewain sided consistently with John until 1215. The subjection of Powys Wenwynwyn was more explicit. Royal opposition to Gwenwynwyn had been made plain in 1198, and the prince had been made to acknowledge his subordination in the agreements of 1199. In response to these indignities, Gwenwynwyn made a considerable nuisance of himself, and he was undoubtedly among the king's enemies from whom William de Braose conquered lands by 1200. He attacked de Braose's lands in 1202 and probably also captured a castle in Gwerthrynion (probably Rhaeadr Gwy) from Roger Mortimer, and there were further hostilities with William de Braose junior in 1204. Gwenwynwyn was joined by Ranulf of Chester against the king in the same year, and these disruptive activities continued until 1208, when Gwenwynwyn ravaged the lands of Peter fitz Herbert, whom John had placed in the march to replace William de Braose. This attack on a royal officer was a step too far, and the king did not hesitate to punish it – Gwenwynwyn was imprisoned on a visit to Shrewsbury, deprived of his lands, and required to give 20 hostages. Yet John was compelled to accept and support Gwenwynwyn as the only serious opponent of Llywelyn throughout this period. He therefore granted him the manor of Ashford in Derbyshire in 1200, and Gwenwynwyn and Maelgwn were summoned together to the royal court in 1204, presumably to devise a common strategy against Gwynedd. Although John initially made no protest when Llywelyn invaded Powys Wenwynwyn as a direct result of the incarceration of Gwenwynwyn in 1208, he was forced to acknowledge his error, and restored Gwenwynwyn forcibly in 1210 – indeed, it was only royal support which enabled Gwenwynwyn to recover his lands, and the same was probably true between 1202 and 1208. Despite Gwenwynwyn's usefulness, however, there was no question of recognition of his pretensions to grandeur. John's renewed support of Powys in 1210 and again temporarily in 1216 was purely for convenience, and he sought to reduce Gwenwynwyn's influence whenever possible. Robert de Vieuxpont, the sheriff of Shrewsbury, had a castle at Mathrafal in 1212 – within a year of Llywelyn's defeat – and a Welsh relieving force was scattered. Powys was now driven to wed its fortunes to those of Gwynedd.

THE ESTABLISHMENT OF GWYNEDD'S SUPREMACY

The weakness of native Wales invited expansion by Gwynedd, whether in the interests of stability or imperialism. Gwenwynwyn sensed the threat in 1201, when John needed to reassure him that Llywelyn had agreed peace, and Llywelyn attacked in 1202, conquering the whole of Powys Wenwynwyn. Failure to obey him was punished harshly – Elise ap Madog was ejected from Penllyn, and only seven *trefi* and the castle of Crogen were restored to him. The occupation was shortlived, not least because of John's support of Gwenwynwyn, but the latter's imprisonment in 1208 allowed Llywelyn to re-conquer the region, only to be repelled in 1210. Gwenwynwyn's fear of Gwynedd was shared by Maelgwn ap Rhys, with whom he allied in 1203, but Maelgwn's dismantling of the castles of Ystrad Meurig, Dineirth and Aberystwyth failed to prevent the conquest of Ceredigion Uwch Aeron by Gwynedd in 1208. Not surprisingly, Maelgwn was relieved when Gwenwynwyn was restored. Llywelyn was widely feared, and his unpopularity with all of his neighbours is shown by the participation of Gwenwynwyn, Maelgwn, Madog ap Gruffudd Maelor, Rhys Gryg, Maredudd ap Rhobert and Hywel ap Gruffudd ap Cynan in the royal expedition of 1211. These men had all been subservient to Llywelyn, and they took the first available opportunity to throw off his rule. Llywelyn's dominant position was fragile; he could not enforce permanent control of Powys and Ceredigion, and his successful campaigns all relied on considerable support from allies, many of whom were less than willing. If he was to become a true leader of the Welsh, Llywelyn needed to win affection as well as fear.

Luckily for Llywelyn, John's increasingly interventionist policy and the cruelties inflicted by some of his officers (notably Robert de Vieuxpont) drove the Welsh into the arms of Gwynedd. The Welsh who slaughtered the sheriff of Gloucester's men in Buellt and destroyed the castle of Builth in 1210 shared a widespread disaffection with royal rule, and Maelgwn and Rhys Gryg burned John's castle at Aberystwyth in 1211. The first decade of John's reign brought a growing realisation among the Welsh that they risked disinheritance whether they supported the king or not, and it was this as much as fear of Gwynedd which eventually persuaded them to transfer their allegiances to Llywelyn. The sense of emergency throughout *pura Wallia* is apparent in the rapid politicisation of the concept of Welsh nationality in the early thirteenth century, and Powys and Deheubarth came to recognise implicitly that complete independence of action was no longer possible. Llywelyn was beginning to assume leadership of the Welsh as a political coalition and as a people.

Such was the fear of intensified royal authority that Gwenwynwyn, Madog ap Gruffudd Maelor, Maelgwn ap Rhys and Maredudd ap Rhobert apparently joined Llywelyn in 1212 during a period when he did not even control the Perfeddwlad, which was recovered with the help of Gwenwynwyn and Maelgwn. By 1215, relations with John reached such a crisis that Maelgwn was even reconciled with his nephews, the sons of Gruffudd, one of whom, Owain, aligned himself with Gwynedd. The confederation of 1212 was revived, and the Welsh made a pact with the English barons, swearing not to make peace with the king until they all received back the castles, lands and rights of which they had been unlawfully deprived. Although this objective was achieved in theory by Magna Carta, it proved necessary to realise the claims by violence. Llywelyn was therefore presented with a further opportunity to enhance his position as a national leader.

At the head of an impressive alliance which now included almost all of the leaders of *pura Wallia*, Llywelyn presided over the expedition which devastated south Wales in 1215. His very involvement in the south – which included the marriage of his daughter, Gwladus, to Reginald de Braose in 1215 – illustrated the radical change in the *status quo*. Unlike the honorary position enjoyed by Owain Gwynedd in 1165, Llywelyn turned his leadership of the Welsh into real political authority. Many of the decisions in the campaign were made by the counsel – or even a council – of lesser princes, with clear implications of Llywelyn's superiority, and most of the Welsh princes were present at Aberdyfi in 1216, where Llywelyn exercised his new authority by formally apportioning Deheubarth between Maelgwn, Rhys Gryg, Rhys Ieuanc and

Owain ap Gruffudd. He was clearly determined to seek and possibly impose a final solution on the interminable confusion in the region, and this was done in such a way that Deheubarth would not regain its former strength. Even if Llywelyn saw Maelgwn's illegitimacy as making him ineligible, the sons of Gruffudd undoubtedly had a better claim to the kingdom than Rhys Gryg, yet it was he who received the *caput* at Dinefwr, and the territories assigned were of roughly equal size, ensuring that no single prince could dominate. The subordination of Deheubarth was confirmed. The poet Prydydd y Moch warned Rhys Gryg of the great power of Llywelyn, and Llywelyn himself – after defeating Rhys in 1220 – contemptuously said of the castle of Dinefwr that it had once been famous, but was now no more than ruins. Moreover, Llywelyn was revolutionising traditional relationships, demanding homage, hostages, oaths, pledges, charters and chirographs, and his supremacy was bolstered by patronage of ecclesiastical foundations throughout native Wales. Gwenwynwyn's revolt in 1216 merely allowed Llywelyn to reinforce his position. Appearing once again at the head of the Welsh, he seized Powys Wenwynwyn, and Gwenwynwyn fled to Ranulf of Chester.

Llywelyn's prestige was increased further by a successful expedition against Reginald de Braose in 1217, when the garrison of Brecon was forced to give five hostages and 100 marks for peace, and the prince ravaged Gower, receiving Reginald's surrender and the castle of Swansea. After giving the castle to Rhys Gryg, he also compelled the Flemings of Dyfed to sue for peace; they offered 20 hostages as surety for a payment of 1,000 marks, and failing that, they would hold their lands of Llywelyn.

Nevertheless, the weaknesses in Llywelyn's position in the south were obvious. The most apparent problem was that until 1217 he had depended substantially on Reginald de Braose, who placed more importance on the recovery of his inheritance than on his friendship with Gwynedd – it was his reconciliation with the king which prompted the 1217 campaign. Significantly, also, many of the Welsh successes were not achieved under the auspices of Gwynedd. In 1215, Rhys Ieuanc and Maelgwn acted of their own accord in subduing all the Welsh of Dyfed (except Cemais) and burning and plundering the castles of Narberth, Maenclochog and Cemais. Rhys continued alone after Maelgwn's alliance with Llywelyn, taking Kidwelly, Loughor, Tal-y-bont, Oystermouth and all the castles of Gower, and subduing Carnwyllion, while Swansea was destroyed by its own garrison. By 1216, Cardigan, Kidwelly and areas of Dyfed were regarded as being under native rule. The dynasty of Rhwng Gwy a Hafren also acted independently, recovering a degree of control in Elfael, where Gwallter Fychan ab Einion Clud held authority throughout the *cantref* in return for his support of Bishop Giles de Braose of Hereford's rebellion against the king. Similarly, the initiative against Reginald in 1217 was taken by Rhys Ieuanc and Owain ap Gruffudd, who captured all of Buellt except the castle of Builth before Llywelyn intervened. Llywelyn never had full control of his military alliance, and the task of maintaining his authority in peacetime would be enormous.

The Nascent Principality of Wales

England was reunited after John's death and the accession of Henry III in 1216, and the Welsh and the rebellious barons were excommunicated by the papal legate Guala in 1217. Llywelyn needed a treaty, but the treaty of Lambeth, which ended hostilities in England, did not directly address Wales – the Welsh had peace, but on condition that all lands, castles and prisoners were to be returned. In effect, this meant unilateral concessions, and the princes did not respond, reportedly saying that they were still bound to an oath. Most importantly, Llywelyn wanted recognition of his supremacy, and he negotiated for more favourable terms while his allies continued the war. In the event, however, although there were many campaigns and negotiations during the following years, he was to be frustrated by a military and constitutional stalemate for the rest of his life.

The young king – or more precisely his regents – accepted Llywelyn's conquests at Worcester in 1218, and the prince performed homage and fealty. Like Rhys ap Gruffudd in the 1170s and 1180s, he was now seen as a quasi-royal official, responsible for ensuring peace in Wales, and it was in this role that he forced Rhys Gryg to do homage to Henry and to hand over Kidwelly, Carnwyllion, Gwidigada and Gower in 1221. Although he conceded the castles of Cardigan and Carmarthen in 1218, Llywelyn was to retain custody during Henry's minority, and he was also given custody of the lands of Gwenwynwyn, who had died in 1216. The only disappointment for the Welsh was that Caerleon was retained by William Marshal. Royal acquiescence in Llywelyn's power was shown in 1220 by the recognition of his son, Dafydd, as his heir by the papal legate Pandulf and the justiciar, Hubert de Burgh. Numerous local disputes did nothing to reduce his prestige, and negotiations continued as normal. Indeed, Henry upheld Llywelyn's partition of Deheubarth, requiring him to see that Rhys Ieuanc was installed at Cardigan in 1221, and Llywelyn was given Rhys's lands when he died the following year. The prince was also on good terms with Ranulf of Chester, who recognised his conquest of Mold and made peace in 1218, and Llywelyn's daughter, Elen, married Ranulf's son, John, as part of a pact in 1222. Nevertheless, although Gwynedd's influence was acknowledged, its supremacy was not. Aware that the Welsh had done homage to Llywelyn, Henry emphasised that this belonged to the king, describing the prince's allies as mere associates, and repeating the assertion that the king's enemies were not to be sheltered in Wales. Llywelyn was far from satisfied.

In 1219, with tension increasing, Pope Honorius III ordered the prince to respect royal rights as he had agreed, and Llywelyn in turn complained that Henry's government often neglected to consult him, and that the king did not honour his promise to conduct negotiations in Wales rather than in England. Furthermore, royal authority was becoming increasingly intrusive. For instance, after Llywelyn dismissed the pleas of Rhys Ieuanc and destroyed his castle of Aberystwyth in 1221, Rhys drew on a principle established in 1201 and sought royal justice, which found against Llywelyn. The essence of Llywelyn's frustration was touched upon in 1220, when he claimed the service and homage of the men of Maelienydd, saying that the king had relinquished all lordship there except homage. This, the prince argued, should be performed by him, since Maelienydd was part of his 'principality' (*principatus*), and he asserted that the matter should be decided 'according to the status of Wales' (*secundum statum Walliae*).[2] Henry, however, considered that the *cantref* should be restored to Hugh Mortimer, who had held it before the war. With some justification, the king saw the 'status of Wales' as representing little more than the pretension of Gwynedd. Mortimer did not press his claims, and settled for a truce, but Llywelyn had indicated his ambition. His desire to rule all the Welsh was demonstrated again by his complaint about the treatment of Welshmen in Dyfed – outside his dominions – in 1220.

Llywelyn's authority within his *principatus* was scarcely homogeneous. He retained Powys Wenwynwyn after 1216, and, although officially merely a custodian after 1218 until Owain and Gruffudd ap Gwenwynwyn reached maturity, he maintained control there until his death. Madog ap Gruffudd Maelor also gave him almost consistent support, and Llywelyn conducted legal proceedings on his behalf against William Pantulf in 1229. Madog's sons deferred to Gwynedd after his death in 1236, and Llywelyn was able to seize the lands of one of them, Maredudd, in 1238. Llywelyn Fawr of Meirionnydd was also subjected, as were Maredudd ap Rhobert of Cydewain, Llywelyn ab Owain Fychan and Owain Fychan of Mechain and the descendants of Owain Brogyntyn in Edeirnion. Yet there were dangerous weaknesses in the hegemony. The devastation of Meirionnydd and Ardudwy by Llywelyn's son, Gruffudd, in 1221 almost led to internecine war, and Llywelyn was forced to resume direct control in these *cantrefi*, where he built a castle (probably Castell y Bere); Gruffudd was imprisoned in 1228. Intervention was also necessary when Madog ap Gruffudd Maelor arranged a marriage between his daughter and Fulk fitz Warin sometime between 1215 and 1227, and Llywelyn still faced problems in the south. As well as his dispute with Rhys Ieuanc, he was obliged to deprive Rhys Gryg of Gower in 1219 and Swansea in 1220, only for Rhys to make a marriage alliance with Gilbert de Clare and re-conquer Gower,

remaining hostile until he was defeated at Carmarthen in 1220, when Llywelyn again took Gower from him. Gwynedd's influence was bolstered by the
marriage of Llywelyn's daughter, Margaret, to John de Braose in 1219, but Llywelyn was forced to alternate his favours between John and Rhys Gryg. There
was also trouble in Dyfed, where, convinced that William Marshal junior was
in breach of the peace of 1218, Llywelyn was goaded to attack in 1220. He took
Narberth, Wiston and Haverfordwest, and ravaged Rhos and Daugleddau, but
Pembroke was saved by a promise to pay £100. Llywelyn's putative principality was an impressive achievement, but tensions and uncertainties such as these
ensured that much of it existed in a continuous state of flux.

The king was understandably not happy with Llywelyn's involvement in the
south, and he accused the prince of breaking the peace. Llywelyn was ordered
to withdraw from Dyfed and to return lands from which he had driven Welsh
lords, and he was reprehended for breaking the recent truce, for failing to appear
for judicial proceedings at Oxford, and for damaging royal lands. The matter was
allowed to rest, since Llywelyn's opposition to William Marshal benefited Henry,
but the prince was still denied recognition of his supremacy. He therefore sought
to create a new bargaining counter in 1223 by capturing the castles of Kinnerley and Whittington in Shropshire, and the situation was inflamed by William
Marshal's recovery of Cardigan, Carmarthen and Emlyn. Gruffudd ap Llywelyn
was sent to the south and Rhys Gryg burned Kidwelly, but William's success
continued, and Llywelyn suffered a further blow when Cynan ap Hywel Sais
defected. The king was eager to resolve the dispute peacefully, but, realising this to
be impossible, he soon determined to defeat Llywelyn. All trade with the Welsh
was prohibited, Llywelyn was excommunicated, and Henry now openly supported William. In turn, Llywelyn besieged Builth and moved into Mabudryd in
Cantref Mawr, while Gruffudd and Rhys Gryg prevented William from returning to Dyfed. The king reacted by fomenting revolt in Powys, and the conflict
was eventually ended by a royal expedition. Llywelyn and his allies throughout
pura Wallia submitted. Kinnerley and Whittington were to be restored, and the
prince received no reparation for his losses, which included Cardigan, Carmarthen, Kidwelly and Montgomery. The war had changed nothing, except to
make the incompatibility of Gwynedd's ambitions and those of the king more
explicit. Henry's construction of a castle at Montgomery indicated that he
expected a prolonged struggle, and the atmosphere was loaded with mistrust.

Llywelyn persisted in proclaiming his status, taking advantage of renewed
dissension in England, and in particular the flight of the rebel Falkes de Breauté
in 1224. Unwilling to provoke direct confrontation, he refused to harbour Falkes, but he did not deny that he had entered Gwynedd for one day. The prince
said that Henry had mistreated Falkes, who did not deserve excommunication.

Moreover, Llywelyn claimed that he was entitled to receive outlaws with impunity in any case, just as the king of Scotland was. The argument was flawed, since he had conceded the right to harbour fugitives in 1201 and 1218, but the assertion was of more significance than the fact.

The king was more concerned to preserve peace and stability than to discuss constitutional issues, and a meeting at Shrewsbury in 1224 resulted in little more than pleasantries and an exchange of gifts: Henry gave Joan and Llywelyn the manors of Rothley in Leicestershire in 1225 and Rayleigh and Condover in Shropshire in 1226, and Llywelyn sent him hunting birds in return. The king co-operated in Llywelyn's attempts to preserve order in Deheubarth, and, apparently at the prince's request, warned William Marshal's bailiff to respect the rights of Maelgwn ap Rhys in 1225. However, Llywelyn's authority in the south was subject to erosion. He had supervised the 1216 partition, but by 1225 he was obliged to ask for a royal commission to adjudicate claims against Maelgwn by Cynan ap Hywel and Owain ap Gruffudd. Once again, his supremacy was compromised, and the king was unable and no doubt unwilling to discuss anything. All Llywelyn could achieve was the renewal of his truce with the marchers. Henry's eagerness that the Welsh should do fealty to Dafydd ap Llywelyn in 1226, and his possible involvement in the papal confirmation of liberties given to Llywelyn by John, may have pleased the prince, but they also served to reinforce the king's status as overlord, able to interfere by offering help in the affairs of his subordinates. Henry was aware of Llywelyn's frustration, and the continued failure to discuss homages brought matters to a head.

In 1228, Llywelyn's persistent stance on homage cost him the manors of Rothley and Condover, which he had been given by the king only a few years before. In this tense atmosphere, Henry established the justiciar, Hubert de Burgh, as a counterpoise to Gwynedd in the march, granting him Arch-enfield and Wormelow in Herefordshire in 1227 and Montgomery in 1228. The rift finally escalated into war in 1228, when some of Hubert's men were set upon by the Welsh after straying into Ceri while clearing the forest around Montgomery. The incursion was apparently unintentional, and Henry was not prepared for hostilities when the men of Ceri reacted by besieging Montgomery. He accepted Llywelyn's apology for the Welsh aggression, and a meeting was arranged, but the prince's frustration was now such that war was unavoidable. Henry therefore gathered a large expeditionary force and led it into Ceri, where a surprise attack was planned, but the royal army suffered heavy casualties after a river crossing proved to be too deep. The monks of Cwm Hir, one of whom had directed the king's soldiers to the supposed ford, were punished by the destruction of several of their granges, but Henry's expedition achieved nothing except the partial completion of work on a new castle.

The king did not resort to violence lightly. He did not allow Llywelyn to be attacked or provoked, relying instead on Hubert's presence to dissuade Welsh attacks. In practice, that presence seems only to have aggravated the situation, but English chroniclers were probably uncharitable to blame Hubert personally; he was not yet fully established in the march when Llywelyn attacked him, and Henry himself blamed the war on the prince's failure to keep his promises. This was an unwanted conflict, and it benefited no-one. Llywelyn retained Ceri, renewed his homage and paid 3,000 marks, and the new royal castle was dismantled rapidly. The prince's only territorial gains were by virtue of his chance capture of William de Braose, who was released in 1229 after giving a ransom of 3,000 marks and a promise to marry his daughter, Isabella, to Dafydd ap Llywelyn, with the castle of Builth and the whole of Buellt as a dowry. Not surprisingly, no progress was made on the question of homage. Despite a revolt in south Wales at Llywelyn's instigation, and despite the prince's crucial role in enabling Maelgwn Fychan ap Maelgwn and Owain ap Gruffudd to capture Cardigan, it was clear that stalemate would continue on the constitutional issue until a new agenda could be devised.

Henry was content with this situation. He continued to sponsor Hubert, giving him Cardigan and Carmarthen in 1229, the lordship of Gower in 1230 and custody of the lordship of Glamorgan and the de Braose lands in 1230 and 1231 respectively. Amicable relations with Llywelyn were also resumed: Condover and Rothley were restored to Joan, and Henry received Dafydd's homage in 1229 for all the lands and rights which would fall to him on Llywelyn's death, promising lands with an annual value of £40 in return. Such was the king's respect and his desire for stability that he did nothing when Llywelyn executed William de Braose in 1230 after finding him in compromising circumstances with Joan, who was imprisoned for a year for her part in the episode. Henry ordered that lands at Totnes in Devon should still pass to Dafydd in dowry, and he regarded William's fate as a mere 'misfortune'.[3] Similarly, neither Llywelyn nor the de Braose family saw any reason why Dafydd's marriage to Isabella should not go ahead. Llywelyn therefore gained a powerful ally and the *cantref* of Buellt in 1230.

In his quest for special status, Llywelyn adopted the title 'prince of Aberffraw and lord of Snowdon' (*princeps de Abbefrau et dominus de Snaudonia*) from 1230. Henry did not object to this, and he thereby recognised implicitly that there had been a change in Llywelyn's status. Llywelyn's propaganda machine was hard at work, and the king may not have been aware that several thirteenth-century redactions of Welsh law insisted that the king of Aberffraw was owed a tribute (*mechteyrn dyled*) by all the rulers of native Wales, and that he alone should make a similar payment to the king. Whatever the theoretical overtones, however, no such payments were ever made, and Llywelyn never made explicit use of the style to justify his position. His ambitions could be achieved only by force, and his opportunity came when William Marshal, the custodian of the de Braose lands, died in 1231. A series of minor disturbances, started by the attempts of a certain Madog Fychan to recover his lands in Brycheiniog, developed into a confrontation between Gwyn ap Goronwy, Llywelyn's constable of Builth, and William's steward of Netherwent. The prince was quick to gather an army, and, after inevitably unproductive meetings with the king, he attacked when Welsh prisoners taken at Montgomery were beheaded by Hubert de Burgh. Henry, not desiring conflict, had Llywelyn excommunicated and deprived him of Rothley again before preparing to fight, while the prince burned Montgomery, Radnor, Hay and Brecon, devastating the surrounding regions and defeating a royal force near Hay. Llywelyn then proceeded into Gwent, burning Caerleon and besieging Newport, and he entered Glamorgan, where Neath was destroyed, Kidwelly was captured, and £40 was extorted from the abbey of Margam. Finally, Cardigan was captured. Llywelyn was now indisputably the leader of all the Welsh of the south except Morgan ap Hywel. Madog Fychan regarded him as his natural lord, and Llywelyn also received the submissions of Rhys ap Gruffudd ab Ifor Bach, Morgan Gam ap Morgan ap Caradog and Morgan's cousin, Hywel ap Maredudd ap Caradog. Henry affirmed Llywelyn's status in 1234 by employing him to ensure that the Welsh of Morgannwg returned lands which they had received illegally from Richard Marshal, the new earl of Pembroke. The prince obeyed, but he still did not have what he wanted, and his tangible gains were minimal. The king's only significant losses were at Neath and Radnor – Cardigan and Kidwelly had only been retaken from the Welsh as recently as 1223 – and only Cardigan remained in Llywelyn's hands. The prince could not maintain his hold on the other captured towns, especially since many of the castles had not fallen. Yet Henry was still unable to dominate the vital middle march. He built a new castle in Elfael at Painscastle, but this was cancelled out by Llywelyn's possession of Buellt, and recent conflicts in the area had shown the limitations of royal military power. English chroniclers complained that the king's army sat watching the construction of one castle while Llywelyn destroyed ten others, and Llywelyn was even believed to have claimed that he feared Henry's piety more than his army.

   Neither Henry nor Llywelyn had any new answers to the problem. Although Hubert de Burgh fell from grace, his position in the march was simply filled by Peter des Rivaux, and, despite the renewal of friendly relations with the king, the prince remained dissatisfied. A truce was arranged, but problems in England prevented the king from being able to offer even a permanent peace, and negotiations continued into 1232. Llywelyn also lost some important allies in that year, when both John de Braose and Ranulf of Chester died, although the latter was succeeded by Llywelyn's son-in-law, John. The prince was driven almost by desperation to make a brief, punitive but fruitless attack on the de Braose lands in 1233, and he was frustrated further by his failure to take full advantage of the revolt of Richard Marshal against the king later in that year – he allied with Richard, who defeated a royal force in an unconventional night attack at Grosmont, but a month-long siege failed to take Brecon Castle, and the prince's joint attack with Rhys Gryg, Owain ap Gruffudd and Maelgwn Fychan on Carmarthen was similarly unsuccessful. Llywelyn had no option but to accept another unambitious peace, which was finally agreed at Middle in Shropshire in 1234. This was merely a restatement of the pre-war *status quo*. Llywelyn retained Cardigan and Builth, which he had held before Richard's revolt, and there was a mutual agreement not to build new castles or to repair old ones. The truce lasted for two years, and it was renewed annually until 1240.

Llywelyn had won peace for the remainder of his lifetime, but the treaty he hoped for had not materialised. The pact of Middle specifically excluded lands, tenements and homages, and the king, while recognising the prince's power and influence, did not acknowledge any alteration in his status. This point was brought home when Morgan Gam, Rhys ap Gruffudd and Hywel ap Maredudd refused to recognise royal justice in 1234 – Henry was forced to accept their demand that their cases should be tried in Llywelyn's court, but he nevertheless did not concede the homages of the Welsh of Morgannwg to Gwynedd. Without royal recognition of Gwynedd's right to Welsh homages, there was no guarantee that Llywelyn's hegemony could survive him.

The Succession Crisis and the Collapse of Gwynedd

Llywelyn's position deteriorated after 1234. Chester reverted to the king on the death of the earl, Llywelyn's ally, in 1237, and the prince himself was an old man. He suffered a stroke and slight paralysis in the same year, and his son Gruffudd revolted once again. Such were Llywelyn's problems that he reportedly placed himself under royal protection, offering the king unconditional military help in return for a guarantee of peace, and the search for support may also have led to marriage with Eve, the daughter of Fulk fitz Warin, in 1239.

The prince made an audacious and somewhat desperate attempt to consolidate his legacy when he sought to procure Welsh homages for Dafydd at Strata Florida in 1238. He was left in no doubt that he would not succeed. Upon hearing of Llywelyn's plan, Henry warned him that it would gravely prejudice royal authority and that it was not consistent with Llywelyn's fealty, and Dafydd was reminded that he held his lands *in capite* and ordered to do homage to the king on pain of forfeiture; a similar message was sent to the other Welsh lords. The question of homage was consequently dropped. The

truce was renewed, and no more than fealty was done when the Welsh came
to Strata Florida later in the year. When Llywelyn died in 1240, his *principatus* of Wales rested on shaky foundations. Although he had dominated Wales,
exacted unprecedented submissions and raised the status of the prince of
Gwynedd to new heights, his three major ambitions – a permanent hegemony, its recognition by the king, and its inheritance in its entirety by his heir
– remained unfulfilled. His supremacy, like that of Gruffudd ap Llywelyn, had
been merely personal in nature, and there was no institutional framework to
maintain it either during his lifetime or after his death.

In an attempt to gain respectability in the wider world, Llywelyn was
determined that his legitimate son Dafydd, a grandson of king John, should
succeed him, although he was younger than the illegitimate Gruffudd. The
emphasis on the importance of legitimacy rather than traditional practice
was intended to impress both a reforming papacy and an acutely socially-
conscious European aristocracy, and Dafydd was accordingly recognised as
heir by Henry in 1220, by Pope Honorius III in 1222 and by the Welsh in
1226. His credentials were finally completed in 1226 when the pope somewhat unconvincingly declared his mother to be legitimate. Llywelyn was fully
entitled under Welsh law to make this choice, but Gruffudd's claim was equally valid, and he rebelled in 1221 and again in 1228, when he was imprisoned
by Llywelyn for six years. He proved such a menace that he was given only
half of Llŷn on his release in 1234. By 1238, this was complemented by Arwystli, Ceri, Cyfeiliog, Mawddwy, Mochnant and Caereinion, and Llywelyn's
weakness allowed Gruffudd to press further claims. Despite being deprived by
Dafydd of all his lands in Powys in 1238, he remained a problem until 1240.

These difficulties provided the king with an opportunity to cripple
Gwynedd and dismantle its hegemony, and his eagerness to do so after
Llywelyn's death was obvious. Dafydd performed homage at Gloucester in
1240, and Henry insisted again that all Welsh homages were reserved to him
– Dafydd's homage was for his own lands, not on behalf of any other prince.
Moreover, the king humiliated Dafydd, recognising him merely as the 'son of
Llywelyn, sometime prince of Aberffraw and lord of Snowdon'.[4] It was made
explicit that all of the Welsh princes were regarded as barons of the king, on
a par with Henry's feudal vassals in England, and all cases where the king's
barons claimed to have been dispossessed by Llywelyn were to be submitted
to arbitration. If Dafydd failed to attend any meeting called by the king, he
would become contumacious – in breach of his feudal obligations to his lord.
Dafydd's status as ruler of Gwynedd was thereby reduced in all respects to
that of an English baron, derived from the king, and Henry also won the right
to challenge Dafydd's tenure of Buellt (which he held by right of dowry),

Powys Wenwynwyn (which Gwynedd had held since 1218) and Cardigan (which had been captured in 1231). Within months of Llywelyn's death, the supremacy of Gwynedd was discredited and undermined.

Dafydd's position was so weak that even the customary title 'prince of North Wales' seemed ambitious, and indeed was not recognised in 1240. The Welsh did homage to Henry, while Maelienydd was restored to Ralph Mortimer, Owain Fychan of Mechain recovered his rights in Mochnant Uwch Rhaeadr, and Kinnerley and the manor of Penmaen in Gower were returned to their previous lords. Walter Marshal also ejected Maelgwn Fychan from the *cwmwd* of Is Coed Is Hirwen and Cardigan – where he rebuilt the castle – and drove Cynan ap Hywel from Ystlwyf and Emlyn. Dafydd's only defence was to hinder the legal procedures by procrastination. By 1241, however, he was able to prevent Owain Fychan from acquiring Mochnant Uwch Rhaeadr, and he also sent troops to resist Mortimer in Maelienydd, while a confederation was made with the brothers of Gruffudd Maelor ap Madog and some of the men of Ceri. Dafydd's position within Gwynedd was also strengthened when his brother Gruffudd was captured and imprisoned in 1240 after being lured to a parley under false pretences.

Henry was determined that Dafydd should not renege on his promises, and sensing the prince's recalcitrance, he issued an ultimatum requiring Dafydd to repair the injuries which he had done to the king. A royal army was assembled, and Henry sought to foster internecine conflict in Gwynedd by championing the cause of Gruffudd, with whom he made a pact in 1241. Dafydd failed to answer the charges against him, and refused to release his brother on the grounds that there could never be peace between them. He was consequently excommunicated, and found himself isolated as the Welsh of Powys, Deheubarth and the middle march all made peace with Henry. Dafydd's counsellors urged him to seek peace, but he was unwilling to release Gruffudd, and the king consequently attacked. Aided by exceptionally dry weather, Henry intercepted Dafydd's retreat around Rhuddlan and forced him to submit after only a week of campaigning.

The treaty of Gwern Eigron which followed the campaign of 1241 transferred Gruffudd, his son, Owain, and a number of hostages into royal custody. Dafydd performed homage, liege homage (*ligantium*) and fealty, and – in the most explicit assertion of royal lordship to date – it was agreed separately that Gwynedd would pass to the king should Dafydd die without an heir. The prince also surrendered Mold, Powys Wenwynwyn, Meirionnydd, Tegeingl and Ellesmere, and he renounced all claims to Welsh homages, swearing also not to accept outlaws. As a final humiliation, he was obliged to pay Henry's war expenses. Furthermore, Henry now imposed the terms he had agreed earlier in the year with Gruffudd, who, prompted by a mixture of self-interest and royal bullying, had made the unprecedented concession that the king was entitled to adjudicate a native Welsh succession dispute. Henry had promised that, once Gruffudd and Owain were released by Dafydd, it would be decided by royal justice whether or not they should be transferred into royal custody, and by Welsh law whether Gruffudd should recover the lands from which he had been ousted. Gruffudd's wife, Senena, promised an annual payment of 600 marks if Gruffudd were restored, and undertook that peace would be maintained with Dafydd. If there should ever be any Welsh rebellion against the king, it was undertaken that Gruffudd and his heirs would help him at their own cost. Moreover, it became clear that Henry intended that Gruffudd should not receive his portion as a simple appanage – it was to be held *in capite*, thus splitting the kingship itself irretrievably into two. This principle owed nothing to genuine native practice, but it was enshrined as the 'custom of Wales', giving the king full powers of intervention in any similar dispute in *pura Wallia*. There is little if any doubt that Henry's mischievous attitude towards Welsh law owed more to expediency than to ignorance, and the significance of his flawed interpretation was not lost on the English chronicler Matthew Paris, who quoted St Matthew in his account of the brothers' rivalry: 'every kingdom divided against itself goes to ruin'.[5] In practice, the legal process between Dafydd and Gruffudd was never initiated, and Gruffudd remained in the Tower of London until his death, but Henry's undermining of Gwynedd and its hegemony was none the less complete for that. He had extended the policy of divide and rule further than ever before, and moreover he had achieved acceptance of his assertion that there were circumstances under which the king might exert direct lordship in *pura Wallia*. This did not mean that Wales now lay open to inevitable domination by the king, however – the destruction of Gwynedd's influence in the south merely allowed Gilbert Marshal to claim the homages of Maelgwn Fychan, Rhys Mechyll and Maredudd ab Owain in Cantref Mawr for himself in 1240. Gilbert failed, but his action demonstrated that all claims and counter-claims depended ultimately on military power. The 1241 *status quo* was anything but permanent.

Defiance, Submission and Recovery

INDEPENDENCE – THE UNFINISHED EXPERIMENT

Royal lordship tightened relentlessly after Gwern Eigron. Henry's request for Dafydd ap Llywelyn and Gruffudd ap Madog to provide 500 troops in Gascony in 1242 was not yet a demand, but Henry's intentions were evident. The appointment of royal justices as an alternative to Welsh and marcher law was unprecedented, and royal commissioners removed Dafydd from Buellt

RHODRI MAWR (d.878)

Hywel Dda

Above left: 1 Rhodri established Gwynedd as a formidable power in Wales, and much of the country was ruled by his descendants for half a millennium. The end of his reign was marked by Scandinavian and Saxon incursions into north Wales.

Above right: 2 Hywel 'the Good' was one of the most powerful Welsh kings, but he could not avoid submitting to Anglo-Saxon overlordship. He became the subject of a hagiographical cult in the early twelfth century, when he was credited with the codification of the Welsh laws.

Rhys ap Tewdwr

Gruffudd ap Cynan

Above left: 3 Rhys established a successful working relationship with William the Conqueror, whom he probably met at St Davids, but his death allowed the Normans to conquer much of south and west Wales.

Above right: 4 Born and bred near Dublin and supported by the Hiberno-Norse, Gruffudd was in many ways an outsider in Gwynedd, but his career and eventual success reveal a great deal about the inherent strength of native Wales.

Gruffudd ap Rhys

Madog ap Maredudd

Above left 5 According to Gerald of Wales, the wildfowl of Llyn Syfaddon (Llangors Lake) confounded two Norman lords by taking flight when Gruffudd asked for their recognition as the rightful ruler of Brycheiniog.

Above right: 6 Madog consolidated Powys against the Normans and the other Welsh kingdoms alike, but it entered into terminal decline after his death.

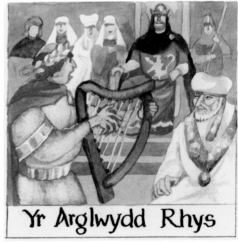

Owain Gwynedd

Yr Arglwydd Rhys

Above left: 7 Owain ap Gruffudd, the first prince to style himself 'prince of Wales', backed up his pretensions by facing down Henry II at the head of a Welsh military coalition.

Above right: 8 'At Christmas in that year, the Lord Rhys ap Gruffudd held court in splendour at Cardigan, in the castle. And he set two kinds of contest there: one between bards and poets, and another between harpists and crowders and pipers and various classes of music-craft' (*Brut y Tywysogyon*, 1176). This event, which was publicised throughout Britain and Ireland for a year beforehand, is sometimes regarded as the first national *eisteddfod*.

Llywelyn Fawr

Gruffudd ap Llywelyn

Above left: 9 Llywelyn ap Iorwerth's alliance with Philip Augustus of France was the first Franco-Welsh treaty. But the prince never got what he really needed: a treaty with the king of England.

Above right: 10 Frustrated with a life of exclusion and imprisonment, Gruffudd tried to escape from the Tower of London. Unfortunately for him, his privileged diet and indolent lifestyle had made him fat, and the sheets he made into a rope for his escape were too short. Matthew Paris says that Gruffudd landed on his head so hard that his neck was crushed between his shoulders.

Dafydd ap Llywelyn

Llywelyn ap Gruffudd

Above left: 11 Dafydd's attempt to persuade the Pope to assume overlordship of Gwynedd was one of only a very few challenges made by Welsh rulers to the overlordship of the king of England.

Above right: 12 Llywelyn the Last, the first and last formally-recognised native Welsh prince of Wales, was killed in a skirmish with English forces near Cilmeri in the Builth area. The exact circumstances remain unclear.

Owain Lawgoch

Owain Glyn Dŵr

Above left: 13 As the last direct descendant of the princes of Gwynedd in the male line, Owain was seen by many in Wales as the 'son of prophecy'. He was assassinated by an English agent at the siege of Mortagne-sur-Mer.

Above right: 14 Glyn Dŵr called himself 'prince of Wales' and adopted the heraldic arms of Owain Lawgoch (four lions rampant counterchanged quarterly *or* and *gules*), but Henry IV never recognised him as more than a rebellious baron. His quixotic revolt and mysterious disappearance gave rise to many legends, including the tradition that he is sleeping in a cave, waiting to return when the hour of need is greatest.

Left: 15 This is the modern view of Aust from Beachley, an ancient crossing point on the Severn. Here Gruffudd ap Llywelyn is said to have greeted Eadward the Confessor – a native Welsh 'king of Wales' meeting on equal terms with an Anglo-Saxon king of England. Times have changed.

16 Ewyas Harold. The motte covered by these trees is the only firmly attested pre-1066 castle in Britain. *Domesday Book* records that it was re-built by William fitz Osbern before 1071, and it was probably Ewyas Harold, which the *Anglo-Saxon Chronicle* says was built by the 'foreigners' in Herefordshire in or before 1051 and inhabited by the 'Frenchmen' in 1052; it was also very likely the castle later described as belonging to Osbern Pentecost. The castle's purpose was to secure south-western Herefordshire, not least against Gruffudd ap Llywelyn, and it was prepared for action against Glyn Dŵr as late as 1403.

Left: 17 The timber defences on this little motte at Ystrad Peithyll – raised around 1110 – lasted only a few years, but they provide an excellent example of the effectiveness of the network of Norman castles in Ceredigion. Gruffudd ap Rhys had no choice but to attack Ystrad Peithyll in 1116, and he burned it to the ground with relative ease. In the meantime, however, the constable was able to send for help to another of Gilbert fitz Richard's castles at Ystrad Meurig, with the result that the larger castle at Llanychaiarn (Aberystwyth) nearby was reinforced before Gruffudd could attack it. The extra troops proved crucial in preventing the Welsh from taking Aberystwyth, showing that even the smallest castle could buy the invaders not just territory, but time.

Below: 18 Coed Grwyne. In the spring of 1136, Richard fitz Gilbert de Clare entered these woods north of Abergavenny accompanied only by a singer and a fiddler, instructing his armed escort to follow behind him. It was a reckless mistake. Somewhere near this spot, he was ambushed and killed by the Welsh of Gwent, triggering a series of Norman reverses throughout south Wales.

19 King Stephen responded to unrest in south Wales by creating a defensible block of territory around Grosmont, Skenfrith and White Castle in Gwent, controlling the open border country between the Black Mountains and the Wye valley. This new lordship of the Three Castles – known to the Welsh as the *Tair Tref* – was granted to Payn fitz John in 1138, and Hubert de Burgh acquired it from the king in 1201 and again in 1219 after having been dispossessed. Hubert undertook extensive work at all three castles, and it was he who replaced the existing wooden fortifications at Skenfrith with the present stone structure.

Left: 20 Henry III was caught by surprise at Grosmont in November 1233 when Richard Marshal of Pembroke – at that time an ally of Llywelyn ap Iorwerth – attacked his army while they slept in camp outside the castle. The king and his men escaped with difficulty to Gloucester.

Below: 21 Dinefwr symbolised the last native Welsh challenge to the dominance of Gwynedd. Under Rhys ap Gruffudd, the power of Deheubarth rivalled that of Gwynedd, allowing some lawyers to assert that Dinefwr was equal in status with Aberffraw. The reality, however, was very different. There is no reliable reference to Dinefwr as a site of any significance before Rhys held it in 1163, and his chief seat seems to have been at Cardigan rather than Dinefwr. Moreover, any pretensions to grandeur were ruined as dynastic squabbles in Deheubarth resulted in the castle changing hands several times between 1195 and 1213. By 1220, Rhys Gryg was compelled to dismantle Dinefwr for fear of Llywelyn ap Iorwerth, but he subsequently built the present keep; most of the rest of the castle dates from after 1282.

Above: 22 Degannwy was the key to Gwynedd for 1,000 years, guarding the Conwy estuary which protected the mountain pastures of Snowdonia and the fertile agricultural land of Môn. There were fortifications here in the Roman period and perhaps earlier, and the site is said to have been inhabited by Maelgwn Gwynedd. It was always a target of English campaigns, and fell to the Mercians, the Normans and the Plantagenet kings of England, only for the Welsh to recover it on successive occasions. The castle was finally demolished by Llywelyn ap Gruffudd after he starved the garrison into submission in 1263, and stone from the ruins may later have been used in the town walls of Conwy. Very little of the masonry survives.

Right: 23 When Llywelyn ap Gruffudd built Dolforwyn in 1273, his purpose was as much political as strategic. The new castle and borough asserted his authority in the middle march and posed a direct military and economic challenge to Roger Mortimer at Montgomery and Gruffudd ap Gwenwynwyn at Welshpool. A royal ban on further work at Dolforwyn allowed Llywelyn to expound on his rights as prince of Wales, but the deteriorating quality of the later masonry work illustrates the increasing financial strains within his principality.

24 Owain Glyn Dŵr won an inspirational victory here on Pumlumon in the summer of 1401, when his small retinue fought their way out of a trap set by a numerically far superior English and Flemish force at Mynydd Hyddgen. Even the foxes here are not always so elusive.

25 On 5 July 1403, John Scudamore, the castellan of Carreg Cennen, sent a desperate letter to the royal receiver at Brecon, warning that all of the king's castles in west Wales were extremely vulnerable to Glyn Dŵr because of a lack of men. Furthermore, Scudamore had met Owain under truce at Dryslwyn the day before, and the prince had failed to promise a safe conduct for his wife and mother-in-law. Carreg Cennen seems to have held out for some time, but it was eventually taken. The fate of Scudamore's family is unknown.

26 The Welsh legend *Kyuranc Lludd a Llefelys* told of two dragons buried at Dinas Emrys beneath this late Roman site in Nant Gwynant near Snowdon, and both *Historia Brittonum* and Geoffrey of Monmouth elaborated upon the story. Vortigern is said to have chosen Dinas Emrys as his residence after he fled from the Saxons, but his efforts to build a palace here were frustrated. Every day, week after week, he would wake to find that the previous day's work on the first tower had collapsed overnight. In the end, he sought the advice of his magicians, and they all agreed that he should sprinkle the hill with the blood of a young orphan boy, born of the fairies. Such a boy was eventually found at Carmarthen, and his name was Myrddin Emrys (or Merlin) – allowing Geoffrey to make the erroneous claim that the name Carmarthen (*Kaermerdin*) means the 'fortress of Merlin'. The boy told Vortigern that the hill contained a pool, beneath which were two sleeping dragons, and he was proved right when Vortigern had the hill excavated and the dragons began to fight. Merlin explained that the white one represented the Saxons, and that although it was gaining the upper hand for the time being, it would soon be defeated by the red dragon, which represented the Britons. Whatever the truth of all this, Dinas Emrys seems to have been an important site in sub-Roman Wales, and both a pool and a tower have been found here, albeit on different parts of the crag. The rectangular stone tower was probably built by Llywelyn ap Iorwerth.

27 Like most Welsh castles in north Wales, the purpose of Castell y Bere was not so much to resist English invasion as to secure Gwynedd internally. It was built by Llywelyn ap Iorwerth when he took Meirionnydd from his son, Gruffudd, in 1221, and it served as the last stronghold of Dafydd ap Gruffudd when he broke out of Gwynedd in March 1283. The castle was occupied by the English, but its importance was greatly diminished by the construction of Harlech, and it was destroyed by the Welsh in 1294.

and Maredudd ap Rhys Gryg from Kidwelly and Gwidigada. Royal intrusions were widely resented, and there was talk of oppression by 1243. Dafydd's cause was also helped by the death of his brother, who fell during an attempt to escape from the Tower in 1244. Henry's plan to divide Gwynedd now revolved around Gruffudd's son, Owain Goch, who did fealty and was promised two *cantrefi* and all the lands due to him by hereditary right. Owain was sent to Chester, but he went no further – Dafydd was now the focus of Welsh discontent, and Henry's only allies in native Wales were Gruffudd ap Madog, Gruffudd ap Gwenwynwyn and Morgan ap Hywel. Seeing his chance, Dafydd seized the initiative within months, invading Cyfeiliog – where he captured Tafolwern – preventing John Lestrange's troops from relieving the castle at Diserth (which had been built in 1241), and harassing the English border.

Having seen Henry's antipathy to Gwynedd, Dafydd did not share his father's desire for a feudal relationship. His own experience taught him that recognition of overlordship amounted to little more than acceptance of increasing and destructive intrusion, and indeed the erosion of the very fabric of native Welsh independence. He therefore resolved to remove himself from royal lordship altogether, and made representations to Pope Innocent IV in 1244 that Gwynedd should become a papal fee for 500 marks *per annum*. Possibly inspired by the example of Reginald of Man, who placed his kingdom under papal patronage in 1219, Dafydd used Honorius III's recognition of his position as heir in the 1220s to claim that he and his kingdom were subject only to the pope. The argument was groundless, but Innocent was sympathetic, and he may have welcomed the opportunity to exercise his theory of papal sovereignty. Henry was accordingly summoned to meet papal commissioners at Caerwys to answer the charge that Dafydd's homage in 1241 had been exacted by force, and that it was therefore void. Inevitably, however, Dafydd's efforts failed. Henry was well aware that Innocent was keen to secure his co-operation against Emperor Frederick II at the council of Lyons in 1245, and he failed to appear to answer the charges. Instead, the king made his own representations to the pope, and his promise to pay his considerable debts to the papacy was enough to induce Innocent to reverse his decision in 1245, saying that Dafydd's predecessors had always been vassals of the king. Matthew Paris commented sardonically that justice had not been achieved without great expenditure, and there was a great deal of truth in his cynicism. Dafydd had shown ingenuity and resolve, but he was out of his depth when caught between the great powers of Europe. The approach to the pope had been exposed as another act of desperation.

Nevertheless, this was a serious attempt to leave the king's lordship. The pope had implicitly recognised the title 'prince of north Wales' – which Henry had failed to acknowledge in 1240, and both ignored and stripped of meaning in 1241 – and Dafydd styled himself 'prince of Wales' in early 1245. He now headed a powerful alliance, as imposing as any headed by his father, and the long list of his followers included not only the Welsh of Powys and Deheubarth but also several native rulers in the march, notably Rhys ap Gruffudd of Senghennydd, Hywel ap Maredudd of Meisgyn and the sons of Morgan Gam of Afan. Between them, the allies defeated Herbert fitz Matthew and Ralph Mortimer, and captured Mold, while the English gained only one victory, near Montgomery. The *de facto* supremacy of Gwynedd was being restored, and Henry did not underestimate it. Whereas he had responded to previous papal requests for tribute by pleading financial hardship, he brought his payments up to date by 1245, and he also resorted to military action against Gwynedd. Dafydd's appeal to the pope was rejected some months before hostilities began, but the war of 1245 was fought in the context of an argument about Welsh independence which had been made more explicit than ever. It seemed that Gwynedd must now prosper or die.

The harshness, brutality and cruelty of the fighting reflected the growing stakes, but the war achieved little. Henry strengthened the castle at Degannwy, but only with difficulty, and the Irish force he sent to ravage Môn suffered severe losses and eventually withdrew. The military stalemate allowed Dafydd to recover some prestige, but it was scarcely a victory for either side. Famine – caused by a trade embargo, the weather and the war itself – reduced both armies to starvation, and a desperate fight broke out when an Irish ship carrying food and wine ran aground near the castle at Degannwy, leading to atrocities by both sides. Moreover, in the words of Matthew Paris, Degannwy remained a thorn in the eye for Gwynedd, and any hope of a revival of the principality was crushed when Dafydd died early in 1246.

Without a leader, Welsh resistance collapsed. Nicholas de Molis, the royal custodian of Carmarthen and Cardigan, already believed that Maredudd ab Owain, Rhys Mechyll and Maredudd ap Rhys were prepared to submit, and, outside Gwynedd, only Hywel ap Maredudd and Maelgwn Fychan failed to make peace – these two were both ejected from their lands. De Molis demonstrated the extent of Welsh capitulation when he took a force into Meirionnydd – where Llywelyn Fawr submitted – and carried on through Snowdonia as far as Degannwy in one of the most dramatic military expeditions in Welsh history. Gwynedd's defeat was complete. It was now in the hands of Owain ap Gruffudd – who had returned from Chester – and his younger brother, Llywelyn, and a territorial division between them was soon made.

Under the terms of Gwern Eigron, Dafydd's lack of an heir and his revolt against Henry meant that Gwynedd should now pass to the king. Henry was unable to assume direct control in practice, since Gwynedd Uwch Conwy was not conquered, but he could exert influence by other means – the hardships of war and the loss of the Perfeddwlad ensured that Gwynedd would not defy him for long. There were also internal pressures: Henry no doubt connived at the sudden emergence of Maredudd ap Rhisiart in Llŷn, and the influential group of men with lands both west and east of the Conwy were keen for peace on the best possible terms. Owain and Llywelyn had no option but to submit.

THE PARTITION AND RE–UNIFICATION OF GWYNEDD

The treaty of Woodstock in 1247 marked the greatest royal success to date, and by the same token it reflected the feebleness of Gwynedd. In an allusion to the terms of 1241, Henry condescendingly pardoned Owain and Llywelyn for making war on him, and the brothers quitclaimed the Perfeddwlad and Mold to the king for ever. These territorial gains, together with a growing share of the march, meant that the king – not the Welsh or the marchers – was now by far the most powerful force in Wales, and he underpinned his position by invest-ing massively in the defence and exploitation of his newly acquired interests. Owain and Llywelyn also did homage and were denied the right to receive Welsh homages, and Henry renewed the threat of forfeiture should they or their heirs revolt. Moreover, Gwynedd was now a royal fee, held on condition of military service – Owain, Llywelyn and their heirs were bound to provide the king, on request, with 1,000 footsoldiers and 24 knights for service in Wales, or 500 footsoldiers for service in the march. Furthermore, although he could not conquer Gwynedd Uwch Conwy, Henry weakened it from within by insisting upon the practical application of the principle of partibility. Homage was accordingly done by both Owain and Llywelyn ap Gruffudd, and the grant of Llŷn to Maredudd ap Rhisiart early in 1247 divided the kingdom into three. Gruffudd's younger sons, Dafydd and Rhodri, provided an excuse for further fragmentation, and Henry took Dafydd's homage in 1253, ordering Llywelyn and Owain to allow him his inheritance 'according to the custom of Wales', knowing that this would cause unrest throughout Gwynedd. In 1254, Dafydd's case was submitted to a royal commission at Chester, which also considered Llywelyn's objections – it continued into 1255, when Llywelyn was summoned to the king, while another commission was appointed to deal with Owain's grievances against Llywelyn. Similarly, Henry sowed the seeds of future tension by promising that Welshmen who held lands in north Wales could continue to hold them as before, knowing that this would inevitably split the loyalties of those who held lands in both Gwynedd Uwch Conwy and the Perfed-dwlad between Gwynedd and the king. Moreover, the agreement that legal cases in Wales should be heard, not at the royal court, but at places designated by royal officials within Wales and the march, to be judged according to Welsh law, was much more than a simple repetition of Magna Carta. Whereas royal officials had previously been empowered to deal with specific issues in *pura Wallia* – namely the restoration of lands and rights in 1215 and the position of Gruffudd ap Llywelyn in 1241 – the 1247 treaty in effect allowed all pleas in native Wales to be submitted to royal courts. This was a significant and novel development, extending the jurisdiction of the king and seriously undermining not just Gwynedd but all of Wales.

Precedents were scarce, but a new principle that pleas between Welshmen should be held in royal courts and judged according to Welsh law (the inter- pretation of which was often flawed) was being carefully formulated. The same was true of the policy of partition, which was applied to Meirionnydd in 1241 – when Llywelyn Fawr and Llywelyn Fychan did homage and paid £40 – and to Ceri in 1245, when Hywel ap Cadwallon and Maredudd ap Maelgwn did homage for only half of the *cantref*. Similarly, Gruffudd ap Madog of Bromfield was made to share his lands equally with his kinsfolk (*consanguineos*) in 1253, 'according to the custom of Wales'. It was no doubt the threat from co-heirs which prompted Gruffudd to swear mutual support with Llywelyn ap Gruf- fudd 'against all men, whether great or small' in 1250.[6] Payments of relief (in re- turn for tenure) were also introduced: Owain ap Maredudd of Cydewain paid 300 marks for seisin of his lands in 1248, and an enquiry was ordered in 1251 to find whether relief (*relevium*) should be paid for Meirionnydd. As early as 1244, Gruffudd ap Madog – who supported the king in 1241 – was concerned at the possibility that new laws were being foisted upon Powys Fadog, and he asked that native laws and privileges might be respected. Shire courts were also introduced at Carmarthen and Cardigan after the death of Gilbert Marshal in 1240, and Rhys Fychan and Maredudd ap Rhys accepted subjection to them when they submitted after 1246. By 1248, there was no dispute about where cases were heard, only about whether Welsh law be used. This was merely part of Henry's intensification of lordship over his dominions as a whole, not least in the march. As an instrument for draining independence away from royal vassals throughout Wales, jurisdiction was as effective as any military conquest, and Henry's success in this respect was so sweeping that Edward I used 1240 as a *terminus a quo* in his dealings with Wales.

The dynastic wounds in Gwynedd needed to be healed quickly, and this prompted Owain and Llywelyn ap Gruffudd to work closely together. They pledged mutual support with Rhys Fychan and Maredudd ap Rhys in 1250 and 1251, and in a symbolic appeal for unity within Gwynedd, their father's body was removed from London to be buried with his own father and brother at Aberconwy in 1248; Llywelyn ap Iorwerth and his sons now lay at peace together. Fraternal co-operation was unlikely to survive the immediate crisis,

however, and Llywelyn, although younger than Owain, emerged as the dominant brother by the 1250s. His superiority in Gwynedd was almost assured
after 1246, as he controlled the mountainous territory of Snowdonia whereas
Owain was confined to the more prosperous but less militarily useful south and
west of Gwynedd. Moreover, the undermining of native custom in the treaty
of 1247 paradoxically contributed in practice to consolidation in Gwynedd.
Frustrated with time-consuming processes of royal justice which they feared
might not work to their advantage, Owain and Dafydd took a more traditional
approach and revolted against Llywelyn in 1255, and his subsequent victory at
Bryn Derwin left him as the sole ruler of Gwynedd Uwch Conwy. With his
brothers imprisoned and their supporters won over by threats and promises,
Llywelyn could begin to look further afield.

In 1256, Llywelyn broke the treaty of Woodstock by invading the Perfeddwlad. His action was largely provoked by Henry's policy of partition, which
created such strains that territorial expansion was almost the only means by
which his younger brothers could be accommodated. It appears that Llywelyn originally intended that the king should provide for Dafydd in the
Perfeddwlad, but the talks failed. Instead, Llywelyn released his brother on the
eve of his attack, clearly hoping that Dafydd would conquer lands for himself.
Such was the prince's concern to avoid further partition that he even offered
the Perfeddwlad to the king in perpetuity in return for recognition as the sole
ruler of Gwynedd. When this came to nothing, an assault on the region by
Gwynedd became almost inevitable.

Llywelyn was aided by considerable resentment of royal rule. The Perfeddwlad had been administered by the justice of Chester since 1247, and it seems
that the rights of tenants who held lands both east and west of the Conwy
were not respected as agreed. Furthermore, although English rule was not new
in Tegeingl, the oppressive activities of John de Grey provoked opposition in
Rhos, Rhufoniog and Dyffryn Clwyd, where royal authority was secured only
by the castles of Degannwy, Rhuddlan and Diserth. De Grey was succeeded in
1251 by Alan la Zouche, who pursued an aggressive policy against Welsh law
and flaunted the money he had taken from the Welsh. Before long, the Welsh
were complaining, and Henry was forced to make concessions. In 1251, he demanded only those services which had been due to Llywelyn ap Iorwerth, and
in 1253 he released the men of the three less-anglicised *cantrefi* from an obligation imposed by la Zouche to serve the king in Gascony. These measures were
not enough, however, and the grant of Chester to Henry's son Edward in 1254
did nothing to ease the problem. Edward's justice of Chester, Geoffrey Langley,
continued la Zouche's efforts to introduce English law in the face of Welsh
refusals to abandon their own native law, and he boasted scornfully that he had

the Welsh under his control. By the time Edward visited the region in person in 1256, the situation was reaching a head. The Welsh of the Perfeddwlad reported the oppression to Llywelyn, saying that they would prefer death in fighting for freedom to the bondage in which they were held under foreign English rule. The prince was assured of widespread support, and he confidently asserted his right to the Perfeddwlad *de iure*.

The Perfeddwlad fell within a week, and Llywelyn's momentum won him control of most of *pura Wallia* within a few months. Llywelyn ap Maredudd was ejected from Meirionnydd, leaving Llywelyn ap Gruffudd supreme from the Dyfi to the Dee by the end of 1256, and the prince soon moved into Deheubarth, putting the 1251 alliance with Maredudd ap Rhys into practice: Maredudd supported him in the Perfeddwlad, and Llywelyn in turn helped Maredudd to recover the inheritance of which he had recently been deprived by Rhys Fychan ap Rhys Mechyll and an English force, and added to it. Maredudd now held the whole of Ystrad Tywi, including Dinefwr, and this success prompted Maredudd ab Owain of Ceredigion to join Llywelyn soon afterwards. Together with these allies, Llywelyn now attacked Powys Wenwynwyn, and, despite Gruffudd ap Madog's allegiance to the king, Gwerthrynion was taken, as was Buellt – which was entrusted to Maredudd ab Owain – while Gruffudd ap Gwenwynwyn was driven out of all his lands except Welshpool, part of the Severn valley and a portion of Caereinion. By the end of 1257, Llywelyn had overthrown the territorial *status quo* of 1241 and 1247, and achieved a supremacy comparable with that of his grandfather. He now needed royal recognition of his feat.

Llywelyn ap Gruffudd:
the Principality of Wales
Won and Lost
1257–1283

Llywelyn ap Gruffudd's Unofficial Principality

By 1258, Llywelyn ap Gruffudd was able to call himself 'prince of Wales' with some credibility, but he received no royal recognition of his position. He would find it no easier to realise the ambition of creating a principality of Wales than had his predecessors.

Gwynedd's supremacy in Deheubarth depended almost entirely upon the support of Maredudd ap Rhys. The king made great efforts to restore Rhys Fychan at Maredudd's expense after Llywelyn's victories in early 1257, but the scheme failed when Stephen Bauzan was routed at Cymerau by Maredudd ap Rhys and Maredudd ab Owain. Nevertheless, Henry's ability to inflame dissension against Llywelyn was clear, and the Welsh victory did not prevent dynastic difficulties in Deheubarth. Rhys Fychan's desertion to Llywelyn before the battle obliged the prince to revise the partition he had made previously with Maredudd, and although a settlement was reached, Maredudd's hopes were sacrificed in the interests of Gwynedd's security. His loyalty was now suspect, and although Llywelyn secured it for a while by taking his fealty in 1258, Maredudd soon broke his faith, necessitating intervention from Gwynedd on two further occasions in the same year. Nonetheless, Llywelyn's position in the south was strong enough to allow him to move into Dyfed in 1257, capturing the castles of Laugharne, Llansteffan, Narberth and Trefdraeth, ravaging the *cantref* of Rhos, taking Nicholas fitz Martin of Cemais prisoner, and seizing his lands. Moreover, his ability to do this was greatly enhanced by a growing sense of Welsh resistance to royal rule.

Henry hoped that a solution could be negotiated, but he soon organised a military campaign, expecting to win the support of Owain and Dafydd ap Gruffudd. His purpose was to recover the Perfeddwlad and to capture Môn and Penllyn. Despite reaching Degannwy, however, he was hampered by the failure of supplies to arrive from either England or Ireland, as well as by disruption in England. The expedition was abandoned with a half-hearted promise to return again and to capture Môn, and Gruffudd ap Madog of Bromfield soon defected to Llywelyn. Henry was more successful in Deheubarth, where Maredudd ap Rhys was enticed to do homage, and was granted all of Ystrad Tywi – except the *cwmwd* of Gwidigada – as well as the *cymydau* of Mabwynion and Gwynionydd in Ceredigion Is Aeron. Although the grant was speculative, the king was able to offer as much as Llywelyn, undertaking not to make reconciliation with Rhys Fychan or Maredudd ab Owain without Maredudd's permission. In addition, Carmarthen and Cardigan seem to have been established as refuges for those who sought to escape Llywelyn.

Llywelyn was now in a position of strength, and in 1258 he adopted the style 'prince of Wales'. His supporters included practically all of the Welsh of *pura Wallia*, and Llywelyn exacted fealty and probably homage from them. At the same time, he introduced himself into the international arena, making a pact with the supporters of Walter Comyn, the earl of Menteith, who had led a palace revolution against Alexander III of Scots in 1251. Neither party would make any agreement with either the king or barons of England or the barons of Scotland without the other's consent (unless they were already in alliance), the Scots would not give Henry military assistance in Wales, and trading links between Wales and Scotland were to be encouraged. Llywelyn could now bargain with Henry for a treaty, and he offered him 4,000 marks for peace. No treaty was made, however. The king's plans to return to Gwynedd with another army were aborted, but Henry's meeting with his disaffected barons at Oxford resulted in nothing of benefit to Gwynedd, and Llywelyn ended the year with no more than recognition of his conquests and a truce. Furthermore, the baronial reforms of 1258 and 1259 meant that he now had to deal with powerful marcher lords at the heart of the English government – Richard de Clare of Gloucester, Humphrey de Bohun of Hereford, James Audley and Roger Mortimer were all members of the Council of Fifteen to which the king was now subject under Simon de Montfort. It was no surprise, therefore, when Llywelyn's request in 1259 for the lands and homages of the Welsh – which he claimed had been held by his grandfather – was rejected, despite his offer of homage, fealty and a number of concessions: these would either be payments of £11,000 to the king, £3,000 to Edward and £2,500 to the queen (at £200 *per annum*), or alternatively a marriage with Henry's niece, the *cymydau* of Prestatyn and Creuddyn (including the castles of Diserth and Degannwy) and either the restoration of lands taken from the marchers or a seven-year truce (together with a payment of £700). Instead, Henry insisted on arranging nothing more than an extension of the truce. Considerable trouble might have been saved for all parties had Llywelyn been recognised as prince of Wales in 1258 or 1259, but Henry's precarious position in England made him unable to make a meaningful treaty. Moreover, Henry was loath to recognise a prince of Wales, who would reserve the homages of the Welsh to himself. Gwynedd and the king were still on a collision course.

In 1260, Llywelyn attempted to force Henry to the negotiating table by attacking Buellt. Both sides were ready to talk, but nothing was agreed beyond the maintenance of the *status quo* of 1258 and the lifting of Henry's trade embargo. The king recognised Llywelyn's *de facto* authority by holding him responsible for all Welsh transgressions of the truce, but a truce was no guarantee of the permanence of Gwynedd's supremacy. From 1260 until 1262, Llywelyn's requests for a peace settlement were met with excuses and procrastination, and, although each side scrupulously made amends for breaches of the truce, border incidents became increasingly frequent. It seemed that Llywelyn was destined to suffer the same endless frustration as his grandfather.

There was no doubt in Henry's mind that Llywelyn was a hostile subordinate, and that his inflated position was illegitimate, even within Gwynedd itself. This much is readily apparent in the king's plans when it was rumoured in 1262 that Llywelyn was dead. Since Owain ap Gruffudd was still alive, Llywelyn was not felt to be the rightful heir to Gwynedd, and his brother Dafydd had no right to succeed him – instead, in the event of Llywelyn's death, the Welsh were to be regarded as 'our enemies', and Dafydd's supposed lordship was described as 'presumptuous'.[1] Gruffudd ap Madog was to be enticed back into the king's fealty and it was to be ensured that Maredudd ap Rhys remained in it, while a large army was to be summoned at Shrewsbury, defence of the whole march was to be organised, and the marchers were to be encouraged to re-conquer the lands they had lost to the Welsh. Above all, it was to be stressed that Welsh homages had always belonged to the king alone, and that it was the prerogative of the king – not the prince – to administer justice in Wales and to determine the heir to Gwynedd. Such implacable opposition – albeit private and unvoiced – gave Llywelyn no option but to go to war again.

The attack by the men of Maelienydd on Roger Mortimer's new castle at Cefnllys in 1262 allowed the prince a chance to intervene in an area of crucial strategic importance. He took the castles of Cefnllys, Bleddfa, Knucklas, Knighton, Norton and Presteigne, and captured the whole of Maelienydd as far as Weobley, Eardisley and Roger Mortimer's lordship of Wigmore. Roger was the sole target of this attack, and this was no coincidence. Llywelyn had complained of his incursions into Powys Fadog earlier in the year, and Mortimer seems to have believed that his claims to Maelienydd were recognised implicitly in the truce. Moreover, Llywelyn's claim that his own complaints were receiving less of the king's attention than those of his opponents suggests a sense that his efforts were being undermined by sympathy towards vested marcher interests. Such suspicions seemed to be justified in 1263 when Mortimer frustrated the king's attempts to reach a settlement with Llywelyn by imprisoning Philip le Bret, the royal messenger who was sent to gain his consent for renewed talks with the prince. Llywelyn and Henry were ready to discuss peace even during the fighting of 1262 and 1263, but Mortimer prevented it. Llywelyn's attack was clearly intended to force Roger, as well as the king, into negotiations.

The assault on Cefnllys obliged Henry to resort to force. There could be no concessions to the Welsh, who had broken the truce and also their homage and fealty. By 1263, the Welsh of Brycheiniog, Blaenllyfni, Elfael, Ystrad Yw and Crickhowell – that is, the whole south-eastern march as far as Abergavenny – were flocking to Llywelyn's side. The men of Brycheiniog even did homage to him, and it was feared that he intended to overrun Gwent. But his army, which included Maredudd ab Owain, Maredudd ap Rhys and Rhys Fychan, was defeated at Abergavenny, and Llywelyn was eager to negotiate. Prospects of peace were destroyed, however, when Henry ordered his son, Edward, to help Mortimer in putting down the revolt. Llywelyn had relied upon the support of Mortimer's tenants in the Maelienydd campaign – indeed, as a self-styled prince of Wales he could scarcely refuse the offer of the allegiance of the Welsh in the march – but this had brought him into direct confrontation with powerful marcher interests. The prince's problems were compounded by the defection of his brother, Dafydd, to the king before Edward and Mortimer took the offensive, and also by the renewed formation of a baronial party against Henry under Simon de Montfort in 1263. Edward's efforts in Wales came to nothing, and parts of the march became a battleground between the English as Roger Clifford, John Giffard, John fitz Alan and others joined Simon. These domestic troubles forced Henry to shelve plans for another Welsh campaign, but they also meant that Llywelyn was once again denied any meaningful recognition.

The unrest did, however, allow Llywelyn to strengthen his position. John fitz Alan, in his search for allies, granted him Dyffryn Tefeidiad in Elfael, and the prince ejected Edward from Degannwy and Carreg Faelan (Diserth). It was rumoured in England that he was in collusion with dissenting marchers as early as 1262, but he did not act in co-operation with de Montfort until their joint attack on Radnor in 1264. Llywelyn was more concerned to consolidate his position in native Wales, and in 1263 he received the grudging homage and fealty of Gruffudd ap Gwenwynwyn, who was driven to support Gwynedd by a dispute with Thomas Corbet over lands in the border *cwmwd* of Gorddwr. The issue had been alive since at least 1252, and, as a supporter of the king, Gruffudd had attacked the castle of Gwyddgrug when Thomas joined the rebels; when Corbet returned to the king's fealty, however, Gruffudd was forced to turn to Llywelyn, who controlled most of his lands. The relationship between Llywelyn and Gruffudd was therefore based firmly on expediency, and their mutual mistrust is shown by the agreement between them that each party would make amends should they fight each other. They also recognised the possibility that Gruffudd might lose Welshpool, which Llywelyn may have intended to capture from him. The fragility of Llywelyn's position was illustrated again when Edward dislodged him from parts of Brycheiniog in 1264, but this seemed of little consequence when Henry and Edward were defeated and captured by de Montfort and his baronial allies at Lewes. Llywelyn's task now was to gain recognition from Simon, and this would not be easy. Although the prince had played an important part in the defeat of the king's marcher allies, including Roger Mortimer, his authority in Wales was still not comprehensive.

De Montfort's priorities had changed. He was no longer a rebel baron looking for allies against the king; as ruler of England, he now inherited Henry's concerns. The new regime seems to have been sympathetic to Llywelyn, but nothing significant was achieved. Llywelyn may have arranged to marry Simon's daughter, Eleanor, at this time, probably in reaction to the defection of Dafydd, who may have been his heir, in 1263. But the treaty he wanted still eluded him. By the time talks began in 1265, Simon faced mounting opposition in the march, and he could not guarantee to uphold any treaty. Llywelyn was even obliged to take hostages from him to ensure good faith, and the king remained helpless in prison. The treaty of Pipton, made between Llywelyn and Simon and sealed by Henry, was practically meaningless, although it revealed both the prince's prestige – he brought the leaders of Powys and Deheubarth with him – and his determination to achieve a revocation of all previous treaties. The king was compelled to recognise the title 'prince of Wales', allowing Llywelyn and the heirs of his body lordship over all the lords of Wales and the whole of the 'principality of Wales', including the recent acquisitions of Elfael Is Mynydd, Ellesmere, Hawarden and Whittington, and Simon was also to help Llywelyn to recover lands such as Montgomery which were legally his, but which were held by his enemies. In return, the prince and his heirs would hold the principality of the king, doing the same services as his predecessors, and paying £20,000 over ten years.

Knowing that the treaty meant nothing, Llywelyn remained wary. Only days after its confirmation, hostilities flared again in England, and de Montfort was killed at Evesham within months. Baronial resistance to Henry was destroyed, and the prince saw that he might soon be able to deal with a unified England. He therefore acted rapidly to establish a bargaining position, capturing Hawarden and routing Hamo Lestrange and Maurice fitz Gerald in north Wales in 1265 and Roger Mortimer in Brycheiniog in 1266. English affairs were now under the discretion of the papal legate Ottobuono, who soon realised that his original brief from Pope Clement IV – to ensure that Llywelyn submitted to the king and renounced all agreements made with de Montfort – was impracticable. The time appeared ripe at last for a treaty. A truce was arranged, but Llywelyn was once again frustrated by Mortimer, whose rivalry with Gilbert de Clare delayed negotiations for two years. Indeed, the prince himself jeopardised his opportunity by his involvement in a similar dispute with Gilbert in 1267. Even when Llywelyn finally met Ottobuono and royal representatives, neither side was confident that the meeting would be fruitful.

The Principality of Wales

THE NATURE OF THE PRINCIPALITY

After days of negotiation at Shrewsbury, Llywelyn met Henry at Rhyd Chwima, a ford over the river Severn near Montgomery. Here, in September 1267, the principality of Wales was formally constituted, and Llywelyn performed homage and fealty for it four days later. The treaty of Montgomery recognised Llywelyn and his heirs as princes of Wales, and thereby marked the first attempt to ensure Anglo-Welsh stability within a constitutional framework. The principality consisted of the homages of all the Welsh of Wales and lordship over all of their lands – with the exception of Maredudd ap Rhys – and it was to be held *in capite*. Llywelyn's elevated position among the princes of *pura Wallia* now had royal sanction at last, and it was envisaged that Henry might eventually sell the prince Maredudd's homage for 5,000 marks. The Perfeddwlad was formally restored to Llywelyn, and he was confirmed in possession of Gwerthrynion, Buellt, Brycheiniog, Cydewain, Ceri and Whittington. Most of the ambitions of Gwynedd had at last been satisfied, and consolidation of its sphere of influence as a political and administrative entity called 'Wales' was now a real prospect.

But Llywelyn now faced many challenges. Not least, he was bound to pay the huge sum of 25,000 marks, which, although it was to be paid in instalments, was sure to strain his resources. In addition, Gruffudd ap Gwenwynwyn was to keep the lands he held before 1263, and, although Llywelyn was given a free hand in restoring Dafydd ap Gruffudd to his inheritance, Dafydd was also to recover the lands he had held before 1263. Moreover, if he was not satisfied with the provisions made for him, Dafydd could appeal to the king, who would send officials to see that justice was done – they were intended merely as observers, but they would very likely advocate Henry's interpretation of 'the laws and customs of Wales'. It seems, therefore, that Henry did not concede his claim of ultimate right to impose his own divisive version of Welsh law. Furthermore, Llywelyn was still forbidden to receive or aid the king's outlaws or enemies. The roles of tenant-in-chief and quasi-independent prince did not sit easily together, and it seems also that Henry deliberately made Llywelyn's rule as difficult as possible by lacing the treaty with bones of contention in the march. No boundaries were placed on the principality; there was no defini-tion of the 'Welsh barons of Wales'; and several territorial clauses were clearly provocative. In Maelienydd, the prince was given the lordship and castle (of Cefnllys?) if he could establish his right there, but Roger Mortimer was also allowed to build a castle there if he pleased. Similarly, although Hawarden was conceded to Robert de Montalt, he was not permitted to build a castle there for 60 years – a provision which almost encouraged Llywelyn to attack that part of the Perfeddwlad. The treaty did not even mention Elfael, despite the homage of Owain ap Maredudd to Llywelyn for Elfael Uwch Mynydd in 1260, and despite Llywelyn's *de facto* control of Elfael Is Mynydd. Llywe-lyn would have to tread extremely carefully if he was to avoid being seen as overstepping the treaty on the one hand, or as failing to fulfil his obligations to the Welsh people as their prince on the other. Conflict in the march was inevitable, and Llywelyn needed a further understanding with the marchers.

THE SEARCH FOR POLITICAL STABILITY

As he left Montgomery, Llywelyn was already distracted by disputes in Mor-gannwg. Hywel ap Maredudd had supported Gwynedd since 1246, and Lly-welyn had been involved in Blaenau Morgannwg since 1262, but he made no concerted effort in the region until 1267. Early in that year, Gruffudd ap Rhys of Senghennydd was captured and imprisoned by Gilbert de Clare, appar-ently in direct response to action by Llywelyn, who claimed Gruffudd's hom-age on the grounds that he was a Welsh baron of Wales. The king's ambigu-ous reaction to this satisfied neither Llywelyn nor Gilbert. Henry explained that Gruffudd was certainly a Welsh lord in Wales, but that his homage had always belonged to the lord of Glamorgan and his lands lay in the 'Englishry'. By 1268, frustration led Gilbert to build a castle at Caerphilly in the *cwmwd* of Senghennydd Is Caeach, and fruitless negotiations continued into 1269, while Llywelyn held Senghennydd Uwch Caeach and the northern part of the *cwmwd* of Meisgyn. In the meantime, Llywelyn was encouraged by the simultaneous case of Maredudd ap Gruffudd, in which the king adjudged that Maredudd's homage for the *cymydau* of Machen (in Gwynllŵg), Edeligion and Llebenydd (in Caerleon) should belong to the prince, despite the fact that these lands were part of the lordship of Glamorgan. The verdict primarily reflected Henry's hostility towards the Clares, but the king had accepted the principle that native lords within the march might be deemed to be tenants of the prince at the expense of the marchers. Nevertheless, in confronting Gilbert, Llywelyn had involved himself needlessly in another dispute, and made a powerful enemy at a time when he could barely afford it.

Edward played a crucial role in Llywelyn's success between 1267 and 1270. Their meetings during the hearings of the Morgannwg cases were noticeably friendly, and it was Edward's need to finance his crusade in 1270 which seems eventually to have persuaded Henry to sell the homage of Maredudd ap Rhys. Edward was by now the chief executive of royal power, and his absence on crusade meant that no binding royal decisions could be made during the remaining 27 months of the old king's reign. Recognising the significance of Edward's departure, Llywelyn asked Henry that all disputes might be settled before Edward left, but he was too late. More worryingly for Llywelyn, friendly relations were now established between Gilbert de Clare and Roger Mortimer, and it was no doubt this influence which prompted Henry to warn the prince in 1270 not to interfere in Gilbert's relations with his vassals. Sensing the changing political climate, Llywelyn attacked and burned the castle of Caerphilly, but Gilbert rebuilt it in 1271, and Henry's attempts to mediate did not prevent Llywelyn from attacking it once again. Llywelyn and Henry arranged for Caerphilly to be taken into royal custody, but Gilbert was not party to the agreement, and he soon reoccupied the castle. An attempt to resolve the matter according to the 1267 treaty in the presence of mutually acceptable arbitrators also failed, and in 1272 the king passed the case on to Edward, the 'friend of the prince',[2] who was said to be on his way home. Having frustrated Llywelyn once again, Henry died in 1272.

Llywelyn also faced problems in Elfael – where he had cause to doubt the loyalty of Iorwerth ap Llywelyn and Meurig ap Gruffudd by 1271 – and Brycheiniog, where the same was true of Einion Sais ap Rhys and Meurig ap Llywelyn. His prospects became bleaker still with the appointment of Roger Mortimer as a key member of Edward I's regency government. Gwynedd was now opposed not only by the most powerful marchers – Mortimer, Clare and de Bohun – but by the royal administration itself, whose animosity was made apparent after Humphrey de Bohun pressed claims in Brycheiniog in 1272. It was declared in 1273 that the *gwlad* belonged to Humphrey, and Llywelyn was warned against attempting to recover his losses. No explanation was given, but Mortimer's private discussions with Robert Burnell and Walter Merton made clear that their only concern was to justify royal intervention in a marcher affair. The spurious argument was adopted that, although Llywelyn held the land of Brycheiniog under the 1267 treaty, there had been no mention of the castles, which should pass to Humphrey. The result was that the prince was now held to be in breach of the treaty. Llywelyn was unaware of the details of this thinking, but he realised that he could not trust the government to respect the treaty. In the absence of his friend, Edward, he therefore ignored the summons to do fealty to the new king in 1273.

Relations were strained further when Llywelyn began to build a castle at Dolforwyn in Cydewain in 1273. Opposition to his creation of a borough there was natural, since it would affect the nearby boroughs of Montgomery and Welshpool, but the prince was soon ordered not to proceed with the castle at all. In response, Llywelyn voiced his own misgivings, saying that he did not believe that Edward would issue such an order. He asked the king to ignore attempts to poison his thoughts, and went on to assert his right and that of his predecessors to build castles and establish markets. Furthermore, he claimed that Roger Mortimer's construction work at Cefnllys was beyond what was allowed by the treaty. The prince's anger was understandable, but his case could not be proven. Roger was fully entitled to build a new castle, and moreover, the vagueness of Llywelyn's own status prevented a clear definition of his rights. It was obvious, nonetheless, that Mortimer, Clare and de Bohun were responsible for a deterioration of Anglo-Welsh relations. In his dissatisfaction with the regime in England, Llywelyn had still not done homage or fealty to the new king when Edward returned to England in 1274.

Homage was an issue on which Edward was not prepared to compromise. It was the single most potent and symbolic instrument of his overlordship, and it had been Llywelyn's only major concession to the king in 1267. Edward was unusually sensitive in matters which touched upon his regal status, and furthermore, he needed to maintain good relations with the marchers, especially Gilbert de Clare. Llywelyn's troublemaking could not be tolerated. For his part, the prince was also very particular – perhaps too particular – about the dignity of his office, and he was certain that his complaints were justified. In different circumstances, the bones of contention might have been removed by negotiation without either side losing face, but the combination of anger, suspicion and pride on both sides made it very difficult to find a solution. The prince had failed to keep up the treaty payments, probably because of his financial difficulties, but this too was turned into a matter of principle. Llywelyn now refused to pay any more until the king upheld the treaty by restoring the lands taken by the marchers, and he raised the temperature of the debate further by failing to attend Edward's coronation. Instead, he insisted on discussions, but his hopes were dashed again when illness – apparently genuine – prevented Edward from meeting him. Subsequent events showed this missed opportunity for reconciliation to be very costly.

The decisive breach came when Dafydd ap Gruffudd and Gruffudd ap Gwenwynwyn sought and were given safe refuge in England after plotting to kill Llywelyn in 1274. Edward connived at their regular border raids, the spoils of which were sold openly in Montgomery and Shrewsbury, and he was even asked for advice on how best to do harm to Llywelyn. The prince was deeply disturbed by the treachery against him, and he naturally resented Edward's support of his enemies. This was an intolerable intrusion into his principality, and he was placed in a dilemma when he was summoned to do homage and fealty in 1275. He needed to make his peace with the king, but he was also very wary of placing his trust in him. In August 1275, Edward waited to receive Llywelyn's homage at Chester while the prince pondered his options at Treuddyn, a mere 12 miles to the west. Both sides seem to have wanted reconciliation, but there was very little room for maneouvre. After deep thought and consultation, Llywelyn resolved not to go to Chester, and Edward returned home in fury. In total, the prince was to refuse five separate demands for homage in 1275 and 1276, and the result was an atmosphere of growing mutual suspicion. Both Edward and Llywelyn became increasingly sensitive, and actions which were intended by one side as bargaining counters came to be regarded by the other as calculated insults. Suspicion turned into mistrust, and mistrust into mutual intransigence. Conflict was becoming inevitable.

Relations were strained to breaking point by Llywelyn's decision in 1275 to act upon an old agreement to marry Eleanor de Montfort. The prince was concerned to make allies and perhaps to reassess his succession plans after the revolt of 1274, but the timing of the marriage suggests that this was also an act of defiance in response to the king's support of his enemies. It was certainly provocative, since Edward's animosity towards the de Montforts had recently been renewed by an incident in southern Italy: his cousin, Henry of Almain, had been sent to seek reconciliation with Simon and Guy, the sons of Simon de Montfort, but they had murdered him in a church. Old wounds were reopened, and it was clear that a Welsh alliance with the de Montforts was very much against the royal interest. Edward's spies kept a close watch on Llywelyn, and it is very likely that the king was aware that something was afoot between Gwynedd and the de Montforts in southern France. It seems that the prince may have decided to marry Eleanor even before his failure to respond to Edward's second request for homage, and this intelligence cannot but have influenced the king's attitude during negotiations throughout the crisis.

Edward was pleased and relieved when Eleanor and her brother, Amaury, who were evidently on their way to Wales, were captured at sea by the men of Bristol late in 1275. He claimed that the incident was entirely providential, and cultivated the impression that he had known nothing about it – but it was very convenient for him nonetheless. Eleanor was imprisoned at Windsor, giving her no opportunity to provide Llywelyn's much-needed heir, and the fact that the couple had already been married by proxy added insult to injury. The prince complained to the papacy, and in response Edward told Pope Adrian V that he regarded the case as an internal English matter; it was not an international dispute, since Llywelyn was merely one of the greater magnates of his kingdom. Moreover, he pointed to the dangers of allowing the de Montforts into England, and cited Llywelyn's repeated failure to do homage as evidence of his unreasonableness. Unless the prince softened his attitude, the king felt himself bound by law and common consent to take firm action against him. For his part, Llywelyn was most aggrieved about Edward's support of Dafydd and Gruffudd, and was equally unwilling to yield.

Llywelyn did not react to further royal summonses, and in May 1276 Edward had him formally condemned. Military operations against him were already under way in Deheubarth, but – at Llywelyn's request – the Archbishop of Canterbury, Robert Kilwardby, checked the king's hand by acting as an intermediary for several months. Increasing tension in the march made his task almost impossible, however, and heated letters continued to be exchanged between Llywelyn and the king. In the meantime, the prince resisted marcher attacks, but he was still willing to offer homage at Oswestry or Montgomery on condition that he received a safe conduct and that Edward promised both to uphold the 1267 treaty and to release Eleanor. Edward, too, was willing to negotiate, but he insisted that homage must be performed unconditionally. In November 1276, Llywelyn was finally declared a rebel for his repeated failure to comply. Yet the king was still ready to consider any representation from the prince, and Kilwardby delayed the sentence of excommunication in order to allow Llywelyn a chance to redeem himself. The prince was prepared to do homage, to do justice to the barons of Wales and the marcher lords, and also to pay as much as 11,000 marks for peace, but he remained uncompromising. He feared imprisonment if he went to England, and he demanded that Roger Mortimer, Dafydd ap Gruffudd and Gruffudd ap Gwenwynwyn should stand as hostages to ensure his safety. Furthermore, he insisted on Eleanor's release, and protested that Edward had now received Llywelyn ap Gruffudd Fychan of Powys Fadog into his protection. The prince insisted that the fairness of his offer should be judged by the king of France, and he urged Edward to recognise his princely status and to put an end to hostilities until negotiations were finished. By 1277, there was little hope of agreement. Llywelyn was excommunicated, and the two sides prepared for war.

The king's military preparations and movements were purposeful, well organised, and executed quickly and on an enormous scale. Edward allowed the marchers a free hand as early as the spring of 1276, and by the time he travelled to Chester to enter the fray himself late in the year they had already taken Powys Wenwynwyn, Gwerthrynion, Ceri, Cydewain, Elfael, Buellt and Brycheiniog. When he eventually moved into Wales, the king followed the strategic approach of his predecessors, and his overwhelming superiority in men and resources ensured that Welsh resistance soon crumbled. Dolforwyn and Dinas Brân were taken early in 1277, and Powys Fadog and Deheubarth soon fell. Llywelyn's principality disintegrated in the face of this onslaught, as his supporters all submitted to the king. Most of Wales was now beholden to Edward, who added Ceredigion and Ystrad Tywi to his territorial acquisitions, and new castles were built at Aberystwyth and Builth. Direct royal lordship in Wales had been raised to a new level once again, and even the seat of the princes of Deheubarth at Dinefwr now became a centre of English rule. Many of Llywelyn's former adherents – including the rulers of Meirionnydd, Powys Fadog, Brycheiniog and Elfael, and indeed his own brother Dafydd – were now in the royal army, and perhaps the most crushing blow of all was the defection of many of the leading men of Gwynedd – including, strikingly, one Gruffudd ab yr Ynad, who may well be identifiable as the Gruffudd ab yr Ynad Coch who was to compose a passionate elegy for Llywelyn a few years later. Edward advanced as far as the Conwy, subjecting the Perfeddwlad, building powerful new castles at Flint and Rhuddlan – as well as others at Hawarden, Hope and Ruthin – and taking possession of the harvest in Môn. Llywelyn was at the king's mercy.

The End of Native Welsh Independence

THE DESTRUCTION OF LLYWELYN'S POWER AND AUTHORITY

Whether or not the fact was apparent to him in 1277, Edward faced a simple choice: he must either crush the principality or allow it eventually to secede from his kingdom. Unrest in England made him particularly keen to assert his authority, and he determined to humiliate Llywelyn as a rebel, to destroy the hegemony of Gwynedd, and to demonstrate that Wales was in his gift. Thus, during the campaign, he drew up a plan by which the prince would be dispossessed, the Perfeddwlad would pass into royal hands, and Gwynedd Uwch Conwy would be partitioned between Owain and Dafydd ap Gruffudd – each of them would do homage, and each would be liable to attend parliament in England. Edward would also retain Môn, and he was ready to hear any claims in Meirionnydd 'according to the laws and customs of Wales'.[3] In the meantime – until a formal peace was achieved – Dafydd was given the *cantrefi* of Dyffryn Clwyd and Rhufoniog. This arrangement suggests that Edward had abandoned hope of conquering Gwynedd Uwch Conwy, and the treaty of Aberconwy in

1277 appears to represent a compromise in some respects at least, since it was accepted that Dafydd would receive no more than lands in the Perfeddwlad.

The treaty destroyed the principality of 1267. Llywelyn submitted to Edward's will, swearing to pay £50,000 and to do fealty after his release from excommunication. The Perfeddwlad was conceded to the king and his heirs in perpetuity, and Edward retained all the lands he had taken in the war except Môn – this was to be held by Llywelyn, but only of the king's special grace for 1,000 marks *per annum*, and it would revert to the king should the prince die without an heir. Llywelyn was free, however, to claim lands which he had lost to men other than the king; such cases would be judged according to the laws and customs either of Wales or of the march, depending upon where the lands lay. He also retained the right to call himself 'prince of Wales', but it was a hollow title. The principality was severely emasculated: Llywelyn kept only Meirionnydd and the almost worthless homages of the lords of Edeirnion – Dafydd ap Gruffudd ab Owain, Elise ap Iorwerth and the sons of Owain ap Bleddyn – and of Rhys Fychan ap Rhys ap Maelgwn. Indeed, Dafydd and Elise may even have been handicaps to Llywelyn, having been imprisoned by him during the war, while Rhys was a landless exile and Meirionnydd was contested by Madog ap Llywelyn Fawr in 1278.

Llywelyn's power within Gwynedd was also weakened, particularly by the provisions made for Dafydd. Although the prince retained Dafydd's hereditary portion in Gwynedd Uwch Conwy for 500 marks *per annum*, this was only for his own lifetime, and Dafydd's lands in the Perfeddwlad would revert to the king when either of the brothers died – they were not heritable by the Welsh. Llywelyn thereby conceded that his authority in Gwynedd was partial, partible and exercised at the king's grace. He was obliged to accommodate his younger brother, Rhodri, as a co-heir – although Rhodri might quitclaim his rights in return for 1,000 marks – and the elder brother, Owain, was to be released from prison; he could then choose either to make peace with Llywelyn or to be transferred into royal custody until his claims received justice according to Welsh law. Owain was in effect a royal bargaining counter, and this was made plain by Edward's statement that, should he be released, Owain could seek his inheritance by whatever means he chose. Despite his insistence on partition, the king recognised Dafydd as the most influential of Llywelyn's brothers, and he accordingly paid relatively little attention to Owain and Rhodri. Although Dafydd had no lands in Gwynedd Uwch Conwy, the treaty ensured by recognising his rights there that his relations with Llywelyn would be difficult. Edward anticipated dissent and took measures to contain it, requiring that Llywelyn should give him ten hostages, and also that 20 men in each *cantref* should swear every year before royal officials to uphold the treaty and to ensure that the prince did the same; if he did not, and if he failed to make amends promptly, they were bound to renounce their allegiance to him. Llywelyn himself was bound to the king in the same way. Although Edward subsequently deleted the payments, Llywelyn's position everywhere was seriously undermined.

Before Christmas 1277, Llywelyn did homage in London, where such matters as the release of prisoners and hostages, the making of amends and the appointment of royal commissioners were dealt with. Edward provided a lavish feast at Rhuddlan in 1278, and it seems to have been around this time that Eleanor was released. Edward assented to her union with Llywelyn, organising an official wedding at Worcester which was attended by Alexander III of Scots and many of the greatest English magnates. There was now a chance that Llywelyn might produce an heir, and Eleanor was encouraged by Edward's kindness. But magnanimity and conviviality could not disguise the inherent conflict between Gwynedd and England.

REPRESSION AND REBELLION: THE LAST YEARS OF GWYNEDD

Two royal commissions were soon appointed. Llywelyn must have begrudged the first, which administered the treaty within Gwynedd, and he was to suffer at the hands of the second, which was to hear and decide legal cases in Wales and the march according to the treaty. Madog ap Llywelyn claimed Meirionnydd immediately, and Llywelyn himself claimed Arwystli against Gruffudd ap Gwenwynwyn. The king optimistically saw this plea as an acceptance of the commissions' role, but tension soon arose when the prince complained that they required him to act inconsistently with Welsh law and custom. Edward insisted that it was usual for cases to be heard at such times and in such places as were designated by royal justices, and he denied any intention to diminish Llywelyn's position. But he was more than willing to remind the prince of his status as a mere baron of the king, and he took every available opportunity to patronise him, interfering in his affairs and issuing veiled threats. Thus Edward assured the prince that he would pay no attention to sinister reports against him as long as he justified his trust, and he advised Llywelyn to act in a manner befitting a prince in his dealings with Bishop Anian of Bangor; royal justices would be despatched to hear any complaints if he did not.

Neither party intended to observe the spirit of the treaty. Within a year, Llywelyn attempted to recover influence in Powys by making terms with Gruffudd ap Gwên, Gruffudd ap Gwenwynwyn's *distain* of Cyfeiliog, who agreed to try to bring his lord back into association with the prince. At the same time, Llywelyn was irritated by a steady stream of legal disputes, many of which betrayed a lack of royal goodwill. He complained that Edward's officials in Genau'r Glyn treated an incursion by huntsmen from Meirionnydd, who were chasing a stag across the Dyfi, as a military attack – this was al-most unheard of, he said, and he demanded that the perpetrators be pun-ished. Similarly, he claimed in 1279 that Reginald Grey, the justice of Ches-ter, distrained him illegally of goods taken from a shipwreck, and the king was less than prompt in ensuring that amends were made. Llywelyn also pro-tested in 1280 that Bogo de Knoville, the justiciar of south Wales, failed to observe the custom of meeting his representatives on territorial boundaries. By 1282, Llywelyn maintained that the treaty had brought him nothing but destruction, claiming that the king disregarded it, and that royal officials were appointed unlawfully to operate in his lands, where they imposed new laws and trampled on his rights. The most important and damaging dispute concerned Arwystli, where the actual question of Llywelyn's rights against Gruffudd ap Gwenwynwyn was never addressed, since it was not agreed under which law it should be decided. The case was opened in 1278 and remained unresolved until Llywelyn's death, having been transformed into an ideological battle.

Customary practice dictated that cases within Wales should be heard according to Welsh law, and a royal inquiry in 1278 found that Welsh law was to be used in cases between Welsh lords. It was stated specifically that Eng-lish law had never been applied in Wales, and it was adjudged that, if a case should arise between a Welsh lord and a marcher lord, the plaintiff should appeal to the king, who was bound to hear the case according to Welsh law. In practice, this meant that Welsh law was to be applied universally in Wales. Indeed, no precise distinction had ever been made between Welsh law and marcher law, and by this time neither the king nor the marchers distinguished between them. The clause in the 1277 treaty which stated that a case should be judged by Welsh law if the lands concerned lay in Wales, and by marcher law if they lay in the march, therefore made a meaningless distinction. Gruf-fudd ap Gwenwynwyn was glad to seize upon it, however, and he claimed that Arwystli lay in the march and that it was therefore not subject to Welsh law. Furthermore, he went on to introduce the contention that English law should be used in cases involving barons of the king in Wales. This was no more than a fallacious legal device intended to skirt around accepted conven-tions, and Gruffudd had employed the same argument – unsuccessfully – in a dispute with Roger Mortimer concerning lands between the Rhiw and the Helygi. In that instance, he had sought justice under English law on the grounds that both he and Mortimer were barons of the king, and his case was rejected in 1281 when the royal justices agreed with Roger that these lands lay in Wales and were therefore subject to Welsh law. For his part, Llywelyn remained insistent that the Arwystli case should be subject to Welsh law, since the lands lay in Wales and both of the litigants were Welsh.

Llywelyn's case was consistent with both customary practice and the treaty. Rather than upholding it, however, Edward chose to overlook important pieces of evidence and turned the issue into one of respect for his authority. The prince, he argued, should expect to be treated as any other litigant and submit himself to the supreme authority of royal jurisdiction. Frustrated by this further humiliation, Llywelyn soon raised the matter to an intellectual and ideological level, asserting that Wales was a province (*provincia*) under royal *imperium*, and that it should therefore be allowed its own laws, as was the case in Gascony, Scotland, Ireland and England. The king could not accept such rhetoric. To do so would have been to abrogate existing royal rights in Wales, since, unlike the other *nationes* mentioned by Llywelyn, Wales was held *in capite*. Edward therefore replied in 1280 that cases in Wales would be heard as they were under his ancestors, that he would not countenance a reduction of royal authority from the time of his ancestors, and that all reasonable and just Welsh laws would be respected. In the meantime, Gruffudd insisted that all cases were subject to English common law in the king's court. Despite all of these diversions, Llywelyn asked the king patiently and politely in 1281 for a swift resolution of the dispute. Once again, Edward placed obstructions in his way, pointing out that Welsh law had not yet been defined – the Chancery would need to be searched and a commission would be sent to Wales to gather evidence. Even when the information was collected, the king merely repeated that the Arwystli case should be decided according to the laws which had been used in the time of his predecessors. Edward was using the case as a means of frustrating and belittling Llywelyn, and perhaps even provoking him.

In 1280, Llywelyn turned in despair to the Archbishop of Canterbury, John Pecham, only to be given the same excuses. Moreover, Pecham added a new moral dimension to the conflict, declaring that many Welsh laws were unacceptable in ecclesiastical eyes, and he conveyed a thinly-veiled threat that a general reform of Welsh law and introduction of English practice was intended. Edward's insistence in 1281 that Llywelyn's original plea for Arwystli was invalid – because he had not received a royal writ – simply provided further proof of English hostility, and a subsequent hearing was fruitless. The prince could only inquire and wait, and by 1282 the urgency of his entreaties was unmistakeable. In Llywelyn's view, Edward was transgressing the treaty, and the prince made known his growing frustration and impatience. Indeed, such was his desire for support that he made an unlikely alliance with Roger Mortimer in 1281. A breakdown in relations was becoming increasingly likely.

Llywelyn's disillusionment was shared by the other leaders of native Wales, with the exception of Gruffudd ap Gwenwynwyn and Rhys ap Maredudd. Dafydd ap Gruffudd was driven to insist upon his right to Welsh law in a dispute concerning the manors of Hope and Estyn, which lay in Wales, and he echoed Llywelyn's point that different laws were used in the king's various territories. Similarly, Rhys Wyndod asserted that, under the 1277 treaty, he should receive Welsh law as a Welshman, and many others – including Gruffudd and Cynan ap Maredudd ab Owain and Llywelyn ap Gruffudd ap Madog – protested that their native rights and privileges were being eroded. This was a reaction against a real threat to indigenous lordships. Royal rule was resented by administrators and princes alike, including Goronwy ap Heilyn, Rhys Fychan ap Rhys ap Maelgwn, and Llywelyn and Hywel ap Rhys Fychan ap Rhys Mechyll, and there were protests against the oppression, greed and injustice of royal officials from the sons of Maredudd ab Owain, Llywelyn ap Gruffudd ap Madog and the men of Rhos, Ystrad Alun, Penllyn and Tegeingl. For these men, allegiance to the king was no longer an attractive proposition, and Gwynedd was already a refuge for Rhys Fychan ap Rhys, Hywel ap Rhys Gryg and Llywelyn ap Rhys Fychan ap Rhys Mechyll. Urged on by an increasing sense of a Welsh identity in the face of adversity, the numbers of Llywelyn's supporters swelled dramatically by 1282.

Discontent flared into an apparently co-ordinated pan-Welsh rebellion in the spring of 1282. Dafydd attacked Hawarden, Flint and Rhuddlan on Palm Sunday, and the men of Penllyn, Edeirnion and Powys Fadog rose simultaneously. Gruffudd ap Maredudd ab Owain took Aberystwyth soon afterwards, while Rhys Fychan ap Rhys ap Maelgwn captured the castles of Llandovery and Carreg Cennen, and then – with Gruffudd – ravaged Ceredigion. The Welsh in the march did not rise – indeed, many of them served in the English forces – but this was a truly national insurrection, fought for the liberation of the whole of *pura Wallia* from English domination. Llywelyn, as prince of Wales, had no choice but to place himself at its head, but it does not seem that he planned or instigated it. He sympathised wholeheartedly with the motives behind the revolt, but he stood to gain little and to lose a great deal from it. The fact that he was expecting an heir by Eleanor was a powerful argument for caution, and the military odds against him were enormous – Gwynedd's resources were not sufficient to defend much more than Gwynedd Uwch Conwy. Moreover, the nature and scale of the revolt obliged Edward to complete his destruction of native Welsh independence. Llywelyn had broken faith with the king, and mounted a serious challenge to royal power in Wales. If he was to survive this war with both his person and his authority intact, he would require exceptional personal qualities and good luck. Several English chroniclers refer to an understanding between Llywelyn and Dafydd, but Llywelyn was not necessarily aware of the plan to rise, and it is unlikely that he was present at the beginning of the campaign. He claimed that he had been ignorant of Dafydd's intentions, and that he merely joined the rebellion when it was already under way. It seems that he went to war only after his last chance of securing the principality's dynastic future had vanished, when Eleanor died while giving birth to a daughter, Gwenllian, in the summer. By June, Llywelyn was fighting in Ceredigion, and he appears to have co-ordinated the whole of the Welsh war effort thereafter.

By this time, the Welsh had been excommunicated and a royal army of unprecedented size had been assembled with remarkable administrative skill. Edward was determined to prevail, however long it might take, and this was the first time that English troops were equipped for a winter campaign in Snowdonia. The king's forces moved slowly but inexorably into the Perfeddwlad, Powys and Deheubarth, and, although Brycheiniog and Powys Fadog proved difficult to subdue, Gruffudd and Cynan ap Maredudd, Rhys Wyndod and Rhys Fychan ap Rhys ap Maelgwn were defeated by the autumn. The offensive now centred on Gwynedd, where Môn was taken and preparations were made for a two-pronged invasion of Snowdonia. The main army made no progress beyond the Conwy, however, and Pecham was allowed to negotiate with Llywelyn. This was a genuine last-minute attempt to make peace, but it was doomed to fail. The king was not in favour of it, the Welsh were intransigent, and Pecham used the opportunity to criticise them for what he saw as their numerous failings and insults against the church. He also made it clear that Llywelyn's position was hopeless. The prince naturally rejected this, and any hope of agreement was lost when the royal force in Môn was routed while attempting to cross the Menai Straits by means of a wooden bridge near Bangor. The Welsh saw this as divine sanction of their cause, and Edward, needing a victory to restore morale, was utterly uncompromising. Dafydd was offered peace on condition that he went to the Holy Land and did not return until summoned, and Llywelyn was offered equally little – Edward refused to negotiate the return of Môn or the Perfeddwlad, demanding that the prince surrender both himself and Gwynedd, and offering him a sizeable estate in England in return. The brothers dismissed these terms with contempt. Edward had intended that the more controversial propositions should be conveyed in secret, but Llywelyn nevertheless presented them to his council, indicating that Gwynedd was united in its determination to fight. Pecham's intervention had merely drawn the Welsh together and established Llywelyn as the primary target of the English attack.

Llywelyn's fate and that of his principality were now almost sealed. Pecham unleashed another tirade against Welsh immorality, and Edward prepared a final offensive. In the meantime, Llywelyn moved south, probably in an attempt to create a second front, and possibly lured by treachery on the part of the Mortimer family. Defeat became inevitable when the prince was killed in a skirmish at Cilmeri in Buellt in December 1282. The royal army moved into Gwynedd with great deliberation, taking Dolwyddelan in January 1283 and moving cautiously but purposefully down the Conwy. The destruction of Welsh independence could not be averted by Dafydd's assumption of the title 'prince of Wales and lord of Snowdon', nor by his grant of the *cantref* of Penweddig in Ceredigion Uwch Aeron to Rhys Fychan ap Rhys ap Maelgwn, nor by his search for help in the middle march as late as May 1283 – his confident marshalling of support that did not exist bore little relation to the reality of chaos, defeat and despair. Most of the Welsh had long since capitulated, and the invasion and subjugation of Gwynedd itself was already well advanced. Dafydd's last sizeable castle, Castell y Bere, was given up to the English in April, and he himself was taken prisoner in June, possibly having been betrayed. The war was over, and the Welsh of each *cantref* in north Wales submitted formally to the king in July, giving hostages and pledging to keep the peace on pain of excommunication. By that time, Dafydd's trial and execution at Shrewsbury had ensured the practical and symbolic extinction of independent native rule in Wales.

In many ways, Dafydd epitomised the duality of Gwynedd's ambitions. He resented losing his inheritance to his brother, and he was always dissatisfied with the lands given him after the successes of 1267. There was a fundamental conflict of interest between Llywelyn's principality and the welfare even of his closest relatives. Dafydd received nothing more from Llywelyn in their 1269 accord than he had held before he deserted him in 1263, and such was the mistrust between the brothers that it was necessary for the bishops of St Asaph and Bangor to mediate between them concerning ambiguities in the agreement. Even then, Llywelyn was reluctant to accept the bishops' interpretation, and he appealed to Pope Gregory X in 1274 for confirmation of it. Yet the timing of Dafydd's more serious outbursts suggests an identification with the principality as well as personal ambition. Although he was the instigator of the 1274 plot, his objective was to become prince – indeed, he may already have been heir. He had seen the problems created by Llywelyn's intervention in the march, and both the plot and his defection in 1263 were most likely protests against this aspect of his brother's policy – he may well have been influenced by the widespread medieval idea that a ruler could be deposed for failure to protect the *regnum*. Dafydd is said to have been instrumental in bringing the prince and the king to terms in 1277, and his precipitous action in 1282 was apparently an attempt to induce Llywelyn to take up arms against dangerously intrusive royal government. His opposition to Llywelyn appears to have reflected policy differences as much as jealous resentment, and it is significant that Dafydd, the arch-rebel who changed sides seven times in 35 years, died as a self-styled prince of Wales. Like his father, who had been excluded from the succession by Llywelyn ap Iorwerth, Dafydd spent most of his life trying to find a constructive role in a world where he was not wanted.

The career of Dafydd ap Llywelyn in the 1240s had shown that a principality of Wales was not feasible without royal support, and the experience of Llywelyn ap Gruffudd demonstrated that dependence on the king could lead to the ruin and destruction of Welsh independence. Llywelyn's failure was to a certain extent the product of unkind circumstances, and the attempt to establish *status Walliae* was undoubtedly rushed. Many of the problems which faced the prince might well have been resolved had they not been overshadowed by the intractable issue of his relations with the king. But it could not have been otherwise, because it was obvious to all parties that the power and prestige to which the princes of Gwynedd aspired were not compatible with their status as tenants-in-chief of the king of England.

8

Conquest and Revolt
1283–c.1415

English Conquest and Welsh Responses

THE EDWARDIAN SETTLEMENT

Edward I was determined to emphasise the completeness and finality of his conquest. Every symbol of Welsh autonomy was to be destroyed. Accordingly, the *regalia* and *insignia* of Gwynedd were removed to England in 1283, and these treasures, which included a crown, jewels, seal matrices and holy relics – notably the *Crux Neoti* or *Croes Naid*, which supposedly contained a piece of the True Cross – were paraded triumphantly through London in 1285. In a further pointed reminder to the Welsh that the rule of their princes had been superseded, Edward established his court in Llywelyn ap Gruffudd's favourite *llysoedd* at Abergwyngregin and Caernarfon. Llywelyn's hall at Aberconwy was converted into an English royal palace, and another of the prince's halls at Ystumgwern was demolished and rebuilt inside a new royal castle at Harlech. Edward's legal right to assume direct rule was undisputed. Llywelyn had held the principality of Wales *in capite*, and his rebellion had made him a contumacious vassal under feudal law. The principality was therefore forfeit, and it escheated to the king. It remained as a constitutional entity, but it was now known simply as the 'land of Wales' (*terra Walliae*).[1] 1283 became the effective limit of legal memory in land law, and the native Welsh principality of Wales was formally extinguished by the Statute of Rhuddlan in 1284. The 'status of Wales' which the princes had fought so hard to create and maintain was officially defunct.

The princely dynasties of native Wales were all but destroyed. Of Llywelyn's family, he and his brothers Dafydd and Owain were dead, and Rhodri had become an English gentleman since quitclaiming his rights in Wales in 1272; he was now known as Sir Roderick fitz Griffin, squire of Malpas, Tatsfield and Bidfield. Llywelyn's baby daughter Gwenllian was sent to the nunnery at Sempringham in Lincolnshire in 1283, and Dafydd's son Owain was imprisoned at Bristol. Neither of them would see the outside world again. Dafydd's daughters were also entered into English nunneries, and all of the surviving heirs of Powys

Fadog were dispossessed, whether they had supported the 1282 rebellion or not. In Deheubarth, all but one of the surviving princes were disinherited, and Rhys Wyndod and his brothers Gruffudd and Llywelyn ap Rhys Fychan all ended their lives in English prisons. Elsewhere, Welsh rulers found their status and privileges eroded even further than they had been already, and some – notably in the middle march – were ousted by the marchers.

Only two senior Welsh lords were allowed to retain their positions, in recognition of their support for the king in 1282. Rhys ap Maredudd augmented his Deheubarth estates with those of his unfortunate relatives in Ystrad Tywi and Ceredigion, and Gruffudd ap Gwenwynwyn was restored to his lands in Powys. When he died in 1286, his marcher lordship – as it had in effect become – was inherited by his son Owain. Some of the minor lords also managed to survive in Edeirnion, Dinmael, Ceredigion, Powys and Morgannwg, but the Welsh aristocracy had been almost obliterated. For decades after 1282, the Welsh poets fell silent. Their patrons had gone, and a generation had been traumatised.

At lower levels of society, however, Wales was still dominated by its traditional native leaders. It was essential for the efficiency of local administration that Welsh expertise should be retained, especially in the *cymydau*, and most of the officials who had served the princes continued to serve the king. These men exercised considerable local authority, and they were succeeded by their heirs as they always had been. In particular, the descendants of Iorwerth ap Gwrgan, the grandfather of Ednyfed Fychan ap Cynwrig (who had been *distain* to the princes of Gwynedd for three decades before 1246), formed a ministerial elite which preserved its influence intact, enjoying a privileged tenure known as that of *Wyrion Eden'* throughout *pura Wallia*. Together with the remnants of the princely dynasties, the members of this native administrative class retained their identity as *uchelwyr*. The king was in no mood to punish them, and he confirmed them in their lands, liberties and offices once they had submitted to him. Many of them, such as Gruffudd ap Tudur, who was given the custody of Dolwyddelan castle in 1284, were to prosper under the new regime. With their position assured, the *uchelwyr* had no practical difficulty in supporting and working with royal officers.

In 1283, all of Gwynedd Uwch Conwy and Ceredigion passed into the king's hand, as did strategic areas around his castles at Hope, Rhuddlan, Conwy and Dinefwr. Edward was now by far the greatest landowner in Wales, and he created new marcher lordships in Denbigh, Dyffryn Clwyd, Bromfield and Yale, Chirk and Cantref Bychan. His chief concern in Wales was to raise money to pay off his debts – many of which had been incurred in conquering the principality – and his government proved very effective in doing so, not least because they based their calculations on the abnormal financial demands made by Llywelyn ap Gruffudd during his last years. As early as 1284, Gwynedd was surveyed in order to determine the obligations and revenues due to the king, and Edward's officers took ever greater rents, taxes and profits of justice as the new regime settled in. Furthermore, in levying a subsidy of one fifteenth of all movables throughout the whole of Wales between 1291 and 1293, the king extended royal prerogatives in the march. In addition, although he was unable to overturn the marchers' right to make war, Edward asserted his authority over them by punishing the earls of Gloucester and Hereford in 1292 for disobeying a royal command to stop fighting each other. Royal rule in every corner of Wales was becoming tighter and more demanding.

New arrangements for the government of north Wales were set out in the Statute of Rhuddlan in 1284. Otto de Grandison was appointed as justiciar at Caernarfon, acting as governor, supreme judge and military commander, and Gwynedd was divided into three counties, namely Anglesey, Caernarfonshire and Merionethshire. Each county was given a sheriff with his own court, and coroners were also introduced, but the *cwmwd* courts were retained, as was much of Welsh civil law. In effect, this dispensation grafted a new tier of government onto the existing administrative structure, but it represented a very pointed implementation of English practice. Welsh *cymydau* were now treated as English hundreds, and the new courts introduced English criminal law and procedures, placing an emphasis upon the king's peace rather private settlement, and upon punishment rather than compensation; there was also an insistence upon the rule of legitimacy in land law. The senior royal officers were accountable to the king – the chamberlain, for instance, submitted his accounts at Westminster – and furthermore, all of the new offices were occupied by Englishmen. There was less drastic change in the royal lands of Carmarthenshire and Cardiganshire, which had been embryonic counties since 1241 (and arguably since the reign of Henry I in the case of Carmarthenshire), but Bogo de Knoville was made justiciar at Carmarthen and a chamberlain was also appointed.

The political and administrative settlement was underpinned by massive military investment. The marchers built new castles during the war of 1282, and existing royal castles were strengthened, while many native Welsh castles were repaired, extended and garrisoned. From 1283, the king also embarked upon the construction of a ring of powerful new castles around Gwynedd, all of which could be supplied easily by ships from Chester, Bristol or Dublin. This was an enormously expensive and complicated logistical undertaking, and it demonstrated Edward's strategic vision, as well as his determination to keep Wales firmly under his control, and his wary regard for the pride and martial skill of his defeated Welsh enemies. Workmen were drafted from almost every county in England, and master craftsmen came from all over Europe; the most notable of them was the chief architect, Master James of St Georges, who was brought from Savoy, possibly because Edward had witnessed his work at Yverdon and Saint-Georges d'Espéranches. The scale and sophistication of the royal castle-building programme exceeded anything that had been seen in Wales before – or indeed anywhere else in the world – and it remains as an unsurpassed example of medieval military architecture. Work at Conwy and Harlech began as soon as possible in 1283 and was completed within a few years, while Caernarfon was designed specifically to remind the Welsh of their subjection. There could be no better reminder that Edward I was the master now.

The final strand of conquest was economic. Increasing prosperity led to the foundation of new towns throughout Europe in the thirteenth century, but the purpose of Edward's plantation boroughs in Wales was overtly political. The royal boroughs which had been incorporated at Aberystwyth, Rhuddlan and Flint after 1276 were complemented by many more after 1283. Most of them took the form of fortified towns, following the pattern of the English *bastides* in Gascony. They nestled in the shadow of the castles, whose constables acted as *ex officio* mayors, and their purpose was to act as secure military supply bases and to place control of trade in the hands of royal officials and English merchants. Settlers from all over England were offered attractive inducements to colonise the boroughs, and the burgesses were granted extensive commercial privileges, while the Welsh were excluded from holding office or living in them. Welsh tenants were often removed from their lands and relocated at less attractive sites, and the boroughs were granted monopolies over buying and selling for many miles around, enforced by hefty fines. Markets and fairs which had been founded by the Welsh princes were allowed to continue, but the new royal boroughs – together with the considerable number which were established by the marchers – ensured that economic power in Wales was taken firmly under English control.

Conquest inevitably led to disaffection. In the south-west, Rhys ap Maredudd had survived 1282 and even profited from it territorially, but he also expected a degree of autonomy, and to be treated with the respect traditionally accorded to native Welsh rulers. Instead, Edward made him quit-claim his ancestral seat at Dinefwr in 1283, and went on to publicly humiliate him for taking possession of his lands before he had received formal investiture from the king. Furthermore, royal officials at Carmarthen and Dinefwr harassed Rhys with constant legal impositions, bureaucracy and extortion. It was more than he could bear. In 1287, he rebelled, only to be crushed in a matter of weeks by a massive show of force. His revolt was reignited briefly in 1288, but it was soon put down again, and Rhys was finally betrayed and hanged in 1292. The dynasty of Deheubarth was effectively extinct, and Rhys's lands were added to Carmarthenshire.

The government learned nothing from the revolt. It had only been a local affair, and even the Welsh seemed keen to put it down – many of them still remembered Rhys's failure to join the rebellion of 1282. Rhys had been motivated merely by personal disappointment, and moreover, he had not intended to reverse the fact of conquest. Nevertheless, his protest highlighted issues which the king would have been well advised to heed. The Welsh were aggrieved at the way their social and legal customs were ignored and overridden by insensitive English officials, and, like local communities everywhere in the Middle Ages, they valued their ability to govern themselves. Many in Wales were used to foreign overlordship, especially in the march, but intrusive government was another matter. The Welsh resented the king's excessive and increasing financial demands as they had resented those imposed by the native princes, and the lack of a well-developed cash economy made it difficult to meet them. There was also anger at the monopolies and discrimination practised in the English boroughs, as well as at the compulsory enlistment of troops for service in Gascony in 1294. The Welsh had little appetite for a change of government, but their grievances were real and urgent, and they wanted them redressed. The king, however, made no attempt to do so, and he complacently reduced the garrisons of some of his castles. He was soon to realise his mistake.

In 1294, Madog ap Llywelyn, whose father had been ejected from Meirionnydd by Llywelyn ap Gruffudd, styled himself prince of Wales and launched a co-ordinated national rebellion, supported by Morgan ap Maredudd of the Gwent dynasty and minor members of the Deheubarth dynasty. Many of the grievances were local – notably against Gilbert de Clare in Glamorgan – but the rebels were united by indignation at the excesses of colonial rule. The deputy justiciar at Carmarthen and the oppressive sheriff of Anglesey were both ambushed and killed in separate incidents, and the rebels then went on the rampage: they attacked the earl of Lincoln near Denbigh; they besieged Harlech, Cricieth and Aberystwyth; they burned Llanfaes; they captured Caernarfon and destroyed government records; and they seized the castles of Denbigh, Ruthin, Hawarden and Morlais. The king abandoned his plans for a campaign in France, and the army he raised to quell the revolt was even greater than that of 1282. Nevertheless, he was forced to spend several months under siege at Conwy in early 1295, after Madog had destroyed his supplies in Llŷn. The castle served its purpose well, however, and it held out with supplies brought in by sea. By the time Edward marched south, the marchers had won important victories in southern and central Wales, and Madog had been defeated by William Beauchamp, the earl of Warwick, at Maes Moydog in Powys.

Edward and the marchers restored order, demanding hostages and fines from their insubordinate tenants. Royal castles were repaired, and work on the uncompleted castle at Caernarfon was given renewed urgency. An entirely new castle was started at Beaumaris in 1295, and to make way for it the whole Welsh town at Llanfaes was removed to Newborough in 1296. But the king was lenient towards the leaders of the revolt. Madog spent the rest of his life in the Tower of London, but he was not executed, and one of his sons became a royal squire, retaining the family's lands in Anglesey. Morgan was pardoned, and within a few years he had been knighted and was leading troops in the king's army. It was now clear that the impetus for revolt had not come from the personal grievances of the distressed aristocracy, but from the complaints of the whole Welsh community, and Edward knew that this was the problem that needed to be addressed. Accordingly, he spoke to the *uchelwyr* and the local Welsh officials, and moreover he listened to them, appointing commissions in 1295 and 1297 to investigate oppression by his officials. He could now present himself convincingly as the defender of his tenants' liberties, but profound tensions remained. The revolt had terrified the inhabitants of the isolated English boroughs, and Edward sought to reassure them by issuing a series of strict prohibitive ordinances against the Welsh. These in turn did nothing to reconcile the Welsh to English rule.

Yet there was a mutual desire for peace and reconciliation. The Welsh had once again proved themselves incapable of sustaining a rebellion in the face of an enemy like Edward, who possessed vast resources, infinite patience, a painstaking attention to detail and unstoppable determination. For his part, Edward needed security in Wales. Madog's revolt had cost him dearly – it contributed to financial and constitutional crises in England in 1296 and 1297 – and the king needed Wales to provide him with money and men for his wars elsewhere. In 1301, Edward's need to provide for his eldest surviving son, Edward of Caernarfon, gave him the opportunity to focus Welsh loyalties by creating him prince of Wales – an office which has generally been conferred upon the monarch's eldest son ever since. The young Edward's principality allowed him to forge close ties of service and reward with his Welsh tenants, and he listened with great sympathy when they petitioned him at Kennington in 1305. His concern for the well-being of the Welsh continued after he acceded to the throne as Edward II in 1307, and he heard further complaints from north and west Wales at Lincoln in 1316. The king's intentions seem to have been good, but this could not disguise the fact that there were a lot of complaints in the principality.

The Welsh in the march were also restless. The lordship of Glamorgan fell into disarray after Gilbert de Clare, the young earl of Gloucester, was killed at Bannockburn in 1314; he had no heir, and the problems this created were such that his widow feigned pregnancy for two years. In the meantime, Glamorgan was badly mismanaged, to the point that Llywelyn Bren, a wealthy descendant of the dynasty of Senghennydd, revolted in 1315. He surrendered in the following year, but a warning had been given. The subservience of the Welsh could not be taken for granted. This message was echoed in the north, and again it was the victory of the Scots at Bannockburn which provided the catalyst. A Scottish fleet was now active in the Irish Sea, and it attacked Holyhead in 1315. When Robert and Edward Bruce invaded Ireland in the same year, there was a real prospect of a Scottish invasion of Wales. Between 1315 and 1317, the Bruces corresponded with Sir Gruffudd Llwyd, the English government's most powerful Welsh servant in north Wales, and Gruffudd promised to help should Edward Bruce land in Wales in person. He was imprisoned for his pains, but not for long, and this fact, together with his long record of loyal service both before and after these events, suggests that he may have acted as an *agent provocateur*. Few of the Welsh were interested in rebellion, but Edward II reinforced the castle garrisons and made sure that the situation was defused by negotiating with prominent Welsh leaders, emphasising that he had been born in Wales, and making concessions similar to those made by his father in the 1290s. There would not be another Welsh revolt for decades.

CONTENTMENT AND RESTLESSNESS

For the most part, the fourteenth century was a time of peace and security in Wales, and there was prosperity and confidence in the towns. Statistical evidence is scarce and difficult to interpret, but it appears that Wales was not noticeably poorer than England during this period – it is possible, for instance, that Anglesey was wealthier than Bedfordshire. Nor were the Welsh excluded from this economic boom. More and more of them were allowed to become burgesses and settle in the plantation boroughs, and the *uchelwyr* enjoyed a wide range of exotic goods, brought from England, Ireland, France, the Low Countries, Spain and Lombardy. Their poets also flourished; Dafydd ap Gwilym, who lived in the middle of the century, is still regarded as the finest Welsh poet, and there is very little hint of misery and oppression in most of his ebullient verses.

The authorities had always believed that Wales was best governed by the Welsh. The sentiment had been voiced in the 1240s, and although the very top tier of government was still an exclusively English preserve, it was only a matter of time before Welshmen were promoted. Sir Gruffudd ap Rhys (or Sir Gruffudd Llwyd) held shrieval office several times in Caernarfonshire, Anglesey and Merionethshire between 1301 and 1327, and Sir Rhys ap Gruffudd was deputy justiciar of the southern principality more than once before his death in the 1350s. These *uchelwyr* were trusted leaders of royal troops over decades, and they were knighted and given substantial territories, offices and privileges for their services. Gruffudd and Rhys both accumulated large landed estates, as did Tudur ab Ithel Fychan in Flintshire, Gwilym ap Gruffudd ap Tudur in Anglesey and Caernarfonshire, and Iorwerth ap Llywarch in the lordship of Denbigh. Other Welshmen, such as Sir Hywel ap Gruffudd and Sir Gregory Sais, amassed great wealth and made a name for themselves fighting in the king's wars from Scotland to Castile. Hywel achieved such fame at Poitiers in 1356 that he became known as Syr Hywel y Fwyall ('Sir Hywel of the Axe'). Many of the *uchelwyr* were more than comfortable with life after conquest.

Not everyone was contented, however. After the accession of Edward III in 1327, and especially after he assumed personal power in 1330, Wales was milked more than ever for money and men. The outbreak of war with France in 1337 meant heavy, frequent and unpopular taxes, as well as economic difficulties, and offices in Wales were used as bribes to satisfy royal creditors. Walter de Mauny was given what amounted to a free hand in Merionethshire after 1341, and the extortion and corruption only worsened after 1343 when the king's eldest son, Edward, the Black Prince, was made prince of Wales. Every available penny was squeezed out of Wales at the expense of Welsh and English tenants alike, and the perpetrators of this misgovernment were not only the English but often the Welsh *uchelwyr*. Complaints of oppression were brought against Sir Gruffudd Llwyd in 1331 and against Ithel ap Cynwrig Sais in Flintshire in the 1350s, and resentment was often expressed in racial terms. It was Englishmen who accused Gruffudd of tyranny, while the Welsh blamed English oppression for their ills. Fears of a Welsh revolt were such that the castles were provisioned against an expected fleet from France in 1338, and the men of Anglesey were rumoured to be plotting with the Scots in 1339. There was a Welsh attack on the fair at St Asaph in 1344, leading to a half-hearted attempt on the castle, and matters reached a head when Henry de Shaldeforde, the prince's attorney in north Wales, was assassinated in Bangor in 1345. All of the burgesses of north Wales bombarded the king with tales of Welsh hostility throughout the country, complaining that it was condoned by the greatest Welshmen in the land – Tudur ap Goronwy, the most senior descendant of Ednyfed Fychan, had led the attack on de Shaldeforde – and claiming that it was hardly safe to move outside their towns. The men of Caernarfon even threatened to pack up and leave if something was not done about it. The king did nothing to address Welsh grievances, and the English burgesses of Beaumaris were only placated when their Welsh counterparts were expelled in 1345. Trouble was being stored up for the future.

The lot of the unfortunate taxpayer in fourteenth-century Wales was made considerably worse by a combination of adverse circumstances. Throughout Europe, a growth in population during the late thirteenth century had reduced the amount of land available for cultivation, with the result that agricultural production was constricted to the point that food shortages became common.

This problem was exacerbated by nature. Colder and wetter weather caused the failure of the harvest across Europe for three consecutive summers after 1315, as well as on numerous other occasions, and there were serious livestock epidemics in the 1320s. Famine was never far away, and it caused widespread social unrest, especially since agricultural prices were in decline. Then came the bubonic plague pandemic known as the Black Death. It originated in central Asia and reached Wales in 1349, wiping out a third or possibly even a half of the population. The plague was particularly virulent in the north, and especially among the bondmen, who tended to live in nucleated communities. Almost all of the bondmen at Degannwy died, and the mortality rate in Dyffryn Clwyd rose fourteen-fold. The country was in despair, and the poet Gruffudd ap Maredudd ap Dafydd was driven to beg God for forgiveness towards Gwynedd. His prayers were only partially answered. Further visitations in 1361 and 1369 ravaged the south, which had escaped the worst in 1349, and there were ten outbreaks altogether before 1420.

The Black Death alleviated the problems of overpopulation, but its effects on social and economic life were deeply disruptive, transforming the relationship between lords and their tenants. There were now too few agricultural tenants to work the land, since many had died or fled. Tenurial vacancies and financial hardship caused small tenements to be sold, and the subsequent creation of large estates accelerated the breakdown of traditional kindred-based free tenure. This in turn created a new class of landless men who were forced to migrate to find work. They often found that their services were not required, since many lords had rented out their unprofitable demesne land to tenants who practised less labour-intensive forms of agriculture. Arable land was given over to grazing, and this in turn forced many mills to close down. The economy was locked into a downward spiral of financial hardship, rural depopulation and insufficient food production. Lordship was now seen primarily as a mechanism for the collection of revenues, and most English lords became absentees, distancing themselves from the poverty of Wales. The burden of rents, taxes and other dues was still borne by the bondmen, however, and they were expected to pay the same as they had before the plague, even though there were now fewer of them. At the same time, the scarcity of labour resulted in higher wages, despite agreements between the marcher lords for the return of fugitive bondmen. The cumulative effect was that both seigneurial revenues and landlord-tenant relations suffered. There was a temporary recovery, but the second half of the fourteenth century was a period of economic slump from which there was no sign of recovery. The financial impact was often severe – the lordship of Ogmore suffered a 30 per cent loss of revenue – and in many cases it proved to be permanent.

Pestilence and economic dislocation caused turmoil throughout Europe. There was a feeling of disorientation as the old order was swept away, and attempts to enforce it provoked resentment and sometimes defiance. Popular revolts swept across the continent, beginning with the *Jacquerie* in France in the 1350s. Many of these movements were religious or social in nature – the Peasants' Revolt which erupted in England in 1381, for example, was a protest by the poor and the unfree against a series of poll taxes – but these elements were absent in Wales. Rather, the focus of most Welsh discontent was English rule. The lower classes were groaning under the burden of English lords, and there was still a creeping nostalgia among the *uchelwyr* for the days of independence. Native tradition prophesied the coming of the *mab darogan* (the 'son of prophecy'), a national deliverer whose name would be Owain, and the time seemed to be ripe in the 1370s, as the French wars had resumed and there was increasing unrest in England. Moreover, such a man existed in France in the person of Owain ap Thomas (or Owain Lawgoch), the great-great-grandson of Llywelyn ap Iorwerth and the great nephew of Llywelyn ap Gruffudd. Sensing the opportunity, Gruffudd ap Maredudd ap Dafydd addressed an *awdl* to Owain, inviting him to come to Wales to recover it for the Welsh. At last, the prospect that a native Welsh dynasty might be restored after nearly a century of colonial rule seemed not only attractive but a practical possibility.

OWAIN LAWGOCH

Owain's grandfather, Rhodri ap Gruffudd, had retired to England as a royal pensioner in 1272, fighting on the side of Edward I in the wars of 1276 and 1282. There is no indication that Rhodri ever went back to Wales, or that he tried to recover his inheritance in Gwynedd after 1282. He played no part in the 1294 revolt, even though his pedigree made him the obvious man to lead it, and the lack of poetry to him suggests that he may no longer have been welcome in Wales; he certainly seems to have lacked any interest in it. His son Thomas, however, was well aware of his roots, even though he spent most of his life in Surrey. He used the lions of Gwynedd on his personal seal, acquired the manor of Dinas in Mechain Is Coed after 1332, and petitioned Edward III in an attempt to recover the family lands in Llŷn. Thomas's efforts were frustrated – possibly by powerful marcher lords – but he performed a great service to Welsh legitimist hopes when he produced a son and called him Owain.

Although he was born in England, Owain seems to have been very proud of his Welsh heritage; even English officials regularly used Welsh nomenclature in referring to him as Owain ap Thomas, whereas his father was known as Thomas Retherik. Owain spent his youth abroad, returning briefly to claim his inheritance in Surrey, Cheshire and Gloucestershire in 1363, and he was in France when the Anglo-French war broke out again in 1369. If he had not already done so, Owain now threw in his lot with the French, and his lands in England were forfeited when he raised a free company of international mercenaries – most of whom were Welshmen – in the service of Charles V. Both Owain and his French masters understood his potential. According to the French chronicler Jean Froissart, Owain asserted that he was the true prince of Wales, and the French knew him as Yvain de Galles. A French invasion of Wales in his name might prove very profitable.

In 1369, an expedition under the command of Owain Lawgoch set out from Harfleur bound for Wales. The timing was not good. The fleet sailed in December, and it was driven back to port by winter gales. Another attempt was made in 1372, but it got no further than Guernsey before Owain was ordered to sail to Castile to seek the urgent support of Henry II in a French attack on La Rochelle. The city was taken, and Owain won a notable victory at Soubise, but there was no invasion of Wales. Proposals for a third attempt with Castilian help came to nothing in 1373, since the French were preoccupied with John of Gaunt's *chevauchée* from Calais to Bordeaux. Plans for an attack on Wales were subsequently dropped. As useful as a second front in Wales might have been, the French never regarded it as more than a sideshow. They now required Owain's services elsewhere, and he was sent to attack the duke of Austria in 1375, only to be defeated by the men of Berne at Fraubrunnen when his men were surprised in their beds at a disused nunnery. For the next three years, Owain campaigned against the English in south-western France. Superficially, at least, it appeared that whatever threat he had posed to the English government in Wales had evaporated.

The English, however, were sufficiently worried about Owain that they sent an agent to assassinate him. By 1378, Owain was besieging Mortagne-sur-Mer on the banks of the Gironde in Poitou, where he was introduced to one John Lamb. Froissart says that Lamb claimed to have come from Wales, where he reported that Owain enjoyed great support, and he won Owain's trust before stabbing him to death one morning while he was combing his hair. The English authorities paid Lamb £20 for his work, indicating that the murder was probably planned at a high political level. There were many reasons to be fearful of Owain. The government had reliable information from its spies, and there had been regular invasion alerts since 1369. Rumours abounded that a Castilian invasion was planned in 1377, and England was now extremely vulnerable, since the new king, Richard II, was a minor who faced mounting political pressure and even treachery within his kingdom. Sir John de Minsterworth – who had defected to the French in 1373 – was captured in 1377, and he confessed that he had planned an attack on Wales with someone who called himself the heir of Wales. Moreover, he wrote a letter which may have named prominent English sympathisers in Owain's cause; it was promptly destroyed by his jailers in the Tower of London. If true, the plot represented a real danger to Richard, and the clampdown was severe. De Minsterworth was executed, and a quarter of his body was put on display at Carmarthen – a gruesome warning to the Welsh in the very part of Wales where any invasion was expected to land. It was against this background that the decision was taken to eliminate Owain Lawgoch.

How much support Owain would have enjoyed had he ever landed in Wales can only be guessed at. Many of the Welsh had a vested interest in preserving the *status quo*, and there were large numbers of Welshmen in the English armies which opposed him in France. But Owain's appeal should not be underestimated. He was seen as the *mab darogan*, and his military prowess was famed throughout Europe. The Bernese, in particular, celebrated their victory over *Yfer von Galeys* for centuries. The French willingness to invest considerable sums in Owain's expeditions suggests very strongly that support was expected to be waiting for him, and Llywelyn ap Cynwrig Ddu claimed that the Welsh had been ready, watching the shore and preparing their weapons in readiness. Gruffudd Sais was convicted in Anglesey of plotting with Owain in 1370, and Rhys ap Roppert and his son Madog were accused in 1374 of communicating with Owain, sending him money and receiving letters from him at Rhuddlan over a period of several years. Numerous Welshmen deserted from the English army to Owain's company, and they were joined by others from all over Wales, and *pura Wallia* in particular. Among the latter were two of the sons of Rhys ap Roppert, one of whom inherited Owain's command after his death. Many of the mercenaries in France were fugitives or adventurers, but some of Owain's troops must have been motivated by higher ideals, and his supporters in Wales included respectable men of substance. Rhys ap Roppert was a prominent *uchelwr* and moreover a nephew of Sir Rhys ap Gruffudd and himself a former sheriff of Flintshire and escheator of Caernarfonshire and Merionethshire. If men like this could be persuaded, Owain's cause had a future. With Owain's death, however, all hope vanished, and the direct male line of Gwynedd was finally extinguished.

CONTINUED DISAFFECTION

Owain Lawgoch was gone, but Welsh grievances remained. In particular, the legal distinctions between the Welsh and the English were becoming intolerable. They were outdated in many respects, but that very fact led to more vigorous enforcement by English authorities who were keen to preserve their privileged status. The boroughs, especially, practised increasing discrimination against the Welsh, and they secured royal support for it by arguing that they were upholding English rule in a dangerous foreign country. In 1366, the burgesses of Beaumaris insisted upon a confirmation of Edward I's anti-Welsh ordinances of 1295, and their example was followed at Conwy, Cricieth and Caernarfon in 1372. In addition, burghal monopolies were extended, and the punishments for infringing them were stiffened, while Welsh burgesses could be harassed into explaining how they – mere Welshmen – had come to enjoy the life of English burghers. Such demeaning measures produced a growing tension between the legal status of Welshmen and what they considered to be their natural entitlement, and Welsh resentment fed English fear. The English of Wales and the marches moaned incessantly about alleged unfair treatment at the hands of Welsh officials, and their complaints assumed an increasingly racial tone. They protested against the dangers of allowing Welshmen to buy land and settle in the towns, and strong measures were taken to prohibit such liberties in the English border counties. There were also accusations of Welsh raids against the English. Community relations were becoming ugly.

There were persistent complaints among the Welsh about misgovernment, extortion and corruption. Like his predecessors, Richard II regarded Wales primarily as a source of patronage and revenue. He imposed his favourites and took heavy taxes, while his successor Henry IV levied equally substantial communal payments. The government's desire for cash also inflamed Welsh sensibilities in matters of the law. According to Welsh law, escheated land – which was forfeited because of an offence, or debt, or the failure of male heirs – was expected to revert to the kin-group, but English lords insisted upon applying English law, which permitted them to distribute the profits however they saw fit – usually to their own coteries. The Welsh felt cheated, especially since the amount of land which came before the courts in this way after the Black Death allowed the wholesale introduction of English forms of landlordship throughout Wales. The preference for English law was not ideological, however, and Welsh law was also used for the authorities' financial gain. The Welsh petitioned repeatedly to be allowed to adopt English procedures relating to the alienation and sale of land, but the king refused, since the existing situation under Welsh law provided him with a steady source of income from licences and fines. Profit was always the overriding motive in the governance of Wales.

Welsh grievances often spilled over into protest, and the targets were almost always boroughs, forests, tolls, mills and the other symbols and symptoms of seigneurial control and exploitation. When the lord of Chirkland died in 1330, his tenants took the opportunity to break down his fences and indulge in illicit hunting and the other privileges of the forest; similarly, in 1401, the villeins of Abergavenny became so incensed with seigneurial oppression that they killed the lord's steward and released several criminals. There were many comparable

cases in fourteenth-century England – indeed complaints like this were common throughout Europe – but in Wales they could be interpreted and portrayed
as the results of English conquest. The truth was that Welsh officials were often
just as oppressive as their English counterparts, and Welsh communities levelled
accusations of misrule and extortion against Rhys ap Roppert, the sheriff of
Flintshire, and Rhys Ddu ap Gruffudd, the sheriff of Cardiganshire. Afterwards,
these men became firm supporters of Owain Lawgoch and Owain Glyn Dŵr
respectively, but the irony was not always appreciated in the increasingly febrile
tension between communities. Any kind of trouble was now almost routinely
interpreted in terms of an adversarial juxtaposition of English and Welsh, and it
was natural in this atmosphere that the English of south Wales were deeply fearful when John Lawrence, the deputy justiciar, was murdered by a Welsh *uchelwr*
in 1385. Similarly, Welsh outrage was inevitable when a prominent *uchelwr* died
in suspicious circumstances while in custody at Carmarthen in 1387. If serious
trouble was to be avoided, a period of calm reflection would be needed.

By the 1390s, however, the social and political climate was anything but
calm. Rapid social and economic change had caused a deterioration of law
and order, worsened by the return of restless soldiers from the wars overseas.
In the late 1380s, it was rumoured that a Castilian spy had been shown the
secrets of all the castles of south-west Wales, and the fevered atmosphere provided sustenance for prophecy and superstition. The *mab darogan* had not yet
come, but he surely would come. The Welsh vaticinatory tradition was supported by millenarian beliefs throughout Europe, which held that bad times
would be followed by the return of a redeemer, heralding a 1,000-year golden
age; alternatively, it was argued by some that the world would end in the year
1400. The excitement and fear generated by such notions was compounded
by a highly unstable political situation in Wales, where Richard II dispossessed
the duke of Gloucester, the earl of Arundel (both of whom were executed)
and the earl of Warwick in 1397. Three of the most powerful marcher lords
had been removed at a stroke, and the political vacuum grew when the duke
of Norfolk and Henry Bolingbroke – the son of John of Gaunt, the duke of
Lancaster – were both exiled in 1398. Furthermore, Roger Mortimer, the earl
of March, died in the same year, and John of Gaunt followed him in 1399.
Finally, the king himself was deposed in 1399, along with his supporters. In
a few short years, a series of political earthquakes all over Wales had severed
the personal ties between lords and tenants which had been nurtured carefully for generations. Nor did Henry Bolingbroke bring stability when he was
crowned as Henry IV in 1399. His right to be king was hotly contested, and
the early years of his reign were dogged by plots, rumours, rebellion, and wars
in Scotland, Ireland and France.

At such a time of confusion and crisis, the Welsh yearned for political direction, and they naturally turned to their traditional political leaders. The *uchelwyr* had suffered less than most of the Welsh population. Indeed, many of them had benefited from the evils of plague and war, enlarging their estates and making their fortunes from plunder and ransoms. But these sources of wealth were drying up, especially after the English defeats in France during the 1370s and the cessation of hostilities in 1389, and most of the *uchelwyr* were anything but immune from the burdens of taxation and discrimination. In addition, there were many complaints among the Welsh clergy, most of whom were drawn from the families of the *uchelwyr*. Well-qualified Welshmen were often unable to gain appointment to ecclesiastical offices, which were granted to the creditors and favourites of the English authorities – only one of the sixteen bishops appointed in Wales between 1372 and 1400 was a Welshman – and the relationship with Canterbury was made more contentious by papal schism after 1378. The clergy also suffered financially. Parochial revenues were appropriated by English monasteries and cathedrals, or else they were siphoned off by pluralist English absentees. Furthermore, inflation reduced the value of fixed clerical incomes, and there was heavy ecclesiastical taxation. Men of education, ability and social standing were being denied advancement, belittled, and fleeced at the same time, and their discontent sometimes flared into direct action and even violence, notably at Oxford University in 1395.

In both the ecclesiastical and the secular spheres, therefore, the leaders of Welsh society had deep grievances. Moreover, many of the secular *uchelwyr* possessed their own military retinues, and service with the king's armies had given them a wealth of military experience – and all this at a time of deep political uncertainty and popular unrest. It was a potent combination, but not an unstoppable one. If the government could address the concerns of the *uchelwyr*, then it was likely that there would be no appetite for serious trouble. If it did not, however – and if there should be some kind of unforeseen problem – then anything might happen.

The Revolt of Owain Glyn Dŵr

A RESPECTABLE PROTEST

In 1399, Owain ap Gruffudd Fychan of Glyndyfrdwy in Merionethshire complained to parliament that his neighbour, Reginald Grey of Dyffryn Clwyd, had seized common land on the boundary between their estates. His petition fell on deaf ears; Grey was one of Henry IV's few allies, and had officiated at his coronation feast. The Evesham chronicler claims that Grey then incriminated Owain by withholding a royal summons for military service against the Scots in 1400, telling the king that Owain had refused to perform it. Whether or not these details are all accurate, Owain was certainly provoked. In September 1400, he had himself proclaimed prince of Wales and raised the standard of revolt at Glyndyfrdwy. His immediate quarrel was local, and all of those present at the proclamation were Owain's own family and friends, but this was more than a marcher spat. The proclamation was almost certainly the fruit of a pre-meditated plan, fuelled by years of resentment, and it held out the promise of an independent Wales under its own legitimate native rulers.

Owain was not a typical rebel. He was used to working within the estab-lishment, not outside of it. His great-great-grandfather, Gruffudd Fychan ap Gruffudd Maelor, had been granted Glyndyfrdwy *in capite* by Edward I in 1283, and Owain – who was often known as Owain Glyn Dŵr – had inherited his relatively privileged and rather archaic status as a baron of Wales, almost ex-empt from the government's financial and legal demands. The family had also acquired Cynllaith, as well as Iscoed and Gwynionydd in Cardiganshire, and they had developed close relations with the earl of Arundel, a powerful marcher neighbour for whom Owain's father had held office in the lordships of Oswes-try and Ellesmere. A number of Owain's relatives married into the march, and his own wife, Margaret, was a daughter of Sir David Hanmer, a chief justice of the King's Bench. Against this background, it was to be expected that Owain would be given the conventional education of an English gentleman as well as the sensibilities of a Welsh *uchelwr*; hence he is said to have studied law at the Inns of Court in London, and he was called as a witness during the celebrated Scrope-Grosvenor case in the Court of Chivalry in 1386. It was also entirely natural that he should become an accomplished soldier in the service of the king and the earl of Arundel, serving at Berwick-upon-Tweed in 1384, in Scotland in 1385, and in the naval victory at Cadzand in 1387. He may also have served Richard II and Henry Bolingbroke in the 1390s. Owain was the very model of respectable conformity, and he had not experienced much of the suffering of his countrymen. He was the wealthiest of what was left of the native Welsh aristocracy, and Iolo Goch sang of his palatial residence at Sycharth. In English terms, his income of up to £70 would have put him among the county gentry. In Welsh terms, however, Owain's significance was much greater than that.

If there was to be a revolt of any size in Wales, Glyn Dŵr was its obvious leader. His pedigree was almost impeccable. He was descended in the male line from the dynasty of Powys, and his mother could trace her descent in the male line from the dynasty of Deheubarth. Furthermore, Owain Lawgoch had died without heirs, and Roger Mortimer – by far the most prominent descendant of Llywelyn ap Iorwerth (through Gwladus Ddu) – was also dead. Owain Glyn Dŵr could therefore put forward a convincing claim to the

legacy of Gwynedd, by virtue of the twelfth-century marriages of Gruffudd Maelor to Angharad ferch Owain Gwynedd and Gruffudd ap Rhys to
Gwenllian ferch Gruffudd ap Cynan. In addition, Owain's cousins in Anglesey, Gwilym and Rhys ap Tudur ap Goronwy, were the senior descendants
of Ednyfed Fychan. Even before the revolt, Iolo Goch saw Glyn Dŵr as the
natural leader of the Welsh, and once it had started, Owain skilfully tapped
into the strong legitimist tendency in native Wales. His genealogy helped him
to attract support in many parts of the country, and it gave him credence
when he presented himself as the *mab darogan*.

Owain's personal reasons for rebellion are less than clear. Before the revolt,
Gruffudd Llwyd compared him with the heroes of the Britons against the
Saxons, thereby reminding him that he was a Welsh prince, but the use of such
conventional poetic idioms did not necessarily imply that he should actually do
anything about the contemporary state of Wales. He certainly identified himself
with the plight of his compatriots, however, and moreover he had suffered his
own personal disappointments. He held no local office, and his prospects looked
bleak after his patrons, Hanmer and Arundel, died in 1387 and 1397 respectively.
Furthermore, Gruffudd complained that Owain had not received the knight-
hood he deserved, unlike a number of his compatriots. Finally, the change of
regime in England and the dispute with Grey may have convinced Owain that
action was required if his ambitions and his dignity were to be respected.

The revolt was probably not intended to go as far as it eventually did. The
use of the title 'prince of Wales' was a provocative evocation of the principality of 1267, but Glyn Dŵr did not use it again for several years. This may have
been because the rising misfired, but it is likely that Owain's ambitions were
more mundane. In 1402, he offered the king his submission in return for no
more than the restoration of his rightful estates, and a petition from the burgesses of Holt some ten years after the revolt was over suggested that he might
have been content with the lordship of Bromfield and Yale, which comprised
much of the old kingdom of Powys Fadog. The use of a grandiose title may
therefore have been intended primarily as a bargaining counter, without any
real intention of creating a tangible principality. In any case, it was a clever
manipulation of discontent in England, since it was a pointed rejection of the
authority of Henry IV, whose eldest son, Henry of Monmouth, had been created prince of Wales in 1399.

Two days after he was declared prince of Wales, Glyn Dŵr led a raid on
Ruthin, going on to attack Denbigh, Rhuddlan, Flint, Hawarden, Holt,
Oswestry and Welshpool. No castles were taken, and the rebels were defeated
a few days later by a Shropshire force under Hugh Burnell, either on the
Fyrnwy or on the Severn. Owain suggested in 1401 that a national revolt had

been planned throughout Wales, but it did not materialise. Gwilym and Rhys
ap Tudur did rise simultaneously in Anglesey, but they were quickly put down
by royal troops, who destroyed the priory of Llanfaes. The king faced little
resistance when he marched his army from Shrewsbury in a circuit through
Bangor, Caernarfon and Mawddwy, and most of the rebels submitted to Henry Percy (also known as Hotspur), the justiciar of north Wales. The Welsh
– including Owain's brother Tudur, as well as others who had witnessed his
proclamation as prince – accepted a general pardon, and dutifully paid communal fines. Only Owain and his closest associates were denied a pardon, and
the Glyn Dŵr and Hanmer lands were confiscated. Owain's shortlived revolt
seemed to be over, and he vanished into hiding. He was now a rebel and an
outlaw, and he seemed to have few supporters left.

The king now had a chance to address Welsh grievances, but he failed to take
it. Henry's position in England was perilous, and both he and parliament had
been decidedly nervous since his seizure of power, enacting harsh legislation
against religious heretics and alien merchants. It was too much to expect a conciliatory attitude towards Wales, especially given the traditional English mistrust
of the Welsh. Indeed, parliament had heard that Welsh students and labourers
had been returning to Wales from England to join the rebels. The dissent might
turn out to be serious, and it needed to be crushed before it gained momentum.
In 1401, parliament therefore introduced a series of penal statutes against the
Welsh, and in particular against the *uchelwyr*. In addition, garrisons at marcher castles were reinforced, and the king imposed more fines, confident that
the leaders of the revolt had been cowed. The Welsh, however, were incensed,
especially since so many of them had already made their peace with the king. A
golden opportunity to defuse decades of resentment had been missed. Rather
than placating the Welsh, the government had made the situation worse.

THE REBELLION FLOURISHES

In April 1401, Gwilym and Rhys ap Tudur took Conwy Castle by a ruse, in
protest at their exclusion from the royal pardon. The return of the castle was
negotiated in a few months, and the pardon was granted, but the incident
highlighted a continuing dissatisfaction in Wales. Glyn Dŵr was not slow to
take advantage of it. Unidentified Welsh forces arose apparently from nowhere,
fighting Hotspur near Cadair Idris, and later against John Charlton, the lord
of Powys. The Welsh were defeated on both occasions, and Charlton almost
captured Owain himself – he did seize his armour – but it was clear that rebellion was not only alive but spreading. Glyn Dŵr was very much at large.
Still in Powys, he defeated the king's troops at Mynydd Hyddgen, and the
Welsh flocked to his cause when he subsequently moved into Cardiganshire.

The revolt seemed to lack central co-ordination, but its local fragmentation made it all the harder to eradicate; as soon as it seemed to be defeated in one area, it flared up again somewhere else. Moreover, it was gaining in strength. Owain's support in Carmarthenshire grew to such proportions that there were rumours that he planned to invade England, and in a letter to Henry Dwn of Kidwelly, Owain declared himself confident that the revolt would lift the burden of English oppression from the shoulders of the Welsh people. The precise political implications of that desire were not made explicit, but it was clearly felt that the king could be brought to the negotiating table.

Henry, however, had no intention of negotiating. He launched a second campaign in October, executing many of Glyn Dŵr's supporters in south Wales and dispossessing many more, especially in Ystrad Tywi. The royal army penetrated deep into west Wales, but Owain refused to give battle, preferring to employ guerrilla tactics; the Welsh were always at their most effective when they remained mobile, elusive, swift and unpredictable, making maximum use of the terrain and the elements. Unable to defeat Glyn Dŵr, the king strengthened his castles and prepared others for defence throughout southern and central Wales. Prisoners were taken, and the monastery at Strata Florida was sacked, but the campaign had failed to achieve its main objective. In the meantime, the Welsh raided Welshpool, before concentrating their efforts in north Wales. Caernarfon was attacked late in 1401, and although Glyn Dŵr failed to take the castle, he now enjoyed effective control throughout Caernarfonshire and Merionethshire – not even the prince of Wales's baggage train was safe. Much of the machinery of English administration in northern and central Wales continued to go through the motions of holding courts and levying dues until as late as Michaelmas 1402, but the government was losing ground rapidly. Most of the castles were holding out, but Henry IV and his parliament could do little more than send them help, and that only sporadically. For the first time, they began to think in terms of a negotiated peace.

Owain was now looking to consolidate his position with foreign alliances. In late 1401, he wrote to Robert III of Scots and to the Irish lords in an attempt to gain support. The prospects seemed good, as the Scots had been keen to exploit trouble in Wales in 1315, 1325, 1335 and 1339, and there had also been a Scottish raid on Beaumaris in 1381. The messenger was executed in Ireland before he could deliver the letters, however, and the king of Scots never sent any military help. Nonetheless, there were regular envoys between the Welsh and the Scots until at least 1408, and two Scots appeared at Caernarfon as late as 1410. Furthermore, Scottish sailors – either pirates or the men of the Lord of the Isles – took Bardsey in 1401, after which a Scottish ship was chased to Milford Haven. The Irish, however, were too disunited to provide any help at all.

Despite these disappointments, the rebels enjoyed great success in 1402. In April, Glyn Dŵr captured Reginald Grey near Ruthin, and held him to ransom; Grey was released later in the year for 10,000 marks, 6,000 of which was paid at once, with his eldest son standing as surety for the rest. Hotspur was recalled from Scotland to oversee the relief of castles in north Wales, but the Welsh seemed unstoppable in the field. The English had tended to dismiss them as unsophisticated irregulars, but that view changed when Glyn Dŵr routed a large English force under Edmund Mortimer at Bryn Glas, near Pilleth in Maelienydd, killing and capturing many of its leaders. Any force which could inflict such a defeat in pitched battle, and so close to the English border, had to be taken very seriously indeed. Moreover, Owain now held a very important prisoner: Edmund Mortimer was more closely related to Richard II than was Henry IV, and he was therefore a natural focus of loyalty for Henry's enemies in England. Owain hoped to profit from this, and he demanded a large ransom, but the king showed no interest in paying it; indeed, he may even have considered Owain to have done him a favour by removing Mortimer from the English political stage. If Henry did entertain such thoughts, however, he underestimated the resourcefulness of both men. Edmund soon married one of Glyn Dŵr's daughters, Cathryn, and informed his colleagues and tenants in the march that he would now uphold Owain's right in Wales. Furthermore, he asserted that if it were true that Richard II was not alive, then his young nephew the earl of March – also called Edmund Mortimer – should become king. With such a powerful ally in tow, Owain was more assured of success than ever, and he confidently expressed a willingness to discuss peace on his own terms, as long as he could meet Hotspur's father – also called Henry – the earl of Northumberland, on the Anglo-Welsh border.

The meeting never happened, because Owain feared for his safety. Instead, encouraged by the king's continued problems in Scotland and France, he struck into Gwent and Glamorgan, where the population rose up in support. The rebels attacked Abergavenny, Usk, Caerleon, Newport and Cardiff, prompting a massive royal campaign in August 1402. The revolt was getting out of hand, and it was to be crushed finally and without mercy. Three armies followed Edward I's strategy of 1282, advancing into Wales from Chester, Shrewsbury and Hereford, but they were all thrown into disarray and driven back by bad weather and Welsh raids. Henry himself was nearly killed when his tent blew down on him in a sudden storm – he was only saved by his armour – and the intensity of the rain, hail and even snow that summer made it seem as though Glyn Dŵr could control the elements. Owain had already proved himself as a formidable soldier and politician, and many Englishmen were now convinced that he was also a magician.

The English in Wales now feared for their lives as well as their status and property, and parliament reacted to their desperate petitions with further measures against the Welsh. The new statutes of 1402 made it plain that the government was profoundly unnerved by the revolt: Welshmen were prevented from acquiring property or holding any office in Wales except that of bishop – a concession to John Trefor, the bishop of St Asaph, who at the time was loyal to the king – and this stipulation was also applied to all of the marcher boroughs and all of the castles in Wales; every castle was now to be garrisoned not merely by Englishmen but by strangers to the district; the Welsh were banned from meeting together in any number; only those loyal to the king were permitted to bear arms or armour in towns or churches; and a number of other measures enacted gratuitous anti-Welsh discrimination. Furthermore, the war against Glyn Dŵr was given a sharper focus when Henry of Monmouth was made the king's deputy in Wales in 1403. Henry immediately ravaged Owain's lands in Cynllaith and Glyndyfrdwy, and he urged his father to give him enough men for a decisive attack. The king, however, was still preoccupied elsewhere. He had defeated the Scots at Homildon Hill in 1402, but he now faced a rebellion in the north of England, led by the Percys. There would be no quick victory anywhere, and perhaps the most significant statute of 1402 was the introduction of an embargo on all trade between Wales and England. The government was preparing itself for a long war of attrition.

It was well advised to do so. In July 1403, Glyn Dŵr launched a major offensive in the Tywi valley, forcing the surrender of Carmarthen and the castles of Llansteffan, Dryslwyn, Newcastle Emlyn and Carreg Cennen. The king's castles at Llandovery and Dinefwr were now isolated, and Owain continued into Pembrokeshire, only to be defeated by Thomas, lord of Carew. The Welsh were also driven off when they attacked Brecon, but they were in the ascendancy, and there were raids and rumours of raids throughout Wales. The revolt was taking a hold on the whole country. Moreover, new horizons opened up for the rebels when the Percys fell out with the king. Owain's enemy Hotspur was now a potential ally; not only was he married to Edmund Mortimer's sister, but the reasons for his quarrel with Henry included the refusal to ransom Mortimer, and his father may even have taken issue with royal policy in Wales. Owain was quick to exploit these channels, and he entered secret negotiations with Hotspur. However, the Welsh were apparently not part of any co-ordinated plan when the Percys raised their own standard of revolt in July 1403. Glyn Dŵr was in Ystrad Tywi at the time, and Henry Percy senior was in the north of England. Before the Percys could join forces, the king reacted with lightning speed and defeated and killed Hotspur at Shrewsbury. In their haste to outmanouevre Henry, the Percys had sown the seeds of their own destruction, not least by making it impossible for Owain to throw his weight behind their cause with any effect – he was sorely missed at Shrewsbury. Their defeat was a blow to Glyn Dŵr, but it is debatable whether any change of king in England would have benefited the Welsh in the long term. As many Welsh rulers had learnt in previous centuries, it was unwise to depend too much on supporters in England, and Owain's failure to appear at Shrewsbury may have belied an equivocal attitude towards his fair-weather friends. There was more cause for comfort closer to home.

By 1403, nearly the whole of Wales was in Glyn Dŵr's hands, and most of the Welsh had joined him. The revolt was driven by the grievances of the *uchelw-yr*, and they were quick to bolster Owain's cause with their private retinues, their military and administrative experience, their personal wealth, their access to revenues, and their extensive and closely-bound networks of families and dependants. Among them were the sons of Tudur ap Goronwy in Anglesey, Rhys Gethin in Dyffryn Conwy, Rhys Ddu ap Gruffudd at Cardigan, William Gwyn ap Rhys Llwyd – a former deputy justiciar of south Wales – at Llansteffan, Henry Dwn at Kidwelly, Hywel ap Tudur ab Ithel Fychan in Flint-shire, and many others. Although they often acted independently, these men all regarded Owain as their leader, and many of them swore fealty to him as prince of Wales in 1403. The revolt also enjoyed the overwhelming – and crucial – backing of the *cwmwd* administrators, most of whom belonged to kin-groups which had exercised local power for centuries, and there were similar levels of support among the clergy. By the end of 1404, John Trefor (the bishop of St Asaph), Lewys ap Ieuan (or Lewis Byford, the bishop of Bangor) and Gruffudd Yonge (the archdeacon of Merioneth) had all joined the rebellion, as had the Augustinian canons of Beddgelert and Bardsey and the Cistercian abbots of Strata Florida, Aberconwy, Whitland and Llantarnam; there were also meetings of Welsh students at Oxford University in favour of the rebels. These men were trained administrators, and between them they possessed vast experience in canon law, secular administration, the papal court and royal diplomatic missions. Glyn Dŵr's principality now had the beginnings of a bureaucratic infrastructure. Furthermore, Owain's appeal extended beyond the leaders and administrators of native Wales. The poor had their grievances too, and they flocked to support the revolt. Many of them were simply following their lords, but there was genu-ine sympathy with the rebels, exemplified by the actions of the carpenter who opened the gates of Conwy Castle to the Welsh in 1401; indeed, all of the castles which fell in Ystrad Tywi during 1403 were taken by similar treachery. Many of the marcher lords also joined Glyn Dŵr, notably Philip Scudamore in Gwent, David Perrott in Pembrokeshire and John Fleming at Ogmore. The rebellion subsumed the grievances of almost every class of person in Wales, and it became a truly national protest under the control and direction of the *uchelwyr*.

The king's only hope of subduing the revolt now lay in direct action. Yet another royal army traversed south Wales in September 1403, following the Usk upstream to Brecon and then striking out to Carmarthen. The Welsh in these areas submitted; castles were repaired and provisioned; and a relieving force was sent to Coety in Glamorgan. But despite the apparent restoration of some degree of order, government policy was proving ineffective. Whenever Henry's expeditions returned home, only the castles held out for him; the rest of the country held out for Glyn Dŵr. Much of Wales was now impassable for the English, and the situation was so desperate at Caernarfon in 1404 that messages could only be sent out of the castle by word of mouth; officials there warned the government that all the Welsh of Caernarfonshire were with the rebels, and that they were likely to raid Anglesey in order to deny the king's troops access to supplies. Even the men of Archenfield and Shropshire were forced to make truces with the Welsh in 1403 and 1404. Glyn Dŵr seemed able to roam the whole country at will.

All was not lost, however. Edward I had shown that there was a solution: it lay in a thorough strategy, pursued with perseverance, which would allow the optimum deployment of the superior resources of the English crown. The trouble was that Henry IV faced so many challenges from all quarters in the early years of his reign that he lacked the time and the money to implement such a policy. Expensive wars and domestic politics distracted his attention, emptied his coffers and sapped his authority, and he lost most of his Welsh revenues to the rebels. Administrative incompetence also took its toll, and in 1404 parliament accused the king of extravagance and financial mismanagement. Moreover, the fragmentation of lordship in Wales made it very difficult to co-ordinate English forces there. Henry was no mean military commander, as the Shrewsbury campaign showed, and he could count himself unlucky with the Welsh weather, but any effective action against the rebels was necessarily local and piecemeal. Furthermore, decades of relative peace in Wales had led to the deterioration of many castles. The result was that many of them were badly in need of repair, their garrisons were reduced to dangerously inadequate levels, and their armouries were in poor condition; the inventory of weapons at Harlech in 1403 was particularly pitiful. Although the castles gave the English a valuable presence in Wales, they could not hold out forever. They had to be reinforced and supplied, and this proved increasingly difficult. Control of the sea was vital in maintaining the coastal castles, and although the English enjoyed superiority there, it was far from uncontested. David Perrott used his ships to harass the king's attempts to relieve Harlech, while the French adventurer Jean d'Espagne provided the rebels with invaluable sea-power, artillery and technical expertise against the castles of Harlech, Caernarfon and Beaumaris. The cumulative effect of these problems was that even some of the strongest English castles in Wales fell in 1403 and 1404: Cricieth was taken first, Aberystwyth and Harlech followed after long sieges, and it is possible that Beaumaris also capitulated to the Welsh. Cardiff also fell, and a Welsh defeat at Campstone near Abergavenny was reversed at Craig y Dorth near Monmouth. The English seemed to be losing their grip on Wales.

The capture of major castles was a huge boost to Welsh morale. The fact that Edward I's great castles were not invincible to Welsh siegecraft confirmed the rebels' military prowess, and moreover it held out the possibility that English rule could be shaken off. Glyn Dŵr now had almost unchallenged control of Wales from Caernarfon to Cardigan, together with secure bases. Furthermore, Harlech castle was a fitting seat for a prince. Owain could now portray himself as a leader of both national and international standing. Accordingly, in 1404, he summoned a parliament at Machynlleth, reminiscent of the councils summoned by the thirteenth-century princes of Gwynedd, and possibly influenced by the parliament at Westminster, which was now an integral part of English government. For the first time since 1282, it was possible to imagine that the Welsh could exercise some degree of autonomy.

If that autonomy was to become permanent, Owain needed foreign recognition – and, more urgently, practical support. France was the most obvious ally. It could offer sea-power, men, money and war machines, and it was a reliable and internationally respected enemy of the English government. In return, Wales offered the French a valuable extra front against England. Already, the French had sought to utilise this avenue of attack in 1339, 1346 and 1359, as well as during the career of Owain Lawgoch. They had also shown an interest in Glyn Dŵr. In 1401, Charles VI – or rather his advisers, since the king had been insane since 1392 – had sent Dafydd ab Ifan Goch to the king of Scots on Owain's behalf, and French pirates had later assisted the Welsh in north Wales and at Kidwelly. French wine and spices were delivered to Llŷn in 1404, and the Machynlleth parliament was attended by envoys from France and its ally, Castile. This was all very encouraging for Owain, and he now saw an opportunity to develop the relationship further. French attacks in the English Channel had been renewed in 1403, and the complexion of the French government changed when Philip the Bold, the duke of Burgundy, died in April 1404. The mood was now much more warlike, and Glyn Dŵr quickly despatched ambassadors to ask the French court for weapons and a military expedition to Wales. He had judged the moment well. In July 1404, Charles VI of France and Owain Glyn Dŵr, prince of Wales, agreed not to make peace with Henry of Lancaster independently of each other, and to promote trade between Wales and France. The French declined to make any promise of military aid, but a fleet of 60 ships soon left for Wales. Bad weather or incompetence prevented it from leaving the Channel, but Owain had won a great political victory: a major European power now recognised him as prince of Wales.

Further possibilities arose in 1405, when the earl of Northumberland plotted with Edmund Mortimer senior to replace Henry IV with Mortimer's namesake, the earl of March. Glyn Dŵr was considered a useful and dependable ally, and the result was the agreement known as the Tripartite Indenture. If implemented, the Indenture would have divided England between Percy and Mortimer, with the earl of March as king. There was no mention of the Mortimers' marcher estates, however, which would apparently have fallen to Glyn Dŵr, who was allotted a sizeable chunk of the English Midlands as well as the whole of Wales. The eastern boundary of Owain's principality was to follow a line from the mouth of the Severn up the river to Worcester, and thence to the Six Ashes on the road between Bridgnorth and Kinver in Shropshire, on to the sources of the Trent and then the Mersey, and down the Mersey to the sea. This amounted to a promise of unprecedented and almost unassailable power for Glyn Dŵr, under which all of the hopes and desires of the Welsh could be answered. It was too good to be true. The plan was so impractically ambitious as to be worthless, at least from the Welsh point of view. Even if Henry IV had been deposed, it was very unlikely in practice that any new king of England – and especially an earl of March – would have countenanced such a formidable principality of Wales. The Indenture was a useful propaganda victory for Glyn Dŵr, but it probably represented little more than a sop thrown out by a cynical Percy and Mortimer to keep their Welsh ally happy. In any event, the plan foundered when the young Edmund Mortimer was arrested at Cheltenham before the projected revolt could begin.

The vision of an independent principality of Wales now floated tantalisingly before Glyn Dŵr, just out of reach. If he did not grasp it soon, it might disappear for ever. He was beginning to suffer serious military setbacks: the Welsh of Gwent and Glamorgan were defeated at Grosmont in May 1405, and an attack on Usk was repelled and then routed at Pwll Melyn, where Owain's brother, Tudur, was killed. In addition, Owain's son Gruffudd was captured – he spent the rest of his life in the Tower of London – as were the prince's secretary, Owain ap Gruffudd ap Rhisiart, and his brother-in-law John Hanmer, in separate incidents. The English were anything but defeated, and the king prepared yet another campaign against Wales, only to be called north to crush the rebellion of Archbishop Scrope of York. Henry was gradually consolidating himself in England, and it did not bode well for the Welsh.

Owain's French alliance had been hampered by disagreement between the dukes of Orléans and Burgundy, but it was given a renewed impetus when the two men were reconciled in the summer of 1405. A second parliament was held at Harlech to raise troops in readiness for the long-awaited French invasion, and also to discuss a possible treaty with Henry IV. In July, a large French fleet sailed from Brest for Milford Haven, where it joined forces with Owain, but the results of the subsequent campaign were mixed. The allies took Haverfordwest – apart from the castle – and they were ignominiously driven off from Tenby by English ships before capturing Cardigan and Carmarthen. What happened next is not clear. A late and somewhat unreliable French source claims that Glyn Dŵr and the French marched eastwards almost as far as Worcester, but this is hard to accept; it would have been the furthest that any foreign army had penetrated into England since 1066, but there is no mention of such a momentous campaign in any of the contemporary sources. Whatever happened between Owain and the French, the alliance was not an unmitigated success. It may, however, have contributed to the failure of another huge royal expedition. This time, the king's ambition was limited to the relief of Coety, but once again he was driven back by the weather, and he suffered the added humiliation of losing his baggage train to Glyn Dŵr.

In November 1405, the French knights went home. They left behind them a large force of infantry, whose presence very likely played a part in persuading the English authorities in southern Pembrokeshire to offer Glyn Dŵr £200 in return for a truce. But the writing was on the wall. Early in 1406, all of the remaining French troops left Wales, and attempts to replace them were half-hearted; only a few more ships were sent, and several of them were captured on the way. There no more major Franco-Welsh operations. The Welsh and the French had been mutually disappointed in each other, and inevitably so, because they wanted different things. Charles VI explained that he would have sent more help if only there had been more response in England from the supporters of the late Richard II. Owain, however, had no interest in involving himself in an invasion of England for its own sake. The war between England and France was not his quarrel. The alliance was always one of convenience, and Glyn Dŵr had to re-learn the old lesson that the French always regarded Wales as an expendable ally. Attacks on Wales might be useful, but they were neither the most direct nor the most effective way to harm England.

A diplomatic alliance was still convenient, however, even if military co-operation was not. In March, Charles wrote to Owain urging him to follow the French and Scots in recognising the schismatic Benedict XIII as pope in Avignon. The English supported Innocent VII in Rome, and Glyn Dŵr – or more particularly his ecclesiastical advisers – immediately saw the French proposition as an opportunity to free the Welsh church from its jurisdictional and economic subjection to Canterbury. Writing back from Pennal in Merionethshire, Owain said that he would give his allegiance to the (anti-)pope in Avignon if Benedict satisfied a series of wide-ranging conditions. In effect, Owain demanded an independent Welsh church, which would constitute a hugely important symbolic, bureaucratic and economic step towards an independent secular principality. Such a radical vision was dear to the hearts of many in Wales, but the proposal elicited no response either from Charles or from Benedict. No-one outside Wales was interested.

Owain's vision was now fading rapidly. With the French alliance effectively defunct, his only supporters outside Wales were the earl of Northumberland and his associate Lord Bardolf, and they had very little to offer. They had been forced to flee from England to Scotland, but the Scots had plotted against them, and they then sought refuge in Wales, only to be defeated by John Charlton, the lord of Powys. In the meantime, large parts of Wales were being lost. Gower, Ystrad Tywi and much of Cardiganshire submitted to the king, and royal troops from Dublin recovered Anglesey; Beaumaris Castle was recaptured, and 2,000 people returned to the king's peace, paying large fines for the privilege of doing so. There was considerable lawlessness in many parts of Wales for a long time after the formal submissions, but it was clear that the revolt was not going to succeed. Sensing victory at last, parliament urged that Prince Henry be given more authority in Wales to crush the rebellion for good. By 1407, English nobles and knights were falling over themselves in their eagerness to share in the spoils which would accompany Glyn Dŵr's long-overdue defeat.

DEFEAT

The decline in Owain's fortunes owed much to an improvement in those of the king. The threat from France was greatly reduced as the French were split by rivalries between the Armagnacs and the Burgundians, and relations with Scotland were more than satisfactory. Robert III's son, James, was intercepted on his way to France in 1406, and when Robert died later in the year the English found themselves enjoying the luxury of holding James I, king of Scots, in their custody. Henry had also overcome most of his enemies in England by this time, and his finances improved markedly after 1405. For the first time, the king could give his undivided attention to Wales, where his son was maturing as a military commander.

Years of rebellion were taking their toll on the Welsh. The financial cost of maintaining large armies, besieging castles and governing a principality was prohibitive, and it could not be met by plunder, ransoms, protection money, or secret donations from England. If Glyn Dŵr was to survive, he needed control over the machinery of government in order to collect revenues for himself. There is evidence that he succeeded in this, at least to some extent. Local administration was in the hands of the rebels, and the Harlech parliament demonstrated a determination to make use of existing fiscal mechanisms, while parts

of the Pennal letter were designed to extend Welsh control over clerical finances. At the same time, however, many of Owain's supporters no doubt viewed
the revolt as an opportunity to continue and indeed extend their oppressive
and extortionate local regimes. Their loyalty may well have come at the price of
allowing them to keep a large share of the revenue they collected. Furthermore,
the administrative structure of Wales was deeply complex and fragmented at the
best of times, and there is no indication that Glyn Dŵr made any attempt to
remedy this. Nor is there any sign that records were ever kept for local courts
or the payment of dues under Welsh control, even if they carried on as normal
in other respects. Slowly but surely, the everyday processes of government were
falling apart. Unless Owain could consolidate his administration during a prolonged period of peace, his principality would never be financially viable.

The English trade embargo was also biting very deep. Although there was
widespread smuggling – it was said, for example, that the men of Gloucestershire and Herefordshire brought food and armour to the Welsh – the harsh
economic restrictions effectively placed the whole of Wales under siege. The
rebels were often short of food and equipment, especially siege engines. There
were French supplies, but many of them were intercepted, and the lack of
resources meant that Welsh military operations were limited in what they
could achieve. Most of them were conducted on a small scale, and obtaining
supplies was often their primary aim. The harsh winter of 1407-8 did nothing to help the Welsh cause. Furthermore, most of Glyn Dŵr's soldiers were
also farmers, and his armies were severely incapacitated at harvest time. Their
numbers might swell to a very respectable 10,000 at times, but the Welsh were
perennially short of manpower, and they could not sustain long campaigns or
sieges. The English, on the other hand, could afford expensive weapons like
cannon, and they could always bring in new troops from somewhere or other.
Their task in this war of attrition was made easier by the fact that communications in Wales run from east to west, and Owain's lack of sea-power also
told against him in the end.

Perhaps the most impressive aspect of the Glyn Dŵr revolt was that it lasted
as long as it did; very few popular rebellions in Europe lasted more than a few
months. As well as being a talented man of action, Owain inspired deep loyalty.
He was never betrayed by his followers, and no-one tried to usurp his position.
This devotion was all the more remarkable because of its cost. Rebellion was
one of the worst imaginable crimes, and the devastation caused by both the rebels and the English made surrender an attractive option if only to regain some
semblance of normality. Yet many – such as Llywelyn ap Gruffudd Fychan of
Caeo, who was executed in Llandovery 1401 – would rather die than inform
against Glyn Dŵr.

As a wealthy *uchelwr*, Llywelyn was a natural supporter of the revolt. Others, however, were not. Many Welshmen opposed it in order to protect their vested interests; they included most of the Welsh burgesses, as well as Maredudd ap Cynwrig, who was captured while collecting the king's taxes at Beaumaris. Some, such as the men of Whittington and Flint, only joined the rebellion under duress. Others hedged their bets: the men of Brecon stated in 1404 that they would submit to the king if he could defeat the rebels in the area, but otherwise they would stay loyal to Glyn Dŵr; similarly, many of Edmund Mortimer's Welsh tenants fought with him at Bryn Glas, only to change sides in the middle of the battle when they saw who was most likely to win. Still others, such as Gruffudd ap Gwilym in north Wales, managed to profit financially from changing sides more than once. Finally, there were many Welshmen whose ancestors had been loyal to the king and the marchers for generations and even centuries. In a world where loyalty to one's lord was paramount, they had no time for an upstart like Glyn Dŵr. There could be only one prince of Wales, and Owain had no right to expect the allegiance of men like Dafydd Gam ap Llywelyn ap Hywel, a descendant of the dynasty of Brycheiniog who lived and died a steadfast supporter of the house of Lancaster. Moreover, even Owain's followers were susceptible to advances from the king – their natural lord – when the revolt faltered.

By 1407, it was faltering. Aberystwyth held out against Prince Henry for several months, and Glyn Dŵr bought time by threatening to have Rhys Ddu executed when he considered surrender, but by the end of the year the castle had fallen. In the meantime, the murder of Louis of Orléans allowed the less belligerent elements in the French court to negotiate peace with England. Despite the promises they had made to Glyn Dŵr in 1404, the French did not now object to the fact that the peace excluded him; instead, they accepted the English assertion that he was a subject of the English realm. Owain lost another ally in 1408, when Henry Percy rebelled again and was finally defeated and killed at Bramham Moor. These allies had long since ceased to be useful, but their removal was a reminder that Owain was becoming increasingly isolated. Even in north Wales, his position was disintegrating. An English bishop was enthroned at Bangor in 1409, and the winter of 1408-9 witnessed a long siege at Harlech. When the castle eventually fell, Owain's wife, daughters and granddaughters were captured and sent to the Tower, together with the sons of Edmund Mortimer – their father had died during the siege. Glyn Dŵr himself escaped, but he had suffered an immense personal, military and political loss. The self-styled prince of Wales was on the run as a hunted outlaw once again.

Failure was now inevitable, but the revolt was not yet defeated. Owain continued raiding in the march in May 1409, and he was not alone. The government believed that there were large numbers of Welsh, French and Scottish troops with him, and marcher officials in Powys, Oswestry, Ruthin and elsewhere found it necessary to make truces with the Welsh in November of that year. In 1410, Glyn Dŵr seems to have been in effective control of the area around his home in Chirkland and Edeirnion, but the rebellion was drawing to a close. The last raid on the English border led to the capture of Rhys Ddu, Philip Scudamore and Rhys ap Tudur in Shropshire in 1410 – they were all executed – and Glyn Dŵr's last recorded act of violence was to seize Dafydd Gam and ransom him in 1412. Even now, however, Owain inspired fear. The government maintained large forces in Wales during 1411 and 1412, and English officials still moved under heavy escort in north and west Wales. In 1413, Henry of Monmouth – now Henry V – offered a pardon to all of the remaining Welsh rebels. He was eager to clear up his outstanding business in Wales in preparation for war with France, and he feared an uprising of Lollard heretics in England. His approaches to the Welsh were therefore conciliatory and even magnanimous, cancelling arrears, dismissing corrupt officers and even offering compensation. There were still cash fines which provoked discontent, but the Welsh were largely reconciled to the king. Most of the *uchelwyr* recovered the lands and privileges they had enjoyed before the revolt, and many were reinstated as royal officials, often on very favourable terms. Henry Dwn, in particular, settled back very quickly into life at Kidwelly after a fine, forfeiture and spells in prison, and he took a quite astounding liberty as a royal official in 1413 when he fined 200 Welshmen for failing to join him in the revolt. The old order in local politics had been restored – if it had ever really changed. By 1415, the inveterate Cardiganshire rebel Maredudd ab Owain was fighting alongside Dafydd Gam and Henry V at Agincourt, and many other former rebels were there as well. The revolt was over.

Glyn Dŵr, however, remained defiant. He was offered a pardon several times in 1415, but he made no response. Gruffudd Yonge was still representing him in France, and Owain's son Maredudd was still keeping the flame of rebellion flickering in the recesses of Caernarfonshire and Merionethshire – he did not accept a pardon until 1421. As late as 1417, fears that the Lollard leader, Sir John Oldcastle, was in league with the Welsh rebels seemed to be confirmed when he was captured in Powys. Glyn Dŵr himself had now disappeared. He was probably dead. There is no evidence that he was alive after 1415, and a pardon offered to Maredudd in 1416 made no mention of his father. Owain may well have retired to stay with his daughter Alice in Herefordshire, but some were of the opinion that he had gone to France, perhaps confusing him with Owain Lawgoch. It is more likely that sympathisers kept the whereabouts of his corpse a secret, in order to prevent any disrespectful treatment.

Glyn Dŵr's rebellion had failed because of the superior resources of the English crown. The English were frustrated and demoralised by the guerilla war, but the Welsh were simply unable to sustain it against the stranglehold of the English castles – most of which never fell – and the economic embargo. Owain made full use of the political opportunities that came his way, but his foreign alliances were ultimately worthless, and the chances of success were always very slim. Glyn Dŵr's failure meant that any prospect for a united, independent Wales under native rule was gone. The government was now faced with a new problem: the revolt had thrown the anomalous relationship between Wales and England into sharp relief, and it had highlighted the administrative fragmentation of the country. In the end, it would be necessary to incorporate Wales formally within the kingdom of England.

9

Medieval Wales and the Welsh

Wales was defined both territorially and psychologically by the English advance into what had been Roman Britain. The fragmentation and diversity of native Wales defied any positive, comprehensive, universally acceptable definition, and only propagandists were ever able to treat the territory to the west of Offa's dyke as though it were a single homogenous block. The cultural affinities within the Romano-British population – often referred to by modern scholars as 'Celtic' and 'sub-Roman' – were widely recognised, as were the differences between the Britons and the Saxons, but the definition of 'Wales' was essentially negative. It was not England, and it was not English, but neither did it incorporate enough of the old Roman diocese of Britannia to be thought of as 'Britain'. In Anglo-Saxon eyes, the Welsh were simply *wælisc* ('foreign'), whereas the Welsh themselves found a shared sense of identity in the memory of dispossession by a common enemy. From these origins developed a national awareness which was integral to the process that created the principality of Wales and culminated in the vision of Owain Glyn Dŵr.

The British Inheritance

CHARACTERISTICS OF NATIVE WALES

It was universally recognised that Wales possessed a distinct 'national' inheritance, characterised by peculiarly Welsh laws and justice, customs and *mores*, as well as the Welsh language. These things transcended political and administrative divisions, distinguishing the Welsh as a separate people (*gens*). From the seventh century, the Welsh often referred to themselves as *Kymry*, a name which seems to have been derived from the Old Welsh *Combrogi* ('fellow countrymen'); this may originally have been a legal term indicating joint proprietorship, and its use in a cultural and political context may have arisen in response to English conquests, or perhaps as an expression of a sense of identity as citizens of a Roman province. The Welsh language was spoken throughout Wales, and it was far more widely understood than any other language. Although the use of Latin was common in the ecclesiastical and legal spheres, the native poets employed the vernacular alone, and one definition of a foreigner was that he was unable to speak Welsh (*anghyfiaith*). Welsh law was also used throughout Wales, and it was apparently first written down in Welsh. Hywel Dda may have been responsible for a codification in the tenth century, and some laws were said to have been amended by Bleddyn ap Cynfyn, but the earliest surviving legal redactions date from the twelfth century, making any speculation about the nature of the 'law of Hywel' before that date very difficult. Moreover, even in the thirteenth century, there were many local variations in customary law, and there is no sign of a common jurisprudence. It was assumed, nevertheless, that Wales was a single unit in legal terms. Welsh culture, society and customs were therefore broadly homogeneous, but it cannot be assumed that any 'national' awareness was drawn from this.

Some common identity in the early medieval period was implicit in the fact that all of the royal lines in Wales claimed descent from Magnus Maximus. The Welsh were also conscious of their shared Christian inheritance, and they used it to identify themselves against pagan Saxons and Vikings. By the eighth century, they distinguished themselves from Christian Saxons by defining themselves as 'Britons', to the extent that a 'History of the Britons' (*Historia Brittonum*) was written in the ninth century. At the same time, the most powerful Welsh rulers were credited with leadership of the Britons. Bede called Cadwallon ap Cadfan 'king of the Britons' (*rex Britonum*), reflecting Welsh usages, and the *Anglo-Saxon Chronicle* and Irish sources followed the same pattern. Such terminology was not entirely meaningless when applied to rulers of extensive territories, such as Hywel Dda or Gruffudd ap Llywelyn. The claims that Hywel was aided by six men from each *cantref* in Wales, and that the law was to be applied throughout Wales, cannot be dismissed out of hand, although they may only date from the twelfth century. Furthermore, the *Latin A* redaction of the laws asserted that Hywel established the 'laws of Britain' (*Britanniae leges*), and the association of Hywel with the law was a clear attempt to emphasise some kind of unity. Nevertheless, such language need not imply any sense of national affiliation, and verifiable contemporary sources are scarce – on the one native Welsh coin which has been discovered, Hywel was simply styled 'king' (*rex*).

There is almost no sign of a common Welsh interest or identity in the early medieval period. The *gwlad* ('country', in the sense of a local area) was a subject of allegiance in the seventh-century *Canu Taliesin* and *Canu Aneirin*, but, even in the late eleventh century, Ieuan ap Sulien made clear that, while his *gens* was that of the Britons, his *patria* was merely Ceredigion – not Britain, Wales, or even Deheubarth. A consciousness of Wales as a territorial whole was growing by the eleventh century, when the term *dextralis Britanniae* (Deheubarth) emerged, and *Pedeir Keinc y Mabinogi* – which were apparently brought together around 1060 – demonstrated a strong awareness of Welsh territorial and cultural integrity. It is very difficult, however, to tell what any of these concepts meant to people, or how different loyalties related to one another. Throughout this period, the chief focus of loyalty was always the leader-follower relationship, and one of the best and earliest illustrations of this appears in Aneirin's account of Mynyddog Mwynfawr and his retinue at the end of the sixth century.

The Romans had treated Britain as a discernable entity, and the Welsh shared a culture which pre-dated Roman rule, but the most potent unifying force was opposition to the English. Having had their autonomous rule confined to the corners of Britain by the Anglo-Saxons, the Welsh became increasingly aware of their identity as 'Britons' by the eighth and ninth centuries. The consciousness of the British past was so strong that several Welsh chronicles record eighth-century battles fought by the Britons of Cornwall and Strath-clyde, and the ninth-century *Historia Brittonum* told of a semi-mythical Ro-mano-British king Arthur, whose enemies were always the Saxons. Similarly, the early tenth-century *Armes Prydein* expressed a common animosity against the English oppressors, who were felt to have no right to the land of Britain, or *Prydein*. In this prophecy poem, the Welsh shared an identity as the *Kymry*, and, with the help of their allies from Scotland, Ireland, Man, Cornwall and Brittany, they would drive the Saxons into the sea, re-conquering the area from Man to Brittany and from Dyfed to Thanet. Such sentiments could scarcely be realised, but they persisted into the twelfth century. Moreover, the definition of Wales (*Cymru*) as a country inhabited by the Welsh (*Cymry*) paralleled the emergence of its neighbour as a unified kingdom of England (*Englalond*) belonging to the English (*Angelcynn*).

For their part, the English viewed the Welsh rather simplistically as a homo-geneous people, essentially barbarous, animal-like and less than proper Chris-tians. Wales was seen as an inhospitable land on the edge of Christendom, and the lifestyle of its people was believed to be inferior, although Gerald of Wales recognised many traits which he regarded as virtues. Gerald was well aware of the contradictions, anomalies and reality of Welsh life, but even he accepted the negative stereotypes as being true.

Implicit in this juxtaposition of Welsh and English was a sense of the in-tegrity of Britain, both geographically and politically. The Welsh acknowl-edged the undeniable supremacy of English power, but the memory of for-mer glories remained. Thus, the first entry in the *Brut* states that the Sax-ons gained the crown of kingship of Britain in 682, and it commemorates

Cadwaladr ap Cadwallon as the last king over the Britons. In the laws, one of the duties of the court poet (*bardd teulu*) was to sing *Unbeynnyaeth Prydeyn* ('the Sovereignty of Britain'), and Dyfnwal ap Moel Mud, a supposed 'king of this island' and holder of the crown of London, was remembered as having ruled a kingdom of over 450,000 square miles. In the *Pedeir Keinc*, both Brân and Caswallon ap Beli held the 'crown of London' (*goron Lundein*), and Brân was buried in London. The Anglo-Norman Geoffrey of Monmouth emphasised the British inheritance in his *Historia regum Britanniae* ('History of the kings of Britain'), saying that the island would be called after Brutus – the legendary Trojan ancestor of the Britons, who led them from captivity in Greece to exile in Britain – and not by the name given to it by the Saxon invaders, who would be ejected. Geoffrey also invented Camber, an alleged second son of Brutus, to explain the name of the *Kymry*. His work contained many fantastic inventions, but his sources included 'a certain very ancient book written in the British language (*lingua Britannica*)',[1] and the Welsh themselves were keen to trace the history of their princes back to Geoffrey's semi-legendary kings, referring to the study of that history as *brut*. Yet, although there was a genuine Welsh consciousness as descendants of the Britons, its extent is unclear – it is impossible to tell, for instance, whether Arthur was a national hero in Wales before Geoffrey popularised him.

The Development of Welsh Self-Awareness

THE PERSISTENCE OF THE BRITISH DIMENSION

Increasing Anglo-Welsh contact made Welsh subordination explicit, especially after the death of Gruffudd ap Llywelyn, and this was often seen in a British context. William I was regarded in Wales as 'king of the Saxons and the Britons and the Scots' and 'king of England and Wales',[2] and Henry I was said to have subdued all the island of Britain with authority vested in him by God – the army he brought to Wales in 1114 was drawn from as far away as Cornwall and Scotland, and the archiepiscopal see of Canterbury claimed metropolitan authority over a similar area. In asserting pan-British overlordship, the Normans relied considerably upon Geoffrey of Monmouth's collection of primarily fictitious Arthurian legends, which appeared around 1136. In both political and literary terms, the Matter of Britain now assumed greater proportions than ever, and the Britain of *Armes Prydein* was soon reconciled with the reality of the twelfth century. Gerald wrote of the 'Island of Britain' in a contemporary sense, and the promulgation of Rhys ap Gruffudd's court in 1176 throughout Wales, England, Scotland and Ireland demonstrated a British consciousness. Similarly, several Welsh romances were inspired by Geoffrey of Monmouth's European setting and Anglo-Norman propaganda: *Chwedyl Gereint uab Erbin*, for example, saw Arthur as a forerunner of the Norman kings, with nine kings as his men, and *Kyuranc Lludd a Llefelys* made it clear that real authority over the Island of Britain rested at London and Oxford. Even the thirteenth-century poets sang of the Welsh princes fighting for the crown of London and sailing their fleets to Caerleon, and Prydydd y Moch made claims for Llywelyn ap Iorwerth which were reminiscent of Geoffrey's Arthur, saying that that the fame of his victory at Aberconwy extended not only across the Bristol Channel but as far as Brittany.

The traditional view of Britain – and especially of Wales as 'the kingdom of the Britons' – remained popular in Welsh literature. As late as 1204, *Annales Cambriae* referred to the Bretons as 'the Armorican Britons' – with the implication that the Welsh were the British Britons – and the poet Cynddelw said that Owain Gwynedd was known at Canterbury for maintaining the privileges of the Britons. *Breudwyt Maxen Wledig* and *Historia Gruffud vab Kenan* both harked back to the Romano-British past, and Gerald of Wales reinforced the myth of Trojan ancestry. Native poets continued to sing of the Old North, and they associated their patrons, however unconvincingly, with *Prydein*. Such praises were offered to Gruffudd ap Cynan, Owain Gwynedd, Rhys ap Gruffudd, Madog ap Maredudd, Dafydd ab Owain, Rhodri ab Owain, Hywel ab Owain and even Einion ap Madog ab Iddon of Powys. This practice reached its height in the eulogies to Llywelyn ap Iorwerth, who was seen as the fulfilment of a prophecy of Merlin (Myrddin) that a man of courage would arise from among the Welsh (*Gymry*); Cynddelw compared him with Arthur, and as the 'ruler of Britain', he was urged to extend his thoughts and possessions to London. In the eyes of the poets, Llywelyn was the inheritor of the tradition of Taliesin. Thus, the princes who implemented radical changes in the Welsh polity were legitimised by reference to a memory of the ancient past, much of which owed more to fantasy than actual history. As the ties of English overlordship tightened, myth and legend played an ever more crucial part in defining who the Welsh were and what they stood for.

The coincidence of this literary revival with the Welsh successes between 1136 and 1155 seems to have caused some alarm in the Anglo-Norman world. Although there was no prospect of the Welsh recovering Britain, the use of the British past in the cause of the Welsh princes posed a clear threat to Anglo-Norman influence in Wales, and it was taken seriously. Five *chansons de geste* with strong ecclesiastical and pro-Norman influences were translated into Welsh in the middle of the twelfth century, apparently with the intention of minimising British-Welsh and anti-English feelings, and Henry II instigated the 'discovery' of 'Arthur's tomb' at Glastonbury, which eventually took place after his death, in 1191. Henry's main incentive in this instance was the abbey's desire to attract pilgrims for financial reasons, but he rarely missed an opportunity to delegitimise Welsh mythologies, and Gerald of Wales relished recalling incidents in Wales where Henry was supposed to have proven the prophecies of Merlin false. The idea of 'Britain' was well understood as a powerful tool in the assertion of Welsh independence, and also in efforts to create a united Welsh nation.

THE CREATION OF A WELSH IDENTITY

By the twelfth century, Wales was taking shape as a geopolitical entity. *Breudwyt Maxen Wledig* viewed it as a whole, and efforts were made to establish an archbishopric of Wales. Gerald of Wales observed that the Dee and the Wye separated Wales from England, and he identified both the Welsh people and the language with a particular territory, which he linked with the British past by systematically replacing the English name *Wallia*, which he considered vulgar, with *Cambria*, after Camber. The name *Kambria* had first appeared in the tenth century as an appellation for Cumbria and Strathclyde, and it was also used by Geoffrey of Monmouth, but Gerald was the first to use it consistently to denote Wales.

Attachment to localities, such as that exhibited in the poetry of Hywel ab Owain Gwynedd, came to be matched by a curious mixture of national and parochial sentiments. The poet Gwalchmai asserted that Madog ap Maredudd was famed from Pumlumon to Caerleon and from Bangor-on-Dee to Meirionnydd and Arwystli, and the expedition through Wales (*kylch Kymry*) embarked upon by the *teulu* of Owain Cyfeiliog ranged over Powys and Gwynedd, but not the south. Moreover, although Hywel ap Goronwy was celebrated in terms of Britain, the ambitious claims made for him by his supporters were confined to Wales, and, more significantly, encompassed Gwynedd, Powys, Deheubarth, Morgannwg, Brycheiniog and the middle march. Such ideas could transcend the fragmentation of the Welsh polity – especially since the poets were not tied to particular dynastic interests – and they became more plausible as Welsh rulers in general broadened their territorial field of action within Wales from the eleventh century onwards.

The Welsh also emerged as a people, not least because of increased interaction with foreigners. The presence of Irish, English and Scandinavians in Wales all reminded the Welsh of their separateness, and the Norman invasions introduced a new element into the equation. The difficulties of describing the Anglo-Norman position in Wales prompted Gerald of Wales to redefine the Welsh as *Kambrenses*, and split identities were commonplace in the march – as late as 1214x1216, charters of the earl of Gloucester could still be addressed to the 'French and English and Welsh of Wales'. Often, however, the distinction

was more negative. Rhigyfarch ap Sulien complained of the tyranny of the
Normans at Llanbadarn in the 1090s, and of their destruction not only of
native Welsh social and cultural values, but of the very dignity of the people.
The revolt in Gwynedd in 1098 was provoked by the 'laws and injustice of
the French',[3] and Gerald was in no doubt that the Welsh would fight for their
patria against hostile peoples. Native chroniclers were convinced that Henry
I intended to destroy even the memory of the name of the Britons in 1114,
and this attitude, which amounted almost to national paranoia, led Gerald to
declare that neither the Welsh language nor the Welsh people would ever be
destroyed. It was a literary convention to praise kings for their feats against
the English, and atrocities such as the Abergavenny massacre in 1175 led to
a tangible deterioration of Anglo-Welsh trust. This process was paralleled
by increasing English prejudice against the Welsh, and also by a substantially
conscious development of English nationality in the twelfth century, which
was given added vigour by the loss of Normandy in 1204.

The tone of Welsh narrative sources also indicates a growing willingness to
unify the Welsh against outsiders, reflecting increasingly xenophobic tendencies common to many societies in later medieval Europe. It was in juxtaposition to non-Welsh-speaking foreigners ('*estrawn genedloedd a rhei agkyfyeith*'),[4]
who were increasingly seen as enemies, that the Welsh came to see themselves
as a people (*cenedl*). The term *cenedl* usually denoted a kindred group, but it
could also be applied to a family, a race, a nation, all of the inhabitants of
Britain, or a species of animals. In *Historia Gruffud vab Kenan*, the Welsh and
the peoples of Ireland and the 'islands of Denmark' all constituted '*genedloed*',[5]
while the Scandinavians, Flemings and 'people' of Sulien ap Rhigyfarch were
described similarly by the *Brut*. Rhys ap Gruffudd was also said to be anxious
to remove the subjection of his people ('*dileu kethiwet y genedyl*') in 1158.[6] At
the same time, the Welsh came to see the Anglo-Normans as the 'English' – a
usage which was paralleled in England itself. The first Normans in Wales were
almost always known as the 'French', and by the 1130s they were *Normanyeit*.
They were regularly distinguished from the English until as late as 1159, but
by the second half of the century they were themselves regarded as English or
Saxons (*Saesson*). The *Brut* first called them *Saesson* in 1198 – when it used the
name three times – and again in 1200, and the fact that each instance referred
to the royal government points to the role of political polarisation in this process. Hywel ap Rhys ap Gruffudd gained the epithet 'Sais' ('Englishman') from
having spent long periods as a hostage in England – as a result of which he is
supposed to have been unable to speak Welsh – and such examples illustrate
both the familiarity of many Welshmen with England and at the same time a
conception among the Welsh of the English nation as a simplistic monolith.

28 Offa's dyke is traditionally supposed to have been built by king Offa 'from sea to sea' to protect Mercia from the Welsh, but modern scholarship suggests that its origins were considerably more complicated than that.

29 William fitz Osbern, lord of Breteuil in Calvados, built Chepstow soon after 1066 to guard the Wye crossing on the coastal route from England into Wales. He seems to have been mindful of Harold Godwinesson's problems in Gwent after 1063, since, unlike the vast majority of Norman castles, Chepstow was provided with a powerful stone keep from the 1070s. Most of the present castle was added during the twelfth and thirteenth centuries.

30 The Roman fort at Cardiff was reinforced against barbarian attacks as imperial rule faltered in Britain, and the site provided an ideal setting for the first Norman castle in Morgannwg, which seems to have been built around 1081. The timber castle was scaled by Ifor Bach when he kidnapped the earl of Gloucester in 1158, and it was replaced by the present stone keep later in the twelfth century.

31 Pembroke was one of the first Norman castles in Wales, and it enjoyed the distinction of never falling to the Welsh. It was founded by Arnulf of Montgomery in 1093 or 1094, and completely rebuilt in stone by William Marshal after 1189. Strategically, Pembroke was vital to the Normans, and the strength of its site was such that it was rarely attacked, although the constable was forced to ransom both himself and the castle during the Glyn Dŵr revolt.

32 Llanychaiarn (Aberystwyth), also known as Tan-y-Castell, Tan-y-Bwlch and possibly Aberrheidol, was the original Norman castle guarding the mouth of the river Ystwyth. Its timber structure was erected around 1110 by Gilbert fitz Richard, the lord of Ceredigion, and it repelled Gruffudd ap Rhys in 1116. *Brut y Tywysogyon* accounts for the Welsh failure by saying that they fought 'like a furious rabble... without a ruler over them', whereas the Normans were well-organised and crafty, provoking the Welsh, remaining steady under attack, feigning retreat and re-deploying swiftly 'as it is the way with the French to do everything with diligence and circumspection'. Llanychaiarn was burned down by Owain Gwynedd and his brother Cadwaladr in 1136, and in later years it was repeatedly taken and rebuilt during the course of dynastic quarrels in Deheubarth, expansion from Gwynedd, and English royal conquest. It was eventually superseded by a new castle in the vicinity (possibly at Plas Crug) early in the thirteenth century.

33 Dolwyddelan Castle is the traditional birthplace of Llywelyn ap Iorwerth, but this castle in Dyffryn Lledr was more likely built by him. In choosing sites for their castles, the thirteenth-century princes of Gwynedd kept them away from the traditional *llys* in each *cwmwd*, thereby emphasising the tightening of their grip on their subjects and the revolutionary nature of their ambitions. Dolwyddelan fell to the English in 1283 and was immediately refortified by Edward I, who provided the new garrison with white clothing as camouflage for winter operations against the Welsh in Snowdonia.

34 Cricieth Castle was built by Llywelyn ap Iorwerth and Llywelyn ap Gruffudd to enforce their control of Eifionydd, and it served as a prison for Gruffudd ap Llywelyn in 1239 and Maredudd ap Rhys Gryg in 1259. Edward I strengthened the fortifications in 1283, and the castle held out during the rebellion of Madog ap Llywelyn, largely because of supplies brought in by sea. In 1404, however, it was destroyed by Glyn Dŵr.

35 The ford of Rhyd Chwima on the Severn witnessed numerous meetings between the Welsh and the king's representatives in the thirteenth century, and the treaty of Montgomery was completed near here in September 1267.

36 Caerphilly mountain formed the boundary between the Norman lordship of Glamorgan and Blaenau Morgannwg until the late 1260s. Then, in 1268, Gilbert ('the Red') de Clare sought to underpin his conquest of Senghennydd in the previous year by building the largest castle in Wales, and one of the largest in Britain. Caerphilly's extensive water defences were probably inspired by those at Kenilworth, where Gilbert had fought for Henry III against the remnants of the de Montfort party in 1266, and the castle made full use of the new concentric design which maximised the concentration of firepower. Before it could be completed, however, it was taken by Llywelyn ap Gruffudd in 1270, and the king arranged a neutral force to hold it pending negotiation. The earl, however, soon regained the castle by a simple ruse. His constable of Cardiff was admitted to Caerphilly on the pretext that he wished to inspect the inventory of arms and other stores, whereupon he immediately opened the gates to Gilbert's men. The castle never fell again in the medieval period, although it was attacked by Morgan ap Maredudd in 1294 and by Llywelyn Bren in 1316.

37 *Above:* Aberystwyth castle, begun by Edward I in 1277 and built by workmen brought from Bristol, replaced the previous castles in the Aberystwyth area and marked the effective end of Llywelyn ap Gruffudd's principality in central Wales. Aberystwyth was still under construction when the Welsh took it in 1282, and it was not finished until 1289; there was also a walled borough, of which no trace remains today except in street names. In 1294, the castle held out for six months after the Welsh killed the constable, and relief eventually arrived by sea. Owain Glyn Dŵr took Aberystwyth in 1404, and he sealed his treaty with Charles VI of France here, but Prince Henry attacked the castle with artillery in 1407 and recaptured it in 1408.

39 Edward I's castle at Harlech was completed in a mere seven years between 1283 and 1290, and its defences were so strong that in 1404 it held out for four months with an under-resourced garrison of just 16 men. Like Beaumaris, it was provided with a fortified sea-dock, and this contributed substantially to its ability to withstand Madog ap Llywelyn's siege in 1294 and 1295. By the same token, it was a sea blockade by the French which eventually allowed the castle to be captured by Glyn Dŵr in 1404. Owain used Harlech as his chief residence until it was re-taken in 1408 or 1409, and he is said to have been formally crowned prince of Wales here. The symbolic importance of Harlech to the Welsh, and also its relationship with the sea, are illustrated in *Pedeir Keinc y Mabinogi*, where the legend of Branwen ferch Lŷr begins with Bendigeidfran, the 'crowned king of this island', looking out from the rock of Harlech to see 13 ships approaching from Ireland.

38 *Opposite below:* Conwy superseded the ancient site at Degannwy, and its military importance is reflected by the fact that Edward I's impressive castle and town walls were completed in four years between 1283 and 1287, requiring the wholesale removal of the abbey of Aberconwy to a site at Maenan further up the Conwy valley. The king originally intended Conwy to be the administrative centre for north Wales, but in the event it never became more than a borough and garrison town. Edward was forced to spend a very frugal New Year here in 1295, when winter storms and a blockade by Madog ap Llywelyn prevented supplies from arriving; it is said that rather than drink the last cask of wine, he shared his men's ration of water mixed with honey. On Good Friday 1401, Gwilym and Rhys ap Tudur took the castle by surprise when the gates were opened to them while the 14-man garrison was at mass.

40 Work on Edward I's castle at Caernarfon began in 1283 on the site of a Norman motte which probably dated from the 1090s. Drawing on Caernarfon's powerful legendary and imperial associations, the king made it his most magnificent castle, intending it to be a royal palace and the seat of his government for north Wales. His son, Edward, the future king and prince of Wales, may have been born in the Eagle Tower in 1284, but the fantasy was shortlived. The borough flourished, but the castle was so massive, complex and expensive that it remained uncompleted for many years, and the Welsh found it relatively easy to sack it in 1294. Even when finished, it became little more than a storehouse. Its superb military architecture was never in doubt, however, and a garrison of 28 withstood several attacks by Glyn Dŵr and his French allies. Town walls were built to protect many of Edward I's new boroughs, but only those at Caernarfon and Conwy have survived more or less intact.

41 Edward I probably planned a castle in the 'beautiful marsh' in Anglesey in 1283, but financial constraints meant that Beaumaris was not built until 1295, after the revolt of Madog ap Llywelyn. It was the last and the largest of Edward's Welsh castles, and Master James of St Georges' most perfectly executed concentric design, but a lack of funds meant that it was never finished. It was attacked only once in the medieval period, when Glyn Dŵr besieged it in 1403.

The delineation of the Welsh as a single separate people was encapsulated by the almost universal substitution of the old name *Cymry* for 'Britons'. *Britones* was used almost without exception in the eleventh century, but its last appearance in *Annales Cambriae* was in 1135. The Welsh were now all placed under the generic term *Kymry*, and to be a *Kemro* or a *Kemraes* constituted a legal status. But the country was not united. Welsh loyalties were directed quite conventionally towards their lords, many of whom were Anglo-Norman, and there was very little sense of common purpose among the native Welsh rulers. As Gerald of Wales pointed out, political unity was essential if Wales was to exert a full influence as a nation. Furthermore, political authority everywhere – especially that of the greater powers – was becoming increasingly territorial, and it was clear that any Welsh unity must be associated with a distinct territorial area.

THE WELSH NATION AS A POLITICAL IDEA

The name *Kymry* first appeared in the *Brut* in the entry for 1124, when it was said that they could not fully accomplish their thoughts. Some frustration at this weakness is implied, and the timing of this adoption of the old name *Kymry*, which had first appeared in a national context in *Armes Prydein*, may not have been coincidental – there were obvious similarities between Æþelstan and Henry I. Thus, the revival of the term seems to reflect a direct assertion of identity against the Normans, and in particular against the pan-British ambitions of the king of England. The concept of political unity as a reaction against the king was made plain under Henry II. The coalition which formed at Corwen in 1165 was conscious of its identity as a Welsh nation, and the English, albeit superficially, were accustomed to view the *Walenses* as a single nation. Symeon of Durham felt it necessary to explain the name *Walenses* ('*Walani, qui et Brittones*' – 'the Welsh, who are the Britons'),[7] but the English came to use it widely in the twelfth century. The Welsh were slower to take it up, but *Annales Cambriae* did so in 1164, when 'all the *Wallenses* of North Wales, South Wales and Powys' rose up and threw off the yoke of the French.[8] This was an unprecedented demonstration of Welsh solidarity, and native chroniclers responded with appropriately novel terminology – not 'the Britons', but 'all of the Welsh' (*yr holl Gymry* and *omnes Wallenses*). The rising brought the *Nortwalensibus* and the *Dextralibus* together in concerted action for the first time, and it could be said that the notion of Wales as a single political entity began to take shape in 1164 and 1165.

Such expressions of national sentiment increased rapidly, generally displacing older forms as the Welsh placed less importance on the past and addressed new ambitions, one of which was political nucleation. The *Kymry* reappeared in the chronicles for 1164, for the first time since 1124, and the usage soon became common. It was said that Henry II sought to destroy 'all of the Welsh'

(*omnium Walensium*) in 1165, and the *Walenses* (or variants) appeared regularly
thereafter. The Welsh began to call Wales *Cymru* with regularity, and they
also adopted the English name *Wallia*, while contemporary writers conveyed
a new element of national consensus – the sale of Cardigan in 1200, for
instance, was allegedly unpopular with the people of all Wales. National identity against the English now permeated Welsh political life. On his death,
Owain Gwynedd was praised as the strength of all Wales, and Cynddelw said
that the poets of *Cymru* would mourn Owain's *teulu*. This use of language
became common: Cynddelw called Rhys ap Gruffudd the shepherd of Wales;
Rhys was styled the unconquered head of all Wales; Gwalchmai said that the
death of Madog ap Maredudd was a loss to Wales; and the *Brut* chronicler
celebrated Maelgwn ap Rhys as the shield and strength of all Wales.

This nationalism was soon applied in practical politics. Gwalchmai's statement
that the land of the *Kymry* was saddened by the difficulties faced by Dafydd ab
Owain, for instance, suggests an identification of pan-Welsh interests. In 1198,
Gwenwynwyn ab Owain sought to 'win for the *Kymry* their original rights and
to restore their bounds to their rightful owners',[9] with help from all the princes
of *Kymry*, and Cardigan was regarded as being of strategic importance for all of
Wales. Most importantly, there were efforts to harness national sentiment to create genuine unity. Owain Gwynedd was well placed to attempt this, and it may
be no coincidence that *Historia Gruffud vab Kenan* was composed around the
1160s, retrospectively making Rhys ap Tewdwr address Owain's father, Gruffudd
ap Cynan, as king of the kings of *Kemry*. Some of the redactions of Welsh law
which fuelled the drive towards unity were also made in the late twelfth century,
while Gerald of Wales's protests against English domination of the Welsh church
and his idea of a 'national' archbishopric were used by Llywelyn ap Iorwerth,
Gwenwynwyn ab Owain, Madog ap Gruffudd Maelor and Maelgwn, Gruffudd, Rhys and Maredudd ap Rhys ap Gruffudd to reassert Welsh solidarity in
1202x1203. Perhaps the most eloquent testimony to the broadening horizons
of native rulers was the diplomatic styles they adopted. After the middle of the
twelfth century, localised styles such as *dux Powisorum* and *Powysorum princeps*
lost popularity, to be succeeded by *Walliarum rex*, *Walliae rex*, *Wallensium princeps*,
princeps Walliae and *Walliarum princeps*. Wales was being reinvented.

Nationality and National Politics

THE DEFINITION OF A WELSH NATION

The thirteenth century saw a crystallisation of nationalities in England, Scotland,
Ireland and Wales, and a distinct marcher identity also emerged. The growth of
English nationalism was of no little consequence in Wales, especially since it was

Edward I who first stirred up racial issues, creating a xenophobic fervour in England for his wars in Wales, Scotland and France. This was often accompanied by moral condemnation, and it fuelled Welsh animosity towards the foreign (*extraneo*) English. Oppressive royal government merely intensified such feelings; many complaints against royal officials in 1282 were specifically against the *Anglicos*, and Llywelyn ap Gruffudd said that the injustice affected all of the Welsh – he in turn was seen as a leader against oppression. The most vivid demonstration of Welsh nationality was the differentiation made in 1282 by Llywelyn and the men of Gwynedd between the political traditions, land, language, laws and customs of Wales and those of England. This might be seen as a combination of mere sentimentality and political expediency – it was part of the last defiant stand of a beleaguered prince – but there was a strong movement towards genuine unity.

Gerald of Wales followed Bishop Bernard of St Davids in describing the Welsh as a *natio*, and they were also said to fight for their *patria* in 1245 and 1257. Both of these terms later came to imply a close association between peoples, land and power, but in this period they were less precise. Generally, in Europe, a *natio* was any political or cultural entity which was not strictly bound to the universal Church or the Holy Roman Empire, and which had no universal basis. A *natio*, like a *gens*, usually denoted people, not land, and it was often determined by place of dwelling, or more especially place of birth. *Patria* could have legal, administrative, religious and emotional connotations. Ecclesiastical concepts of the Holy Empire and the Body of the Church led to increasingly territorialised interpretations of the idea, and by the twelfth century it was often identifiable with a kingdom (*regnum*), although this was not always the case. The terms *natio*, *patria* and *gens* were widely used, but they could convey different shades of meaning in different contexts. Gerald, for example, understood the *Kambrenses* to be the indigenous population of Wales – the 'Britons' – but he said that the marchers were also Welsh, if not by descent ('*nacione Kambrensis non cognacione*'),[10] and it is interesting by way of comparison that most of the 'English' and 'Scots' aristocracy in the twelfth and thirteenth centuries were of Norman French descent. Social, economic and tenurial ties were far more important to most people than any nation, but the nature and extent of the politicisation and integration of the Welsh *natio* and *patria* were vital factors in determining the fortunes of the imperial ambitions of Gwynedd.

Birth, language and law were the only universally accepted definitions of a Welshman. Llywelyn ap Gruffudd and Rhys Wyndod argued that it was as men of the Welsh condition (*condicionis Wallensice*) that they were entitled to Welsh law, and Edward I saw his enemies in 1282 as people of the Welsh tongue (*generibus lingua Walensis*). Similarly, Gruffudd Maelor ap Madog was Welsh by '*natione, genere et lingua*', and Dafydd ap Gruffudd was said to have been captured by men of his own tongue ('*per homines lingue sue*') in 1283.[11] Nevertheless, although the Welsh were identified by their language, and used it to emphasise their separateness – the poet Dafydd Benfras, for instance, boasted that he never knew English, and revelled in the linguistic distinctness of north Wales – neither birth nor language were seen as symbols of Welsh nationhood in any more positive sense. The case of law was somewhat different, since it was to become a crucial part of attempts by Gwynedd to create a Welsh polity in the thirteenth century.

One of the functions of the native literary tradition was to give meaning to the Welsh past and future. It had been shown – notably in Normandy – that nations could be created by the invention of a 'national' past, and it is therefore noteworthy that Welsh poetry and chronicles shared the same values. This was undoubtedly stimulated by the private interests of the aristocracy, but that alone does not explain the depth and longevity of the common tradition. The past has often been used throughout history to provide legitimacy and a continuum to justify the present, and medieval Welsh poetry seems to have been part of this tendency, illustrating a growing sense of Welsh unity. Among a growing tide of references to *Kymry*, Prydydd y Moch said that Hywel ap Gruffudd ap Cynan fought for Wales, and that Gruffudd ap Hywel ab Owain was a protector of *Gymry*, while Dafydd Benfras saw the death of Gruffudd ap Llywelyn in 1244 as a blow for the whole of Wales – Gruffudd was associated with heroes from all the major kingdoms, and he was seen as the 'dawn of Wales' ('*gwawr Cymru*')[12] – almost a messianic hope. Even more extravagant claims included Llygad Gŵr's assertion that Llywelyn ap Gruffudd ruled as far as Cornwall, and Einion Wan even compared Gruffudd ap Llywelyn ap Iorwerth with Charlemagne. Sir Gruffudd Llwyd went so far as to envisage the defeat of the English and the division of Britain between the Scots and the Welsh in 1316, reminding Robert Bruce that the Welsh and Scots alike had been disinherited and oppressed by the English, and Owain Glyn Dŵr repeated these sentiments in 1401. Nevertheless, although such rhetoric offers a valuable political insight, it should not always be taken at face value; Edward Bruce's pan-Celtic rhetoric in 1315, for example, was neither realistic nor honest, and much of the poets' language was driven by literary hyperbole.

Essentially, the political Welsh nation was created not by rhetoric but by a shared experience under institutions, whether temporal or spiritual. Llywelyn ap Iorwerth indicated the importance of ecclesiastical institutions in engendering Welsh nationhood when he said that Gerald of Wales's fight for an archbishopric of St Davids would be remembered 'as long as Wales shall stand',[13] and it was opposition to royal government which united the Welsh in 1241, 1256 and 1282. It was also the king who provoked them to react with one accord in 1211. Equally significant was the development of a national 'state' under the aegis of Gwynedd. Allegiance to Gwynedd was now synonymous with allegiance to Wales. Cynddelw described Llywelyn ap Iorwerth's army as 'true Welshmen' ('*guir Cymry*' – which could also be read as 'the men of Wales'),[14] and Rhys Gryg 'deserted the Welsh' – namely Llywelyn's confederation – in 1213. Similarly, Maredudd ap Rhys's homage to Henry III in 1258 angered the *Walenses*, and his infidelity was seen to trouble all of Wales. Loyalties were now held to be clear-cut between Wales-Gwynedd and the king. The point was made succinctly by Prydydd y Moch, who, in attempting to justify Llywelyn ap Iorwerth's conquest of Powys, asked whether a French conqueror was preferable to a Welsh one: '*ai gwell Ffranc no ffrawddus Gymro?*'.[15] The fact that the force employed by Llywelyn ap Gruffudd to punish Gruffudd ap Gwenwynwyn for his treachery in 1274 was described as the host of all Wales illustrated the real and potential growth of national sentiment under a single ruler.

THE PRINCIPALITY OF WALES

The pretension to rule over the whole of Wales was shared by a number of kingdoms. It was Gwynedd, however, which achieved supremacy after 1215, and the significance of this was not lost on contemporaries. Henry III recognised the predominance of Gwynedd, and Dafydd Benfras hailed Llywelyn ap Iorwerth as the supreme head of Wales (*kemry*) – he also said that the death of Dafydd ap Llywelyn was sad for Wales, and he saw Llywelyn ap Gruffudd as the ruler of '*Cymru fawr*'.[16] Elsewhere, Dafydd ap Llywelyn was also remembered as the shield of Wales. Furthermore, Gwynedd inspired widespread support: Dafydd was hailed as the love of Wales, and the Welsh reportedly followed Llywelyn in 1257 as though glued to him. Not surprisingly, Llywelyn's assumption of the title 'prince of Wales' was anticipated and elaborated by the literary propagandists. They applied the title 'king of Wales' (*brenin Cymry*) to Llywelyn ap Iorwerth, Dafydd ap Llywelyn and Llywelyn ap Gruffudd, and Llywelyn ap Iorwerth was seen as prince of all Wales (*princeps totius Walliae*) as early as 1218. The poets played a vital propagandist role in Wales, as they did in other medieval societies, and the poems of Dafydd Benfras in particular seem to represent an attempt by Gwynedd to invent a kingship of Wales. Nevertheless, the task was hampered on all sides by tradition.

One of the few means available to create unity was law. It was in the late twelfth century or early thirteenth century that the earliest surviving redactions of Welsh laws were made, providing powerful propaganda for Gwynedd's domination of a united Wales. Hywel Dda was seen as prince of all Wales ('*tywyssawc Kemry oll*'), the laws themselves were the 'laws and customs of Wales' ('*kyfreitheu a defodeu Kymry*'),[17] and the prologues implicitly sanctioned the universal application of one native law throughout Wales – the laws were

applicable to Gwynedd, Powys and Deheubarth, which were seen as parts of
a whole. Such unity was superficial, however, and the appeal to tradition was
necessarily limited, since the aim of the princes was to revolutionise Wales.
Furthermore, closer links in the march and with Anglo-Norman royalty
necessitated a reassessment of traditional prejudices. Nevertheless, law proved
to be a crucial instrument in the assertion of a more comprehensive Welsh
nationality. Growing English pressure made it essential that Wales should
become a consolidated, progressive unit with a homogeneous population
under a single prince, and it was important to insist upon the rights and dignity
of native authority if such an entity was to be recognised constitutionally. The
main battleground over which this was disputed was the status of Welsh law.

Law was inconspicuous in Welsh political life until 1201, when Llywelyn
ap Iorwerth and John distinguished between *lex Walliae* and *lex Angliae*. Welsh
law did not ideally suit the imperial aims of Gwynedd, since it possessed no
'national' consistency or exclusivity – it was a law for the Welsh rather than
for Wales, and it did not have the monolithic, clear-cut quality attributed to
it after 1278. This vagueness was made plain to an inquisition in 1278, which
heard simply that Welsh law ought to prevail 'as far as the power of the Welsh
extends'[18] – furthermore, the jurors could not recall it ever being used before
royal justices. The Welsh had occasionally asserted their right to native law in
the 1240s, and the revolt in 1257 was reportedly against a royal threat to Welsh
law and lands, but the king was generally tolerant and respectful towards it.
Indeed, Henry III placed great importance on Welsh law, albeit mischievously.
Similarly, although Edward I made jurisdiction into a key issue in 1278, it had
never been disputed before that date. Discontent against English rule in the
1240s and 1250s was rooted more in resentment of misgovernment and foreign
laws than in any concept of a common sovereign Welsh jurisdiction.

Llywelyn ap Gruffudd's appeal to Welsh nationality after 1277 was prompted
directly by the dismemberment of his principality – in other words, the desire
for self-preservation. This was a conflict over the status and mastery of Wales,
and it was recognised that the legal controversy was intended by the prince
to divert attention away from the feudal issue, and by the king to emphasise
his claims to sovereignty. The tone of Llywelyn's propaganda campaign was
set by his demand that he be allowed Welsh law in the Arwystli case in 1278,
and his technically dubious claim that Wales should be allowed its own laws
was echoed by Dafydd ap Gruffudd, Rhys Fychan and Owain and Llywelyn
ap Gruffudd Maelor. The law was now presented as an emblem of Welsh nationality, with the native language included for good measure. Thus, when he
was offered lands in England, Llywelyn replied that he could never live in a
country where the language, laws and customs would be foreign to him, and

this stance was firmly supported by the *populus* of Gwynedd, who declared that they would never do homage to a foreigner who was ignorant of their language, customs and laws, even if the prince should do so. In this sense, the war of 1282 was fought as a national uprising. As positions polarised, Llywelyn repeatedly stressed his descent from Camber, son of Brutus, but he was dismissed by the English as the 'dregs of the Trojans' ('*faex Trojanorum*').[19] He traced the jurisdictional independence of Gwynedd back to the time of Brutus, and the law of Hywel was seen in England as 'his (Llywelyn's) law' by 1279.[20] The prince's claim that it was the 'common law' of Wales, and his flawed contention that it had been conceded by Edward to all the Welsh as their law, were clearly intended to oblige all the Welsh to support him. Thus, the insistence on 'national identity' in 1282 was merely a means of upholding Gwynedd's claims to regalian rights; Welsh nationality had been appropriated by Gwynedd.

Many of the weaknesses of Llywelyn's principality stemmed from the failure to define its extent. The 1267 treaty had merely distinguished between '*Anglorum et Wallensium*',[21] and the prince's ambitions in the march were linked closely to his position as leader of 'the Welsh'. His attack on Abergavenny in 1256, for instance, was characterised by the presence of 'all the men of the Welsh tongue' from the neighbouring marcher lordships. Furthermore, although the rebels in 1282 certainly saw themselves as Welshmen, and worked together as such, Llywelyn's principality was never fully established beyond Gwynedd. Rhys ap Maredudd was praised as the 'brave dragon of Deheubarth' for his resistance to Gwynedd, and the *Brut* hinted at the strength of local affinities when it commemorated Llywelyn's ally, Maredudd ab Owain, as the defender of all Deheubarth. Such localism was not a peculiarly Welsh phenomenon. In France and Germany, too, the consensus was that it was better to fight for a local *patria* than for larger units. Although they rose as one nation in 1282, the Welsh rarely thought of themselves as such, and in later times Llywelyn and his forebears were easily overlooked in the search for a national Welsh past. Even so, the achievements of Gwynedd in the thirteenth century meant that Wales was accepted as a political concept, notably in Edward I's declaration in 1284 that he now ruled Wales.

The reaction to Llywelyn's death in 1282 was informed at a profound psychological level by Geoffrey of Monmouth and the Welsh prophetic poetry which had preceded him. For the Welsh, the prophecies of Merlin offered hope that they would one day be rid of English rule, and in that sense, Llywelyn's death was a cataclysmic disaster: 'and then all of Wales was cast to the ground'.[22] For the English, the idea that Arthur would return and drive out the usurping Saxons posed a direct challenge to their domination of Britain. Although it was not a practical likelihood, the knowledge that the original Britons still inhabited western Britain, and that they still harboured these

hopes, was unsettling, and this perhaps accounts for the triumphalism, brutality and special pleading in the treatment of Llywelyn after his death. Mindful
of the legends which surrounded such figures as Arthur and Frederick Bar-
barossa, whose bodies were never found and who were expected to return
again to save their people, Edward went out of his way to prove that Llywelyn
and all that he represented were indisputably dead. The prince's head was
displayed before the king's army, and it was then crowned with ivy and placed
on the Tower of London in mock fulfilment of Merlin's prophecy that the
Britons would once again be crowned in London. Some English chroniclers
even went as far as to claim that Edward's victory fulfilled the prophecy that
the monarchy of all Britain would be re-established.

The original Arthurian legend – that of the British hero against Saxon invasion – had been turned neatly on its head. This was part of a long process by
which British history was already being hijacked by the English state. More
than half a millennium before 1282, Bede had grafted the history of the Angles
and Saxons onto that of Roman Britain, and Geoffrey had later appropriated
Arthur as a king of England, tracing the origins of Norman kingship in England
back beyond the Romans to the ancient British kings. Faced with the incon-
venient existence of the Welsh and their claims regarding Britain, the English
countered simply by denying that there was a problem. As early as the tenth
century, the Anglo-Saxon chronicler Æðelweard asserted that Britain was now
called England, and his claim was to be repeated many times throughout the
Middle Ages. While the Welsh clung to Arthur and the Matter of Britain in the
hope of deliverance, the English disarmed the mythology by removing it from
its context and adopting it, with the result that Arthur acquired a reputation as
one of the greatest kings of England – and by extension, an Englishman. This
Anglo centric version of the Arthurian story became a romance of continental
chivalry, and it was eventually embraced by the whole of western Christendom.
Richard I – who himself entered chivalric mythology as *Coeur de Lion* – supposedly possessed 'Arthur's sword called *Caliburn* by the Britons'[23] – at the time
'Arthur's tomb' was uncovered at Glastonbury in 1191, and Edward I was also
heavily involved in the Arthurian cult, ordering the tomb to be reopened in
1278, and the remains to be transferred and re-interred. Roger Mortimer even
claimed descent from Arthur, and held a round table in 1279. It was not difficult,
therefore, for Edward to present himself as an English Arthur, intent on recovering Arthur's supposed dominion over the whole of Britain. Wales and the Welsh
had been written out of history and relegated to the margins.

After Llywelyn's defeat, Edward appropriated the dignity of Gwynedd to the
crown of England, and in doing so destroyed the last vestiges of native Welsh
sovereignty. In 1283, he seized the *regalia* and *insignia* of Gwynedd, associating

himself with a hero of Welsh legend by having the body of the Roman emperor Constantine discovered at Caernarfon and re-interred there. He was also careful to ensure that the polygonal towers and bands of coloured masonry in Caernarfon castle closely resembled both the fifth-century walls of Constantinople (known by this time as Byzantium) and the many-coloured towers in the dream of the emperor Macsen (Magnus Maximus) in *Breudwyt Maxen Wledic*. The allusion to imperial Rome and to *Maxen Wledic* was driven home by the addition of eagles to the battlements, and the Arthurian image was completed by the holding of a round table at Nefyn in 1284 and the removal of the 'crown of Arthur' to England. Welsh nationality was finally subservient to the English state.

Conquest and Nationality

ASSIMILATION AND DISCRIMINATION

The experience of conquest and colonisation brought Gwynedd into a process of contact and accommodation with English values and practices which was already well advanced in many other parts of Wales and the marches. The Welsh were not denied the benefits of English law, as the Irish were, and they were keen to adopt many aspects of it. Trial by jury and final concord became popular, and the freedom of alienation and entail under English land law allowed Welshmen unprecedented control in the restriction and transferral of inheritance. Similarly, the English often made use of Welsh law when it suited them. The result was an eclectic and kaleidoscopic variety of local practices, and in some parts of the south-east there emerged a hybrid land law whereby English forms of tenure co-existed with Welsh inheritance practices. At the same time, the land market allowed the English to encroach into the Welshries, while the Welsh settled increasingly in the Englishries, including some of the English plantation boroughs. By 1330, most of the burgesses at Aberystwyth and Beaumaris were Welsh. Intermarriage was more common than ever, and English surnames became widespread. Some came in with the settlers, and others were adopted by the Welsh in a bid for respectability. Owain ap Gruffudd ap Gwenwynwyn of Trallwng, for instance, preferred to be known in certain circles as Owen de la Pole, and the lords of Afan changed their name to d'Avene. The need for acceptance also encouraged many Englishmen to adopt Welsh names, and it was common for people to have both an English name and a Welsh name, making life easier in both communities. The cross-fertilisation and assimilation of cultures gained momentum in the fourteenth century, as Welshmen attended English universities and English lords patronised Welsh poets. By 1400, the Welsh had adopted a host of English manners and habits, including clothing styles, urban life and private gardens.

Both socially and economically, the more anglicised parts of Wales were now in many ways barely distinguishable from southern England.

But Wales was not a part of England, and neither did it have any institutional integrity of its own. The country was deeply fragmented between the various royal lands – which were administered separately from one another – and forty or so marcher lordships. The Statute of Rhuddlan, for example, did not apply to the march, or even to the royal lordships of Montgomery and Builth, and the new county of Flintshire was officially part of the lordship of Chester. This was the legacy of centuries of piecemeal conquest, and it meant that there was no common jurisdictional authority, no legal uniformity, no general taxation (except once in the early 1290s) and no Welsh government. More than ever, it was difficult to think of Wales except as a state of mind or a geographical expression.

For most of the Welsh, the conquest of 1283 signified little more in their daily lives than a change of tax collectors. Indeed, for most it did not even mean that, since their obligations, loyalties and identities were bound up in their existing relationships, either with the marcher lords or with local *uchelwyr*. When there was no choice but to transfer allegiances to a new lord, the ruling classes had always been adept at doing so, and it was entirely natural that the *uchelwyr* who had dominated government at the local level before 1282 should continue to do so under their new masters. Although they were denied access to the very highest public offices, Welshmen such as Sir Gruffudd Llwyd, Sir Rhys ap Gruffudd, Sir Hywel ap Gruffudd and Goronwy ap Tudur became prominent in the English administration in Wales during the fourteenth century. Many became sheriffs and, like Rhydderch ap Ieuan Llwyd in Cardiganshire, served as loyal government officials at the same time as providing patronage for a golden age of composition, preservation and organisation of Welsh poetry, much of which harked back to former glories. Nor was there any contradiction in the fact that Iolo Goch could sing with equal conviction to Sir Rhys ap Gruffudd, Edward III, Roger Mortimer, Owain Glyn Dŵr and possibly Owain Lawgoch, since *uchelwyr*, political patrons, native Welsh heroes and descendants of the thirteenth-century princes were all integral parts of the poets' world. There was an inevitable emotional conflict between the present and the past, but the Welsh were well used to living with it.

The process of moulding the Welsh into loyal subjects of the king of England was given constitutional form when Edward of Caernarfon was made prince of Wales at Lincoln in 1301. He had been born in Wales in 1284 – possibly at Caernarfon castle – and it was claimed in Tudor times that his father had presented him to the Welsh at that time as their own prince who could speak no English. Whimsical as this story may be, it correctly identified both the government's eagerness to win acceptance and the Welsh willingness to give it. As prince of Wales, Edward made a point of employing Welshmen in his household as knights, squires and minstrels, and the Welsh of the principality followed him loyally until his death. He was their lord, and they were prepared to fight and die for him. Other Welshmen followed other lords: the men of Roger Mortimer's Welsh lordships, for instance, fought with him against the unpopular royal favourite Hugh Despenser and also against the king himself after 1321. Loyalty had always been defined by the personal ties of lordship above all else.

Wales was now an important source of soldiers for the king's campaigns. Welshmen had served in royal armies for hundreds of years, and on a large scale since the twelfth century, but the practice now assumed new dimensions. Welsh troops were first used *en masse* by Edward I against William Wallace at Falkirk in 1298, and they became essential to the English wars in France and Scotland, comprising half or more of the king's armies in 1297, 1332 and 1334. Falkirk showed that the English were already mastering the longbow themselves and making it their own, but Welsh archery proved crucial in celebrated English victories at Crécy, Poitiers and Agincourt, and it was during the Crécy campaign in 1346 that some Welsh units were first issued with green and white uniforms and wore leeks in their caps, probably for disciplinary purposes. The Welsh thereby became the first soldiers in Europe to wear a national uniform, but their cause was not the independence of their native land; rather, they fought for Edward III's claim to the duchy of Aquitaine and the kingdom of France.

Nevertheless, any impression of cheerful co-existence and co-operation was tempered by a fundamental inequality. There was never any room for doubt that the Welsh were a conquered people. In introducing English law in 1284, the statute of Rhuddlan extinguished the rights of Welshmen to appeal to their own customs, laws and liberties, and a rigid legal distinction was drawn between the Welsh and the English. They were often dealt with in separate courts, and tried by juries composed entirely of members of their own nationality; they could choose different procedures and rules; the financial dues they paid reflected the sharp contrast between the communal nature of Welsh society and the more individualist economy of the English settlers; and even their labour dues were often registered separately. The discrepancies between English and Welsh law could be exploited with profit by both sides, but they were used just as often to emphasise the separateness of the two communities. This was particularly true with regard to the transfer and inheritance of land, where it had long since been received wisdom that the Welsh practised partibility between co-heirs and the rejection of descent through females, in preference to the English practices of primogeniture and descent through the female line in the absence of male heirs. In legal terms these observations were

true, but they were often misinterpreted, and moreover they became rigor-
ously-enforced stereotypes, despite being a far from accurate representation
of what many Welshmen actually wanted. Moreover, the decision whether to
accord a person Welsh or English status could be very arbitrary in a country
where practical distinctions were becoming increasingly blurred.

Psychologically, therefore, Wales was inhabited by two very separate peoples,
and the fact that they increasingly lived cheek by jowl only intensified their
mutual resentment and suspicion. In the English boroughs, the burgesses guard-
ed their privileged status jealously and exploited it ruthlessly, enforcing trading
monopolies, excluding the Welsh – while forcing them to trade in the towns
– and sometimes removing them to less desirable land. Such injustices contributed to the revolt of Madog ap Llywelyn in 1294, in reaction to which Edward
I introduced more stringent discrimination against the Welsh in 1295. They were
now prohibited from carrying arms within the towns of north Wales, and also
from living in them; and they could not assemble without the permission of the
king. These measures could be justified in terms of security in a newly conquered
country, and they fell into disuse in more peaceful times, but the element of fear
and racial intolerance could not be disguised. Both conquerors and conquered
were now convinced that their fears and prejudices were well-founded.

The Anglo-Welsh divide was further entrenched by the absenteeism of many
English landlords. Their sensitivities to their Welsh tenants were dulled by distance, and their preoccupation with lands in England helped to prevent them
from going native. Furthermore, there was now a more confident and aggressive
English nationalism which disapproved of anyone becoming less English, and the
reign of Edward III saw increasing tension between native Welsh communities
and the boroughs. Ethnic relations deteriorated to the point that some individuals practised outright racism with impunity. A bishop of Bangor, Thomas Ring-
stead, stipulated that his bequest of £100 to the cathedral should be cancelled if
a Welshman succeeded him, and he specifically excluded the Welsh from a grant
of another £100 intended to enable the poor of the diocese to gain an education at Oxford and Cambridge. In a similar vein, English border counties took
steps to penalise Welsh settlers in England in the late fourteenth century, simply
because they were Welsh. Under different circumstances, it might have been a
sign of harmony that English lords sought to uphold Welsh law while the Welsh
were attracted to English law. The reality, however, was that the authorities insisted upon whatever rules best suited their own financial greed, and to that
end they were prepared to impose an increasingly arbitrary form of apartheid.
Nowhere was that attitude more pronounced than in the boroughs. Here, in the
very front line of the English presence in Wales, it was openly declared that the
Welsh were to be regarded as foreigners (*forinseci*) in their own country.

THE SON OF PROPHECY

The Welsh had enjoyed a long history of independence, and they bitterly resented being treated as a conquered people. Their grievances were no longer local, but national, and they were sustained not only by contemporary oppression but by a longing for the world that had been ended by foreign conquest. This allowed – and indeed almost required – Madog ap Llywelyn, Owain Lawgoch and Owain Glyn Dŵr to arrogate authority to themselves by adopting the style 'prince of Wales'. The Welsh had very long memories. A Glamorgan *uchelwr* recalled in 1365 that his ancestors had been dispossessed by Robert fitz Hamo in the 1090s, and the pragmatism of most Welshmen in coming to terms with daily realities did not preclude a deep and heartfelt regret for ancient losses. It is difficult to measure the degree of anti-English feeling in the fourteenth century, but an *awdl* sung to Rhys Gethin around 1400 makes plain the continued awareness of the British past, of the displacement of the Welsh by the English, and of daily tyranny: '*lle bu'r Brython, Saeson sydd, a'r boen ar Gymru beunydd*'.[24]

There was less warfare in fourteenth-century Wales than there had been at any previous time in the country's history, but there was always a fear that the Welsh might revolt. One English chronicler said that they suffered from a long-standing madness, whereby they would wait quietly for years before suddenly erupting in a violent lust for war. Others attributed the Welsh tendency to rebel to lightheadedness (*levitas cervicosa*), but it was generally agreed that it was derived from their deep-seated belief in the prophecies of Merlin. Welsh poets still made routine references to the Matter of Britain – Gruffudd Llwyd comparing Owain Glyn Dŵr with Uthr Bendragon, for example – and at the turn of the fifteenth century Hopcyn ap Thomas of Ynysdawe owned a manuscript of Geoffrey of Monmouth's *Historia regum Britanniae* to which had been appended a section lamenting the present exile of the Britons in their own country. It was an old poetic tradition in Wales that the past could be linked with the present, and that future successes against the English could be prophesied. This vaticination, known variously as *canu darogan* or *cywyddau brud*, was often very obscure and allusive, but those very qualities suggest a shared knowledge among the Welsh. Prophetic poetry was often pressed into service as political propaganda, especially after the twelfth century, and some of the names given to the sons and grandsons of Gruffudd ap Cynan – Cadwallon, Owain, Cadwaladr, Rhun, Maelgwn, Cynan, Rhodri, Hywel and Cunedda – may well have alluded to this shared sense of past and future.

Much of this poetry was addressed to the national saviour known as the *mab darogan*. He was often called Owain; he was sometimes associated with the dynasty of Gwynedd; and his coming would be accompanied by signs and portents. The origins of this tradition are not known, but the belief that a warlike redeemer would arise to overthrow the existing order can be found in the works of many Welsh poets between the ninth and thirteenth centuries. These ideas were usually passed off rather dubiously as the work of Merlin and Taliesin, and they also appear in Geoffrey of Monmouth's *Historia regum Britanniae, Prophetia Merlini* ('Prophecies of Merlin') and *Vita Merlini* ('Life of Merlin'). According to this tradition, Owain was fifth in a line of redeemer heroes, the others being Hiriell, Cynan, Cadwaladr and Arthur, of whom only Cadwaladr is a reliably attested historical figure. Owain himself did not emerge even as a literary character until the thirteenth century, when he became the most frequently invoked deliverer, and the *canu darogan* to him was renewed with increased vigour in the fourteenth century by such poets as Y Bardd Cwsg, Rhys Fardd, Y Bergam, Adda Fras and Goronwy Ddu. It may be that this was nothing more than a literary fashion; on the other hand, myth and prophecy may have been the only meaningful way in which the profundity of a conquered nation's past and future could be understood. The truth probably lies somewhere in between. What is certain is that the promise of the *mab darogan* kept Welsh spirits alive when all else seemed lost.

Owain Lawgoch never came to Wales, and there is no conclusive evidence that he could speak Welsh, but the Welsh poets and their patrons were well aware of both his existence and his significance. Here was a famous soldier called Owain, the last direct descendant of the princes of Gwynedd in the male line; he must surely be the *mab darogan*. Y Bergam sang of a man in France who would avenge his father with an army, and the Anglesey poet Gruffudd ap Maredudd ap Dafydd urged Owain to come to Wales in order to drive the Saxons out of Britain with great slaughter. Another poem (sometimes attributed to Iolo Goch) proclaimed that it had been wrong to kill Owain's uncles – a thinly veiled reference to his great-uncles Llywelyn and Dafydd ap Gruffudd. The poet drew upon the traditional imagery of red and white dragons representing the Britons and the Saxons, first found in *Historia Brittonum*, and he foretold that the avenging Owain would land at St Davids or in Anglesey. Furthermore, the appeal of Owain ap Thomas was given added mystery and romance by his association with Ieuan Wyn – a kinsman who was known to the French as *Le Poursuivant de l'Amour* – and by Owain's own nickname 'Lawgoch' ('Red hand'). The term *llawgoch* was usually applied to murderers, and in Ireland a red mark on the hand was sometimes seen as a messianic symbol, as it was in the case of Cathal Croibhdhearg in the early thirteenth century. Stories in Guernsey also attributed the name to a wound Owain was supposed to have received there in 1372, clearly ignorant of the fact that it is attested as early as 1370. The true explanation of Owain's name was probably more mundane. Dafydd ab Edmwnd, Dafydd Llwyd and Lewys Môn all sang to him as Owain Frych ('the Speckled'), indicating that his distinctive marking may have been no more than a birthmark or freckles.

The men who circulated the subversion relating to Owain were much more than nostalgic romantics or troublemakers. The poets and their close associates were *uchelwyr*, and as such they were responsible, hard-headed and influential figures with a vested interest in the *status quo*: Gruffudd ap Maredudd ap Dafydd, for instance, was *rhaglaw* of Talybolion and a member of the Penmynydd dynasty. Faced with mounting social, economic and political problems in the late fourteenth century, these men turned to Owain Lawgoch not simply because of a fond hope that the prophesied Owain might yet come, but because Owain ap Thomas seemed to offer a genuine practical solution.

Owain's failure elicited a number of reactions. Llywelyn ap Cynwrig Ddu articulated the high hopes and expectations that had been aroused, and the disappointment that many must have felt when Owain did not come. Some found the death of a promised redeemer impossible to accept. He had never been seen in Wales alive or dead, so it was easy to believe that he was asleep in a cave, waiting for the call when the time was right. Others took a more prosaic approach. Llywelyn ap Cynwrig Ddu poured scorn on Merlin, Taliesin and the other prophets who had all been proved wrong. Moreover, he argued, it was obvious that Owain Lawgoch had not been the *mab darogan*, since the portents which were supposed to precede Owain's arrival had not manifested themselves – no trumpets had been blown, there had been no flood in Dublin, and no comet had been seen. Another Owain would come, and this time there would be war.

Another Owain did come, and there was war. But unlike Owain Lawgoch, Owain Glyn Dŵr was not exhorted by the poets to take up the mantle of redeemer. Gruffudd Llwyd tried gentle persuasion in ambiguous language, but it may have been felt that, whereas it was acceptable to incite a mercenary in the pay of a foreign king to take precipitous action, it was irresponsible to encourage a respectable *uchelwr* to do the same. If such an attitude existed, it may have changed after 1400, but it is not recorded; all of the extant poems to Glyn Dŵr were composed before the beginning of his revolt. No later ones survive, possibly because of their incriminating nature.

If Glyn Dŵr was to succeed, it was essential that he should be seen to fulfil the prophecies. Whether the poets encouraged him or not, he was well aware of the prophetic tradition, and he made full use of it from the outset. Indeed, he seems to have taken a great personal interest in it: Crach Ffinnant – who is described in 1400 as his 'prophet' – served with him at Berwick as early as 1384. The need for support throughout Wales might explain why Owain insisted on his status as the *mab darogan* rather than as the legitimate heir to Gwynedd or any of the other old kingdoms, but it is clear that he and many of his followers saw the whole revolt in terms of prophecy. Crach Ffinnant was present at Owain's proclamation as prince of Wales in 1400, and when the prophesied comet appeared early in 1402 it was immediately interpreted as the third great star of history, after the Star of Bethlehem and that which portended the greatness of Arthur's father, Uthr Bendragon. In 1403, Owain consulted Hopcyn ap Thomas, a recognised expert on prophecy, and on being informed that he would be captured under a black banner between Gower and Carmarthen, he stayed away from the area.

The emphasis on prophecy was even carried into Glyn Dŵr's diplomatic business at the highest level. His ambassadors told the French that he was the heir of Owain Lawgoch, and the clauses relating to Wales in the Tripartite Indenture were impregnated with prophetic allusions. However politically unrealistic the document was, the delineation of the Percy and Mortimer lands was expressed in conventional terms based upon the administrative definitions of English counties. Owain's territory, however, was described in much less mundane language. It was bounded by the Severn – the legendary boundary between Leogria and Cambria – and more strikingly by *Ynn Mei-gion* ('the Ashes of Meigion'), whose significance stemmed from a prophetic dialogue between Merlin and his sister Gwenddydd in which these six ash trees were named as a place where Welsh warriors mustered in the heart of England; it may also be relevant that a place called Meigen was tradition-ally associated with a victory of Cadwallon ap Cadfan over the Saxons in the seventh century. Furthermore, a tripartite division of England and Wales was strongly reminiscent of *Teir Ynys Prydein* ('the Three Realms of Britain') in *Trioedd Ynys Prydein* ('the Triads of the Island of Britain'). The prophetic tradition also informed Owain's entreaties to the Scots in 1401. His letter to Robert III emphasised that they were both descendants of British kings, since the Scots traced their ancestry to Albanactus, a brother of Camber, and it pointed out moreover that it had been prophesied that the Britons would overthrow the Saxons with Scottish support. This seemed a powerful argu-ment, but Owain was lucky that the letter never reached its destination, for it contained a serious diplomatic gaffe: the Scots had very recently decided to rethink their origins in reaction to an English contention that they owed homage to the English descendants of Locrinus, the eldest son of Brutus, and they now traced their kings back to Scota, a daughter of Pharaoh.

Fanciful as much of this may seem, it was deeply important. Prophecy, ancient history and superstition exercised more than a curious fascination in the medieval world; they touched upon a society's core beliefs about its identity and its prospects, and they were taken extremely seriously. Henry IV feared Welsh prophecy so much that he banned popular gatherings of poets and minstrels in 1402, and the prophets sustained the spirit and vitality of the Glyn Dŵr revolt even after its leader was dead. Owain had no identifiable grave, and a Tudor copy of a Welsh chronicle attributed to 1422 (which may not be genuine) reported that, although many believed that he had died, the seers maintained that he did not.

The Glyn Dŵr Revolt and the Welsh Nation

A DIVIDED NATION

The popular perception of the Glyn Dŵr revolt was that it was a war between all of the Welsh and the English. In 1401, Owain told Henry Dwn that they were embarked upon delivering the Welsh people from their captivity under the English, and he voiced similar sentiments in his letters to the French in 1403 and 1404, saying that the English had oppressed the Welsh for generations. Similarly, in 1406 he told Charles VI that Wales had been trodden underfoot by barbaric Saxon madness, and he called for the war against the English to be given the status of a crusade. Such language did nothing to reassure English communities in Wales, and the mutual fear and loathing of the enemy allowed many in England to believe that Welsh women mutilated the corpses of English soldiers after the battle of Bryn Glas. Glyn Dŵr himself recognised the climate of fear that prevailed in 1402, alluding to an English belief that he wanted to destroy the whole English people. Such concerns were unfounded and hysterical, but the strength of the rebellion coupled with its reliance on Merlinic prophecy inevitably made the English feel very uncomfortable.

One of the chief complaints of the Welsh was discrimination against them, but their revolt merely persuaded the English authorities that anti-Welsh legislation needed to be made more comprehensive than ever before. Many of Henry IV's ordinances of 1401 and 1402 reiterated previous measures which had long since fallen into abeyance, but some of them echoed the overt racism of English policy in Ireland, where the Statute of Kilkenny in 1366 had penalised and demonised the Irish simply for being Irish. Any English person accused of a crime by any Welsh person was to be tried only by English judges and an English jury; all convicted Welsh felons were to be summarily executed; and any Englishman who took a Welsh wife was to forfeit his rights. Adam of Usk even claimed that a decree for the destruction of the Welsh language was considered. Similarly, Prince Henry's ordinances for Chester in 1403 included a provision that any Welshman found within the city walls after dark was liable to be decapitated. Such draconian measures could not be justified on the grounds of law and order, even in a time of rebellion. Far from freeing the Welsh, Glyn Dŵr's revolt had ensured that anti-Welsh sentiment became

more institutionalised, and some of the Welsh may have withheld their support from him or even opposed him in anticipation of the government's reaction. All of the discriminative laws passed against the Welsh since 1283 were
revived, entrenched and enshrined in borough charters throughout Wales and
the English borders, with new ones added for good measure. They were not
formally repealed for centuries – if at all. Furthermore, any Welshman who
wished to make his way in the world now had to petition for denizenship, or
English status, and Gwilym ap Gruffudd of Penrhyn in Caernarfonshire successfully did so only by making the patently false claim that all of his ancestors
had been 'mere English'. Any ambitious Welshman was now required by law
to deny that he was Welsh.

The revolt also created and deepened social and political rifts among the
Welsh themselves. Inevitably, many English settlers in Wales, including marchers and especially burgesses, fought against Glyn Dŵr, but the rebellion was also
opposed by many Welsh burgesses, such as Thomas ap Dafydd of Brecon, who
saw it as a threat to their livelihoods. Large numbers of Welshmen resisted Glyn
Dŵr for a variety of reasons. Some looked out for their own personal gain or
safety, while others remained loyal to their existing lords, and others still were
equivocal and tried to remain neutral. Dafydd Gam ap Llywelyn ap Hywel was
a constant and prominent enemy of the rebellion; Bleddyn ap Madog Gryg
spied for Prince Henry against Glyn Dŵr; Iorwerth ab Ithel guided a force
which attacked the rebels near Caerwys; and it was later believed that Owain's
own cousin, Hywel Sele of Nannau, tried to kill him. Furthermore, many families were divided against themselves. In Maelienydd, for instance, Maredudd
ap Madog refused to join Glyn Dŵr even though his kinsmen did, and
Robert ap Maredudd ap Ieuan supported the rebels while his brother Ieuan
died defending Caernarfon for the king – as did Hwlcyn Llwyd ap Tudur
Goch. As is always the case in a civil war, the rebellion was deeply divisive.

In addition, many remembered the revolt primarily for the devastation
wrought by both sides across Wales and the borders. This may have been
unfair, since many of the problems for which it was blamed were symptoms of
the pre-existing economic situation, and the revolt was no more destructive
than other contemporary wars – it hardly stands comparison with the Hundred Years War, for example. But such associations nevertheless reveal a deep-
seated unease about the consequences of rebellion. Even more significantly,
Glyn Dŵr had failed to provide a viable blueprint for a secular principality.
Certainly, he had his grand vision, together with the ecclesiastical bureau-
crats who would have provided the backbone of any administration, but the
proposals laid out in the Pennal letter were never implemented properly, and
the country was still deeply fragmented. Apart from the Harlech parliament,

which was attended by four men from every *cwmwd* in Wales, there is no indication that Owain had any workable national administrative framework or even any kind of reliable central control. His principality was even more disjointed and incoherent than that of the thirteenth-century princes, and although the ambition to achieve a pan-Welsh governmental structure was there, the means of achieving it were not. Nor was it reasonable to expect that they should be, especially during a time of unrest; after all, the Welsh were fighting to rid themselves of English rule, not to replace it with a new centralised bureaucracy. Centuries – indeed millennia – of local particularism could not be swept away in a few years.

A NATIONAL VISION

Yet Glyn Dŵr and his advisers established for the first time a vision of government for a unified, separate Wales. This was expressed most coherently in the Pennal letter of 1406, in which Owain envisaged what amounted to his own independent Welsh ecclesiastical bureaucracy, free from English control. His conditions for supporting the Avignon papacy centred upon the jurisdictional and economic independence of the Welsh church from Canterbury, and also upon the creation of an archbishop of St Davids. The new archdiocese was to incorporate the English dioceses of Exeter, Bath, Hereford, Worcester and Lichfield, over which it was supposed to have had authority between the time of David (Dewi) himself and that of Samson of Dol, his twenty-fifth successor. Furthermore, the pope was to appoint only Welsh-speakers to ecclesiastical benefices, and he was to allow the establishment of two universities, one each in north and south Wales. These demands echoed the concerns of princes across Europe. The desire to manipulate appointments was universal, and the appropriation of ecclesiastical revenues was a common complaint. Universities were also regarded as prerequisites of a fifteenth-century state, and the Glyn Dŵr programme may have been inspired by the recent foundation of such institutions at Heidelberg and Leipzig. Similarly, Owain asked that his own chapel be granted jurisdictional independence from diocesan control, as other European rulers had for theirs. This was a vision of an independent Wales which could hold its head up among the princes of Europe.

For all its fragmentation, Glyn Dŵr's Wales also possessed an unprecedented unity. Like Llywelyn ap Gruffudd, Owain could be seen as the last native Welshman to claim the title 'prince of Wales'; he referred to his predecessors and successors as princes of Wales; and he repeatedly spoke of Wales and the Welsh as his country, his people, and his subjects. But Glyn Dŵr was a truly national leader in a way that none of his predecessors ever was. He controlled more of Wales than anyone had ever done – almost the whole country – and he was the first Welsh leader to enjoy the willing support (or at least the acquiescence) of most Welsh people, and in every corner of Wales; hence it was that the men of Shropshire agreed a truce with 'Wales' – rather than with Glyn Dŵr or the rebels – in 1403. Despite the local origins of the revolt, both its extent and its appeal were national. Whereas the thirteenth-century princes of Gwynedd had faced resistance to their imperialist expansion, Owain's movement promised unity and deliverance. Furthermore, it could not be ignored by anyone in Wales, and it gained international recognition. Glyn Dŵr did for the Welsh what Wallace and Bruce did for the Scots, what Jeanne d'Arc did for the French, and what Jan Hus did for the Bohemians – he gave them respect, belief and an acute sense of who they were. In that sense, he succeeded.

Despite some of his anti-English language, Glyn Dŵr's targets in practice were political and economic rather than racial. Ruthin – the rebels' first target – was an English borough, but it was heavily populated by Welsh families, and Owain's decision to attack on a market day ensured that many (perhaps most) of the people in town that day were Welsh. The attack was a blow against the centre of Reginald Grey's power at the time when it was most vulnerable; nationality was not an issue. Racial discrimination was almost invisible in Glyn Dŵr's political programme, the only possible exception being the insistence that every cleric in Wales should speak Welsh. Again, however, the purpose was economic. Pluralist absentees from England had fleeced Welsh benefices for years, and it was now intended that Welsh dues should remain in Wales. The language barrier certainly excluded new English immigrants, but most members of the marcher families had fluent Welsh, and many of them were sympathetic to the rebels while remaining fiercely proud of their origins. Some of them died in Owain's cause, and Owain himself may have spent his last years at the home of his marcher son-in-law John Scudamore, at Monnington Straddel in the Dore valley in Herefordshire. Glyn Dŵr was alive to the positive aspects of English rule, and he stopped short of demanding a return to Welsh law, recognising the value placed by many Welshmen on English law – his own grandfather, Gruffudd ap Madog ap Gruffudd Fychan, had benefited from the English practices of entail and freedom of alienation. Amidst all the fear and rhetoric, the rebellion offered some hope of a more cosmopolitan, inclusive, respectful, reasonable and tolerant Wales.

After his death, Glyn Dŵr became a powerful symbol of the Welsh nation. His strength as a figurehead was derived from the fact that he was not fighting to preserve independence, but rather to win freedom for a people who had not known it during their lifetimes. Later generations used his legacy to come to terms with their own place in the new order, especially after the Act of Union with England in 1536, and he became a folk hero, at least for the common people – the gentry sought to preserve their respectability by trying to forget him. Many tales became attached to his name, adding to his reputation as a warrior and out-law, as well as to his supposed mastery of all the arts of trickery and magic. Stories about both the historical and the mythological Glyn Dŵr can still be found throughout Wales today, and he inhabits the same realm as Merlin, Arthur, Robin Hood, Cú Chulainn and Fionn mac Cumhaill – enigmatic and heroic characters whose historical existence or otherwise is less important than their myth. Like Owain Lawgoch, Glyn Dŵr is said by some to be waiting in a cave with his men, and he is still a focus of Welsh nationalism. He has been regarded since the nineteenth century as the greatest Welsh national hero, not least because his vision of national unity and education, together with his underdog status and his championing of oppressed minorities, is attractive to modern tastes.

A NEW WORLD

Paradoxically, Glyn Dŵr's success as a national focus and especially as the *mab darogan* was possible only because of the absence of a native institutional or governmental framework in Wales. Had such a political culture existed in post-conquest Wales, it would have provided both an outlet and practical solutions for Welsh grievances. Instead, the Welsh had no option but to rely on the governmentally less reliable instruments of violence and prophecy. The political and administrative machinery necessary for independent native Welsh action had been dismantled beyond repair after 1283, and it had to be recreated almost from nothing. This proved almost impossible to achieve, but the Welsh could still dream. The chronicler Elis Gruffudd, writing in 1548, re-corded a folktale in which Glyn Dŵr met the Cistercian abbot of Valle Crucis one morning on the Berwyn mountains; when Owain remarked that the abbot was up early, the abbot replied that it was Glyn Dŵr who had risen early – 100 years too early to be the prophesied saviour of Wales. It was a comforting story. In truth, however, he was several hundred years too late.

Welsh independence was gone, and even the poets acknowledged as much. They persisted with their prophecies, but their loyalties now lay with William Herbert, Edmund and Jasper Tudor, and later Henry Tudor. Just as Iolo Goch had sung to Roger Mortimer, so the Welsh now focused their hopes on Englishmen of royal Welsh stock. The Welsh nation now had to define itself within the context of conquest rather than against it. In itself, the process of doing so was anything but new, but the Welsh now had to accept final and apparently irreversible defeat.

At the Battle of Bosworth in 1485, Henry Tudor raised a standard which had never been seen before. Its background was green and white, to emphasise Henry's Welsh blood as a descendant of Tudur ap Goronwy of Penmynydd. Its emblem, moreover, was the red dragon of the Britons, borrowed straight from *Historia Brittonum* and the writings of Geoffrey of Monmouth. At last, the dragon of prophecy was fighting for the crown of London, and winning it. But that dragon had long since been appropriated by the English. The Black Prince displayed it at Crécy, and another of Henry Tudor's standards at Bosworth bore the arms of Saint George. His battlecry was also 'Saint George'. The prize was no longer Welsh independence, but the crown of England – on English terms.

Long before the Glyn Dŵr revolt began, Wales was already undergoing a profound economic, political, administrative, social and cultural orientation towards England. That process led towards the integration of Wales and England, and when the two countries eventually became formally united in 1536 it became more difficult than ever – and perhaps impossible – to regain native independence; whether that would be practical or even desirable would be a question for future generations. Yet, although the autonomous kingdoms of native Wales were gone for good, the Welsh people were not. Gerald of Wales spoke for Welshmen across the millennia when he recorded the supposed words of an old man living at Pencader in Cantref Mawr who joined Henry II's campaign against Rhys ap Gruffudd in 1163. Encouraged by the man's complicity against his fellow countrymen, the king asked him what he thought of the royal army. This was the reply:

> My lord king, this nation may now be harassed, weakened and decimated by your soldiery, as it has so often been by others in former times; but it will never be totally destroyed by the wrath of man, unless at the same time it is punished by the wrath of God. Whatever else may come to pass, I do not think that on the Day of Direst Judgement any race other the Welsh, or any other language, will give answer to the Supreme Judge of all for this small corner of the earth.[25]

The Nature, Practice and Loss of Independence

The independence that the Welsh had enjoyed for centuries depended ultimately on the inherent strength and flexibility of their native political institutions, and in particular the effectiveness and status of kingship. This in turn was affected by a number of factors, including inheritance practices, the changing balance of power within Wales, the development of a pan-Welsh polity, and the relationship between Welsh rulers and the king of England.

Tradition, Stability and Fluidity

KINGLY AUTHORITY AND POWER

Political authority in early Wales could be measured in several ways: the exercise of leadership and control over people, access to and control of economic resources, and the ability to make and enforce laws. It might take time for a ruler to assert himself in these ways, especially after a military seizure of power, but it was these attributes which ultimately defined the quality of his rule, and they were possessed most commonly by kings. It was kings who dominated political life, and according to *Pedeir Keinc y Mabinogi*, the quality of their rule could also be measured in terms of their discernment, personal affability and generosity. Although Welsh kingdoms lacked size and sophistication, there was no doubt that they were kingdoms. Until the twelfth century, both native and foreign observers invariably referred to kings and kingdoms in Wales, often using the Latin terms (*rex* and *regnum*) which were universally employed to denote kings and kingdoms anywhere in Europe.

Welsh kingship was an ancient institution. According to the laws, every land needed a king (*brenin*), who was said to own (*byey*) his country (*gwlad*), and archaic elements remained deeply ingrained, preserving a sense that there was a connection between kings and the natural elements. *Llyfr Cyfnerth* asserted that a bad lord brought disaster, for example, and Hywel Foel ap Griffri said that the earth was 'fruitless' ('*diffrwyth*') after the death of Owain ap Gruffudd ap Llywelyn.[1] These themes echoed the situation in Ireland, where evidence for the survival of 'Celtic' kingship – harking back to the fifth century and earlier – is stronger. In Irish kingdoms, just rule was believed to bring prosperity, health, fertility, good weather, peace at home and victory abroad, whereas bad rule would be punished by the opposite. Traces of the ancient 'king's raid', whereby a king ravaged neighbouring kingdoms for plunder upon assuming his kingdom, also survived in Ireland and Scotland as late as the thirteenth century, and medieval Wales witnessed numerous attacks which might be seen as reminiscent of this practice. Any symbolic significance is never made explicit, however, and if there was a conscious tradition, it is hard to distinguish it from pragmatic politics.

Very little is known of the inauguration rituals of Welsh kings. Such ceremonies were and are an essential official recognition of political authority throughout the world, and it follows that they almost certainly existed in medieval Wales. Llywelyn ap Iorwerth was seen to have a marriage (*priodas*) with the island of Britain, suggesting an element of the idea – again found in Ireland and Scotland, as well as in Norway, France and India – that the king symbolically married his kingdom, and this also appears in the *Pedeir Keinc*, where Rhiannon appears only in the presence of the rightful king, and loses her status when she loses the rightful heir. More modern forms of inauguration are hard to detect, however. Welsh princes certainly possessed *regalia* – which in 1283 included 'Arthur's crown', the *Croes Naid* and a golden coronet, together with jewels and other relics – and they were also enthroned, but they lacked the coronation and anointing which were the hallmark and essence of contemporary European kingship. Gildas suggests that the Britons may have had unction along Old Testament lines in the sixth century, but, even if this persisted in the thirteenth-century principality, anointing alone did not carry the weight of consecration by coronation. The distinction in the *Pedeir Keinc* between a king (*brenhin*) and a crowned king (*brenhin corunawc*) was a significant one, and it is noteworthy that the first attested Welsh *garlonde* was worn by Dafydd ap Llywelyn at the humiliation of Gwynedd at Gloucester in 1240. A crown alone – rather than a coronet – denoted royal prerogative, and, from the tenth century, it was anointing which distinguished between a king (*rex*) and a prince (*princeps*).

Welsh kingship was neither backward nor impotent, however. By way of comparison, the Scots (who also lacked coronation and anointing) maintained the independence of their monarchy from that of England until the seventeenth century and theoretically until the eighteenth. It was in degree rather than in nature that kingships differed – everywhere, they drew on tradition, pragmatism and ecclesiastical guidelines as expediency required. The original 'Celtic' office of king (**rix*), for instance, was a dynamic institution, starting as a primarily sacral role but demonstrating centralising tendencies as it came to denote a war leader. Furthermore, Welsh law allowed native kings most of the prerogatives of medieval monarchs, many of which were borrowed from the Anglo-Saxons, who in turn adopted many ideas from continental Europe.

Nevertheless, it was no easy task for any king in Wales to gain control of his dominions, given the unsophisticated nature of monarchy and administration. It is not even clear whether kings ruled pre-defined communities, or whether those communities were formed by the actions of kings themselves after their accession to power. Although a territorialised administrative structure of *cantrefi* and *cymydau* was developing before 1066, there is very little evidence for it in areas like Morgannwg, and the concept of centralised authority is not found in Wales until the arrival of the Normans, who revived the ecclesiastical idea of the *caput* (or 'head' of a lordship) – a legacy of Roman rule – and brought the castle.

The greatest problem was the traditional nature of the economy. The common currency was livestock, and the tributes paid by Maredudd ap Bleddyn (1121), Rhys ap Gruffudd (1171) and Llywelyn ap Iorwerth (1201) consisted not of cash but of thousands of animals. Even the success of William Rufus's campaigns was judged by the Welsh in terms of how many cattle he took, and as late as 1241, only one third of the 600 mark payment agreed between Henry III and Senena for the restoration of her husband Gruffudd ap Llywelyn was in cash, the rest consisting of cattle and horses. Rather than investment in commercial and economic development, the preferred method of gaining wealth was often simply to go raiding, as Maredudd ab Owain seems to have done when he removed relics from Môn to Ceredigion and Dyfed in 987, and as Bleddyn ap Cynfyn and many others are known to have done.

Other weaknesses in native Wales included a slowness in adopting modern military technology – the first Welshman known to have thought of building a castle, for instance, is Cadwgan ap Bleddyn in 1111 – and, more fundamentally, a lack of social adherence to native kings. The ruler-client relationship was traditionally a primarily military one, but this aspect of it seems to have been weakened by the use of external military aid, and clients grew more powerful as a result. Gruffudd ap Cynan's warband in 1081 was described as an association (*gedymdeithas*), implying an absence of strong bonds of leadership, and the fact that Welsh society was less hierarchically defined than that of the Anglo-Normans meant that Welsh kings had less freedom of action. The development of groups of noblemen (*uchelwyr*), outside the traditional social structure of the kin group and the royal household warband (*teulu*), naturally clashed with the interests of kings, and aristocratic defiance was not unusual. The men of Gwent killed Einion ab Owain in 984 and trapped Gruffudd ap Llywelyn in 1047, and the *uchelwyr* of Ystrad Tywi killed Bleddyn ap Cynfyn in 1075 – furthermore, Iago ab Idwal was even killed by his own men in 1039, and Gruffudd ap Llywelyn by his in 1063. Finally, kings were further hampered by the lack of a territorial definition of kingship. Gruffudd ap Cynan's influence was thought to have increased when the men of Rhos sought his protection, and this prompts the question of whether his power outside Gwynedd Uwch Conwy was measured in lands or in supporters. Llywelyn ap Gruffudd's relationship with the march raises similar issues, and the ambiguity of the treaty of Montgomery in this respect owed as much to uncertainty within Wales as to deliberate mischief on the part of Henry III.

The failure of Welsh rulers to improve the machinery of government and administration contrasted sharply with the progress made in England. This could work to their advantage, however. Whereas the highly sophisticated kingdom of England was conquered by the Normans in a few years, the painfully slow colonisation of Wales was due largely to the absence of workable native systems which could be adopted by the invaders. But the preference for raids and military alliances over institutional and economic development was to prove a significant handicap, and perhaps even a fatal one. There were developments in bureaucracy and centralised administration, and also a growth of existing towns after the Roman period, but there was very little new urbanisation before the arrival of the Normans. Moreover, whereas the monetary system and international trade which had been a feature of Roman Britain were either maintained or revived in most of the rest of Europe, in Wales they were lost after the sixth century. There was a lack of movable wealth, and this, combined with the plundering of Wales by outsiders and the failure of native rulers to exploit the country's economic potential, ensured that it remained relatively impoverished. There was a greater focus after the twelfth century on control of resources such as rents, the profits of justice and the sale of economic surpluses, but it was too little, too late. An economically wealthy territorial core was essential to the creation of successful kingdoms in England, Scotland and France, but the heartland of the principality of Wales lay not in the lush pastures of Gwent and Morgannwg, nor in the fertile land of Ystrad Tywi and Dyfed, nor even in the uplands of Powys and Ceredigion, but in the harsh mountains of Gwynedd and the relatively poor soil of Môn. Furthermore, when economic growth began in earnest in later medieval Wales, most of it took place in areas under Anglo-Norman control – this was almost exclusively the case in the development of urban centres, for example, the rare exceptions being Welsh boroughs such as Llanfaes, Llanrwst, Nefyn and Pwllheli. Throughout the period of Welsh independence, even the most successful native kings and princes were hamstrung by the lack of resources in the country they ruled. Although they became very adept at building, defending and attacking castles, they were never able to match the financial might and architectural skill apparent in Gilbert de Clare's castle at Caerphilly, let alone the chain of castles constructed by Edward I. Without resources, any political ambition was very difficult to realise.

DISORDER AND ORDER

The most striking aspect of the Welsh polity was its apparent confusion. This was especially evident between the ninth and eleventh centuries, and in particular in Morgannwg and Gwent, where aristocratic families displaced existing dynasties and founded new ones in the tenth century. Throughout Wales, the aristocracy was ready to defy kings, creating an impression of anarchy in Anglo-Norman eyes, and doing little to encourage political consolidation in pre-Norman Wales.

Disruptive as the arrival of the Normans was, it was not they who introduced upheaval and disorder into Wales. Nor did they invent the concept that Welsh kingdoms could be conquered – they had been annexed and split apart for centuries. Deheubarth was an invention only 150 years old in 1066, and it was not unusual for the king of one region to stake claims in others. Segments of the Gwynedd dynasty held rule in most parts of Wales in the tenth and eleventh centuries, and there is no evidence for any king of Powys in the eleventh century who did not also have rule in Gwynedd. Hywel Dda was king of Deheubarth, Gwynedd and probably also Powys, while Maredudd ab Owain ruled Gwynedd and Deheubarth, and Gruffudd ap Llywelyn held Gwynedd, Deheubarth, Powys, Morgannwg and probably Gwent. Gruffudd ap Rhydd-erch originated in Ergyng and Gwent Uwch Coed, but still assumed king-ship in Deheubarth, ruling the whole of the south – an achievement possibly emulated by Rhys ap Tewdwr – and his son, Caradog ap Gruffudd, pressed claims for Gwynllŵg, Gwent and Deheubarth, and reportedly held Ystrad Tywi. Gruffudd ap Llywelyn came from a dynasty which had its origins in Dyfed, but he came to prominence by taking control of Powys and Gwynedd. Similarly, Maredudd and Rhys ab Owain of Deheubarth asserted themselves in Brychein-iog in the 1060s, and Bleddyn ap Cynfyn began his career as king of Gwynedd but was seen by posterity as the head of the Powys dynasty; he was succeeded in Gwynedd by Trahaearn ap Caradog of Arwystli. All of the major dynasties took part in scrambles for power in Morgannwg and Deheubarth in the 1070s, and they were all represented at Mynydd Carn in 1081. Cadwgan ap Bleddyn also sought lands in both Gwynedd and Ceredigion in the 1090s, and Gruffudd ap Rhys claimed Brycheiniog. Indeed, for centuries the term 'kingdom' (*regnum* or *gwlad*) usually denoted a sphere of influence rather than any specific territorial area. Geographical definitions were becoming more common by the eleventh century, but kings could still be described as rulers either of groups of people, or of areas, or in areas. Although the north-west, the south-west and the south-east were continuously prominent in focusing political activity throughout the medieval period, the very idea of what a kingdom was, and exactly where, seems to have been fairly malleable until the later Middle Ages. In the ninth century, for instance, it appears that the kings of Glywysing and Gwent co-existed side

by side, and in some areas even had authority over the same territory, while the
'kingdom' of Rhwng Gwy a Hafren which emerged in the twelfth century was
little more than a loosely-bound conglomeration of petty kingdoms controlled
by a single dynasty.

The immediate impression is one of chronic instability, but this is in many
ways superficial. Attacks on neighbours were invariably carried out in regions
which were already unstable, and power was becoming increasingly territorialised. It became common for poets to suggest a lord's power by the extent of
his lands, and the same process gave rise to the distinction between Wales and
the march, which first appears in the Pipe Rolls in 1195. Most importantly,
Welsh kingdoms were extraordinarily resilient. Dyfed and Morgannwg maintained stable identities for centuries, and Gwynedd in particular could claim a
continuous geographical and (to a lesser extent) dynastic history from the fifth
century to the thirteenth. Despite dynastic problems, each of the three major
kingdoms retained its dynasty until 1282. Whereas the Anglo-Normans forcibly imposed candidates – usually natives – for kingship in Ireland, and Richard fitz Gilbert even claimed the kingship of Leinster for himself, this is not
known to have occurred in Wales. The supremacy of Gwynedd was not prevented by disruption in the late eleventh century, or by dynastic conflict after
1170, or by the exclusion of Llywelyn ap Iorwerth's father on the grounds of an
archaic tradition, and similarly, the line of Cynfyn ap Gwerstan survived in Powys from 1063 until after 1282 despite partitions, opposition from its neighbours,
conquest, changes of allegiance, rebellion, forfeiture and a dynastic bloodbath.
Furthermore, despite all of the apparent weaknesses of the Welsh kingdoms, no
brand new ones are known to have emerged after the seventh century. Wales
as a whole possessed some kind of stability, and individual kingdoms were well
equipped to survive. Indeed, given native inheritance practices, this kind of polity was arguably no more vulnerable than a unified kingdom – a single strong
ruler could vanish overnight, as Harold Godwinesson did at Hastings, and pre-
dictability might therefore be preferable to solidity. Nevertheless, survival alone
was not always enough. In the rapidly centralising world of the twelfth and thirteenth centuries, many native rulers, and ultimately the prince of Wales himself,
faced an increasingly stark choice between being live rats or dead lions.

The Struggle for Supremacy

KINGS, PRINCES, LORDS AND BARONS

There were significant changes in the nomenclature of native political
authority from the eleventh century onwards, reflecting both the increasing
influence of England and changes in the status quo within Wales, as well as

developments across Europe. Although Welsh rulers were given no title at all most of the time, the term 'king' (*rex*) was reserved for prominent figures by the late twelfth century – the *Brut* referred only to Owain Gwynedd, Madog ap Maredudd and Maredudd ap Gruffudd ap Rhys as kings, and *Annales Cambriae* saw nobody but Owain as a *rex*. Lesser rulers underwent a severe reduction of status. Hywel ap Ieuaf, for instance, was *rex Arewestli* in 1141x1143, but he was demoted to *dominus de Arewistil* by 1143x1151; he was known by the latter title in 1177x1185, and by 1197 his son, Meurig, was simply *de Arwistil*. It is interesting, however, that Bishop Alan of Bangor was prepared to refer to Hywel as *rex Arwistili* as late as 1195x1196.

From the middle of the twelfth century, even the greatest Welsh rulers made increasing use of the title 'prince' (*princeps*). In the European context, *princeps* and *rex* had once been of equal stature, but *princeps* became subordinate long before the twelfth century, so the exclusive use of 'prince' in the *Brut* for native leaders after 1157 might appear to suggest that *rex* was abandoned in the face of English power under Henry II. However, the transition was neither comprehensive nor clear-cut. Some confusion over the position of the leading Welshmen at the council of Oxford in 1177 is suggested by the use of both *rex* and *regulus* ('ruler') to describe them, but this does not necessarily imply a loss of status. Roger of Howden, who used the term *regulus* for 1177, was not sure of his terminology – he called Gruffudd ap Rhys 'rege de Suthwales' in 1200,[2] and he referred to Rhys ap Gruffudd both as a *regulus* and as a *rex*. Although the styles *princeps* of north and south Wales came to be used, they were anything but consistent, and even royal sources called Dafydd ab Owain *rex Norwallie* in 1194. In practice, the Anglo-Norman chronicler Florence of Worcester's dictum that there were no more kings in Wales after 1093 was ignored by both the Welsh and the English.

The adoption of the style *princeps* was nevertheless significant. The term itself, and the related form 'principality' (*principatus*), conveyed a sense of pre-eminence, but they were unusual and unclear in meaning. In Europe, a *princeps* was usually simply a 'ruler', essentially the same as a 'lord' (*dominus*), but in Wales the term seems to have represented an attempt to redefine the nature of native authority. The Welsh equivalent, *tywysog*, did not necessarily convey more than the sense of an individual's leadership, and it did not appear in the laws. It may have been a translation of *dux* ('leader') – the *Brut* called the dukes of Normandy, Burgundy and Austria '*tywysog*', and Llywelyn ap Iorwerth was styled *dux Norwallie* several times – and in that case it might seem to amount to demotion. But many sources give a very different impression. Henry II complained to Pope Alexander III that Owain Gwynedd called himself a *princeps* in 1165, and the English chronicler William of Newburgh said that the Welsh were as insolent as *principi* in 1157, suggesting that the new title was if anything an assertion of power. The Welsh were apparently defying conventional definitions of their authority by inventing a new one, playing on the fact that *princeps* might describe kings, lords or abbots without being common and without being consistently either general or specific. 'Prince', and therefore 'principality', could be defined as circumstances warranted.

This change appears to have been motivated primarily by the realisation that native authority must be made into a kingdom or principality in order to survive, and the existence of such a process is evident in the territorialisation of power and the creation of a clear identity. Stronger kingdoms could do this more effectively than weaker ones. Madog ap Maredudd occasionally styled himself king of Powys (*rex Powissensium*) rather than leader of the Powysians (*dux Powisorum*), as his father had done, but the kings of Gwynedd adopted territorialised forms more quickly and confidently – Gruffudd ap Cynan was *regis Guenedotie* and *Gruffut Gwynet*, both Owain Gwynedd and Llywelyn ap Iorwerth were *tywyssawc Gwynedd* and *princeps Norwallie*, and Dafydd ab Owain was *rex Norwallie*. In addition, the adoption of nomenclature such as *dominus* reflected the extension of lordship (*dominium*) within kingdoms. Seemingly humble titles such as 'lord' may have asserted a far closer sense of direct lordship than more grandiose styles. Indeed, in the laws, the term *arglwydd* (the Welsh form of *dominus*) had no legal connotation of subordination to any higher authority.

Ambitious titles were not merely honorary. They denoted power, and, significantly, they were used by only one member of each dynasty at a time. In this light, it might seem that the transition from *rex* to *princeps* represented an increase in the power of some families, rather than a decrease, so that a thirteenth-century Welsh *princeps* was in fact superior to a twelfth-century *rex*. Titles now reflected not royalty, but executive power. From the late twelfth century, only members of the leading dynasties were entitled *princeps* in the chronicles, and the last non-Gwynedd ruler to style himself a *princeps* was Gwenwynwyn ab Owain in 1200x1206. As Gwynedd became dominant, the other princes tended to appear in groups, signifying their inferior status, and their titles were reduced accordingly. Madog ap Maredudd appeared as a *tywyssawc* only once in the *Brut*, and even on his death he was a mere *arglwyd* (lord), while Einion ab Anarawd was no more than a *dux* in 1163. The rise of Gwynedd was accompanied by a dramatic reduction in the status of its satellites. In 1209, Llywelyn ap Iorwerth referred to 'our fellow princes' (*conprincibus nostris*),[3] and all the native rulers, including Llywelyn, were styled *dux* in the early thirteenth century – as late as 1214, they all appeared as both *ducibus* and *principibus*. But Llywelyn emerged as a *princeps* after 1215 while his allies remained as *duces*. By 1237, he was seen as *princeps Walliae*.

The last reference to minor rulers as 'princes' in the *Brut* was in 1257, after which they became barons and lords. Again, the relationship between titles and power is clear: they were *principes-tywyssogyon* when they submitted to Dafydd ap Llywelyn in 1238, but they were reduced to *barones-barwneit* by Henry III in 1240. When the king's grip on Wales was loosened in 1244, they became 'princes' again. The assertion of royal power caused Maredudd ap Rhys and Maredudd ab Owain to be seen as *barones* in 1257, and their implicit subjection was turned to the advantage of Gwynedd in 1267. The dynasty of Gwynedd had outstripped its rivals in defining and asserting itself, and its princely title was now expanded beyond Gwynedd. If the principality of Wales was to be viable, however, it was necessary to exceed the tradition of pan-Welsh supremacy upon which it drew.

OVERLORDSHIP OF WALES

There is little evidence for any form of dependence relationship between rulers in early medieval Wales. If the king of one *regnum* conquered another, as Rhodri Mawr took Powys and Ceredigion, he simply became king there as well, displacing the incumbent. He did not become an overking over the two kingdoms, and he did not unite one kingdom with another. There was therefore no tendency towards the creation of a kingdom of Wales, as there was in England during the ninth and tenth centuries. Yet there was always a sense that kings of Gwynedd had some kind of superiority in Wales. Gildas saw Maelgwn Gwynedd as the most important of the British kings, and Maelgwn's successors were often regarded by Welsh, English and Irish sources alike as 'kings of the Britons', and as the natural leaders of the Welsh in war. The kings of Gwynedd also operated outside their own kingdom to a degree not matched by their rivals. In the eleventh century, Gruffudd ap Llywelyn achieved a greater supremacy than any ruler before him, and he could call upon the resources of Gwynedd, Powys and Deheubarth, but – despite being accorded the title 'king of Wales' by contemporaries – he could not unite Wales, and the years after his death suggest that chaos was the norm. Similarly, although both Bleddyn ap Cynfyn and Rhys ap Tewdwr are said to have held 'the kingdom of the Britons', this probably reflects their stature as the most prominent native bastions against Norman invasion rather than any wider hegemony on the scale enjoyed by some of their predecessors.

Nevertheless, the concept of overkingship associated with tribute and military service was known to the Welsh from their experience of English and possibly Scandinavian overlordship as early as the tenth century, and it could be applied from within Wales as well as from outside. Tribute was taken regularly from Môn in the late tenth century, for instance, suggesting both that tribute-taking was a normal activity and that more effective means of raising it were being developed, and some territorial rulers were depicted in eleventh-century charters as subject to others. Furthermore, whereas the movements of earlier rulers had been confined to the corners of Wales, the territorial range covered by Welsh kings increased dramatically in the tenth and eleventh centuries. The sons of Idwal ranged over Powys, Dyfed and Gwynedd in the 950s; Maredudd ab Owain was in Ceredigion, Dyfed, Glamorgan and Gwynedd at the turn of the eleventh century; Gruffudd ap Llywelyn operated in Powys, Ceredigion, Ystrad Tywi, Hereford and Gwynedd between 1039 and 1055; and a number of other equally ambitious, if less successful, rulers attempted to impose their influence outside their own immediate localities. The stage upon which political activity was conducted now included the whole of Wales.

By the late twelfth century, unitary rule over all of Wales began to become a genuine ambition. Gerald of Wales maintained that the Welsh should unite in the interests of mutual security and submit to one good prince, and he blamed their disunity largely on their inability to accept a single king. This vision was shared by native secular leaders in the late twelfth century, and the role of Gwynedd in leading Welsh resistance in 1165 and 1210 put it at the forefront of moves towards unification. Owain Gwynedd called himself king and prince of both Wales and the Welsh in the 1160s, and *Historia Gruffudd vab Kenan* – which probably dates from the same period – portrayed Gruffudd ap Cynan as 'king of the kings of Wales'.[4] The poet Gwilym Ryfel similarly indicated a desire to place Gwynedd at the apex of a Welsh hierarchy when he said that God gave Dafydd ab Owain a place above other chieftains (*pennaethau*). Gwynedd did not assume this role because it was intrinsically more innovative than other kingdoms, however – indeed, it lay in the traditionally more conservative highland zone of Wales. Rather, Gwynedd owed its position largely to the fact that it was simply the most stable Welsh kingdom in the twelfth and thirteenth centuries. Deheubarth also aspired to rule over Wales – Rhys ap Gruffudd styled himself 'prince of Wales' (*princeps Walliae*) and 'prince of the Welsh' (*Walliarum princeps*), and he was called 'head of all Wales' (*tocius Wallie capud*), while his son, Gruffudd, was also mourned as the rightful 'prince of Wales' (*Kambrie princeps, Kambrie monarchiam* or *tywyssawc Kymry*) in 1201 – but infighting among the dynasty meant that these ambitions came to nothing.

The events of the early thirteenth century ensured that overlordship would belong to Gwynedd. Although not necessarily the wealthiest kingdom in Wales, Gwynedd had been consistently prominent for centuries by virtue of its military strength. That strength had always depended to a large degree upon the mountainous geography of Snowdonia and the pastures of Môn, and the relative power of Gwynedd grew as the other Welsh kingdoms succumbed to English incursions. By 1216, Llywelyn ap Iorwerth could claim to be prince of the whole of Wales – *tocius Wallie monarchiam*, and later *princeps totius Walliae* and *tywyssawc Kymry* – and the poets insistently saluted the dynasty of Gwynedd as kings of Wales. The prologues of *Llyfr Iorwerth*, which probably date from the time of Llywelyn ap Iorwerth, also called Hywel Dda *tywyssawc* of all Wales. Nevertheless, despite the mention of tribute (*mechteyrn dyled*) due to Aberffraw, the laws did not usually give prominence to Gwynedd, and each kingdom was generally seen as self-sufficient. Indeed, Dinefwr was also given superior status in southern redactions, although *Llyfr Iorwerth* said that gold could only be given to Aberffraw, which generally received the most attention. The complexities of the propaganda war are illustrated by the fact that even the English government retrospectively called Dafydd ab Owain *rex Walliae* in 1221.

The precedents for overlordship within Wales were few. Gwynedd had taken tribute from other parts of Wales on occasion, and hostages were another customary means of asserting dominance, but this never amounted to more than a tenuous superiority. Lacking the economic, geographical, political and military good fortune which attended the creation of centralised kingdoms in England, Scotland and France, the Welsh consequently lacked the institution of national kingship which made it possible for the king of Scots to exercise authority beyond the territories which came under his own direct lordship – he ruled over many ethnic groups throughout the whole of Scotland while styling himself merely 'king of Scotia' (that is, the eastern seaboard from the Firth of Forth to the Moray Firth). The efforts of most Welsh rulers to achieve wide hegemonies are more reminiscent of the kings of Tara, who were unable to give practical effect to their claim to rule the whole of Ireland, giving rise to the delicately understated idea of the *rí hErend co fressabra* – 'king of Ireland with opposition'.

The obvious means of achieving more direct control was military conquest. Welsh law, however, did not accept simple possession (*goresgyn*) as sufficient grounds for ownership or right, and a dichotomy emerged over the validity of unlawful conquest. Many princes were encouraged to take armies beyond the boundaries of their patrimony and to take possession of areas to which they had no legal claim, and they were probably mindful of the need to break with tradition in the furtherance of dynastic interests. But there remained powerful arguments against such action. Cynddelw warned that only God was entitled to take another's property for himself ('*nid meddwl meddu hefyd namyn Dduw ddim o'r byd*'), and Elidir Sais advised Llywelyn ap Iorwerth to be cautious about extending his power across boundaries: '*ystyrwch pan dreisych dros ffin*'.[5] Traditional concepts of legitimate acquisition stood in the way of political unity.

Inheritance Practices, Consolidation and Fragmentation

UNITARY SUCCESSION

Political unity also depended upon innovation in the inheritance of king-doms. Welsh kingship was transmitted dynastically from at least the sixth cen-tury, but this in itself did not ensure stability. To address the problem of politi-cal instability, inheritance practices developed significantly in the later Middle Ages, following a tendency throughout Europe to concentrate power in the hands of a single segment of a single dynasty. Customary practice was merely the product of years of dynastic self-interest.

Gerald of Wales believed that Welsh succession practices were inherently divisive and destructive, but he missed the crucial point that whereas land could be divided, kingship usually could not. He failed to distinguish between the in-heritance of land and of kingdoms, or between contested and partible succes-sion, and his condemnation of Wales probably derived from a bias against the alleged political ineptitude of 'barbarian' frontier peoples. In practice, succes-sion practices reflected instability as much as they caused it, and the Welsh laws made it clear that kingship was supposed to be passed on intact, rather than being divided like the lands of free men – there was only one heir, and only one kingship. Except under exceptional circumstances, Welsh kingship was never partible, and even when territorial fragmentation was unavoidable it was a common desire to reunify the patrimony. Inheritance practices were not well-defined or immutable, however, and the tendency towards indivisibility of kingship was the product of a long process of change throughout Europe. The ultimate criteria in the develop-ment towards impartibility and primogeniture were expediency and precedent.

The idea of the designated king (*rex designatus*) was widespread in Europe, and the *Brut* was aware of the status of Henry, the son of Henry II, as having been designated heir in his father's lifetime. Welsh law provided for the selec-tion of an heir, called a *gwrthrych* or *edlyng* – although contemporary jurists disagreed about whether there could be more than one – and it appears that some twelfth-century Welsh kings selected a single heir. The encomium in the *Brut* for Rhun, the eldest son of Owain Gwynedd, on his death in 1146 sug-gests that he may have been regarded as Owain's heir, and another of Owain's sons, Hywel, was seen by the poet Peryf ap Cydifor to be '*yn gorwedd ar yr aerfa*' – literally, 'lying in the heir's place' – before his death in 1170.[6] Cynddelw saw the death of Llywelyn ap Madog ap Maredudd in 1160 as more disastrous than that of his father, referring to him as an *aer*, and the *Brut* said that the hope of all Powys had lain in him. None of these men can be shown indisputably to have been designated, but the sense of desolation on their deaths, and the dynastic chaos which followed, suggest that they played an important role. Gruffudd ap Rhys was certainly designated heir to Deheubarth in 1197, and he was still regarded as such in some quarters in 1201. Similarly, Dafydd ap Llywelyn was designated heir to Gwynedd, and swore homage to the king in this capacity during his father's lifetime, and Gruffudd ap Gwenwynwyn selected his son, Owain, to inherit his full authority in 1278. It is also possible that Dafydd ap Gruffudd was intended to succeed Llywelyn ap Gruffudd. Steps were being taken throughout Wales to ensure that rulership of king-doms remained in the hands of a narrow dynastic group. Nevertheless, no medieval succession was entirely smooth, and the fact that the Welsh did not inaugurate their heirs, as Henry II did, deprived their successors of a much-needed extra support. Moreover, the existence of a designated heir did not necessarily reflect dynastic stability, and might even imply the opposite – in Ireland, for instance, the position of heir (*rígdamna* or *tánaise*) between the tenth and twelfth centuries was very likely a sort of guarantee that kingship would change hands between powerful segments or even dynasties, and prob-ably denoted the head of the main segment not in possession of the kingship. Furthermore, in the case of Wales it is not clear whether there was always an heir, or whether the king was obliged to choose one, or even whether the selection of heirs was exclusively the prerogative of the king.

THE PROBLEMS OF MULTIPLE ELIGIBILITY

The fundamental purpose of Welsh dynasties was to preserve the integrity of kingship. Within that outline, however, ideas of unitary succession and provi-sion for failed contenders were very flexible. The designation of an heir could not always prevent territorial partition, and in extreme cases – such as Powys in the 1190s – kingdoms could even be split. The problem was not partibility, but multiplicity of eligibility.

The laws did not agree on the kin limits for eligibility to kingship. Those eligible – known as the *membra regis* or *aelodau'r brenin* (the 'members of the king') – could include sons, nephews and cousins of the king, but the laws record confusion over whether each one was an *edlyng*, or whether the *edlyng* was merely the one to whom the king gave 'hope and prospect' (*gobeyth a gurthrych*). Furthermore, eligibility was in fact wider than was prescribed in the laws. Some idea of the number of the *membra regis* is given by the fact that land law was based on a kin-group of four generations, and *galanas* (a form of compensation payment) was payable by seven degrees of kin. Inheritance rules for kingship did not always follow those for property, but the extent of the *membra regis* was apparently considerable, and the ability to cultivate a convincing genealogy was very important. Gerald's observation that the Welsh were obsessed with tracing their ancestry back some six or seven generations is therefore not surprising. Each royal son or cousin produced a new dynastic segment, each with its own claim, and inter-segmentary rivalry could be very fierce. In Gwynedd between 951 and 985, for example, the sons of Idwal first fought the sons of Hywel (the great-grandsons of Rhodri Mawr) before fighting each other, and their sons in turn followed suit.

The pragmatic elasticity of how the *membra regis* were defined, and of what constituted legitimate rule, is revealed by the ability of *Historia Gruffud vab Kenan* both to vilify Gruffudd ap Llywelyn as a usurper against the family of Gruffudd ap Cynan and to use him as a legitimising association in the same cause, and the proliferation of dynastic segments after the tenth century complicated eligibility still further. Large numbers of candidates could emerge in a succession dispute, often with tenuous claims. Deheubarth, for instance, was controlled by distant segments between 1044 and 1063 and in the 1070s, and the emergence of Owain and Uchdryd ab Edwin in Gwynedd after 1098 is particularly intriguing. They may have been sons of Edwin ap Goronwy ab Einion ab Owain ap Hywel Dda, who may have held lands in Tegeingl in 1086, but this in itself does not explain their appearance with the Norman invaders of Gwynedd in 1098, nor the fact that Owain's son, Goronwy, held a powerful position in Gwynedd as late as 1114. Gruffudd ap Cynan found it necessary to marry Angharad, a daughter of Owain, in order to make his task easier, and Owain Gwynedd also married into the family. It appears therefore that the sons of Edwin were able to press a convincing claim to Gwynedd despite the genealogical distance between them and the recent rulers of the kingdom. Some Irish kingships passed remarkably often to people outside the four-generation kin-group, and the point is underlined by the success of Gruffudd ap Cynan. His grandfather had been king of Gwynedd before 1039, but Gruffudd lived his early life apparently unnoticed by his Welsh contemporaries. Despite the *Historia*'s retrospective claim that he was regarded as the rightful heir to Gwynedd, Gruffudd was in fact the least well-known of the combatants at Mynydd Carn in 1081, and his claim was based almost entirely on his distant royal descent and the probably fictitious assertion that his father had been king of Gwynedd.

In practice, it seems that royal lineage was the only prerequisite for candidates for Welsh kingship. This was not exceptional in medieval Europe, and it was not surprising in view of the potential number of *membra regis*, which was increased still further by widespread royal polygamy and an inclusive rule of legitimacy. The dynasty, rather than the individual, was heir, and such wide eligibility inevitably meant that those on the fringes were likely to mount particularly determined challenges. Ultimately, however, any claimant's chances depended upon his access to resources. It was often the case that no segment could keep its grip on power for long, and the appearance of more remote relatives was a sure measure of the weakness of a dynasty. Strong kings were usually succeeded by their immediate relations, especially sons and brothers, and often nephews of the previous incumbent's predecessor. The kingship of Gwynedd, for example, passed directly from father to son for four generations after Rhodri Mawr, and its incumbents remained within five generations of Idwal Foel ab Anarawd ap Rhodri Mawr from the ninth century to the eleventh. Similarly, the kings of Deheubarth in the same period could all trace their ancestry to Owain ap Hywel Dda within four generations. Most notably, all but four of the rulers in both north and south-west Wales between the last quarter of the ninth century and the third quarter of the eleventh century hailed from the line of Rhodri Mawr, and the need for some kind of identification with this nexus is clear in the poet Meilyr's description of Gruffudd ap Cynan as the 'strength of Rhodri' ('*nerth rodri*').[7]

This dynasty was clearly important, but very little is known about it in the ninth and tenth centuries, and it is difficult even to establish precisely where its members ruled in the tenth century. Other dynasties appear just as prominent in the period before 950, and many eleventh-century rulers were either from uncertain backgrounds or linked only indirectly to Rhodri. Every part of Wales except Morgannwg came under 'intrusive' rulers from other dynasties in that period. These 'intruders' were not mere aberrations – some of them, such as Bleddyn ap Cynfyn, established powerful dynasties. Although Rhodri's heirs held substantial power, there is no indication that descent from Rhodri was ever a mark of inherent legitimacy or a prerequisite for kingship. Indeed, the concept of 'intrusive' rulers seems to have been either unknown to the Welsh chroniclers or of little consequence to them, since they rarely identify them as such. The succession to Gwynedd was far from smooth between 1075 and 1098, when none of the claimants were sons or grandsons of the previous incumbent. Yet no comment is passed by *Annales Cambriae* or the *Brut* about the suitability or otherwise of candidates. A closer examination of the genealogical claims reveals that, although there was no descent in the male line, all of the incumbents were related more or less distantly, often through their mothers. Moreover, a study of the degree of kinship between each incumbent and his immediate predecessor in eleventh-century Gwynedd, based on descent from a common ancestor who had rule, is revealing. To arrive at such an ancestor, most incumbents had to go back at least three generations, and in some cases six. A man like Gruffudd ap Cynan – who was linked to his predecessor Trahaearn ap Caradog at a distance of two generations – was anything but a rank outsider, despite his failure to play any part in the politics of Gwynedd for 18 years after the death of Gruffudd ap Llywelyn.

Succession was determined not by order of precedence but by the balance of power. In Gwynedd, both Dafydd ab Owain and Llywelyn ap Gruffudd challenged successfully against better-qualified opposition, and even those such as Owain Gwynedd and Llywelyn ap Iorwerth, who had as good a theo-retical case as their rivals, had to fight their way to power. There are count-less other examples of disputed succession, but this level of violent opposi-tion must be seen in light of the fact that dynastic warfare was a widespread phenomenon throughout medieval Europe, and that every king of England before the thirteenth century found it necessary to resort to violence against his rivals before or during the early stages of his reign. In this context, for all its problems, the succession of Dafydd ap Llywelyn was relatively smooth.

The Norman conquerors were well aware of these realities in Welsh political life. Gerald of Wales relates that Miles fitz Walter, the earl of Hereford and lord of Brycheiniog, once teased Gruffudd ap Rhys ap Tewdwr about his royal pretensions, quoting an old saying that all the wildfowl of Llangors lake would burst into song should the rightful ruler of Brycheiniog come to the lake. To prove the point, having addressed the birds themselves without effect, Miles and Payn fitz John of Ewyas challenged Gruffudd to do the same. According to Gerald, they were astounded when the lake erupted in a chorus of birdsong. Henry I, however, is said to have remarked that he was not at all surprised by this. Gruffudd was the rightful lord, he acknowledged, but the Normans held the power and could use it as they wished. There was no need to elaborate further. It was accepted by all as a matter of fact that neither genealogy, entreaties to kinsmen nor the apparent ability to influence wild-fowl were sufficient to press a claim, and Gruffudd's authority was only accepted after a military campaign in 1136. In the laws, one of the definitions of an heir was 'he who should rule after the king' – in practice, whether his rivals were Welsh or Norman, there was no guarantee that he would.

If only by sheer force, strong dynastic segments were able to retain power. Within these segments, the practice of designation tended to favour linear succession, from father to son. As in the rest of Europe, linear succession in Wales evolved over time, but it was not easy to maintain unless, like the Pre-myslid dynasty in Bohemia in the thirteenth century, each successive king produced only one son. No major Welsh dynasty was so fortunate, and linear succession was very rare in Wales. There was also a considerable degree of luck involved in the success of any candidate. Gruffudd ap Cynan, for instance, benefited from the decision of Llywarch ap Trahaearn, Uchdryd ab Edwin and the sons of Bleddyn ap Cynfyn (after 1098) to involve themselves in the politics of Powys rather than Gwynedd, and also from the deaths of Meurig and Griffri ap Trahaearn at the hands of Owain ap Cadwgan in 1106, not to mention the defeat of the Norman earls by the king of Norway. Strong rulers made the most of their luck, and they were able to consolidate their position and appease ecclesiastical critics by restricting inheritance to one segment. This necessarily required the diminishing of the *membra regis*, which was achieved in a variety of ways.

METHODS OF REMOVING THE *MEMBRA REGIS* FROM CONTENTION

The most obvious way of eliminating opposition was to kill them. This was a regular occurrence until the early twelfth century, but the preferred method thereafter was mutilation. This allowed the victim to remain alive – and thereby lessened the degree of ecclesiastical condemnation – while disqualifying relatives from eligibility. *Llyfr Blegywryd* stated that blind, deaf and crippled candidates should be excluded, and this apparently ancient tradition – it may have originated from pre-Christian notions of virility and fertility – seems to have been extended to other disfigurements. Iorwerth Drwyndwn ('Flat nose') was deemed ineligible because of a minor physical deformity, and Maredudd Ddall ('the Blind') ap Rhys ap Gruffudd was apparently excluded because of mutilation; the same may also have been true of the Cynwrig ap Rhys who was mutilated by the king in 1165. It was not impossible for the son of a blemished candidate to assert claims successfully – Llywelyn ap Iorwerth demonstrated this – but mutilation generally condemned a man to the political wilderness. Castration, in particular, could incapacitate a segment. Llywelyn ap Iorwerth continued to rule after a stroke and slight paralysis in 1237, but instances of rulers who succeeded despite natural disfigurements, such as Morgan Gam ('the Crooked'), were rare. Dynastic mutilation was especially popular in the twelfth century, but, along with assassination, it was gradually superseded by more sophisticated practices.

Rivals could be removed from the political sphere by an enforced *clericatus*, whereby they were entered forcibly into monasteries. This useful resource seems to have been used by Rhys ap Gruffudd on his brother, Cadell, who died at Strata Florida, and by Llywelyn ap Iorwerth on Gruffudd ap Cynan ab Owain, who died at Aberconwy. Another means of disposing of rivals was imprisonment, and it may be significant that Owain Gwynedd was first called *tywyssawc Gwynedd* in the *Brut* when he imprisoned his son, Cynan, in 1150 – he went on to strengthen his position further by expelling his brother, Cadwaladr, imprisoning Cadfan ap Cadwaladr, and then mutilating another nephew, Cunedda ap Cadwallon. Similarly, Dafydd ab Owain incarcerated his brothers Maelgwn and Rhodri. Gruffudd ap Llywelyn ap Iorwerth and his son, Owain, were also imprisoned several times by the princes of Gwynedd, and the effort to exclude Gruffudd underlay his father's invocation of the principle of legitimacy.

Less violent was the process of mediatisation, by which *membra regis* could be subsumed within the non-royal aristocracy. According to the laws, the privileges of the *membra regis* were only the same as those of the king for as long as they remained without land. Once they took land, their rights were

merely those associated with that land. Unsuccessful segments were inevitably demoted where linear succession was practised, and the more prominent members of the princely kin, including the designated heir, were usually
given land. It was therefore possible to reduce all of them to the status of
freemen under a single sovereign ruler, and unsuccessful *membra regis* were
often accommodated in the aristocracy of princely service. In this way, Gruffudd ap Rhodri served Llywelyn ap Iorwerth by the 1220s, and Einion ap
Caradog, a great-grandson of Rhodri ab Owain, was in the entourage of
Llywelyn ap Gruffudd in 1258. Rhisiart ap Cadwaladr, apparently a son of
Cadwaladr ap Gruffudd, and possibly the father of Maredudd ap Rhisiart, was
rhaglaw of Dinllaen in Llŷn, and Dafydd ap Gruffudd was the *penteulu* (or *dux
familie* – the leader of the warband) of two of his brothers, Owain and then
Llywelyn. The king's relatives were also provided with ecclesiastical posts, or
simply allowed to merge into the aristocracy. Finally, there was dispossession.
The more remote *membra regis* did not always get even a *cwmwd*, and Rhys ap
Gruffudd went a stage further by planning to disinherit his daughter and all of
his grandchildren. As kings often gave substantial lands to non-royal *priodorion*,
the less wealthy royalty could quickly be subsumed into the aristocracy.

Such centralisation of power was fraught with difficulties, however. When
Madog ap Maredudd attempted to completely dispossess his younger brother,
Iorwerth Goch – leaving him 'without anything' (*heb dim*), with neither honour (*anryded*) nor possession (*medyant*) – he provoked a violent response, and
the poet Hywel Foel ap Griffri no doubt spoke for many *membra regis* when
he protested that no-one but God was entitled to dispossess a man: '*ny uet
namyn duw digyfoethi dyn*'.[8] Violent and extreme actions might successfully
limit the *membra regis*, but they jeopardised territorial integrity. Strong kingship required both of these things.

MEANS OF PRESERVING TERRITORIAL INTEGRITY

From the early Middle Ages, Welsh kings usually divided their lands between
their sons. There was no need for rigid adherence to either unitary or partible
succession, however – it was possible to combine them. In France, the designation of one son and the provision of territorial appanages for the rest around the
fringes of the kingdom usually worked well for the Capetian and Valois kings in
their efforts to strengthen central authority, and versions of this were practised
in Wales. Gruffudd ap Cynan's grant of his border *cantrefi* to his sons seems to
have been a primarily military decision, but dynastic considerations were also
crucial. Similarly, Owain Gwynedd entrusted Ceredigion Is Aeron to his son,
Hywel, and Ceredigion Uwch Aeron and Meirionnydd to his brother, Cadwaladr, clearly intending to divert their attentions away from Gwynedd. Owain

Cyfeiliog also seems to have given lands to his son, Gwenwynwyn, by 1185, and Madog ap Gwenwynwyn held Mawddwy as an appanage in 1263.

Appanages were in part an acknowledgement of the limitations of government. Just as several kings of France created appanages simply because their effective authority could not cover such wide territories, so Llywelyn ap Iorwerth had no option but to treat his conquests in Powys Wenwynwyn and Meirionnydd in this way. Moreover, he was obliged to provide for his disinherited son, Gruffudd, and he made repeated attempts to install Gruffudd in lands to which the line of Cynan ab Owain had claims. Rhys ap Gruffudd seems to have been similarly reluctant or unable simply to imprison his excluded son Maelgwn. The risks of such a policy were clear. Appanages could provide a power-base for potential contenders, and the Welsh, like the French, sensibly gave only acquisitions – rather than the patrimonial inheritance – as appanages. It was only in exceptional circumstances, however, that the holders of appanages rebelled. The division of Powys after 1160, for instance, was a rejection of the arrangements made on the death of Madog ap Maredudd, but it would not have occurred had the heir not been killed. Similarly, Gruffudd ap Llywelyn's dissatisfaction was with his father's novel succession plans, not with his appanage, and Maredudd ap Rhisiart's revival of the claim of Cadwaladr ap Gruffudd to Llŷn owed more to the disruptive policies of Henry III than to any inherent weakness in the practice of appanage. On the whole, appanages probably strengthened central authority. They could be recovered, if necessary, and they seem to have actively restricted inheritance to kingship. The granting of appanages also bound both the grantees and their lands closer to the king by defining his lordship more specifically, however loose this might be in practice. As in France, appanages signified not weakness and a diffusion of authority but an ambition to tighten central authority and control. Whether or not there was any real increase in power is debatable, however.

The combination of linear succession, territorial integrity and centralised authority was not impossible to achieve, and came nearest to realisation in the practice of parage – parallelled in England and France – by which lands were divided more or less equally between sons, one of whom was given prominence. Llywelyn ap Iorwerth's re-apportioning of Powys Fadog between the four sons of Madog ap Gruffudd Maelor on their father's death in 1236 seems to have been a case of parage, and Gruffudd ap Madog also apparently intended to institute parage on his death in 1269. In Powys Wenwynwyn, too, Gruffudd ap Gwenwynwyn planned in 1278 to give the inheritance to his eldest son, Owain, while the other five sons received parages. Owain was to be the only tenant-in-chief, and he would have jurisdictional and tenurial rights throughout his brothers' lands. This may have been a move towards the English practice of 'entail', but not necessarily so, as it was fully in accordance with native Welsh practice.

Dynastic unity was always inherent in the parage, despite the division of lands, and Henry III's interpretation of Welsh law as divisive flew in the face of Welsh tradition. A striking example of the way in which parages preserved both territorial and dynastic integrity amidst apparent fragmentation is found in Poland in the twelfth and thirteenth centuries. In 1138, Boleslav III gave parages to four of his sons, the eldest of whom received the suzerain principality of Cracow – which contained the *caput* – and other lands and rights which gave him a predominant position. The desired unity did not materialise, however, and Poland was split. It was now united only by the church and the nominal supremacy of Cracow, and was threatened by enormous decentralising pressures which included the nobility, inadequate administration, negligible resources and numerous ethnic divisions which meant that the peoples near Prussia, Bohemia, Russia and Germany had more in common with those on the other side of the border than with other members of the Polish kingdom. The division seemed permanent and irreversible, but all of the minor princes consistently regarded the suzerain principality as their superior, and Przemyslav II finally restored unity in 1288. Despite its superficial divisiveness, the fragmentation of Poland after 1138 was in spirit anything but a departure from unity.

The practice of parage on eldest sons was entirely compatible with the long-standing Welsh tradition of *droit d'aînesse* (the 'right of seniority'), by which sons of an elder brother were eligible even if their father were incapacitated. Llywelyn ap Iorwerth's claim to Gwynedd was grounded in this principle, since eligibility passed to him through the excluded Iorwerth Drwyndwn after the death of Hywel ab Owain in 1170. Because of his youth and the exclusion of his father, not to mention the *de facto* power of Dafydd ab Owain, it is not surprising that there is no secular reference to Llywelyn as heir, but customary practice made it clear that he had a greater right than his uncles and cousins to the kingship. After Llywelyn, Gruffudd ap Cynan ab Owain was the eldest surviving, active and eligible descendant of Owain Gwynedd, and he apparently held the kingship after 1194. He was succeeded by Llywelyn. Similarly, the claim of Rhys Ieuanc and Owain ap Gruffudd against Maelgwn ap Rhys in Deheubarth stemmed from the fact that they were the sons of the eldest son of Rhys ap Gruffudd. Another example was the dispute between the descendants of Trahaearn ap Caradog in Arwystli in the early twelfth century, which was caused primarily by the death of Trahaearn's eldest sons, Meurig and Griffri, in 1106. The bloodbath which followed seems essentially to have been conducted on three levels. It was partly a contest between the sons of Llywarch and Owain – the surviving sons of Trahaearn – and those of their two dead brothers; the sons of Meurig and Griffri were attempting to assert *droit d'aînesse*. It was also partly an effort by the sons of Owain to oust those of Llywarch on the same principle. Finally, it was a struggle among the sons of each brother – each son would benefit from the elimination of his elder brothers. Thus, Maredudd ap Llywarch killed the son of Meurig, and also blinded Maredudd and Griffri, the sons of Griffri, while Owain's son, Ieuaf, blinded his two brothers, and then killed both of Llywarch's eldest sons, Iorwerth and Maredudd, only to be killed himself by the remaining sons of Llywarch, the eldest of whom, Madog, was killed by an unidentified first cousin called Meurig – possibly a son of Meurig ap Trahaearn, asserting *droit d'aînesse* – who in turn was mutilated by an unknown party. As is often the case with apparently indiscrimate murders, there was method in the madness.

Droit d'aînesse also seems to have been influential in the succession crisis in Powys in the early twelfth century, and similar considerations apparently motivated Hywel ap Iorwerth's mutilation of his uncle, Owain Pencarn – the younger brother of Iorwerth ab Owain – in 1175. Owain Cyfeiliog was another who appears to have acted on the principle in his bid for southern Powys. His father, Gruffudd ap Maredudd, was the eldest son of Maredudd ap Bleddyn, but his death in 1128 – before that of Maredudd – allowed the kingship to pass to his younger brother, Madog. That Madog was nevertheless induced to give Cyfeiliog to Owain and his brother, Meurig, suggests recognition of their right according to *droit d'aînesse*.

However loosely, Welsh inheritance practices were moving towards a restriction of eligibility and a consequent concentration of power in fewer and fewer hands. Whatever form it took, and however gradually and erratically it evolved, this could only mean greater political stability. Nevertheless, even when all of the native forms of dynastic elimination were operated, damaging disputes could and did occur. 1137 was the last occasion on which an eldest surviving legitimate son succeeded to Gwynedd, and even as prince of Wales, Llywelyn ap Gruffudd was obliged to recognise his brothers' rights to lands. Indeed, his failure to find a wife before 1275 suggests an understanding that Dafydd's support was dependent upon acceptance of his position as heir, and it was no coincidence that Dafydd's revolt in 1274 persuaded Llywelyn to take up his longstanding undertaking to marry Eleanor de Montfort in the hope of an heir of his body. The issue of Dafydd's inheritance was a perennial problem for Llywelyn, and it played a crucial part in his downfall. Domestic problems such as this proved to be a major obstacle to the success of the principality of Gwynedd.

Centralisation and Tension in the Hegemony of Gwynedd

THE CONSOLIDATION OF OVERLORDSHIP

The supremacy of Gwynedd was aided by the existence of a sense that there was a need for native Welsh unity – if only temporary – and a related tendency towards a common identity. Moreover, the examples of Scotland and Ireland showed that political centralisation in Britain and Ireland was not held back by some archaic 'Celtic' traditionalism. The position of Gwynedd was unique and hard to define, but the princes' aim in essence was to bind the other Welsh to them, and thus to create what can be termed a pan-Welsh state – in other words, a new coercive organisation within defined territorial limits, differentiated from other forms of socio-political organisation as an executive agency and a central source of authority. Such an entity could be brought into existence in many ways. In England, for instance, unity was the product of a combination of common legal, cultural, political and administrative ties, made possible as lesser kings were deprived of their status by more powerful ones. Other states evolved in different ways, and it was the task of the princes of Gwynedd to find ways of creating a state in the circumstances which prevailed in thirteenth-century Wales.

Revolution in medieval government necessarily came from the top, and the ideological bedrock of the state was provided by lawyers. Thirteenth-century Welsh law encapsulated the superiority (*superioritas*) of Gwynedd in the conception of tribute known as *mechteyrn dyled*, and it also accepted a king's right to make legal amendments; in this, the princes may have been influenced by the dictum of the English lawyer Henry de Bracton that 'what pleases the prince has the power of law' ('*quod principi placuit, legis habet vigorem*').[9] Llywelyn ap Iorwerth certainly put this principle into practice when, for example, he manipulated the succession to Deheubarth in 1216.

This superiority was underlined by Llywelyn's 'council' (*consilio*) of the princes of Wales in 1212, which was often repeated, notably in 1216 and 1238. Llywelyn emphasised his power and authority by summoning the princes to the execution of William de Braose in 1230, and the dominance of Gwynedd was pressed further by Llywelyn ap Gruffudd, who exercised the right to confirm grants by his tenants – he is known to have confirmed a grant of the *cwmwd* of Anhuniog in Ceredigion Uwch Aeron by Maredudd ab Owain in 1273, and this was probably not the only example of its kind. He also seems to have influenced the original plans for the succession to Powys Fadog in 1269. It cannot be assumed, however, that it was normal for the prince to interfere in the territorial or dynastic arrangements of his clients.

Gwynedd's empire was well equipped to be firm in dealing with its recalcitrant members. Llywelyn ap Gruffudd tried and imprisoned Maredudd ap Rhys for infidelity in 1259, and in 1263 Gruffudd ap Gwenwynwyn was bound to accept that any case against him would be heard immediately by Llywelyn's court, but that, should Gruffudd have any complaint against Llywelyn, he must not make any accusation until it could be proven – if it was not, he would be liable to give compensation. When Gruffudd and his son

Owain fell foul of the prince in 1274, it was made especially clear that both they and their lands were subject to his jurisdiction – this was in accordance with the provision in the laws that a man should forfeit his inheritance (*tref y tat*) for the crime of treachery against his lord (*brat argluyd*), which included plots and rebellions. The prince left no room for doubt that even the greatest native magnates were bound by their oaths to him, and that his authority gave him both ultimate power over their lands and the benefit of any doubt concerning their loyalty. In this sense, Llywelyn elevated himself to the status of lord over the Welsh. It was unity and seigneurial allegiance, more than anything else, upon which the principality depended.

The most important part of the creation of a centralised polity was the taking of homage, since it was this which transformed a leader into a lord and a follower into a tenant. All of the elements of Bracton's definition of homage – that it was done by the will of both parties, and broken if either desired it, while the duties of the lord to the tenant were as great as those of the tenant to the lord – are found under Llywelyn ap Gruffudd. Furthermore, there was a tendency towards the classical European model of feudalism (if such a thing can be said to have existed). Both Llywelyn ap Iorwerth and Llywelyn ap Gruffudd exacted homage, and the latter insisted that the Welsh barons and their heirs held their lands of him and his heirs. Gruffudd ap Gwenwynwyn's submission in 1263 bore a particularly close resemblance to European feudalism, when he did homage and set up a relationship of lord and tenant in the form of a *finalis concordia*. This was not the only example, and forms of homage and fealty were not uncommon by the middle of the thirteenth century.

It may be that this 'feudalisation' was a product of the need to preserve political independence from the king of England, and Owain Gwynedd may have been one of its earliest and strongest advocates, but it seems that there was already a brand of 'feudalism' native and peculiar to Wales. The laws said that there could be no land without a king, that every man was the man (*gwr*) of a king, and that the bond between a king and his man transcended that between a man and his kindred bond. *Gwrogaeth* (often translated as 'homage') was therefore bound up with the ownership (*priodolder*) of land, and this might be interpreted as a form of feudal tenure. Welsh investiture practice resembled feudal enfeoffment, and the lord's rights – including the authority to deprive a man of land if he failed to pay tribute, if he died without an heir within four degrees of consanguinity, or if he committed felony or treason – were very similar to feudal incidents. This begs the question: what was 'feudal'? The answer, if the term is to have any meaning in this context, must surely be that only practices found in post-1066 France and England but not in pre-1066 Wales could be feudal.

By this reckoning, the Welsh concept of the 'man' was not feudal. In *Pedeir Keinc y Mabinogi*, Teirnon Twryf Uliant was on good terms with Pwyll, having previously been Pwyll's man. In Anglo-Norman feudal practice, however, a man was always his lord's man, and to renounce a lord was a sign of hostility. It appears, then, that the bond between Pwyll and Teirnon was not based on Anglo-Norman feudalism. *Gwr* clearly meant something else. Similar problems are raised by the term *gwrogaeth*. It is sometimes found in the *Pedeir Keinc* connected with the idea that land was held of the king, but it is difficult to say whether the contract was feudal or personal. Even in England under the first Norman kings, demands for homage – such as the 1086 Salisbury oath – were rare, and the king had no automatic right to it, so it cannot be expected that the Welsh were familiar with any strict concept of homage. In the *Pedeir Keinc*, Pwyll and Arawn made a *kerenyd*, which was a legal relationship of peace between kings, and this was probably typical of concords between Welsh rulers. Similarly, the *gwrogaeth* performed to Pwyll by Hafgan's men, who then became his men (*gwyr*), was probably more like submission-allegiance than later forms of homage, and this was undoubtedly true of the other occasions on which this term was employed. Welsh vassalage was not so much 'feudal' as a native institution, with elements similar to Anglo-Saxon and Irish practices.

There are, however, indications that European feudalism was present by the twelfth century. The authority attributed to Welsh kings in the *Pedeir Keinc* seems to show the influence of the legal powers of twelfth-century kings of England, for instance in homicide cases and the giving and releasing of hostages, and a charter in *Liber Landavensis* which may date from as early as 1045 described Caradog ap Rhiwallon as one of the 'counts' (*comitibus*) of Meurig of Morgannwg. *Llyfr Colan* referred to the office of 'barony' (*uayrony*), and it was thought to be plausible that a man could have been a 'baron' of Gruffudd ap Cynan. *Braint Teilo* has an early-twelfth-century charter referring to a late-tenth-century exemption of the church and bishops of Llandaf from military service to the king of Morgannwg, and a charter of *c*.950x1090 also mentions military service, while the late-eleventh-century *Vita Cadoci* says that Gwynllŵg sent men for three days and three nights to serve the same king. Significantly, also, the term *feudum* was applied to land in Morgannwg held of Morgan ap Caradog by Robert ap Gwion in 1197x1203. Some form of military service was agreed upon when Cadwgan ap Bleddyn gave Meirionnydd to Uchdryd ab Edwin in 1116 on condition that he should help him and his sons against opposition, and similarly, according to the twelfth-century *Historia*, Gruffudd ap Cynan gave the sons of Merwydd in Llŷn, and also Tewdwr and Collwyn in Môn, a gift called *kyuarwys* after they joined him and Gwrgeneu ap Seisyll in a military alliance. *Kyuarwys* probably represents some sort of tribal rights, which were usually given to an innate Welshman (*bonhedyc kanhuynaul*), a category which the laws say encompassed clergy, *priodorion* and the king's court (*llys*). Yet the recipients of Gruffudd's gift do not seem to fit any of these descriptions, and it is possible that he was rewarding them for military service. Many if not all of these relationships were considerably less well-defined than any truly 'feudal' contract, but there was nevertheless a tradition of hierarchical political relationships upon which the princes of Gwynedd could draw.

THE CENTRALISATION OF POWER WITHIN GWYNEDD

This introduction of new ideas was parallelled by attempts to eradicate the traditional practices which hampered the princes within Gwynedd itself. Dafydd ap Llywelyn's status as the son of a daughter of the king of England was an advantage in the wider world, but Welsh law allowed the full free Welsh status of a *bonhedyc kanhuynaul* only to those with two Welsh parents. Such anomalies did not sit easily with the ambitions of Gwynedd. There was considerable potential for the greater concentration of power in the hands of the prince, however, since, in comparison with other countries, the state's role was not well developed. Welsh kings in the early medieval period were primarily military leaders, and their governmental functions were limited. Central government was acquiring greater responsibilities by the tenth century, but the kin-group (*cenedl*) still played a crucial role, and the widespread use of the bloodfeud – a form of decentralised social control – was characteristic of a stateless society. Similarly, according to the laws, the *cenedl* and the state competed for the terms and profits of justice which accrued from the settlement of crimes. Welsh law fell into the juristic category of *Volksrecht* ('people's law'), which did not lay great stress on royal power, as opposed to the *Kaisersrecht* or *Königsrecht* ('king's law') of both England and Scotland, where it was emphasised that both civil and common law were imposed by the state.

Gwynedd was far from the only European kingdom to suffer from these problems, however, and the princes were able to improve their position so that by 1282 the *cenedl* and the *gwelygordd* were merely administrative instruments for financial and judicial control. *Galanas* – the traditional payment made between kin-groups in cases of personal injury – was abolished by Dafydd ap Llywelyn, allowing the state to take responsibility for homicide cases, and Llywelyn ap Iorwerth and especially Llywelyn ap Gruffudd preferred inquisition to traditional law and procedures. They also interfered in tenurial arrangements for their own benefit, and Llywelyn ap Gruffudd seems to have practised escheat, by which property reverted to the prince in the absence of legal heirs. This centralisation was not all the work of the princes. *Galanas* was virtually obsolete by the late twelfth century, and it was often paid by the individual rather than the kindred – in these circumstances, the main aim of the state was not to destroy the old system but to see it work smoothly. Furthermore, far from being a novel imposition, the idea that the state was the guardian of individual rights was an essential characteristic of *priodolder* tenure. The transition to the prince's 'feudal' suzerainty over land was hardly a quantum leap. Similarly, the increasing popularity of English forms of tenure and trial by jury in the thirteenth century seems to have occurred voluntarily rather than under political pressure, and Welsh law was scarcely affected by the administrative changes. Overall, the state and the kindred existed side by side fairly comfortably. Indeed, it was sometimes better for the prince not to exercise his powers to the full – Llywelyn ap Iorwerth was able to circumvent legal theory by permanently alienating kin-lands in the Perfeddwlad, but it was often more profitable not to, since the kin-groups had to pay a fee for permission should they wish to alienate land themselves.

There was undoubtedly full potential in medieval Wales for political growth parallel to that found elsewhere in Europe. However, the simple increase of central administration alone was never sufficient to increase princely control, and it was necessary to allow power to other parties. Most importantly, the dynamism of Gwynedd's empire relied as much upon the scarce and often contradictory resources of tradition as upon the prince's immediate power. The march of the state was anything but irresistible, and in particular, the absence of a tradition of a Welsh state was a fundamental handicap in the attempt to establish and maintain a principality of Wales.

THE INTERNAL WEAKNESSES OF THE PRINCIPALITY OF WALES

The Welsh showed considerable respect for law, custom and the church, but they were not inclined to accept central authority, and they did not like outsiders ruling over them. This was probably why the English saw them as untrustworthy, and it posed a serious problem for Gwynedd's authority beyond the frontiers of its heartland. Gerald of Wales said that Gruffudd ap Llywelyn oppressed all of Wales with tyranny, and the *Historia* claims that the men of Gwynedd were outraged at being ruled by Trahaearn ap Caradog of Arwystli and Cynwrig ap Rhiwallon ap Cynfyn of Powys. Gruffudd ap Cynan told the men of Môn and Arfon that he reclaimed Gwynedd as their rightful lord against usurpers from elsewhere, and Madog ap Maelgwn of Maelienydd said that his men would never want any prince over them. That Gwynedd never overcame such sentiments is evident from the lack of a single official contemporary interpretation of the growth of the principality of Wales. The *Cronica de Wallia*, for example – a Deheubarth chronicle which was probably written by a supporter of Rhys ap Maredudd – did not mention the treaty of Montgomery, and referred to Llywelyn ap Gruffudd only as *princeps Northwallie* after 1277. The speed with which Llywelyn's supporters deserted him, particularly in 1276, is testament to the depth of their loyalty – or rather the lack of it – towards the principality of Wales.

There was no attempt to abolish rival kingships. Llywelyn ap Iorwerth's conquest of Powys was justified primarily by reference to his descent from a previous king there, Madog ap Maredudd, and, although Prydydd y Moch called Llywelyn king (*ri*) of the south, and Llygad Gŵr asserted Llywelyn ap Gruffudd's right to Dinefwr, the reality was that the latter was simply the 'leader of the people of Powys and the South' ('*llywydyr pobyl Powys a'r Deheu*').[10] He was more than merely a leader, since he held the *tair talaith* ('three diadems') of Wales, associated by the poets with Aberffraw, Dinefwr and Mathrafal, but Gwynedd was unable to unite them into one. Furthermore, even during Llywelyn ap Iorwerth's triumphs in 1215, Maelgwn ap Rhys was called 'true chief of the princes of South Wales' ('*principes uero Suthwallie capite*'),[11] and Gwynedd was unable to deprive even the dynasty of Meirionnydd of power completely – the latent dangers of this situation were eventually realised in the rebellion of Madog ap Llywelyn against Edward I in 1294. The prince could not destroy either his clients or their authority, and he was often forced to rely upon their consent, notably during military operations in 1215 and in making the decision to hang William de Braose in 1230. The tenuous and anomalous nature of Gwynedd's authority was illustrated by the case of Maredudd ap Rhys. Llywelyn apparently took Maredudd's son, Rhys, as a hostage, imprisoned him, and confiscated Maredudd's castles before 1258, but Maredudd turned to the king for support in 1257, and Llywelyn received no more than fealty in 1258, when he was forced to promise not to implement many of the terms he had previously imposed on Maredudd. Similarly, Llywelyn's relationship with Gruffudd ap Gwenwynwyn was strained. Indeed, Gruffudd, together with his son, Owain, and Dafydd ap Gruffudd, plotted to kill Llywelyn in 1274, only to be foiled by the weather.

Yet Llywelyn overcame the revolt and used the opportunity to demonstrate his mastery. When he became aware of the plot, he immediately dispossessed Gruffudd of Arwystli, the lands between the Dyfi and the Dulas in Cyfeiliog and the lands between the Rhiw and the Helygi, and he took Owain as a hostage. Llywelyn was lenient at first, restoring Gruffudd to his lands on condition that twenty-five of his men swore to remain loyal should he ever prove disloyal again. The prince may have been waiting to assess the opposition, but it seems that he was simply unaware of the rebels' intentions until the end of the year. Upon learning the full truth, Llywelyn was shocked, and he took much more decisive action when Gruffudd imprisoned his messengers. The prince captured and burned

Gruffudd's castle of Welshpool, repossessed all of Gruffudd's lands, and began legal proceedings against him. Gruffudd then followed Dafydd in flight to England.

Resistance from the lesser princes was inevitable, since centralisation meant that they stood to lose out whether ruled by Gwynedd or the king. Rebellions were therefore not necessarily a sign of impending disaster. Far from undermining authority, revolts often keep systems together by identifying the central authority as the upholder of order, and it is worth noting in this respect that the 1274 rebellion was apparently an attempt to oust the incumbent prince rather than to destroy the principality. Llywelyn's demonstration of his power over the rebels also did his prestige no harm at all – the message to his other clients was clear. Parallels can be found in England, where the Plantagenet dynasty survived and increased its power despite numerous rebellions including the humiliation of Magna Carta and the baronial revolt led by Simon de Montfort, and similar problems were faced and overcome by Conrad of Jerusalem, Sancho II of Portugal, James I of Aragon and Alfonso X of Castile. Most galling for the Welsh, perhaps, was the success of Henry IV in outfighting, outwitting and ultimately outlasting all of the most serious challenges to his authority.

The prince's authority over the principality was severely restricted. As lord, he was in theory entitled to rights of military service, various renders and jurisdiction throughout the whole principality, but this was difficult to enforce in practice. Although the thirteenth-century princes introduced *pennaethium*, which was a form of service intended to make Powys and Deheubarth into tenants-in-chief, even Llywelyn ap Gruffudd was unable to commit his subordinates outside Gwynedd to more than mutual support in war. The prince could not dictate terms, and his 'confederations' were characterised more by distrust than by fidelity. Tenure by military service was an essential characteristic of English and continental feudalism, but this was lacking in native Wales. Apart from the introduction of a provision in the thirteenth century that the prince of Gwynedd would pay for service outside Wales (which it might be possible to interpret as the beginnings of knights' fees), the process of binding the prince and his barons by feudal contract was not well developed.

If the rulers of Gwynedd hoped that expansion to the south could provide an economic base for their empire, they were disappointed. They received the profits of justice throughout the principality, but there was no question of raising substantial resources from any territory except Gwynedd, and there is no evidence that *mechteyrn dyled* was ever paid. As a result, the princes rarely left Gwynedd, upon which the impossible burden of financing the entire principality of Wales fell. The royal officials who levied unpopular heavy taxes in the Perfeddwlad in 1256 asserted quite plausibly that they were merely following the custom of Llywelyn ap Iorwerth, and Llywelyn ap Gruffudd was compelled to intensify resource management in a highly intervention-ist manner which included seizing land, introducing and raising taxes, and increasing traditional obligations. Gwynedd's economic problems were a se-rious handicap. The loyalty of troops often depended as much on the ability to pay them as on ties of lordship, and Llywelyn ap Gruffudd was committed to vast expenditure on treaty obligations and military resources, which seem to have included mercenaries and modern war machines. Against all this, his annual income was probably no more than a meagre £5,000, and the cash he needed to pay the king was a scarce commodity in a poor country.

Such strains, together with the centralisation of power and the pressures exerted by the king of England, naturally provoked unrest in Gwynedd. Bishop Anian of St Asaph was a persistent opponent of Llywelyn from 1269, primarily because of the restriction of his privileges, and Archbishop Pecham collected numerous complaints (*gravamina*) from the people of Gwynedd against the prince in 1282. Discontent was never far from the surface, even in the heart-land of the principality. The 1274 plot was regarded by all as a very credible threat to the prince, and there was further treachery against Llywelyn by some of his most trusted supporters in the belfry at Bangor Cathedral in 1282.

The principality's most significant weakness was the limitation of its jurisdic-tion. There seems to have been a slow, gradual and irregular centralisation of justice, and the prince's *distain* appeared occasionally as the 'justice of Wales', but the influence of his court was small compared with that of the local *cwmwd* courts, and there is no sign that cases could be transferred to the higher court. Thus, when Llywelyn ap Gruffudd fought the king for jurisdiction after 1278, he had few precedents from which to argue. This was a serious defect, since law was the most powerful weapon available to any feudal ruler in Europe by the thirteenth century; the extent of his demesne was determined by that of his jurisdiction, which accounted for nearly all of his sovereignty. Without a wide jurisdiction, the lands, wealth, adherents, liberty (*libertas*), dignity (*dignitas*) and rights (*iura*) of the principality were ultimately as nothing.

In attempting to create a Welsh state, Gwynedd suffered particularly from the diametrical opposition between the feudal and the theocratic dimensions of kingship. The theocratic idea allowed a king's will (*voluntas*) to make the law on the grounds that it was implicitly sanctioned by God, whereas feudal lordship required the explicit consent of his tenants-in-chief, because it was fundamentally contractual. This caused problems throughout Europe, but the tensions it caused in Wales were enormous, since neither dimension had been properly developed. The contradictions could be dissolved in the need for the prince to take the role of military leader, but this only occurred occasionally, and moreover the lack of an integrated Welsh state meant that it was only under exceptional circumstances that Gwynedd could assume leadership of the Welsh in war. The princes' dilemma was that the 'feudalisation' of Wales under Gwynedd demanded change at the same time as the maintenance of territory and authority required the preservation of the *status quo*. Moreover, the power of medieval rulers lay not in 'constitutional' resources, but in the doctrine of sovereignty and consistent action upon the assumption that such authority was possessed. If sovereignty was to be asserted, the Welsh princes needed regality (*regalitas*).

Regality and Homage: Wales and England

Welsh kings were entirely independent after the departure of the Romans, but that position gradually became muddied as they submitted to the kings of Wessex. At first, there were few negative practical implications in submitting to an English king. Any powerful man was seen both to deserve honour and to radiate it onto those around him. Hence the Irish were keen to call the Holy Roman Emperor Charlemagne their 'lord', and they referred to the Emperors Henry II and Conrad II in Germany as '*rí in domain*' – 'king of the world' – without any reflection on their real authority. But Wales was not as far removed from England as Ireland was from continental Europe, and Welsh rulers found themselves within the growing orbit of English power. The act of submission, intended originally as a means of securing mutual co-operation, set precedents which would eventually compromise and destroy the notion of Welsh independence. The payment of tribute and the provision of military support weakened Welsh kings by deflecting their resources to England as early as the tenth century, and from the eleventh century until 1283, and also during the Glyn Dŵr revolt, the dichotomy between the implementation of pan-Welsh lordship and the acceptance of closer English overlordship became an issue which dominated Anglo-Welsh relations.

An important part of the assertion of native Welsh authority was social climbing. Gruffudd ap Llywelyn's marriage to Ealdgyþ of Mercia was one of the earliest instances of a Welsh ruler marrying into the march, and many more followed after the arrival of the Normans, allowing the Welsh to join an aristocratic society which was linked across Britain and Ireland and even further afield. Rhys ap Gruffudd and Llywelyn ap Iorwerth were leading exponents of this practice, and Gerald of Wales was very proud of both the Norman and the Welsh sides of his pedigree. But the princes of Gwynedd wanted more – they intended to set their dynasty above the rest of the Welsh. This is what Llywelyn ap Iorwerth had in mind when he told Madog ap Maelgwn of Maelienydd and his associates that as they respected him, so they should respect his relatives. Gwynedd had visions of European stature. Llywelyn's approaches to the papacy, with their ostentatious (if disingenuous) deference towards canon law and papal jurisdiction, were part of a drive towards European respectability, and the chroniclers' euphoric reaction to the treaty of Montgomery in 1267 demonstrated the dramatic expansion of Gwynedd's horizons – in the same year, and quite uncharacteristically, the *Brut* also reported the deaths of the son and grandson of Emperor Frederick II in Apulia at the hands of the king of Sicily, the capture of Antioch, and the ravaging of Armenia by the sultan of Cairo.

The Welsh did not, however, enjoy the close dynastic links with royalty which distinguished and bound together the highest level of European society, and the plans revealed by Henry III in 1262 for the destruction of Gwynedd made it clear that Llywelyn ap Gruffudd was not regarded as an equal. Certainly, Dafydd ab Owain's marriage to Emma brought him hoped-for English support, and Dafydd ap Llywelyn's status as a grandson of John was an important asset, while Eleanor de Montfort – Henry's niece – gave Gwenllian, the daughter of Llywelyn ap Gruffudd, an impressive pedigree, but the full potential of such marriages never materialised. Eleanor, for example, was given no chance to improve Llywelyn's relations with Edward I, and despite the *kudos* gained from Dafydd ap Llywelyn's position – he was known to Henry III's administration as 'the lord king's nephew' – his father's attempts to gain respectability by preferring the legitimate son of Plantagenet blood as his heir at the expense of the illegitimate elder brother Gruffudd created a situation which eventually allowed the king to impose an unprecedented degree of subjection. Llywelyn's favouritism towards Dafydd was entirely in line with royal policy, and this had been made clear in 1211 when John imposed terms specifying that all Llywelyn's lands would escheat to the king should he die without an heir by Joan. John's charter was rescinded in 1215, but it is not surprising that integration with the Angevins seems to have caused some resentment in Wales – neither Joan nor Emma was mentioned by the court poets. Moreover, the princes were only ever able to marry illegitimate or discredited members of the English royal family. Unlike the Scots, they were never permitted to enter the highest flights of European society.

They were able to bring themselves onto the European stage in other ways, nonetheless. A desire to conform to wider standards and to achieve international respectability was evident in the redaction of Welsh law and the condemnations of local variations, as well as in the princes' patronage of the church. Alliances with the French and the Scots also showed outward vision, and the making of a Franco-Welsh treaty in 1212 was especially impressive in view of the fact that there had been no English foreign treaties until the reign of Henry I. The search for political legitimacy also led to approaches to the papacy in the thirteenth century, including several appeals by Llywelyn ap Iorwerth and most notably by

Dafydd ap Llywelyn in 1244. Nevertheless, English influence in Rome inevitably made such contacts worthless. The Scots suffered from the same problem – whereas Haakon IV of Norway was granted anointing and coronation by the pope in 1247, the Scots were unable to secure the same privileges from Honorius III in 1221 or Innocent IV in 1251 because of the pope's reluctance to do anything prejudicial to the status of the king of England.

The state of Gwynedd also suffered from its lack of *regalitas*. Each Welsh king ruled a *regnum*, but this did not in itself necessarily indicate royal status, since, from the middle of the twelfth century, the term *regnum* did not always imply rule by a *rex* – rather, it could denote royal government, authority, power, influence, dominion, rule, sovereignty, or merely a territory or possession. The authority of a king was exemplified in the *Legend of Fulk fitz Warin*, where John claimed the right to capture fugitives and punish those who harboured them simply because 'I am king' ('*je su roy*').[12] Such prerogatives were conferred largely by the sacerdotal aspects of kingship, or as Shakespeare was to put it, the 'divinity that doth hedge a king' – a king received his authority by divine ordination, and it was this that made him a suzerain lord. Whereas the kings of England styled themselves kings by the grace of God (*Dei gratia*) from 1172, the *regalitas* of Gwynedd in the wider principality was based on no higher authority than conquest and popular consent. Although Llywelyn ap Iorwerth occasionally styled himself prince of north Wales *Dei gratia*, the princes could not afford to offend the king, who was so important to their plans. The need to appease the king probably also underlay the apparent failure even to attempt to obtain anointing and coronation, which would have been valuable acquisitions. Moreover, although Gwynedd possessed *regalia*, they did not amount to *regalitas*, and neither were they symbols of a single Welsh principality. Wales knew nothing like the sophistication of the English monarchy, where a twelfth-century legal abstraction linked the idea of kingship with that of the community of the realm by making a distinction between the king and the crown. Owain Gwynedd pre-empted the kings of England in his use of the first person plural (which the Angevins adopted in 1189), and many Welsh rulers followed suit, but no other recognisably regal style was used in the correspondence of the princes during the thirteenth century.

Furthermore, there was no clear link between the institution of kingship in Wales and the dynasties and lands of individual kings. Unlike the kings of Scots, Llywelyn ap Gruffudd was obliged to fight simply to be recognised as sole ruler of Gwynedd, and the principality he ruled in 1267 was a very new creation. Whereas the pedigree of Alexander III was linked with the kingship of the Scots when it was read by a Gaelic *seanchaidh* at his inauguration in 1249, Llywelyn's authority was associated not with the principality but with the fact that he was a son of Gruffudd ap Llywelyn. The poet Dafydd Benfras saw his assumption of rule as the creation of a new scenario, rather than a continuation of princely rule, and the succession to the office of prince was never made synonymous with the inheritance of lands. The only meaningful bond between a Welsh ruler and his authority was the idea that kingship was a possession. When Rhys ap Gruffudd claimed Deheubarth as its *proprietarius princeps*, he was referring to the legal term *priodor*, which was rooted in the principle that no title to land was fully established until transmitted within a kin-group for four generations. Similarly, Gruffudd ap Cynan was welcomed by the men of Gwynedd – '*tref y dat*' (his inheritance, but literally 'his father's home') – as their '*hargluyd priodaur*', while his enemies were '*ampriodoryon*'. Gwynedd was Gruffudd's inheritance ('*tref tat*') and propriety ('*priodolder*');[13] his kingship (*brenhiniaeth*) seems to have been separate from these, a remote abstraction of much less practical use. In short, the Welsh had no *regalitas* in the European sense – they were not kings in the full sense of the word, and their authority depended ultimately upon their ability to assert the regality of their position at home.

NATIVE REGALITY AND '*STATUS WALLIAE*'

The status of Welsh rulers was based primarily on their *braint* ('privilege') within their own lordships. The means of exercising this authority was the *cwmwd*, a unit of territory which was bound up with the institutions of lordship. The *Brut* always saw conquests in terms of *cymydau* and *cantrefi* (their larger counterparts), and it was by indigenous units that the Normans moved into Wales, building a castle in each of the *cymydau* of Ceredigion and Dyfed. Contrary to the impression given by the laws, however, regality did not inhere in the *cwmwd* – by the twelfth century, the *cwmwd* and the *cantref* were merely administrative divisions intended to extend and enforce central authority. Nevertheless, the value of native *braint* was such that Edward I based his authority in Wales after 1282 on the local institutions of the indigenous principality. The marchers also seem to have adopted many Welsh institutions, and some idea of the nature of native liberties can be gained from the extent of marcher rights – *libertas marchie*, as they were called in 1291 – which included all of the prerogatives of royal lordships, including courts and other jurisdictions, a seal, powers to issue writs and warrants, to appoint justices and to make treaties and wars, and rights to treasure trove, wrecks and escheat of traitors' lands. A description of the rights of Welsh barons in the *Quo Warranto* proceedings of 1344 similarly included free courts, the goods of felons convicted within a baron's lordship and the right to dispose of them, free gallows, the right of wreck, fines for shedding blood, the right to raise hue and cry, and many more. The laws also referred to a right of plunder, and it is also clear

– despite references to conciliar consent – that the thirteenth-century princes of Gwynedd exercised the right to correct and amend the law.

The exercise of these liberties depended ultimately upon the ability to withstand the attempts of outsiders to intervene, and this was equally true for great lords and small ones. The balance of power at any given moment was crucial in determining who could do what. In 1238, for example, Llywelyn ap Iorwerth was able to deprive Maredudd ap Madog ap Gruffudd Maelor of his lands after Maredudd killed his own brother, Gruffudd Iâl, whereas Henry III found himself compelled to allow the Welsh lords of Maelienydd the right to fight Ralph Mortimer after the expiry of a truce in 1241. In England, there was no right to fight without royal permission, but *de facto* power was a much greater consideration than legal niceties in Wales and the march. Hence the earls of Gloucester and Hereford claimed the right to make private war in the march in 1292, prompting Edward I to try to assert a royal prerogative to prohibit it. The authority of the princes was derived from the practicalities of convenience and expediency as much as from native custom, and that custom could give them the sanctity of tradition only because it had been defined by those very practicalities.

The first Statute of Westminster confirmed in 1275 that the king's writ did not run in the march – a conclusion which was repeated in 1335 – and Gilbert de Clare undoubtedly echoed the thoughts of marchers and native Welsh rulers alike when he claimed in 1281 to hold his lands and liberties in the march by virtue of the conquests of his ancestors and himself. In the same vein, Richard de Clare adopted regalian rights and even introduced a criminal offence against his dignity (*laesae maiestatis*) in the 1240s. The lord of Glamorgan was described in quasi-royal terms, and Gilbert de Clare claimed to hold his lands as by royal right, while William de Braose made similar claims in the lordship of Brecon. In this sense, a vestige of Welsh independence was to survive until the first Act of Union in 1536, when Henry VIII finally abolished marcher lordships and implemented royal government throughout Wales for the first time. The situation in *pura Wallia*, like that in the march, was primarily military and political, not constitutional. War was neither a right nor a privilege, but a necessity. Wales and the march were beyond the reach of regularly enforceable royal authority, and regality was therefore autogenous. In modern parlance, this was Welsh independence. This had been the foundation of native rule in Britain since the departure of the Romans, and it lay at the heart of the principality of Gwynedd, which first appeared as such in 1201. The principality consisted of no more than Gwynedd at first, but it came to include a wider empire, and its prerogatives came to be expressed as the prince's rights (*iura*), a term which combined the concepts of kingship and *regnum*.

Anglo-Welsh tensions in the thirteenth century placed great importance upon the interpretation of the prince's *iura*. Owain Gwynedd and his predecessors were under relatively little pressure from the king of England, and they consequently felt little need to make specific claims for their dignity. Llywelyn ap Iorwerth, however, faced mounting interference from the king, and responded by insisting upon what he termed the 'status of Wales' (*status Wallie*). Both he and his grandson declared parity with the king of Scots, and Llywelyn ap Gruffudd in particular attempted to convey a sense that the unity of Wales was symbolised and encapsulated in his person – he was extremely sensitive to infringements of his *iura*, even insisting that the validity of his claims should be adjudicated by no less a person than the king of France. The princes of Gwynedd claimed numerous privileges against the king in this period, including the rights to meet the king on the border, to harbour the king's fugitives, to punish royal subjects for infringements of the princely *dignitas*, to build castles and establish markets within their own boundaries, to retain the spoils of war and to take possession of wrecks. When called upon to justify his construction of a castle at Dolforwyn in 1273, Llywelyn ap Gruffudd replied pointedly that he and his ancestors had always had these rights; he did not need to declare his intention to the king, let alone ask for permission.

Many of these assertions could be substantiated by reference to ancient custom, but others were quite impudent. Llywelyn ap Iorwerth was inaccurate in saying that the Scots could receive outlaws from England with impunity, since Maol-Coluim Ceann Mór had been forced to promise not to harbour the enemies of William I in 1072, and the prince's claims for himself with regard to this issue ran counter to his own promises to the king in 1201 and 1218. Whatever the validity of the princes' contentious claims, however, they amounted to an assertion of prerogatives more substantial than those of the English palatinates of Durham and Chester, which themselves were microcosmic kingdoms in many ways. Moreover, the authority of Gwynedd was clearly autogenous. In this context, John made an important concession when he sent the Archbishop of Canterbury and the justiciar to take Llywelyn ap Iorwerth's homage on the border in 1201. This was known in Europe as *hommage de paix*, or the performance of homage on a border, with connotations of peace and concord between equals. Such agreements differed from *hommage vassalique* in that they contained no clear subordination or feudal obligations, and examples included the relations of the dukes of Normandy with France, Anjou, Maine and Brittany, as well as the relationship between England and Scotland. Maol-Coluim Ceann Mór, for instance, refused to meet William Rufus except on the border, and both Llywelyn ap Iorwerth and Llywelyn ap Gruffudd were keen to avoid meeting the king or his officials anywhere except on the boundaries of their own territories. Similarly, both Gruffudd ap Llywelyn and Owain Glyn Dŵr showed a desire to meet with the king or his representatives on the border. Hence, despite the explicit disparity in status between the king of England and the prince of Wales, Llywelyn ap Gruffudd's *iura* were sufficient to ensure that the treaty of Montgomery was executed not at a royal residence in England, as had been the custom with many previous Anglo-Welsh agreements, but at a ford on the river Severn which marked the border between England and Wales. Thereafter, nearly all of Llywelyn's meetings with royal officials were conducted on the border.

Both socially and legally, then, Llywelyn occupied a position which merited great honour, and he was treated accordingly by Edward I at his wedding in 1278, despite his crushing defeat in 1277. In some ways, the radical alteration of Anglo-Welsh relations at Montgomery invalidated precedents from before 1267, but tenancy under the king was not necessarily a weakness. The rise of the *principatus* in tenth-century France stemmed from just such origins, showing that the key to power was not in its source but in its execution. Gwynedd's attempt to assert *regalitas* should now be placed in its European context.

PRINCELY SELF-PROMOTION: SOME EUROPEAN SIDELIGHTS

The Lombard glossator Papias declared in the middle of the eleventh century that princes and dukes could occasionally be called kings, and by the twelfth century the Lombards claimed that duchies, marquisates and counties were *regales dignitates* – that is, they possessed regal liberties. Although the only recognised secular sovereign was the Holy Roman Emperor, there were many claims throughout Europe from the twelfth century onwards that any king was an emperor in his kingdom (*imperator in regno suo*), and the principle received papal approval in 1202, when Innocent III stated that France was not subject to the empire either *de facto* or *de iure*. The subsequent debate about imperial overlordship necessarily touched upon the issue of sovereignty, and it was widely held that national sovereignty overrode that of the empire. In 1255, Johannes de Blanosco said that rebellion against the king of France was a *crimen laesae maiestatis*, since 'a king in his kingdom is a *princeps*' ('*rex in regnum suo princeps est*'),[14] and Petrus Jacobi claimed that, rather than being subject to the empire, France was federated to it. Similarly, the thirteenth-century kings of Naples asserted their own *imperium*, arguing that the terms *imperator, rex* and *princeps* were essentially synonymous, while the Sicilians described their king as '*princeps in regno*' in the early fourteenth century.[15] In Burgundy, Philippe de Beaumanoir claimed in the fourteenth century that 'every baron is sovereign in his barony',[16] and he envisaged a hierarchy of sovereignties which would give the emperor more *superioritas* than *supremitas*. Such arguments set ideological precedents for the loosening of overlordship throughout Europe.

These ideas may have filtered into Wales, and they may even have been adopted. They were certainly as applicable to the *imperium* of England as to that of Germany, and there were many channels through which they might come. Welsh diplomats, messengers and hostages frequented the English court regularly, and education in mainland Europe became increasingly popular in the twelfth century. Whereas Sulien ap Rhigyfarch was educated in Scotland and Ireland, and his sons at Llanbadarn Fawr, Gerald of Wales studied in Paris, and many of his Welsh contemporaries went to Oxford. The most prominent before 1282 were Thomas Wallensis (the archdeacon of Lincoln and bishop of St Davids) and John Wallensis (Archbishop Pecham's emissary to Wales), and it is safe to assume that Oxford learning and ideas found their way into Wales. It seems that there were sufficient attractions in Wales to bring exiled scholars back. Gerald returned, as did the Oxford graduates Geoffrey of Monmouth, Adam of Wales – both bishops of St Asaph – and Bishop Richard of Bangor. Cuhelyn (or Alexander), the cross-bearer of Archbishop Thomas Becket and interpreter for Archbishop Baldwin in 1188, was archdeacon of Bangor, and there were many educated men among the clerks who served the princes, although the only Oxford-educated Welshman to take sides in an internal political conflict in Wales before 1282 was Richard of Bangor. Intellectual input from abroad was useful to the princes, but it was not essential. Any great feudatory anywhere could be seen as a petty king ruling a petty kingdom, so awareness of continental ideas was not a prerequisite for the assertion of Gwynedd's claims.

In France, it was not theoretical debate but the practical weakness of the king which encouraged the princes to strive for independent power. The dukes of Aquitaine, for instance, stayed aloof from the king, amassing enormous power in territories which stretched as far south as Granada. This allowed Fulbert of Chartres to address Duke William V with terms – such as *princeps* – which were reserved strictly for royalty, and the thirteenth-century dukes seem to have imitated royal inauguration ceremonies. Similarly, in the tenth century, Count Fulk of Anjou recognised only a few of his fiefs as held of the king, and Geoffrey of Anjou later styled himself *princeps*. Despite the lack of an historical antecedent, which contributed to disintegration of their power in the eleventh century, the counts recovered their position in the twelfth century. In the same way, Angoulême resisted royal intervention from the tenth century until 1141, and Normandy was exceptionally centralised and independent by 1100 – indeed, the duke of Normandy had more power in his own demesne than the king of France had in his.

Nevertheless, the potential of emerging principalities in France was restricted steadily as the king asserted his dominant position after the tenth century. By the end of the thirteenth century, Poitou, Normandy, Anjou, Maine, Touraine, Toulouse, Blois and Champagne were all incorporated into the royal demesne, and the only significant survivors were Gascony, Flanders, Brittany and Burgundy. The process of centralisation and subjection was inexorable.

The homage relationship of the counts of Brittany with the king of France was not fully formalised until the thirteenth century, and they were therefore able to style themselves *rex, monarchus* and *princeps*. By the 1330s, it was argued that they were *principes* who recognised no superior, and the Breton counts established practical and theoretical independence in the fourteenth and fifteenth centuries, assuming most of the prerogatives of a sovereign prince, including coronation and *laesae maiestatis*. The dukes of Burgundy also grew in power while maintaining minimal contact with the king. Despite relative ineffectiveness at first, the dukes rose to prominence in the fifteenth century, marrying into the house of Castile and founding the dynasty of Portugal. This was aided by a growth of central government generally, and the fact that Burgundy's neighbours were weak at that time – France was merely a vague conglomeration and Germany was no more than an idea. As a result, Philip the Good was able to play a crucial role in France, adopting the style *Dei gratia* and virtually controlling the monarchy while the king, Charles VI, went insane. Philip's absence from Agincourt in 1415 was a major contribution to the French defeat, and he developed a close alliance with England after 1420. The success of this arrangement owed much to the fact that, unlike Welsh alliances with the French, it was grounded in considerable common trading interests as well as a common antipathy to the enemy. All of this meant that the Burgundians could move at ease in the highest political circles, establishing alliances and dynastic links which encompassed Aragon, Castile, Milan, Florence, Sardinia, Hungary, Poland, Portugal, Scotland, Prussia, Venice, Genoa, Naples, Bohemia, Sicily, Cyprus, Norway, Denmark, Russia, Austria, Lombardy and many more. By the middle of the 1470s, the Burgundian court was the diplomatic centre of Europe.

Like Gwynedd, Burgundy's neighbours usually regarded it as an upstart, but its demise was due to self-inflicted problems rather than to external pressure. It was the overambition of Charles the Bold and territorial partition – reminiscent of the problems of Llywelyn ap Gruffudd – which finally humbled the Burgundian dukes. An even more striking similarity with Gwynedd was the dukes' lack of a single title to encapsulate their authority, and the fact that Philip the Good's attempt to make himself a king in 1444 depended upon the support of the king of France. Charles the Bold was able to negotiate equality with the emperor, and a coronation by Frederick III was arranged, but the duke lost his chance because of his continual insistence on new conditions.

As a result, despite his vast territories, influential court and powerful allies, Charles had no official title, and the duchy died with him. Although the prince of Wales at least had a title, the comparison between Charles's demands and the claims of *status Walliae* is obvious. Like the Welsh, the French princes generally had no legal, spiritual or traditional means of proclaiming independent authority. However convincing their *de facto* power might be, they were always bound as part of the *regnum Franciae* which eventually engulfed them.

Elsewhere, it was shown to be possible to press autonomy as far as kingship itself. Poland, for example, owed theoretical allegiance to the papacy and the empire in the eleventh century, but it maintained *de facto* power, with the result that Boleslav II was crowned king in 1076 without needing either imperial or papal authority. In 1109, Boleslav III refused the request of Emperor Henry V that he should give half of Poland to his brother, Zbigniev, and that an annual tribute to the emperor should be made – he resisted an imperial campaign, and had Zbigniev blinded and exiled. Although imperial authority was occasionally imposed successfully, and the coronation of Przemyslav II in 1295 was achieved only with papal consent, the influence of both the empire and the papacy in Poland had undeniably been undermined.

The dukes of Bohemia also won royal status for themselves. Bohemia was very different from Wales in that it was never directly subject to imperial officials, and ducal power was never derived from the empire. Nor was there a distinction between the land and the subjects over which the duke ruled, and no authority had the right to limit his rights. Rather than invalidating the comparison, however, the relative strength of Bohemia adds weight to the conclusions which can be drawn.

Despite its lack of homogeneity in the early medieval period, Bohemia was subdued and united by a Moravian, Svatapluk, who made himself king in the 870s. This kingdom was destroyed by the Magyars, however, and it became a duchy under the empire, but a centralised state evolved in the tenth century, and Moravia was annexed around 1029. The emperor was entitled to confer the title of king of Bohemia in the eleventh and twelfth centuries, but, despite frequent and determined attempts to intervene, especially in 1182, he never established any formal right to do so. Bohemian independence in the appointment of rulers was unparalleled in the empire, which lost all influence in the succession there by the thirteenth century. Although Emperor Frederick I made Moravia independent of Bohemia in 1182, Henry Bretislav recovered it in 1197, and the Premyslid dynasty ruled in unbroken and unchallenged succession thereafter. The dukes began to invest bishops of Prague – who were supposed to hold their fief of the emperor – and disturbances in the empire allowed Premysl Ottokar I to make himself king in 1198 under the auspices of Philip of Swabia. The title was confirmed as hereditary by Pope Innocent III in 1207 and by Emperor Frederick II in 1212, and Waclaw I seceded from the empire and allied with the duke of Austria in 1239. This was followed by the acquisition of huge territories, including Austria in 1254 and Carinthia in 1269 – largely due to the breakdown of the empire – and in 1272, Premysl

Ottokar II became a candidate for emperor. By this time, the Bohemians'
duty to support imperial campaigns had long since been overlooked. The
sometime dukes of Bohemia had not only made themselves kings but raised
themselves almost to the highest tier of European politics.

Yet neither Bohemia nor Poland could reject imperial authority completely.
As late as 1276, Premysl Ottokar II of Bohemia was outlawed and disinherited
by Emperor Rudolf I, and Waclaw II was placed under imperial trustees in
1278. When he became king of Poland as well in 1300, Waclaw was crowned
by the emperor, as was his son in Hungary in 1301. Even in Poland and
Bohemia, then, upstart kings could not escape their feudal superiors, and
official recognition of their status as kings ultimately guaranteed nothing. It is
as well to bear this in mind in the case of Gwynedd.

WELSH SUBMISSION AND SUBJECTION

The Welsh were subordinate to the king of England from the ninth century,
but the relationship remained ill-defined until the thirteenth century. The king
enjoyed an increasing degree of superiority, but the Welsh always derived their
authority from their own indigenous sources. Cadwgan ap Bleddyn, for example,
paid Henry I for his *kyuoeth* – literally his land or 'wealth' – in 1110, but not for his
status, which was both royal and autogenous. The king received his first firmly-
attested Welsh hostage from Iorwerth ap Bleddyn in 1110, after which the practice became common. This marked an intensification of overlordship, but Welsh
subordination before the twelfth century meant very little more than submission
and the promise to supply military support and occasionally tribute. Welsh kings
did not enjoy their authority as part of any contractual relationship of dependence, and for some 300 years before the reign of Henry II there was no change
in the terminology employed in submissions. Nor was it particularly demeaning
when Owain ap Cadwgan (1114), Hywel Sais (1173) and Llywelyn ap Iorwerth
(1209) accompanied the king on his campaigns. The kings of Scots did the same,
and there was no question of a serious threat to their authority when Alexander
I joined Henry I in Wales in 1114, or when David I served with Stephen in 1141,
or when Malcolm IV accompanied Henry II in 1159 and 1165 – indeed, William
I never promised military service and never performed homage, even though
he was humiliated by Henry II in 1174 and by John in 1209. The king took his
overlordship over the Welsh very seriously, but it is likely that he felt no need
to assert it beyond a certain point, not least because he lacked the governance
to do so – Henry II, for example, may well have regarded his relationship with
the Welsh in the same light (albeit in reverse) as his position in France, where he
recognised the overlordship of Louis VII but the relationship went no further.
Nevertheless, closer Anglo-Welsh links in the late twelfth century led to greater

Welsh subjection. Whatever the terms of individual agreements, there was always a blurred line between a medieval treaty and a feudal contract, and it was seen in Deheubarth in 1197 that the sanction of the king might even become necessary in such private internal Welsh affairs as the inauguration of native rulers.

Royal superiority was aided by the Welsh concept of a pan-British over-king. In the laws, the tribute of *mechteyrn dyled* was due to the king of London, of whom Welsh lands were held, and in the *Pedeir Keinc*, Pryderi submitted to Caswallon ap Beli at Oxford. Thus, when William I was called 'king of the English and of Wales', there were echoes of Arthur, 'king of the kings of Britain'.[17] Furthermore, there was a general conception of a hierarchy of kings. The poet Meilyr, for instance, referred to God as the 'king of kings', and also called him '*rieu rwyf eluyt*' – 'sovereign lord of the world'.[18] The Welsh therefore accepted the theoretical legitimacy of English supremacy, however grudgingly. Moreover, Gerald of Wales wrote of 'Wales, which is part of the kingdom of England, and not in itself a kingdom' ('*Wallia quidem portio est regni Anglicani, et non per se regnum*'),[19] and he said that he himself, a native of Dyfed, was born in the *regnum Angliae*. Wales was not a kingdom, and more-over, although it was not in England, it was nevertheless part of the *regnum* of the king of England – a differentiation expressed by the *Brut* when it described Hubert Walter as 'justiciar of all England and of all the kingdom'.[20] Whatever its merits *de facto*, therefore, Llywelyn ap Gruffudd's claim in 1273 that Edward I knew that 'the rights of our principality' ('*iura principatus nostri*') were entirely separate from those of England ran counter to accepted wisdom.[21] More importantly, Llywelyn never disputed the fact that he was a tenant of the king of England, and Gwynedd's claim to Welsh homages was therefore a major problem – in the king's eyes, all of the Welsh princes were always tenants-in-chief until 1267.

The crux of the problem was that the princes of Gwynedd had no choice but to do homage. This severely compromised their quasi-royal dignity – especially since the concept of homage (*homagium*) became more legally bind-ing throughout Europe from the late eleventh century – and the sovereignty and *regalitas* they desired could not be achieved simply by insistence on custom-ary liberties. Although Henry III promised to 'magnify' (*magnificare*) Llywelyn ap Gruffudd in 1267, he had no intention of allowing him to be more than a glorified baron, and the Welsh *regalia* were never conferred by the king. Hom-age and *regalitas* were virtually incompatible, but Gwynedd had no choice but to look to England for recognition. Appeals to the pope and alliances with the Scots and the French were fruitless, since Wales was too small and in the wrong place geographically to be of any lasting use to them. The French wanted con-trol of the English Channel, and they therefore allied with the Scots against the English in 1295 but not with Madog ap Llywelyn in 1294 – this factor also helps to explain their half-hearted military support for Owain Glyn Dŵr. Expediency dictated that there was to be no 'Auld Alliance' between Wales and France. Successful European rulers, such as those of Brittany, Bohemia and Poland, were all able to play off emperors, popes and powerful kings against each other because of their geographical positions, but Wales did not enjoy that luxury, and Owain Gwynedd's apparent recognition of Louis VII as his overlord was therefore never likely to lead anywhere – the king of England was the only lord to whom the Welsh could turn. The only alternative was to join the forces opposed to the ruling power in England, which was always a precarious course of action. Consequently, whereas it was the consistent policy of the Scots to avoid doing homage for Scotland, Llywelyn ap Gruffudd depended upon the explicit recognition that he held his principality of the king, and he was anxious to perform homage, although only in circumstances which were not demeaning to him. Under these circumstances, it was inevitable that his dealings with the king would often be fraught with tension. While Alexander III was secure enough in his relationship with Edward I that he gained prestige from his attendance at Edward's coronation, Llywelyn feared for his position and stayed away. Indeed, the Welsh were never prominent at the English court, and in this there was a marked contrast with Scotland: Edgar, king of Scots, carried the sword for William Rufus at his crown-wearing in 1099, David I was the first to swear allegiance to Matilda in 1127, and William I carried the sword at the coronation of Richard I in 1194. The markedly inferior status of Welsh rulers meant that the continental idea that princes could secede from the *imperium* of their overlords simply by disobedience and *de facto* power was entirely inappropriate to Wales.

This inferiority placed intolerable restrictions upon Gwynedd, similar in effect if not in detail to those in force in Ireland. Like Llywelyn ap Gruffudd, Ruaidhrí O Conchobhair of Connacht attempted to establish his patrimony as a heritable fee held *in capite* of the king, but – unlike Llywelyn – his status as a king was always recognised. In 1175, the treaty of Windsor made Ruaidhrí the 'liege man' of Henry II, and more importantly, the intermediary between Henry and the Irish kings; no homage was performed, since the Irish never became tenants-in-chief. Similarly, in 1215, John allowed Cathal Croibhdhearg many incidents of jurisdiction, as well as recognition for himself and his heirs. Connacht might therefore appear to have been in at least as strong a position as Gwynedd, and the consequences are instructive. Under pressure from the government of Henry III, the *regalitas* of Connacht was diminished rapidly, and the kingdom forfeited to the king in 1226. Native authority then withered away, to the point that the English no longer recognised the Irish as kings by the fourteenth century. Clearly, the king could not be relied upon to protect

the *regalitas* of his subordinates, since he placed expediency before the hon-
ouring of agreements. Edward I almost said as much when dealing with Wales
in 1280, declaring that he would always follow the advice of his prelates and
magnates, according to God and justice, but that it was unlikely that such pru-
dent men would give advice dissonant with reason. 'Reason' was substantially
what the king wanted it to be, and a principality of Wales which damaged his
authority was not reasonable in royal eyes. The subjection of both Gwynedd
and Connacht was bound to result in their eventual destruction by the centralising monarchy of England. Despite the differences between the two cases,
and despite suspicions of bad faith, the demise of both was inexorable. Just as
the Angevins' recognition of Capetian suzerainty over their lands in France
allowed Philip Augustus of France to justify his capture of Normandy in 1204,
so Welsh submission to England laid the foundations of the process which led
to 1282. Only by not accepting a superior authority could independence be
upheld. To be allowed the title of prince or even king signified almost nothing
in itself, as the kings of Poland, Bohemia and Connacht could testify.

The king generally did not go out of his way to destroy the authority of the
Welsh until the thirteenth century, and this was in keeping with his policy in
Scotland and Ireland. Henry II showed little interest in Ireland beyond dealing with the situation created by the involvement of his marcher barons there,
and he interfered only three times in Scottish affairs – and then by invitation.
The main aim of English kings in Scotland was simply to maintain a peaceful border, although John pushed overlordship harder in his desire to obtain
Scottish resources for his French wars. Claims to the homage of the Scots
were introduced only in about 1237, apparently merely as a bargaining counter, and the demands for homage in 1235, 1251 and 1278 were all defied, while
Edward I respected the status of the king of Scots in the 1270s and 1280s.
Overlordship of Britain and Ireland was asserted, maintained and extended,
but that was very different from the implementation of direct lordship. The
logic which required Edward I to conquer Gwynedd in 1282 owed more to a
particularly Welsh situation than to any imperative derived from his relations
with Scotland and Ireland.

Advances in record keeping and legal precision intensified the spotlight on
Welsh subjection from the twelfth century onwards, and Gwynedd's inferior
position meant that the Welsh could take their appeals above the prince to a
higher authority – the prince was often not their superior in legal matters.
A similar situation existed in Scotland, where Edward I offered to help in a
succession crisis in 1290 and used it to stress his position as suzerain, requiring John Balliol to perform homage and to provide military service while
Edward set himself up as a court of appeal. The resulting conflict led to the

Scots' crushing defeat in the war of 1296, and it is worth noting in this context that royal opposition to Gwynedd in the thirteenth century was generally far more implacable and formidable than it was to the Scots; whereas the Scots had peace with the king after 1235 and an unchallenged jurisdiction, Gwynedd's case was the opposite, and the king's military resources were increased massively under Henry III. The plot against Llywelyn in 1274 also demonstrated the impossibility of separating the internal affairs of Wales from those of England. The prospects of Gwynedd were not good.

By the later Middle Ages, the English firmly believed that they were destined to rule the whole of Britain. This idea had been promoted by Bede, who was primarily interested in ecclesiastical domination, and in later centuries it was taken up by the kings of Wessex. In seeking to bind together the newly created kingdom of England, Eadgar presented himself as emperor of the kings and people of Britain, and both Æþelstan and Eadward the Confessor styled themselves kings of the whole of Britain. The Welsh submission to Eadgar in 973 was made all the more powerful in its symbolism by the king's recent coronation at Bath – rather than at the usual site of West Saxon consecrations at Kingston-upon-Thames – recalling memories of Roman rule, and with them, perhaps, the notion of a single ruler of Britannia. By the eleventh century, English clerical circles regarded the authority of the king of England as an *imperium*, which Eadward the Confessor was considered to enjoy over the Welsh. The practical effect of that *imperium* was limited in 1063, but the *imperium* of Edward I which Llywelyn ap Gruffudd acknowledged in 1279 was a very different thing. By the thirteenth century, *imperium* essentially meant that a ruler had no superior power on earth, and there was therefore ample justification for Pecham's claim – with which the king agreed in 1280 – that royal rights must prevail over subjects' customs. *Imperium* now legitimised the steady erosion of Welsh liberties. Llywelyn ap Iorwerth was required to give up the right to harbour fugitives in 1201, and he came under pressure to meet the king outside his own boundaries in 1219, while Henry III introduced crushing obligations in the 1240s which triggered a series of royal intrusions into Welsh internal affairs. In the thirteenth century, all of the Welsh were treated more and more like the king's feudal tenants in England, and Llywelyn ap Gruffudd was left in no doubt that executive power in Wales belonged ultimately with the king, especially after 1277. By 1280, the prince even found that he needed royal licence to grant lands in Glyndyfrdwy in Edeirnion, within his own principality.

Intrusive royal overlordship was countered by Llywelyn's emphasis in 1282 on the right of his ancestors to jurisdiction in Gwynedd. This, together with Edward I's assertion of sovereignty over Welsh law, demonstrated that it was jurisdiction, rather than the status of Welsh law, which was at stake. Admittedly, the question of Welsh law did not surface fully until 1278, when it proved a very useful weapon in complicating and frustrating cases relating to royal jurisdiction, but the issue was more profound. The prince had his own laws, but he could be summoned before royal justices wherever, whenever and however they liked. In this respect, his authority was reduced to that of an English baron. Since jurisdiction was the essence of sovereignty, Llywelyn saw this as a fundamental denial of his status, and he went so far as to say that he was more concerned about the potential disgrace to himself as prince if he lost the Arwystli case in 1281x1282 than any profit to be gained from the *cantref* itself. That Llywelyn's humiliation was precisely the king's intention was shown in 1282 by his insulting offer of estates in England to a prince whose life's ambition had been to raise himself and Gwynedd above mere baronial status.

The only way to resist the claims of *imperium* was to counter them with equally supreme independent power. The thirteenth-century kings of France were a case in point, as they were able to resist domination from the Holy Roman Empire only because they possessed both *regalitas* and *de facto* power. These qualities ensured independence without any need to resort to argument, but the Welsh rarely had either of them in any great quantity, and never both at the same time. Welsh independence was therefore always open to question. Nor was there much prospect of escape from this situation. If the prince of Wales was to assert sovereignty, he would require military, economic, diplomatic and constitutional resources for which there was simply no potential in Wales. The only alternative was to accept unacceptable royal intrusions. The inexorability of tightening English lordship was illustrated in 1283, when Dafydd ap Gruffudd was convicted of high treason (*regiae majestatis laesione*) and sentenced to be hanged, drawn and quartered as a common traitor. Blame cannot be apportioned for this development, since both the Welsh and the English appreciated that what made kingship strong was not strict observance of the letter of the law, but licence. Like all politicians, the Welsh princes, the marcher lords and the king were often guilty of exaggerating their claims. The Angevin kings, in particular, owed much of their success to their ability to exceed the law rather than observing it, and there was no mention of 'marcher rights' until Henry III began to contest them in the 1240s. For their part, the marchers, like the Welsh, were all too aware that their position was defined by nothing more or less than seigneurial power, and they resisted royal intrusions fiercely – Walter Clifford even made a royal messenger eat his message, seal and all, in 1250. This was the political world in which the princes of Gwynedd lived, and they were as adept at manipulating it as any of their contemporaries. They knew both the stakes and the risks.

Was Welsh Independence Viable?

The ambitions of Gwynedd and the king were mutually exclusive, and the king's ability to crush attempts to create a wide native Welsh hegemony was shown as early as 1063. Llywelyn ap Gruffudd's need to assert his *libertas* as a quasi-royal ruler of Wales, while avoiding provoking conflict with his tenants and neighbours by imposing unacceptable restraints and intrusions upon their own liberties, placed him in an almost impossible position, and the principality was a cause of great anxiety to the king – Edward I described it in 1285 as a 'snake lying in the grass'.[22] It is not surprising, therefore, that the principality was destroyed within 16 years of the treaty of Montgomery. Rather, it must be wondered whether it was possible to meet the enormous challenges which faced Llywelyn in 1267. His principality was crippled by its economic dependence on Gwynedd, and furthermore the counteraction between the internal and external fragility of the principality was self-perpetuating. Even had the princes created a stable, independent polity, they invited the destruction of their dynasty by the king. Moreover, European comparisons such as Aquitaine in the tenth and eleventh centuries showed that, even if sub-kingdoms succeeded in separating themselves from a central authority such as the king of France, the result was often a disintegration of their own internal unity.

Like the French princes, the rulers of Gwynedd always lacked a clear constitutional status, and they consequently found themselves open to charges of both tyranny and usurpation. Their authority could probably have been increased in time; Poland, for instance, was unified despite the lack of a national kingship or a central council, and despite the fact that the only unifying factors were the church and the royal dynasty (both of which were new in many regions). Furthermore, the kings of France showed that it was not impossible to overcome a lack of jurisdiction in outlying provinces. Nor was devolution of power necessarily a weakness, since a policy of circumscribed devolved jurisdictions – equivalent to mediatisation – in Deheubarth and Powys would have enhanced rather than harmed the *regnum* of Gwynedd. The alternative – to allow local rulers power – was also not entirely detrimental, since it would provide important buffer zones against the king. Examples of successful fragmented kingdoms included the seventh-century *regnum Fran-corum* – which was more a commonwealth of Neustria, Austrasia and Burgun-dy than a single kingdom – and Scotland, where the king rarely involved him-self in Caithness and Orkney until the late twelfth century. Moreover, while devolution could lead to disintegration under weak rulers, the experience on the continent was that it could equally be used by strong ones to create unity by dissipating local frustrations. Even the absence of an integrated economic system in Wales might work in the princes' favour, since their inability to impose consistently extortionate financial burdens reduced the chances that special interest groups might seek outright independence from the higher authority. However, it remains that success depended upon the princes' ability to distance or even free themselves from their feudal superior.

In this respect, the nearest parallels to Wales were in Scotland. Galloway, for instance, was ruled by a semi-independent prince in the early twelfth century, but it succumbed to the king of Scots in 1235. Similarly, the Mac Domhnaill lords of the Isles in the fourteenth and fifteenth centuries created a centralised polity with what almost amounted to full sovereignty. They seem to have dealt with the king of Scots as equals, but, like the Welsh, they were on the fringe of a greater power. They could neither break away nor become accepted as an integral part of the kingdom of the Scots, and the only possible outcomes were independence or de-struction. It was arguably better, then, to accept royal overlordship. In France, Ger-many and Burgundy, too, real power was best achieved by helping – or pretending to help – the king. For example, an attempt by Paulus to establish Languedoc as an independent kingdom in the seventh century failed, whereas Lupus, in Aquitaine, continued to recognise the king and was able to accumulate enormous power, since the king had no pretext for intervention. There were many other cases like this in the seventh, eighth and ninth centuries, including Frisia, Swabia, Alsace, Languedoc, Flanders, Normandy, Brittany, Lorraine, Gascony, Burgundy, Saxony, Thuringia and Bavaria. Indeed, the Frankish empire was eventually destroyed not by the king's overt enemies but by his numerous 'faithful' followers.

The last independent Welsh princes, however, were not dealing with the Frankish empire, but with a large, powerful and sophisticated thirteenth-century nation state. Moreover, although the Welsh had grown in power, the fastest-growing power was the king, and the relatively small territorial area of Britain made it all the more difficult to evade royal influence. The princes of Gwynedd, like the Lords of the Isles, found themselves increasingly squeezed out as power in the island of Britain was gradually arrogated to the kings of England and Scotland. Paradoxically, this problem became worse as the Welsh princes achieved more influence themselves. The extent of their dominions gave them no choice but to confront royal and marcher interests head-on, and the prince of Wales in particular could not avoid involving himself in the march – as leader of the Welsh, he was obliged to respond to native requests for intervention.

Under these circumstances, and bearing in mind the internal divisions within Wales, a unified independent Welsh state may well have been unfeasible as early as the seventh century, and certainly after the eleventh. If Llywelyn ap Iorwerth and Llywelyn ap Gruffudd could not create such a state, Owain Glyn Dŵr's attempt to do so after more than a century of conquest was unlikely to succeed, despite his great skill in using all of the tools of nation-building and statecraft at his disposal. Owain encountered nearly all of the problems experienced by his thirteenth-century predecessors, and in addition he faced the fact that native Welsh regality was now further away than ever. Even the title of prince was presumptuous in 1400 – it belonged under feudal law to Henry of Monmouth – and Henry IV never regarded Glyn Dŵr as other than a mere baron. The revolt officially made him nothing more than a rebel and an outlaw, and even the French declined to recognise his authority as being *dei gratia*. Owain did acquire some of the trappings of a prince, however, including a chancellor, a secretary and great and privy seals, and he made good use of formal diplomatic protocol, dating letters by his regnal year and styling himself *dei gratia princeps Wallie* in his correspondence with Charles VI in 1404; Charles went so far as to call him a 'cousin'. Together with Owain's adoption of the heraldic arms of Owain Lawgoch (rather than his own family's lion rampant of Powys), these affectations represented a conscious attempt to emulate the thirteenth-century principality of Wales.

Posturing was all very well, but Glyn Dŵr was well aware that sovereignty, regality and international respectability could only be achieved by becoming a sovereign lord, and this explains the breathtaking ambition of his programme. It may even be that he hoped to sever all the ties of English overlordship; certainly, the particular and crucial question of whether to perform homage to the king of England for his principality was never explicitly discussed. The details of Owain's thinking are not known. Perhaps he saw his putative principality as a merely symbolic creation, designed to force the king to address Welsh complaints; alternatively, he may have envisaged a new negotiated principality similar to that created by the treaty of Montgomery. It is almost certainly the case that his ambitions waxed and waned with his political and military fortunes. He was prepared to submit to the king in the early years of his revolt, but his attitude in later years was defiant, and the question of royal overlordship was neatly avoided because Owain did not recognise Henry IV – 'Henry of Lancaster' as he always called him – as the legitimate king of England. There was no ambiguity in the relationship, however, when the Welsh were received back into the king's peace with royal pardons.

Glyn Dŵr's vision was necessary and attractive precisely because the forces ranged against it were so formidable. His appeal to tradition and to prophecy resonated with the most cherished hopes of the Welsh as a people, but ultimately it was little more than a veil which could be drawn over the fact that genuine independence from the overlordship of the king of England was simply not practical. If that really was Owain's aim, it was a forlorn hope. For all his achievement and inspirational vision, Owain's position both *de facto* and *de iure* was never clearly defined, always open to question, continually shifting and never comprehensive. In the long term, English embargos and castles, together with the cumulative effects of more than a century of colonisation, ensured that he was never likely to succeed in breaking free of English rule. Indeed, it had been apparent for centuries that Welsh attempts to leave English overlordship – such as those made by Owain Gwynedd and Dafydd ap Llywelyn – were always tinged with either brinkmanship or desperation.

It remains, nonetheless, that the Welsh preserved their independence with remarkable tenacity. They survived the Saxon and Irish incursions during and after the fall of the Roman empire; they resisted both the Vikings and the expansion of Wessex more successfully than did their Mercian and Northumbrian neighbours; they withstood Norman incursions more effectively than did the kingdom of England; and Gwynedd maintained its independence from direct royal lordship long after much of Ireland and France was subjected to the king of England. Most tellingly of all, Gwynedd was the very last piece of the western Roman empire to fall to barbarian invasion, and also the very last to remain under the rule of the people who had inhabited it before the Romans arrived.

Notes

Where references have been abbreviated, full details can be found in the bibliography.

INTRODUCTION
1 *Historia Gruffud vab Kenan* p.15
2 *Brut y Tywysogyon (Peniarth MS 20 version)*, 1213

CHAPTER 1: THE ORIGINS AND GROWTH OF WELSH KINGDOMS
1 *Brut y Tywysogyon (Peniarth MS 20 version)*, 916
2 *Annales Cambriae* s.a. 950; see also *Brut y Tywysogyon (Peniarth MS 20 version)*, 949
3 *Brut y Tywysogyon (Peniarth MS 20 version)* s.a. 998
4 Ibid. s.a. 1020

CHAPTER 2: WALES AND THE ANGLO–SAXONS
1 Asser, *Life of king Alfred* p.71
2 *Anglo-Saxon Chronicle*, 830
3 Asser, *Life of king Alfred* p.96
4 *Anglo-Saxon Chronicle* s.a. 1055
5 Roger of Howden, *Chronica* i p.102; J.E. Lloyd, *Wales and the coming of the Normans* (*Transactions of the Honourable Society of Cymmrodorion* 1899–1900) p.149
6 *Anglo-Saxon Chronicle* s.a. 1065
7 Ibid. s.a. 1061
8 Geoffrey Gaimar, *L'Estoire des Engleis*, ed. A. Bell (Oxford 1960) v p.5084

CHAPTER 3: WALES AND THE VIKINGS
1 *Brut y Tywysogyon (Peniarth MS 20 version)* s.a. 970
2 Ibid. s.a. 1107
3 *Historia Gruffud vab Kenan* p.30
4 *Brut y Tywysogyon (Peniarth MS 20 version)* s.a. 1116, 1134

CHAPTER 4: NORMAN CONQUEST AND WELSH RESISTANCE
1 *Domesday Book* i p.186b
2 *Chronicon ex chronicis* ii p.31
3 *Brut y Tywysogyon (Peniarth MS 20 version)* s.a. 1073, s.a. 1076
4 *Brut y Tywysogyon ('Red Book of Hergest' version)* ed. T. Jones (Cardiff 1955) s.a. 1092
5 *Brut y Tywysogyon (Peniarth MS 20 version)* s.a. 1135
6 *Domesday Book* i p.179b
7 *Brut y Tywysogyon (Peniarth MS 20 version)* s.a. 1134, s.a. 1156, s.a. 1113
8 Ibid. s.a. 1113
9 Ibid. s.a. 1112
10 Ibid. s.a. 1101

CHAPTER 5: THE BALANCE OF POWER AND ITS DESTRUCTION
1 *Annales de Margam* (in *Annales Monastici*, ed. H.R. Luard [5 vols. London 1864–69] i) p.15
2 *Brut y Tywysogyon (Peniarth MS 20 version)*, 1171, 1172
3 Benedict of Peterborough, *Gesta regis Henrici secundis*, ed. W. Stubbs (London 1867) i p.162
4 Roger of Howden, *Chronica* iii p.23
5 *Materials for the history of Thomas Becket*, ed. J.C. Robertson (7 vols. London 1881) v p.239
6 *Annales Cambriae*, 1197

CHAPTER 6: LLYWELYN AP IORWERTH AND HIS LEGACY

1 *Foedera, conventiones, litterae, etc.*, ed. T. Rymer and R. Sanderson (4 vols. London 1816–69) I i p.84
2 *Royal and other letters illustrative of the reign of Henry III*, ed. W.W. Shirley (2 vols. London 1866) i pp.122–23; *Calendar of Ancient Correspondence* pp.8–9
3 *Close Rolls* i p.368
4 Idem iv p.240
5 Matthew Paris, *Chronica majora* iv p.151 (Matthew 12:25)
6 *Littere Wallie* p.148

CHAPTER 7: LLYWELYN AP GRUFFUDD: THE PRINCIPALITY OF WALES WON AND LOST

1 *Close Rolls* xii pp.142–43, 144
2 *Calendar of Ancient Correspondence* pp.9–10; *Cartae et alia munimenta quae ad dominium de Glamorgancia pertinent*, ed. G.T. Clark (5 vols. Cardiff 1910) iii pp.765–67
3 *Littere Wallie* pp.103–4

CHAPTER 8: CONQUEST AND REVOLT

1 *Monasticon Anglicanum*, ed. W. Dugdale ([2nd ed. J. Caley, H. Ellis and B. Bondinel] 6 vols. London 1817–30) iv 660

CHAPTER 9: MEDIEVAL WALES AND THE WELSH

1 Geoffrey of Monmouth, *The history of the kings of Britain*, pp.51, 258
2 *Brut y Tywysogyon (Peniarth MS 20 version)* s.a. 1085, s.a. 1079; *Liber Landavensis* p.274
3 *Brut y Tywysogyon (Peniarth MS 20 version)* s.a. 1096
4 *Historia Gruffud vab Kenan* pp.30–31
5 Ibid. p.21
6 *Brut y Tywysogyon (Peniarth MS 20 version)* s.a. 1157
7 Symeon of Durham, *Historia regum* (in *Opera omnia*), ed. T. Arnold (2 vols. London 1882-85) ii p.177
8 *Annales Cambriae* s.a. 1165
9 *Brut y Tywysogyon (Peniarth MS 20 version),* 1198
10 Giraldus Cambrensis, *Opera* v p.321
11 Matthew Paris, *Chronica majora* v p.613; *Calendar of Welsh Rolls* (in *Calendar of the Chancery Rolls, Various* v 1277–1326) (London 1912) p.281; *Chronicon ex chronicis* ii p.229; *Registrum Johannis de Pontissara* p.632
12 *Myvyrian Archaeology of Wales* p.221
13 Giraldus Cambrensis, *Opera* iii p.209
14 *Myvyrian Archaeology of Wales* p.175
15 *Llawysgrif Hendregadredd* p.275
16 *Myvyrian Archaeology of Wales* p.224
17 *Llyfr Iorwerth*, ed. A. Rhys William (Cardiff 1960) §1; *Llyfr Blegywryd*, ed. S. J. Williams and J.E. Powell (Cardiff 1961) p.1
18 *Calendar of Inquisitions Miscellaneous 1216–1422* (London 1916) i no.1109
19 William Rishanger, *Chronica et annales*, ed. H.T. Riley (London 1865) p.101; *Annales Cestriensis*, ed. R.G. Christie (Record Society of Lancashire and Cheshire 1886), 1282; Ranulf Higden, *Polychronicon*, ed. C. Babington and J.R. Lumby (9 vols. London 1872) viii pp.266–68; Henry de Knighton, *Chronicon*, ed. J.R. Lumby (London 1889) i p.274
20 *Calendar of Ancient Correspondence* p.59
21 *Littere Wallie* p.1
22 *Brenhinedd y Saeson*, ed. and trans. T. Jones (Cardiff 1971), 1282
23 Benedict of Peterborough, *Gesta regis Henrici secundis*, ed. W. Stubbs (2 vols. London 1867) ii p.159
24 *Cywyddau Iolo Goch ac eraill* ed. H. Lewis, T. Roberts and I. Williams (Cardiff 1937) p.109
25 Giraldus Cambrensis, *Opera* vi p.227; Gerald of Wales, *The journey through Wales/The description of Wales* p.274

CHAPTER 10: THE NATURE, PRACTICE AND LOSS OF INDEPENDENCE

1 *Myvyrian Archaeology of Wales* p.267
2 Roger of Howden, *Chronica* iv p.142
3 K. Williams-Jones, Llywelyn's charter to Cymer Abbey in 1209 (*Journal of the Merionethshire Historical Society* iii 1957-60) p.54
4 *Historia Gruffud vab Kenan* p.13
5 *Myvyrian Archaeology of Wales* p.240
6 *Llawysgrif Hendregadredd* p.332
7 Meilyr's elegy for Gruffudd ap Cynan p.265
8 *Myvyrian Archaeology of Wales* p.267
9 F. Schulz, 'Bracton on kingship' (*English Historical Review* lx 1945) p.139
10 *Llawysgrif Hendregadredd* p.219
11 *Cronica de Wallia*, ed. T. Jones (*Bulletin of the Board of Celtic Studies* xii 1946-48) pp.27-44, s.a. 1214
12 *Fouke le fitz Waryn*, ed. E.J. Hathaway, P.T. Ricketts, C.A. Robson and A.D. Wilshere (Oxford 1975) p.34
13 *Historia Gruffud vab Kenan* p.7
14 W. Ullmann, 'The development of the medieval idea of sovereignty' (*English Historical Review* lxiv 1949) p.11
15 Ibid. pp.18-28
16 C.T. Wood, *The French appanages and the Capetian monarchy 1224-1378* (Harvard 1966) p.82
17 *Brut y Tywysogyon (Peniarth MS 20 version)* s.a. 1079; *Liber Landavensis* p.274; *Historia Gruffud vab Kenan* p.11
18 Meilyr's elegy for Gruffudd ap Cynan p.263
19 Giraldus Cambrensis, *Opera* iii p.166
20 *Brut y Tywysogyon (Peniarth MS 20 version)*, 1196
21 *Calendar of Ancient Correspondence* p.86
22 *Registrum Johannis de Pontissara* p.443

Maps

1 Major Welsh kingdoms and political units

2 Other territorial divisions

Genealogical Tables

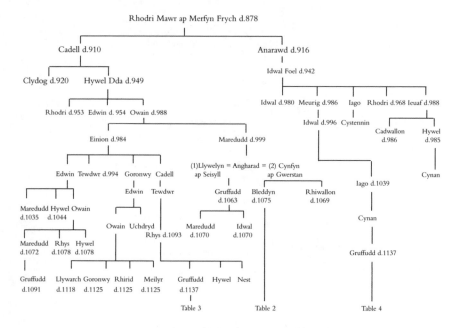

1 Descendants of Rhodri Mawr (Gwynedd and Deheubarth)

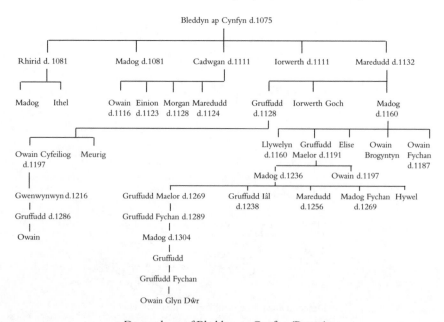

2 Descendants of Bleddyn ap Cynfyn (Powys)

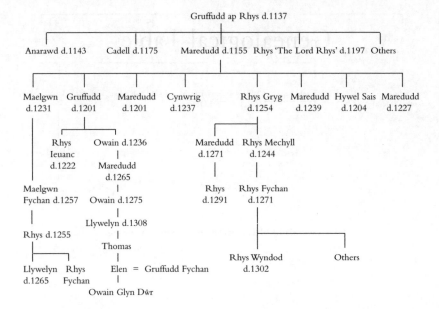

3 Descendants of Gruffudd ap Rhys (Deheubarth)

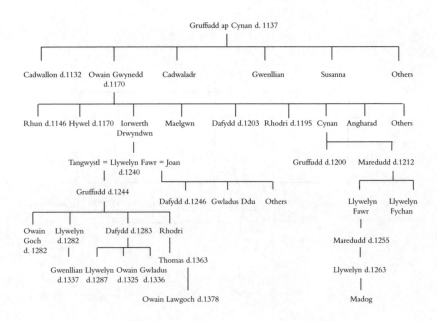

4 Descendants of Gruffudd ap Cynan (Gwynedd)

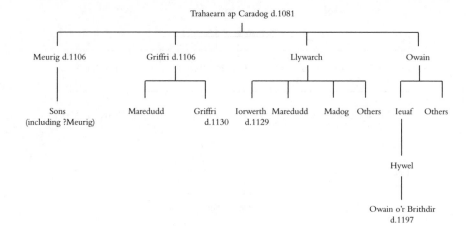

5 Descendants of Trahaearn ap Caradog (Arwystli)

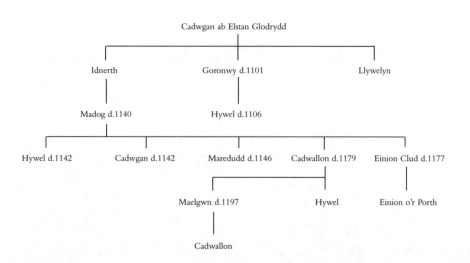

6 Descendants of Cadwgan ab Elstan Glodrydd (Rhwng Gwy a Hafren)

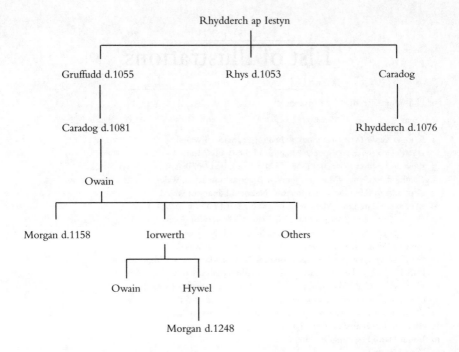

7 Descendants of Rhydderch ap Iestyn (Gwynllŵg)

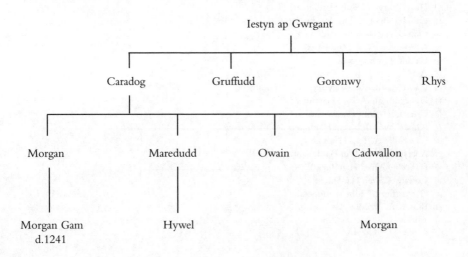

8 Descendants of Iestyn ap Gwrgant (Morgannwg)

List of Illustrations

The illustrations are artists' impressions.

Select Bibliography

This bibliography is intended as a starting point for the general reader. The emphasis is on authoritative English-language works which are not too specialised and are available relatively easily; inevitably, many valuable contributions to the study of medieval Wales have had to be left out. However, by following the bibliographical references provided in the works which have been listed, readers will be able to access a wide range of academic publications relating to many aspects of the Welsh wars of independence, as well as the primary sources upon which any study of this period is based.

Anglo-Saxon Chronicle, ed. and trans. D. Whitelock (London 1961; revised impression 1965)

Annales Cambriae, ed. J. Williams ab Ithel (London 1860)

Armes Prydein, ed. I. Williams and trans. R. Bromwich (Dublin 1972)

Asser, *Life of king Alfred*, ed. and trans. S.D. Keynes and M. Lapidge (in *Alfred the Great* [Harmondsworth 1983])

R.S. Babcock, 'Rhys ap Tewdwr, king of Deheubarth' (*Anglo-Norman Studies* 16 1994) 21–35

F. Barlow, *Edward the Confessor* (London 1970)

F. Barlow, *William Rufus* (London 1983)

G.W.S. Barrow, *Scotland and her neighbours in the Middle Ages* (London 1992)

G.W.S. Barrow, 'Wales and Scotland in the Middle Ages' (*Welsh History Review* 10 1981) 302–19

R. Bartlett, *Gerald of Wales 1146-1223* (Oxford 1982)

R. Bartlett, *The making of Europe: conquest, colonisation and cultural change 950–1350* (London 1993)

P.C. Bartrum, *Welsh genealogies AD 300–1400* (8 vols. Cardiff 1974)

Bede, A *history of the English Church and people*, ed. and trans. L. Sherley-Price (Harmondsworth 1983)

J.H. Beeler, 'Castles and strategy in Norman and early Angevin England' (*Speculum* 31 1956) 581–601

Brut y Tywysogyon, Peniarth MS 20 version, ed. and trans. T. Jones (Cardiff 1952)

F.J. Byrne, *Irish kings and high kings* (London 1973)

Calendar of Ancient Correspondence concerning Wales, ed. J.G. Edwards (Cardiff 1935)

The Cambridge Medieval History, ed. J.R. Tanner, C.W. Previté-Orton and Z.N. Brooke (Cambridge 1936): 5 *Contest of empire and papacy*; 6 *Victory of the papacy*

A.D. Carr, '"The last and weakest of his line": Dafydd ap Gruffudd, the last prince of Wales' (*Welsh History Review* 19 1999) 375–99

A.D. Carr, *Llywelyn ap Gruffudd* (Cardiff 1982)

A.D. Carr, *Owen of Wales: the end of the house of Gwynedd* (Cardiff 1991)

A.D. Carr, *Medieval Wales* (London 1995)

B.G. Charles, *Old Norse relations with Wales* (London 1934)

Chronicon ex chronicis (Florence of Worcester, *Chronicon ex chronicis*), ed. B. Thorpe (2 vols. London 1848–49)

M.T. Clanchy, *England and its rulers 1066–1272: foreign lordship and national identity* (London 1983)

Close Rolls (London 1902–38)

P. Contamine, *War in the Middle Ages* (Oxford 1984)

P. Courtney, 'The Norman invasion of Gwent: a reassessment' (*Journal of Medieval History* 12 1986) 297–313

F.G. Cowley, *The monastic order in south Wales 1066–1349* (Cardiff 1977)

D. Crouch, *The image of aristocracy in Britain 1000–1300* (London 1992)

D. Crouch, 'The march and the Welsh kings' (in *The anarchy of king Stephen's reign* [ed. E. King] Oxford 1994) 255–89

D. Crouch, 'The slow death of kingship in Glamorgan 1067–1158' (*Morgannwg* 29 1985) 20–41

E. Curtis, 'The fitz Rerys, Welsh lords of Cloghran, Co. Dublin' (*County Louth Archaeological Journal* 1921) 13–16

K.R. Dark, *Civitas to kingdom: British political continuity 300–800* (Leicester 1994)

J. Davies, *A history of Wales* (London 1993)

M. Davies, 'Gruffudd ap Llywelyn, king of Wales' (*Welsh History Review* 21 2002) 207–48

R.R. Davies (ed.), *The British Isles 1100–1500: comparisons, contrasts and connections* (Edinburgh 1988)

R.R. Davies, *Conquest, co-existence and change: Wales 1063–1415* (Oxford 1987; reprinted in 1991 as *The age of conquest: Wales 1063–1415*)

R. R. Davies, *Domination and conquest: the experience of Ireland, Scotland and Wales 1100–1300* (Cambridge 1990)

R.R. Davies, *The first English empire: power and identities in the British Isles 1093–1343* (Oxford 2000)

R.R. Davies, 'Henry I and Wales' (in *Studies in medieval history presented to R.H.C. Davis* [ed. H. Mayr-Harting and R.I. Moore] Hambledon 1985) 132–47

R.R. Davies, *Historical perception: Celts and Saxons* (Cardiff 1979)

R.R. Davies, 'Kings, lords and liberties in the march of Wales' (*Transactions of the Royal Historical Society* 29 1979) 41–61

R.R. Davies, *Lordship and society in the march of Wales 1282–1400* (Oxford 1978)

R.R. Davies, *The revolt of Owain Glyn Dŵr* (Oxford 1995)

R.R. Davies, R.A. Griffiths, I.G. Jones and K.O. Morgan (ed.), *Welsh society and nationhood* (Cardiff 1984)

W. Davies, *Patterns of power in early Wales* (Oxford 1990)

W. Davies, *Wales in the early Middle Ages* (Leicester 1982)

R.H.C. Davis, *King Stephen 1135–54* (London 1967)

Domesday Book, ed. J. Morris (35 vols in 40. Chichester 1975–86)

D.C. Douglas, *William the Conqueror* (London 1964)

D.N. Dumville, 'Sub-Roman Britain: history and legend' (*History* 62 1977) 173–92

J. Dunbabin, *France in the making 843–1180* (Oxford 1985)

A.A.M. Duncan, *Scotland: the making of the kingdom* (Edinburgh 1975)

J.G. Edwards, 'Madog ap Llywelyn: the Welsh leader in 1294–95' (*Bulletin of the Board of Celtic Studies* 13 1950) 207–10

J.G. Edwards, 'The Normans and the Welsh march' (*Proceedings of the British Academy* 42 1956) 155–77

R. Frame, *The political development of the British Isles 1100–1400* (Oxford 1990)

H. Fulton, 'Tenth century Wales and *Armes Prydein*' (*Transactions of the Honourable Society of Cymmrodorion* 7 2001) 5–18

Geoffrey of Monmouth, *The history of the kings of Britain*, ed. L. Thorpe (Harmondsworth 1982)

Gerald of Wales, *The journey through Wales/The description of Wales*, ed. and trans. L. Thorpe (Harmondsworth 1980)

J. Gillingham, 'Conquering the barbarians: war and chivalry in twelfth century Britain' (*Haskins Society Journal* 4 1992) 67–84

J. Gillingham, 'Henry II, Richard I and the lord Rhys' (*Peritia* 10 1996) 225–36

J. Gillingham and J. C. Holt (ed.), *War and government in the Middle Ages* (Cambridge 1984)

Giraldus Cambrensis, *Opera*, ed. J. S. Brewer, J. F. Dimock and G. F. Warner (8 vols. London 1861–91)

Glamorgan County History, ed. T. B. Pugh (Cardiff 1971): 3 *The Middle Ages*

R.A. Griffiths, *Conquerors and conquered in medieval Wales* (Stroud 1994)

R.A. Griffiths, 'The revolt of Rhys ap Maredudd 1287–88' (*Welsh History Review* 3 1966) 121–43

E.M. Hallam, *Capetian France 987–1328* (Oxford 1980)

E.R. Henken, *National redeemer: Owain Glyndŵr in Welsh tradition* (Cardiff 1996)

N.J. Higham, 'Medieval "overkingship" in Wales: the earliest evidence' (*Welsh History Review* 16 1992) 145–59

D. Hill and M. Worthington, *Offa's Dyke: history and guide* (Stroud 2003)

Historia Gruffud vab Kenan, ed. D. S. Evans (Cardiff 1977)

B.W. Holden, 'The making of the middle march of Wales 1066–1250' (*Welsh History Review* 20 2000) 207–26

C. Warren Hollister, *Henry I* (Yale 2001)

C. Warren Hollister, *Monarchy, magnates and institutions in the Anglo-Norman world* (London 1986)

M. Howell, 'Regalian right in Wales and the march: the relation of theory to practice' (*Welsh History Review* 7 1975) 269–88

B.T. Hudson, 'The destruction of Gruffudd ap Llywelyn' (*Welsh History Review* 15 1990–91) 331–50

K. Hughes, *Celtic Britain in the early Middle Ages* (Woodbridge 1980)

D. Jenkins (ed.), *Hywel Dda: the law* (Llandysul 1986)

D. Jenkins, 'Kings, lords and princes: the nomenclature of authority in thirteenth-century Wales' (*Bulletin of the Board of Celtic Studies* 26 1976) 451–62

J.E.A. Jolliffe, *Angevin kingship* (London 1963)

G.R.J. Jones, 'The defences of Gwynedd in the thirteenth century' (*Transactions of the Caernarfonshire Historical Society* 30 1969) 29–43

M. Jones and M.Vale (ed.), *England and her neighbours 1066–1453: essays in honour of Pierre Chaplais* (London 1989)

N.A. Jones and H. Pryce (ed.), *Yr Arglwydd Rhys* (Cardiff 1996)

W.R. Jones, 'The image of the barbarian in medieval Europe' (*Comparative Studies in Society and History* 13 1971) 376–407

D.J. Cathcart King, *Castellarium Anglicanum* (2 vols. London 1983)

D.J. Cathcart King, 'The defence of Wales 1067–1153' (*Archaeologia Cambrensis* 126 1977) 1–16

P. Latimer, 'Henry II's campaign against the Welsh in 1165' (*Welsh History Review* 14 1988–89) 523–52

J. Le Patourel, *The Norman empire* (Oxford 1976)

J. Le Patourel, 'The Plantagenet dominions' (*History* 50 1965) 289–308

A.W. Lewis, 'The Capetian appanages and the nature of the French kingdom' (*Journal of Medieval History* 2 1976) 119–34

C.W. Lewis, 'The treaty of Woodstock 1247: its background and significance' (*Welsh History Review* 2 1964–65) 37–65

K.J. Leyser, *Medieval Germany and its neighbours 950–1250* (London 1982)

Liber Landavensis: text of the Book of Llandav, ed. J. Rhŷs and J. Gwenogvryn Evans (Oxford 1893; facsimile edition Aberystwyth 1979)

Littere Wallie, ed. J. G. Edwards (Cardiff 1940)

H.R. Loyn, *The making of the English nation* (London 1991)

H.R. Loyn, *The Vikings in Britain* (London 1977)

H.R. Loyn, *The Vikings in Wales* (London 1977)

H.R. Loyn, 'Wales and England in the tenth century: the context of the Æþelstan charters' (*Welsh History Review* 10 1981) 283–301

Llawysgrif Hendregadredd, ed. T. Morris-Jones and T.H. Parry Williams (Cardiff 1933)

J.E. Lloyd, *A history of Wales from the earliest times to the Edwardian conquest* (2 vols. 3rd edition, London 1939)

J.E. Lloyd, *Owen Glendower* (Oxford 1931)

R.S. Loomis, *Wales and the Arthurian legend* (Cardiff 1956)

J. Lydon (ed.), *The English in medieval Ireland* (Dublin 1984)

W.J. McCann, 'The Welsh view of the Normans in the eleventh and twelfth centuries' (*Transactions of the Honourable Society of Cymmrodorion* 1991) 39–67

J.F.A. Mason, 'Roger of Montgomery and his sons' (*Transactions of the Royal Historical Society* 13 1963) 1–28

Matthew Paris, *Chronica majora*, ed. H. R. Luard (7 vols. London 1872–73)

K.L. Maund, 'Cynan ap Iago and the killing of Gruffudd ap Llywelyn' (*Cambridge Medieval Celtic Studies* 10 1985) 57–65

K.L. Maund, 'Dynastic segmentation and Gwynedd c. 950–c. 1000' (*Studia Celtica* 32 1998) 155–67

K.L. Maund (ed.), *Gruffudd ap Cynan: a collaborative biography* (Woodbridge 1996)

K. L. Maund, *Ireland, Wales and England in the eleventh century* (Woodbridge 1991)

K.L. Maund, 'Trahaearn ap Caradog: legitimate usurper?' (*Welsh History Review* 13 1987) 468–76

K.L. Maund, *The Welsh kings: the medieval rulers of Wales* (Stroud 2000)

Meilyr's elegy for Gruffudd ap Cynan, ed. and trans. A. French (*Études Celtique* xvi 1979) 263–81

T.W. Moody (ed.), *Nationality and the pursuit of national independence* (Belfast 1978)

J.E. Morris, *The Welsh wars of king Edward I* (Oxford 1901)

The Myvyrian Archaeology of Wales, ed. O. Jones, E. Williams and W.O. Pughe (Denbigh 1870)

L.H. Nelson, *The Normans in south Wales 1070–1171* (London 1966)

The New History of Ireland ([ed. A. Cosgrove] Oxford 1987)

D.Ó Corráin, *Ireland before the Normans* (Dublin 1972)

Orkneyinga Saga, ed. and trans. H. Pálsson and P. Edwards (Harmondsworth 1981)

Hugh Owen, 'Warfare in pre-Edwardian Wales' (*Transactions of the Anglesey Antiquarian Society* 1940) 32–45

T. Jones Pierce, *Medieval Welsh society* ([ed. J. Beverley Smith] Cardiff 1972)

A.L. Poole, *From Domesday Book to Magna Carta* (Oxford 1954)

M. Prestwich, *Edward I* (London 1988)

H. Pryce, 'Owain Gwynedd and Louis VII: the Franco-Welsh diplomacy of the first prince of Wales' (*Welsh History Review* 19 1998) 1–28

W. Rees, *Historical atlas of Wales* (Cardiff 1951)

Registrum Johannis de Pontissara episcopi Wyntoniensis, ed. C. Deedes (London 1915)

S. Reynolds, *Kingdoms and communities in western Europe 900–1300* (Oxford 1984)

M. Rhys-Griffiths, 'The military career and affinity of Henry, Prince of Wales, 1399–1413' (Oxford MLitt, 1980)

M. Richter, 'Dafydd ap Llywelyn' (*Welsh History Review* 5 1971) 205–19

M. Richter, 'The first century of Anglo-Irish relations' (*History* 59 1974) 195–210

M. Richter, *Giraldus Cambrensis: the growth of the Welsh nation* (2nd ed., Aberystwyth 1976)

A.J. Roderick, 'Marriage and politics in Wales 1066–1282' (*Welsh History Review* 4 1968) 3–20

Roger of Howden, *Chronica*, ed. W. Stubbs (4 vols. London 1868)

I. Rowlands, 'The making of the march: aspects of the Norman settlement in Dyfed' (*Anglo-Norman Studies* 3 1980) 142–57, 221–25

P.H. Sawyer and I.N. Wood (ed.), *Early medieval kingship* (Leeds 1977)

K. Simms, *From kings to warlords* (Woodbridge 1987)

J. Beverley Smith, 'Dynastic succession in medieval Wales' (*Bulletin of the Board of Celtic Studies* 33 1986) 199–232

J. Beverley Smith, 'Gruffudd Llwyd and the Celtic alliance 1315–18' (*Bulletin of the Board of Celtic Studies* 26 1976) 463–78

J. Beverley Smith, 'The legal position of Wales in the Middle Ages' (in *Law-making and law-makers in British history* [ed. A. Harding] London 1980) 21–53

J. Beverley Smith, *Llywelyn ap Gruffudd, prince of Wales* (Cardiff 1998)

J. Beverley Smith, 'The middle march in the thirteenth century' (*Bulletin of the Board of Celtic Studies* 24 1970–72) 77–93

J. Beverley Smith, *Offra principis Wallie domino regi* (*Bulletin of the Board of Celtic Studies* 21 1966) 362–67

J. Beverley Smith, 'The origins of the revolt of Rhys ap Maredudd' (*Bulletin of the Board of Celtic Studies* 21 1964–66) 151–63

J. Beverley Smith, 'Owain Gwynedd' (*Transactions of the Caernarfonshire Historical Society* 32 1971) 8–17

J. Beverley Smith, 'The succession to Welsh princely inheritance: the evidence reconsidered' (in *The British Isles* [ed. R.R. Davies]) 64–81

J. Beverley Smith, 'The Statute of Wales 1284' (*Welsh History Review* 10 1981) 127–54

R.W. Southern, *Medieval humanism* (London 1978)

F.M. Stenton, *Anglo-Saxon England* (Oxford 1985)

D. Stephenson, *The governance of Gwynedd* (Cardiff 1984)

D. Stephenson, 'The politics of Powys Wenwynwyn in the thirteenth century' (*Cambridge Medieval Celtic Studies* 7 1984) 39–61

A.J. Taylor, *The king's works in Wales 1277–1330* (London 1974)

R.F. Treharne, 'The Franco-Welsh treaty of alliance in 1212' (*Bulletin of the Board of Celtic Studies* 18 1958) 60–75

R.V. Turner, *King John* (London 1994)

R. Turvey, 'The defences of twelfth-century Deheubarth and the castle strategy of the Lord Rhys' (*Archaeologia Cambrensis* 144 1995) 103–32

R. Turvey, *The Welsh princes 1063–1283* (London 2002)

W. Ullmann, 'The development of the medieval idea of sovereignty' (*English Historical Review* 64 1949) 1–33

R. Vaughan, *Valois Burgundy* (London 1975)

W.L. Warren, *Henry II* (London 1973)

W.L. Warren, *King John* (London 1960)

K.F. Werner, 'Kingdom and principality in twelfth-century France' (in *Medieval nobility* [ed. T. Reuter] Oxford 1978) 243–90

A.G. Williams, 'Norman lordship in south-east Wales during the reign of William I' (*Welsh History Review* 16 1993) 445–66

D.H. Williams, *The Welsh Cistercians* (Pontypool 1969)

G. Williams, *Owain Glyndŵr* (Cardiff 1993)

G. Williams, 'Prophecy, poetry and politics in medieval and Tudor Wales' (in *British government and administration* [ed. H. Hearder and H.R. Loyn] Cardiff 1974) 71–86

G.A. Williams, 'The succession to Gwynedd 1238–47' (*Bulletin of the Board of Celtic Studies* 20 1964) 393–413

H. Wolfram, 'The shaping of the early medieval kingdom' (*Viator* 1 1970) 1–20

H. Wolfram, 'The shaping of the early medieval principality' (*Viator* 2 1971) 35–51

D. Wyatt, 'Gruffudd ap Cynan and the Hiberno-Norse world' (*Welsh History Review* 19 1999) 595–617

Index

Only subjects which are dealt with in detail in the text have been indexed, together with some other prominent people, places and events. Most of the subjects which may be inferred from chapter headings and sub-headings have been omitted.

The Tempus History of Wales

Series Editor
Professor Gareth Williams, University of Glamorgan

Our curiosity about the past remains insatiable. Interest in the Welsh past is no exception, and exists not only among the Welsh themselves. Partly as the consequence of a general resurgence of interest in the Celts, partly because of the rapidly changing nature of the social and physical landscape of Wales itself, the history of a Wales that was or may have been continually attracts new audiences. While scholarly research finds outlets in academic publishing and leaned journals, its specialist findings are not always accessible to the general reader, who could often benefit from a broader synoptic view. Valuable and often innovative studies in community, family and special-interest history are enthusiastically pursued outside the academy, too. Established scholars and younger researchers will contribute to this new series aimed at illuminating aspects of the Welsh past for a wide readership.

Published
David Moore, *The Welsh Wars of Independence: c.410-c.1415*
'Beautifully written, subtle and remarkably perceptive... a major re-examination of a thousand years of Welsh history' John Davies, author of *The History of Wales*

Commissioned
Matthew Griffiths, *Tudor Wales 1440-1640*
Ioan Matthews, *The Welsh Valleys: A Social & Industrial History*
Nia Powell, *The Renaissance in Wales*
Keith Strange, *Iron Metropolis: Life in a Welsh Industrial Town*
Richard Suggett, *Welsh Witches & Wizards: A History of Magic and Witchcraft in Wales*
Eryn White, *The Welsh Bible*

Further titles are in preparation

If you are interested in purchasing other books published by Tempus,
or in case you have difficulty finding any Tempus books in your local bookshop,
you can also place orders directly through our website
www.tempus-publishing.com